THE TROUBLESHOOTERS

Project lead, setting and rules design
Krister Sundelin

Editor
Brandon Bowling

Proofreaders
Magnus Bergqvist, Brandon Bowling, Oscar Falk,
Leif Eriksson, Staffan Johansson, Mikko Kauppinen,
Laszlo Stadler

Cover art
Ronja Melin, Krister Sundelin

Interior art
Ronja Melin, Elinore Rönning, Theodor Rönnudd,
Krister Sundelin, David Öqvist

Graphic design and layout
Dan Algstrand of Stockholm Kartell

Producers
Paul Dali, Anton Wahnström

Playtesters
Dan Algstrand, Marco Behrmann, Magnus Bergqvist, Anders Blixt,
Måns Broman, Paul Dali, Andreas Ekeroot, Emma Fahlström,
Niklas Fröjd, Per Fröjd, Gustaf Gadd, Rickard von Haugwitz, Petter Nallo,
Joakim Nes Olsson, Johan Osbjer, Jonas Schiött, Krister Sundelin,
Anton Vikström, Thomas Wegebrand

Special thanks
Colin Chapman, Peter Eriksson, Björn Hellqvist, Tobias Junghöfer

Helmgast
Marco Behrmann, Paul Dali, Martin Fröjd, Niklas Fröjd, Petter Nallo,
Krister Sundelin, Anton Wahnström

Arkhane Asylum
Raphaël Crouzat, Romain Darmon, Fabien Marteau, Mathieu Saintout

Printed by	**ISBN**
BALTO print, Lithuania	978-1-912743-77-3

FOREWORD

"You have talked about making a journey," Yoko's mom said. *"Make it and come back healed."*
  "Yes, to the stars," Yoko replied. *"Where a girl with blue skin and golden hair awaits…"*
  "You see? Your dreams are returning!"

Those lines made me curious when I read the final panels of the *Yoko Tsuno* comic book "Daughter of the Wind" back in 1983.

Yoko Tsuno was not my first contact with French and Belgian comics, *bande dessinée* or *bédé* – that honour probably goes to *Astérix*, *The Smurfs*, *Tintin* and *Spirou et Fantasio* – but she quickly became one of my favourite comic book heroes. Sadly the books were not easy to get in Sweden when I grew up. It would be years before I learned about the blue-skinned Vineans in Yoko's universe, so for a long time, I wondered who Yoko was talking about.

Tintin and *Spirou et Fantasio* were much easier to find in bookstores – and together with Yoko they formed an oasis in the comics desert that was Sweden in the 1970s and early 1980s. They were published irregularly, you couldn't subscribe to them, and they were not always available in the stores.

But they were so much more varied than the "normal" comics we had. They were set in the future. In the past. In space. In magic worlds. And even if they were set here and now, it was a much more exciting "here and now", with robots, flying cars, aliens, time travel, shrinking beams, and even magic. They were almost always about somewhat *ordinary* people having extraordinary adventures. They were the door to a much more fantastic world.

About the year when I read those *Yoko Tsuno* panels, a new door into the fantastic opened before me: roleplaying games. They allowed me to not just peek into these fantastic realms, but actually enter them. They let me act out my dreams and – in a certain sense – bring them to life.

It is now some 35 years after those doors opened. Albert Barille's cartoon *Il était une fois… l'espace* has appeared on Netflix. Luc Besson made his live action version of *Valerian*. I brushed off my rusty school French to enjoy the live action versions of *Spirou et Fantasio* and *Gaston Lagaffe*. *Valérian et Laureline*, *Spirou et Fantasio*, *Yoko Tsuno*, *Blake & Mortimer* and many more are being translated and published in Swedish.

As bédé re-entered my life, it suddenly hit me: why isn't there a roleplaying game like this?!! Why isn't there a way of making those particular dreams come true?

Well, now there is. I hope you will enjoy it.

INTRODUCTION

You may have noticed that this is *not* a comic book. It's a *tabletop roleplaying game*, albeit one that is inspired by comic books.

If you haven't played tabletop roleplaying games before, welcome to a new and exciting hobby!

This is a game of imagination, where the story is created through conversations with the other participants. You and a group of friends sit down together and create a story about exciting adventures, inspired mostly by Belgian and French comics like *Spirou et Fantasio*, *Tintin*, *Yoko Tsuno* and many others. There's no winning in tabletop roleplaying, only the creation of stories.

This book contains rules, ideas and guidelines for creating such stories, and will guide you through setting up and running a game of the Troubleshooters on your own.

> Hello! I'm Elektra, professional rally driver for the ERF Oil team. I'm one of the best in the field, good enough to compete with world-class drivers. And with a car like the Lancia, I'm among the best of the best.

ELEKTRA AMBROSIA

> Being one of very few girls in the sport makes me a lot more popular in the media, though. Nobody knows the top drivers of the other teams by name, and nobody could point them out in a crowd. But everyone knows who Elektra Ambrosia is!

> However, being at the centre of attention sometimes pulls me into adventures outside the rally track. Luckily, I don't have to face these adventures on my own.

Skills: Alertness 65%, Credit 45%, Endurance 65%, Engineering 65%, Machinery 45%, Melee 45%, Search 45%, Status 45%, Strength 45%, Vehicles 75%, Willpower 65%; other Skills 15%
Vitality: 5
Abilities: Born Behind the Wheel, Been Everywhere
Complications: Overconfident
Languages: Greek (native); English, French (fluent)
Plot Hooks: Media Darling
Gear kits: Racing car (signature), Film camera, Mechanic's toolbox, Wad of cash, Beach wear

YURIKA MISHIDA

 Yurika is one of my best friends. She's a Japanese photo-journalist on long term assignment to France from her newspaper in Japan. She is very good at noticing the little things, has incredible attention to detail and an eye for the eye-catching. And she knows everybody! She's also a judo black belt, and more than one intoxicated fondler has taken a short, involuntary flight into the Seine.

Skills: Alertness 65%, Charm 45%, Contacts 75%, Investigation 65%, Languages 45%, Melee 45%, Prestidigitation 45%, Search 65%, Status 45%, Subterfuge 65%, Vehicles 45%; other Skills 15%
Vitality: 5
Abilities: Press Credentials, Judo Blackbelt
Complications: Code of Honour (the truth must be known)
Languages: Japanese (native), English, French, German (fluent)
Plot Hooks: Looking for a Case, Foreign
Gear kits: Camera (signature), Tape recorder, Sports car, Furisode (formal long-sleeve kimono), Film camera

 Paul never had that much respect for the law. He started off in the French Maquis during the war, stealing guns from the Germans and blowing up trains and bridges. It's a miracle that he got away, but he learned to do stuff out of sight of the authorities.

He still uses those skills for a little smuggling and a little burglary and larceny. Well, more than a little. But he's a good man, and he never allows ordinary people to get caught in the crossfire. Sometimes I think he sees himself as a French Robin Hood.

PAUL MARCHAND

Skills: Agility 65%, Alertness 45%, Charm 45%, Investigation 45%, Melee 45%, Prestidigitation 65%, Search 65%, Security 75%, Sneak 65%, Subterfuge 45%, Vehicles 45%; other Skills 15%
Vitality: 6
Abilities: Lock-Picker, Sixth Sense
Complications: Bad Reputation
Languages: French (native), English (fluent)
Plot Hooks: Do-Gooder, Looking for an Adventure
Gear kits: Lockpicks (signature), Flashlight, Binoculars, Disguise kit, Compact car

HARRY FITZROY

I had Harry as a map reader for a while, but he got bored of rally and set off on something else. He's an alpinist, a yachtsman, a rider – anything that can satisfy his sense of adventure. He's an ex-officer and the epitome of the British gentleman adventurer, and as such he has access to the top layers of society. Unfortunately, he's also a bit too fond of whisky.

Skills: Agility 65%, Alertness 45%, Contacts 65%, Credit 45%, Endurance 65%, Languages 45%, Ranged Combat 45%, Search 45%, Survival 75%, Vehicles 45%, Willpower 65%; other Skills 15%
Vitality: 6
Abilities: Peerage, Been Everywhere, Bushman
Complications: Honest, Drunkard
Languages: English (native), French, Latin (fluent)
Plot Hooks: Friends in High Places, Looking for the Past
Gear kits: Hiking gear (signature), Survival gear, Hunting rifle, Off-road vehicle, Camping gear

I don't know of anyone that can be as cool under fire as Frida, and she's possibly the only girl that is faster than me, but only because she cheats: she is a Swedish Air Force fighter pilot.

Currently, she's assigned to the Swedish representation to the European Economic Community and NATO. She often complains about the coffee here – she wants her coffee to come in pints and taste like tar.

Skills: Agility 45%, Alertness 65%, Charm 45%, Endurance 65%, Investigation 45%, Melee 45%, Ranged Combat 75%, Red Tape 45%, Strength 45%, Subterfuge 65%, Vehicles 65%; other Skills 15%
Vitality: 6
Abilities: Pilot, Military Rank (Captain), Fighter Pilot
Complications: Code of Honour, Patriot
Languages: Swedish (native), English, French (fluent)
Plot Hooks: Secret Service
Gear kits: Parade uniform, Handgun, Pocket pistol (signature), Radio set, Bicycle

ANNI-FRID "FRIDA" BÄCKSTRÖM

Éloïse is a genius in electronics and science, despite her youth. I would even say that she is a bit of a mad scientist – had I not stopped her, she would probably have built a time machine out of the Lancia. She definitely needs to get out more.

Éloïses's dad just disappeared some years ago, and her mom works full-time, so I guess I have become an extra big sister to her.

ÉLOÏSE GIRAUD

Skills: Contacts 45%, Electronics 65%, Engineering 45%, Investigation 75%, Languages 45%, Medicine 65%, Melee 45%, Science 65%, Search 65%, Security 45%, Willpower 45%; other Skills 15%
Vitality: 5
Abilities: Tech Wiz, Young, Mad Inventor
Complications: Underage, Sleepy
Languages: French, German (native), English (fluent)
Plot Hooks: I Owe You, Arch-Enemy: The Octopus
Gear kits: Electronics toolbox (signature), Chemistry lab set, Moped, Walkie-talkie, Ski gear

Those pesky adventurers have crossed the path of me, Graf von Zadrith, Number Two of the Octopus, over and over again! They have foiled my plans for world domination more times than I can count.

They always throw a monkey-wrench into our operations, no matter if it is salvaging the secrets of a sunken submarine in South-East Asia, exploring a hidden temple in the Himalayas, infiltrating the French Government using a mind-control field, or raiding an Inca tomb in the Andes. They are always there to stop us, always the thorn in our side!

And I warn you to not take part in their adventures and become one of...

GRAF VON ZADRITH

THE TROUBLES

SHOOTERS

 ...because if you do, you will face the wrath of the Octopus.

WHAT THIS GAME IS ABOUT

 So what does a troubleshooter do? For starters, we're not an organisation of any kind. We're just a group of friends living adventurous lives. Sometimes we find ourselves in trouble and have to, well, troubleshoot.

"Troubleshooters" is a moniker that some people in the police, press, intelligence community and military use for any group of people like us: adventurous friends who happens to fix problems by doing the right thing.

Me, Yurika, Paul and the others are not the only troubleshooters out there. You're about to become one of them, and discover firsthand what that entails.

THIS DOESN'T LOOK LIKE A COMIC BOOK!

True. This is not a comic book. It is a roleplaying game inspired by comic books.

There is a chance that this is your first roleplaying game. If that is the case, you may be wondering how a game can be a book.

A roleplaying game is a game of imagination. It's a game in which the players create stories together. The game is played mostly in the minds of participants with the aid of forms and tokens, dice, and rules (like the ones in this book) for arbitration and interpretation.

You have already met me and the others. Whenever you see one of us like this, that's us talking directly to you. We do that when we want to give you our view of things, or when we present an example of how things are done.

I'm graf Albrecht Vogelin Erwin von Zadrith, Number Two of the Octopus and soon to be leader of the world. When you see me, I'm talking as the Director of Operations of a Troubleshooters game, telling you how a proper Director should control the world!

HOW TO READ THIS BOOK

This is *The Troubleshooters* core book. It contains rules, procedures, stats and a description of this roleplaying game. The first part, which you are reading now, is about the genre of the game and what tabletop roleplaying is.

The next part is about the characters of the game, how to make them, and the stats and values that describe them. Of course you use this part to create your character, but odds are you will need to reference it during the course of the game as well.

The third part is about procedures: how to handle actions and fights, how to influence the story using **Story**

Points, how to advance your character, and what your character will do between sessions.

The fourth part is for the host of the game, called the Director of Operations, or just the Director.

PLAYING THE GAME

The Troubleshooters is a roleplaying game, in which you create your own comic book-style stories. Playing a tabletop roleplaying game is a bit like improvised theatre, but without a stage. Instead, the scene is described through conversation among those sitting around the table, sometimes using props like maps and miniatures.

In this game, players will pretend to be heroes in a comic book setting, as if they were the main characters of a comic book like Spirou et Fantasio or Tintin. Each player takes the role of one character, either one of the characters presented earlier in the book, or one that they make up on their own. It's up to you.

One of you, referred to as the Director of Operations, will moderate the game. You will give the game direction by preparing adventures, story outlines and challenges for the players, or using a prepared adventure where someone else has already done the basic job of creating the story outline and challenges.

The rest of you take the roles of made-up characters who work together to overcome the challenges and solve the problems in the adventure. As a player, you tell the other participants what your character does and says. The others respond and describe what their characters are doing. In that process, the story unfolds.

At all times, you get to make choices (that's why we call it a "game"). You decide what your character will say and do. You lend her your voice to talk as her, and you describe her actions. Those actions have consequences.

Some of the consequences are decided by the reactions of the other players and their characters or moderated by the Director of Operations. Some of the consequences, in particularly those that require impartial moderation, are decided using rules and dice.

WHAT IS A DIRECTOR OF OPERATIONS?

One player has to take a special role, that of the Director of Operations.

The Director of Operations, more commonly called the Director, has an outline of the basic plot of the story and guides the players through it, taking the roles of any people that their characters may encounter along the way. The Director also sets up scenes, creates challenges and describes the action and events in the game.

The Director has one more job, and that is to be a referee and moderator of the rules, making sure that the game itself is fair and enjoyable for all the players.

As anyone who has ever played "let's pretend" knows, sometimes there will be a situation where two descriptions are in conflict ("*Bang! You're dead!*" – "*No, I'm not!*"). There are two ways of resolving such conflicts. Either you can ask the Director of Operations, or you can use the rules. The Director often resolves such conflicts using common sense and her judgment of what's best for the continued enjoyment of all participants. In other cases, the Director will use the rules to arbitrate such conflicts.

WHAT YOU NEED

In addition to this book, there are a few things you need.

- **Dice:** A set of dice consists of at least half a dozen six-sided dice, and two ten-sided dice. You will need at least one set. Traditionally, players often have their own dice. There is an official Troubleshooters dice set available in game stores, but any set will do.
- **Passports:** The Passport is a booklet in which you keep track of your character and her adventures. You can find sets of Passports in game stores. There is also an Emergency Passport available for download at the Helmgast website to print, free of charge.
- **Pencil and eraser:** To take notes. They can also be used for drawing.
- **Friends:** *The Troubleshooters* is suitable for one Director of Operations and 2–6 players.
- **A place to play:** A table in the kitchen or dining room works fine.

Optionally, you can also get:

- **Extra core books:** Although not necessary, having more than one core book available increases the flow during play, since one player hogging the core book does not stop other players from looking things up. It is definitely an advantage while creating characters.

- **Adventure books:** Adventure books contain prepared scenarios for you to use. They are for the Director of Operations' eyes only. You can do without them, but if so, you'll have to do the preparation on your own.
- **Miniature figures and battlemaps:** Miniatures and battlemaps are not necessary either, but they are useful for making the situation more clear.
- **Snacks and drinks:** Refreshments are nice, but they carry the risk of spilling and leaving marks on paper and books.
- **Directors' Display:** The Display hides the Director of Operations' secrets from the other players as well as having reference information handy for the Director.
- **Gear cards:** Gear cards make it easier to handle gear and equipment. Each card has reference information about one gear kit. These are available in game stores.
- **Vitality and Story Point tokens:** You can track **Vitality** and **Story Points** by taking notes, but having tokens makes it a little bit easier.

HOW DOES IT WORK?

As we stated earlier, the game is played as a conversation.

In the following example, the characters have been tracking down a secret base of the criminal organisation the Octopus. It is an underground complex under Matterhorn. The main entrance is heavily guarded, but they have heard about an emergency exit that they could use.

The locals in Breuil-Cervinia, the ski resort where the characters are staying, have noticed some unmarked all-terrain trucks going up and down the mountain on a little-used side-road.

 Following the directions, you find a track leading up into the alpine forest. Matterhorn rises sharply above you, hidden in mist and clouds and there is a chill wind blowing. It starts to pour down, and Paul, your 2CV isn't exactly built for off-road conditions.

 That means making a task check, right?

 It does. A difficult one.

 Let me take the wheel. If I can drive a Morris through the desert to Dakar, I should be able to take a 2CV on this lousy road.

 Right, we switch places.

 Great. Elektra, the track is muddy and steep, so I want a Drive task check down two pips, because of the conditions. If you fail, you have to walk.

 Hah! Look at that! 66! Success and **Good Karma**. And a **Story Point** to me! And an experience check!

 Heh. Okay, as you drive on the narrow track, suddenly there's a crack and boom!

Lightning strikes a pole next to the road, and the surveillance camera and sensor array at the top goes up in smoke. So you're probably still undetected and you don't have to make a **Sneak check** to get past it.

Surveillance camera, huh? That means that we're on the right track.

Eventually, you reach the end of the track. Someone has drilled and blasted away the mountain to create a platform and a v-shaped cut in the mountain side, and lined the cut with concrete. It's all painted in green and dark olive to hide it. At the far end of the cut, there's a huge blast door with an embossed Octopus logotype.

This must be it. I get my pistol out and secure the platform and blast door.

I get out of the way since I'm in the front seat, but I too get my pistol out. I'm on my guard.

Okay, I want an **Alertness task check** from Paul, and a **Search task check** from Frida.

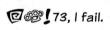 73, I fail.

09 here, which is a success, despite the low odds. I have **Search** 15.

Paul, you don't notice anything strange. There might not have been anything strange in the first place, but if there were, you wouldn't notice it. Frida, the platform is secured. The only way here is from through the blast door, the track you travelled, and possibly dropping down on the platform from above, but that would require a master alpinist.

Thank you. At last we have found their secret base. How do we get in?

Through the door, obviously. I try to pick the lock.

There isn't one.

What?

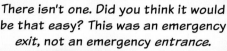
There isn't one. Did you think it would be that easy? This was an emergency exit, not an emergency *entrance*.

So we came here for nothing?

There ought to be an air intake somewhere. In bunkers, the air intake is often the emergency exit. I search for one. 28 on a **Search task check**.

Uh, yes, there is one. But there are three problems: there is a sturdy padlock on the steel grille, it's way up on the wall so you can't reach it, and the hole is too small for you.

Don't worry. I have a plan! I drive the car to the wall and park it right under the air intake. That should be enough for Paul to reach the padlock to open it. If it is not enough for Paul to reach the padlock from the roof of the car, our Swedish Amazon can lift him.

Hey, I'm an officer in the Swedish air force, not a ladder.

Can we do it?

Well, first I want a **Strength task check** from Frida, and then a **Prestidigitation task check** from Paul. If she doesn't make it, your **Prestidigitation task check** will be at −2 pips.

Meh. 75, fail.

Hold still, woman! I can't reach! But I roll 47, a success despite the higher difficulty.

So you open the steel grille. But it's still too small for you.

 Not a problem. Éloïse, your turn!

 What?

 What?

 It is obviously too small for me or Frida, but not for our skinny teen mad inventor. I spend two **Story Points** if necessary to make it so.

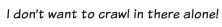 Sigh. Okay, why not?

 I don't want to crawl in there alone!

 Don't worry, we'll tie this rope around you and pull you out if you're stuck. And here, take the flashlight.

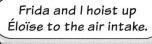 Frida and I hoist up Éloïse to the air intake.

 Waah! It's dark in here!

 And it's very very tight. I want an **Agility task check** to avoid getting stuck.

 40. That's a fail. But I'm like, Young and skinny, so I spend a **Story Point** to flip that to 04, and wiggle through anyway.

 Usually, Young allows you to spend a **Story Point** to be ignored by adults, but okay, I'll allow it this once.

 I could spend another **Story Point** if you want to play by the rules.

 No, that's okay. You squeeze through and crawl on, and find an opening into the corridor leading to the exit.

 Is there anyone there?

 No, it's empty.

 Then I drop down into the corridor. I look around for anything unusual, anyone detecting me, security cameras and things like that.

 Make a **Search task check**.

 41. Success.

 No, nothing here, unless I secretly made the check more difficult.

 Let's hope not. I untie myself, go down the corridor to the door and open it. Is it a lock wheel, like a bank vault?

Yes. On the outside, the door swings open, and a grimy Éloïse greets you. The corridor goes straight into the mountain. What do you do?

Well, we're here for a purpose. I take the lead.

Deep inside the mountain, a red lamp lights up on a control panel, indicating that the emergency exit door has opened from an alarm circuit that Éloïse failed to notice because her Search task check was in fact more difficult. Von Zadrith plans to send security personnel to look into what set off the alarm and stop any intruders…

What happens next? That's for you to find out, if your characters ever sneak into an Octopus base through the hidden back door.

HOW DO I START?

The first thing to do is to appoint one person as the Director of Operations. It's often the person that buys the game. As a Director, the best way to start is to familiarise yourself with the rules and the story of the first adventure, and then just try it out.

THE PARADIGM OF THE GAME

The Troubleshooters is a roleplaying game about action, adventure and mystery in a fictional European 1960s–1970s setting in the style of mainly Belgian and French comics, also known as bande dessinée or bédé.

If you have not read Belgian or French comics, do not despair! This game is inspired by them, not based on them. There is a certain paradigm of the game that's actually pretty easy to understand:

> *The Troubleshooters* is about good friends, competent in their fields of expertise, who have fun, exciting and light-hearted adventures together, in Europe and other exotic locations.

It's that simple.

Sources of inspiration

If you think *Tintin*, *Yoko Tsuno*, *Spirou et Fantasio*, or *Franka*, you're definitely in the right ballpark. If you haven't read any of them, you really should! Some of them are still published, and many of them are being translated and republished as anthologies in English.

Other sources of inspiration are the television shows *The Saint*, *Carmen Sandiego* and *Lupin III*, and *The Man from UNCLE*.

ADVENTURE!

This game is about adventure! *The Troubleshooters* will take you all over the world, and sometimes even beyond. There will be danger and challenges, but through teamwork and smart thinking, you can overcome them.

ACTION!

The Troubleshooters has car chases, fisticuffs and shootouts. It has heists and daring stunts.

Despite the danger and the action, *The Troubleshooters* isn't deadly or gritty. In this game, your character doesn't die unless that's what you want or you do something really stupid. Characters are more likely to be knocked unconscious, or disappear from the scene, or be taken prisoner. In fact, being taken prisoner is a staple of the genre. You choose if incoming damage will just knock you unconscious or hurt you for real, or even kill you.

COMPETENT CAST

The player characters of *The Troubleshooters* are beyond the norm. They are often jack-of-all-trades sorts that can hold their own in many different areas, as well as competent specialists in their own fields. They can have exotic origins or specialise in exotic fields or trades, and above all, they embrace the adventure!

Although considerably above average, the player characters are not superheroes. The story may stretch their feats a bit, but it's more of an exaggeration of the real and the possible than something unreal or impossible. The unreal and impossible is left for superhero comics.

FUN AND FRIENDSHIP

The Troubleshooters is not a grimdark or even a dark game. On the contrary, the colours are bright, the tone is light, and it is full of humour, jokes and gags.

There's not much room for intrigue and enmity among the player characters, beyond friendly competition. They are friends, working together towards a common goal and helping each other when they get into trouble. The characters have their weaknesses and things won't always go their way, but making enemies of one another isn't meant to be a major point of conflict.

IN THE PAST, WHEN IT WAS BETTER

The game is set in an alternate 1960s to 1970s and mainly in Europe. It has been a few decades since the War, and Europe has recovered.

It is an era of glamour, optimism and technological advances. Everyone can afford a car and drive to wherever they want. Jumbo passenger jets have shrunk the world. You can call anyone anywhere through transatlantic cables and even satellite calls. People are even reaching for the Moon!

That doesn't mean that everything is perfect. Far from it: Europe is divided by the Iron Curtain. There was less equality between the sexes, the fight for civil liberties for minorities sometimes became violent, and homosexuality was seen as a disease. The Western and Eastern blocs do have their occasional showdowns, often in the form of proxy wars or proxy revolutions around the globe.

There is petty crime and organised crime. There are conspiracies and secret societies, and in the shadows, the organisation known as the Octopus vies for world domination. But despite all these problems, there is a sense that the world is improving.

EUROCENTRIC AND METROPOLITAN

The Troubleshooters is an international game. Its focus is on Europe, because Europe is diverse and full of exotic locations that are within reach by train or car.

Europe has a very diverse legacy, from castles in the Rhine valley to small principalities forgotten along the borders of their bigger neighbours; from remote villages in the Alps to the skyscrapers of Europe's capitals; from wine chateaus in France to glittering casinos on the Riviera.

Often, the game leaves Europe for even more exotic venues. Even a trip to the other side of the Iron Curtain means entering another world. With the new supersonic jets, it's not that big a deal to go to the far side of the world. Jumbo jets offer long distance air travel in comfort (economy air travel with passengers packed like sardines is not yet invented). And even if this jet set lifestyle is growing, cruise ships still cross the oceans in style.

INTERNATIONAL COOPERATION

International cooperation is very much in vogue in Europe. France and Germany, once bitter enemies, initiated the European Coal and Steel Community which then expanded to the European Economic Community. France and Britain cooperated to create the first supersonic jetliner – the name "Concorde" even means "harmony" – just recently entering service. France and Japan launched the first moon mission in 1964 using the atomic rocket Kaguyahime. Now, France and Japan are talking about building a Paris-Lyon *Shinkansen* line.

International teams of characters are not only possible in *The Troubleshooters*, they are even encouraged! It is an easy way of adding some cultural diversity to a group, and it may even make some adventures easier.

ROLEPLAYING ETIQUETTE

Like most other activities, roleplaying has a social code to help everyone have a good time.

RESPECT THE DIRECTOR

The Director is there to guide you through the story and help you create it. Many hours were probably spent preparing for the evening. Appreciate that work: don't sabotage the game by your character's actions, and respect the Director's interpretation and arbitration of the rules.

RESPECT THE PLAYERS

As the Director, your job is to make the game fun, not to beat the players. Your goal is therefore to challenge them. Challenges shouldn't be impossible, but they shouldn't be an automatic success either.

The players also have ideas for the stories about their characters. They are here for those stories. Respect that, and let the players influence the stories, directly through the actions of their characters as well as indirectly through the design of their characters.

While you have a lot of control over the story, the players have minds of their own. Be prepared for when the players don't act according to your plan. In fact, the collaborative storytelling of roleplaying is a big part of the fun. If the players take you by surprise, they give you ideas you would not otherwise have had. Don't reject these gifts just because they're unexpected.

RESPECT THE FLOW

Nothing breaks the mood of a thrilling action scene faster than someone saying "*no, I should have made that hit because the rules on page 115 say…*" Rules lawyering is disrespectful of everyone else's time. Rather, accept that what's done is done, and hold the discussion for after the session.

It isn't just rules discussions that may break the flow. So could a bad joke, non-game talk, and just about anything that is not focused on the unfolding story. The flow is a precious thing. Respect it when you have it.

RESPECT THE LIMELIGHT

Different sessions will focus on different characters. If you want the other players to give you the limelight, you also have to be willing to let them shine.

BE PREPARED

As a player, you should be familiar with your character's Abilities, Skills, Complications and gear. You should know how often they can be used and what they do. You should also do your best to remember the things you encounter in the game – people, places, events.

As a Director, being prepared means plotting adventures and preparing for unexpected turns. It also means that you should know the rules, at least to the point where you can determine how things should work and answer the players' questions.

DICE AND STUFF

The Troubleshooters uses six-sided dice and percentile dice. You will need at least half a dozen six-sided dice. Ordinary dice will do, but there are custom dice for *The Troubleshooters* that have a circle on the 4 and 5 sides, and an explosion symbol on the 6 side.

Dice code	Meaning	Used in
d%	Percentile dice	Task checks, some tables
Nd6	Sum of N six-sided dice	
NdP	Pool of N six-sided dice	Soak rolls, Recovery rolls
NdX	Pool of N exploding six-sided dice	Damage rolls

Percentile rolls: All task checks use the percentile dice, abbreviated "**d%**".

For the percentile dice, you use two ten-sided dice to give you a random number between 1 and 100. You read one of the dice as the **Tens** (there are ten-sided dice with the numbers 00, 10, and so on up to 90), and the other as the **Ones**. The result 00 and 0 (or 0 and 0) should be read as "100".

Keep track of the outcome of the individual dice. We sometimes use the **Tens** or the **Ones** of a **d%** roll.

- The **Tens** die gives you a random number between 0 and 9, unless you roll exactly 100 ("0 and 0" or "00 and 0"), in which case the **Tens** counts as 10. **Tens** can be capped by your Skill value if they are used on a successful roll.
- The **Ones** die also gives you a random number between 0 and 9, but there is no special case for 100. The random number is mostly independent from Skill value. **Ones** are often used in conjunction with difficulty.

Most of the time, percentile rolls are used for task checks. In a task check, you compare the random number to a Skill value to determine success or failure. Sometimes, percentile rolls are used for table lookups.

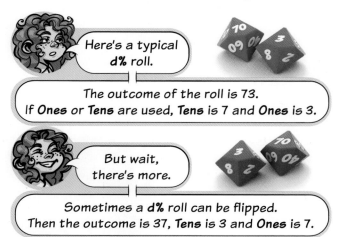

Here's a typical **d%** roll.

The outcome of the roll is 73. If Ones or Tens are used, Tens is 7 and Ones is 3.

But wait, there's more.

Sometimes a **d%** roll can be flipped. Then the outcome is 37, Tens is 3 and Ones is 7.

Six-sided dice: Six-sided dice, commonly called **d6s**, are used for many rolls that are not task checks, specifically damage, soak and recovery rolls. If you roll several **d6s**, the amount of dice is a number before the "**d6**" code.

And this is a **3d6** roll.
1 + 4 + 3 means an outcome of 8.
Boring!

Sum of dice (Nd6): If **d6s** are used and it is not for a Damage, Soak or Recovery roll, you just roll the dice and add them together.

Damage rolls (NdX): Damage rolls are used to inflict damage, and range from **2dX** for unarmed attacks to up to **7dX** for machine guns. You use six-sided dice as an exploding dice pool for damage rolls. "Exploding dice" means that if you roll 6s, you roll additional dice.

- Roll N number of six-sided dice.
- If you roll any sixes, roll one additional **dX** for every six you got. Keep doing this until you no longer roll any sixes.
- Each die that shows a 4–6 equals 1 point of **Vitality** loss.

This is me shooting at an Octopus brute and inflicting **5dX** damage.

The 6 explodes, so I roll another **dX**. It too comes up as 6, so I roll yet another **dX** and get a 3.

These are not counted towards the **Vitality** loss.

These four dice mean that I inflicted 4 points of **Vitality** loss.

Soak and Recovery rolls (NdP): Soak rolls are used to reduce incoming **Vitality** loss, usually from armour. Recovery rolls are used to recover lost **Vitality**. Soak rolls are uncommon, while Recovery rolls happen more frequently.

Like Damage rolls, you use six-sided dice as a dice pool for Soak and Recovery rolls, but unlike Damage rolls, Soak or Recovery rolls never explode.

- Roll N number of six-sided dice.
- Each die that shows a 4–6 equals 1 point of Soak or Recovery.

My brute has a **2dP** bulletproof vest, and rolls 3 and 6.

The 3 doesn't count, but the 6 does.
The 6 doesn't explode as it is not a Damage roll.
The vest soaks 1 point of **Vitality** loss.

THE CUSTOM DICE

The custom dice set has seven six-sided dice and two ten-sided dice.

The six-sided dice have the numbers 1–6 instead of dots. The faces 4–6 are different from the rest to use for Damage, Soak and Recovery.

- The faces 4 and 5 have a circle on them, to indicate that these count as 1 point of **Vitality** loss, Soak and Recovery.
- The 6 face has an explosion symbol on it, to indicate that this side counts as 1 point of **Vitality** loss, Soak and Recovery, and that it explodes in the case of Damage rolls.

TERMS AND GLOSSARY

These terms are often used in *The Troubleshooters*.

Action: An attempt to do something. It may be resolved using dice, or by the Director's moderation.

Cast character: A character controlled by one of the players.

Challenge: An action that is complex, takes time, and/or uses several Skills, and has a more impactful outcome than ordinary actions. They are resolved using three to five task checks.

Condition: Each of these signals that a specific effect is in play for a character, for instance **Wounded** or **Intoxicated**.

Damage roll: A roll of six-sided dice to determine damage.

Director: Short for Director of Operations. Other games would call this player the Gamemaster, Dungeon Master, Storyteller or Referee.

Director character: A character or creature controlled by the Director.

Downtime: The time between adventures. Between each adventure, you get downtime periods, which you can use to train, travel, socialise and invent things.

Experience check: A check made to improve a Skill.

Experience tick: A tick that allows you one chance to make either an experience check or a learning check.

Flip a check: In some situations, you can flip the dice roll of a task check, reading it in reverse so that, for instance, a dice roll of 73 becomes a dice roll of 37.

Gear kit: A bundled set of equipment or gear. You can have five gear kits at any time.

Initiative: Turns are evaluated in a round in initiative order, from highest to lowest.

Karma: An exceptional result. **Karma** can be Good or Bad. You get **Good Karma** if the **Ones** and **Tens** of a task check are equal and the task check succeeds; and **Bad Karma** if the **Ones** and **Tens** of a task check are equal and the task check fails. You also get one **Story Point** every time you get **Good** or **Bad Karma**.

Modifier: Modifiers make task checks easier or harder, by looking at the **Ones** of task checks. An up modifier makes it possible to succeed even if you roll higher than the Skill value, and a down modifier may make you fail even if you roll equal to or below the Skill value.

Opposed check: Testing one task check against another task check. You have to roll equal to or lower than the Skill value, but above what the opponent rolls.

Plot Hook: Something that pulls your character into the adventure.

Recovery roll: A roll to regain lost **Vitality**, either as a result of catching your breath or getting support from a friendly character.

Scene: A place in space and time where something interesting happens.

Skill: There are 28 areas of expertise, known as Skills. Each has a percentage value between 15 and 106, measuring how good you are.

Soak roll: A roll to absorb or otherwise shrug off incoming damage. You can make a Soak roll if you have some kind of protection or stay behind light cover.

Story Point: **Story Points** are used by players to buy influence in the story. You get **Story Points** for activating Complications, getting **Karma**, doing cool things, and being caught. You **spend Story Points** to activate Abilities, flip checks, and add things to the story.

Tags: Tags indicate specific qualities of gear, equipment, weapons, and enemies.

Task check: A dice roll to check whether a task succeeds or not. You want to roll equal to or below your Skill value.

Turn: In a fight scene, each character takes a turn in initiative order. On each turn, you get to do a number of actions. A single turn is roughly what happens in one comic panel.

Vitality: A measure of energy, willpower and physical prowess. When **Vitality** runs out, you're **Out Cold**.

Zone: Places of interest are divided into zones for handling movement, types of terrain, line of sight and so on. Zones are almost only used in fight scenes.

THE CAST

Now that you know who we are, it's time to talk about you: who you are, what you're good at, what your dreams are, who your friends are and how you'll function within a group.

You are going to step into a world of adventure and action, and you need to know where you are to know where you are going.

The journey will take you all over the world. You never know where you will end up or what will happen there. But it's important to understand your abilities and your limitations when tackling an adventure. And that's what we're about to take a look at.

Do you have your passport ready? Because we're going now!

WHAT IS A CHARACTER

In traditional roleplaying games – such as *The Troubleshooters* – the character is the means through which the player interacts with and experiences the setting. It is your role, your vessel through which you contribute to the creation of the common story.

Your character has two components: the game stats in the Passport, which are used with the rules to determine the direction of the story; and the description, which could consist of all kinds of things, such as a character's portrait, background story, description of their appearance, or journals chronicling adventures you've had with your friends.

This combination of story and game stats is your character, and through it you act and participate in *The Troubleshooters*.

24

The Passport
The Passport is where you keep track of your character's journey. You can use the 32-page Passport booklet available in stores, or the simplified double-sided Emergency Passport form that you can download from our website.

WHAT MAKES A GOOD CHARACTER

The Troubleshooters is not a game of intrigue and conspiracies. It's a game of fun, friendship and adventure. While tension between the characters is good drama, it's not the kind of drama that *The Troubleshooters* aims for. If you prefer it, by all means, go ahead and play the game that way.

However, the game is designed around the idea of a group of friends helping each other and cooperating to achieve a common goal. In this mode, tension between characters is just there to spice things up and to differentiate the characters, not to drive the story.

A good character in *The Troubleshooters*:

● Is competent and can do her job
● Does not replace any other character, but brings something unique to the group
● Has plenty of reasons to get involved in adventures, sometimes willingly, but even kicking and screaming will do
● Allows for character growth and development
● Has weaknesses that can be used to enhance the story or make the game more interesting
● Is fun to interact with
● And most important, is fun to play!

WHAT THE STATS MEAN

The core game stats in *The Troubleshooters* are the Skills and **Max Vitality**. These allow you to perform actions and take hits.

In addition, there are the story mechanism stats: **Plot Hooks**, Traits, Abilities, Complications, and **Story Points**, that allow you to influence the way events unfold.

Finally, there are Tags, especially on equipment, that define their special characteristics in game terms. Protective gear also has a Protection stat, and weapons have a Damage stat.

PLOT HOOKS

Plot Hooks are used to get your character into adventures. They also help define each character's individual motivations.

There's a list of 11 possible **Plot Hooks**, and each character has one or two from that list. Adventure modules will have startup handouts for four to six of the **Plot Hooks**, and the director uses one or two of them to start the adventure. The other players are encouraged to play it up and help make the **Plot Hook** characters feel truly special.

Plot Hooks could be used for homebrew adventures as well.

SKILLS

Skills are measured on a percentile scale. The lowest Skill value you can have is 15. Theoretically, the highest value you can have in any Skill is 106. The highest starting value is 85.

When making a task check, you try to roll lower than or equal to the Skill value in order to succeed. In an opposed check, you also want to roll higher than your opponent's roll. The outcome of task checks are binary – you succeed or you don't, or in the case of opposed checks, you win or you don't – but it is good to regard higher rolls as "better" or more successful than lower ones, even if there is no specific rule that says this. That way, you get a bit of extra input when narrating the outcome, plus you train yourself to handle opposed checks.

Next to each Skill value is an improvement checkbox. Check this when you use the Skill in a meaningful way. You don't have to succeed, or even actually make the task check, just so long as the attempt moves the plot forward. However, if you use the Skill just to put a mark in the checkbox, you don't get the improvement check. You can only have one check per Skill at any given time.

VITALITY

Vitality is a measure of your energy, capacity to withstand injury, defence ability, guard, pain threshold, et cetera. You have a current **Vitality** and a **Max Vitality**. Your starting **Max Vitality** is set by the Template you pick for your character and has a value between 4 and 7. Most characters will have **Max Vitality** 5.

You lose current **Vitality** when you are hit and suffer damage. When you run out of **Vitality**, you're **Out Cold**. You regain current **Vitality** by taking a breather, or when the fight is over. Your current **Vitality** can never be higher than your **Max Vitality**.

Your **Max Vitality** can be temporarily lowered if you are exhausted, poisoned, et cetera. **Max Vitality** is restored when the Condition that lowered **Max Vitality** is dropped.

Since current **Vitality** will change often, we recommend using some tokens like beads or counters to keep track of it, rather than constantly having to erase and rewrite the number.

ABILITIES

Abilities are special rules that enable you to do things most people can't. Some of them are for combat, some are for other situations. There's often some conditions attached: usually it will cost a number of **Story Points** to activate the Ability.

Abilities have a tier, depending on what prerequisites they have. Tier 0 Abilities have no prerequisites, while tier 1 Abilities require that you have a minimum Skill value in one or more Skills. When creating characters, you can pick tier 1 Abilities even if you don't have the required Skill value.

Each Template has five Abilities to pick from. You normally start with two of them.

COMPLICATIONS

Like Abilities, Complications are special rules, but instead of enabling you to do things, they limit you in fun and interesting ways. When a Complication is triggered, it may give you one or more **Story Points**.

Each Template has three Complications to pick from. You start with one.

STORY POINTS

Story Points are the "currency" you spend to influence the events of the story and buy yourself advantages. You start each session with **4 Story Points**.

You **gain Story Points** by activating your Complications, getting captured, rolling a **Karma** result on a task check, or changing a successful task check into a failure.

There is a cap on **Story Points**: you can't have more than 12.

DAMAGE

Whenever you fight and hit the opponent, you inflict damage. Damage is measured as a number of **d6s**, usually between **3d6** and **5d6** for close combat weapons, and **4d6** to **7d6** for firearms. In a fistfight or other unarmed fight, your base damage is **2d6**, but can occasionally be higher if you use Abilities. Each 4–6 you roll inflicts 1 point of **Vitality** loss.

Damage rolls are open-ended: meaning that whenever you roll 6s, you roll one additional **d6** for every 6 you roll. Repeat until you don't roll 6s on the additional dice. This is sometimes referred to as exploding dice.

PROTECTION

Most people don't wear protective gear. It's generally only worn in very special situations. Bodyguards, some public figures, and police in riot gear may wear a bullet-proof vest. Soldiers wear helmets. Some specialist combat roles, like door gunners in helicopters, may wear heavy protective gear. And there are occasions when a character might don a medieval knight's armour to sneak around a castle. But other than that, protective gear is very unusual.

Protective gear has a protection value, measured in a number of **d6s**. A soldier's helmet or a public figure's bulletproof vest has a protection value of **1d6**, while a medieval knight's armour has a protection value of **3d6**.

When hit, you roll a number of dice equal to the protection value. This is called a Soak roll. Each 4–6 cancels out, or soaks up, 1 point of **Vitality** loss.

Protection dice are not open-ended.

Protective gear has some disadvantages. It limits your Initiative roll, for instance. It also takes time to put on, from an action for a simple bulletproof vest to half-an-hour for a knight's armour. Finally, it may limit your movement and obstruct your senses, making **Agility** or **Alertness check**s more difficult.

TAGS

Weapons, protective gear and a lot of other items can have one or more tags. Tags work a bit like Abilities: they are special rules that can be activated in certain situations where they are an advantage or disadvantage to the weapon.

LANGUAGES

Languages are binary: you're fluent or you're not. If you're not fluent, your ability to communicate is limited by whether or not you succeed at a task check with the Skill **Languages**. If you are fluent, you rarely have to use the Skill **Languages** to get your point across.

Most characters know two or three languages. French and English, plus the native tongue of your character's home country if not anglophone or francophone. It is actually very likely that your character isn't a native English speaker – after all, the game is set in Europe and the cast is international.

SESSION ZERO

A good way to start a *Troubleshooters* campaign is by having a Session Zero. In this session, the Directors and players meet up, talk about the campaign and discuss what it will be about. The goal is to leave Session Zero with a clear consensus of what the campaign will be like, what expectations you and the other players have, and finished characters.

Here's a sample agenda for Session Zero:

- The Director tells the players what kind of campaign he has in mind.
- The group brainstorms about the team and the campaign:
  - Theme
  - Expectations
  - Characters
  - Roles within the team
  - Location
- The players create their characters.
- The players create a team from their characters.
- Start playing!

My idea for the campaign is based on independent do-gooders battling the Octopus, a bit like The Saint vs SPECTRE.

There is a world conspiracy that the characters oppose, but they are not secret agents. Instead, they're a bit like "underworld freelancers", not tied to any government.

I tell the players my idea, and they start to brainstorm around it.

CREATING A TEAM

The Troubleshooters is not one of those games where you conspire against other player characters. Your team doesn't have to be an organised formal team with a hierarchy – being friends who go on adventures together is enough.

You work reasonably well together. There may be tensions, arguments and differences, just like in any other group, and acting out such tensions may heighten the experience. But team conflicts and intrigues are not the point of the game.

With that in mind, go ahead and create a team.

THEME

One important decision regards the theme of the campaign and how the team fits into that. This may be the Director's decision, or it could be made collectively by the group.

CURIOUS ADVENTURERS

This is the most common theme for *The Troubleshooters*. The characters are just friends, and sometimes they're dragged into adventures by their own curiosity or as a result of job assignments.

- Archaeologists stumble upon historical or anthropological artifacts, for instance famous lost art, secrets from the War or previous dynasties, historic objects, or local myths.
- Journalists investigate an interesting story, which leads to an unexpected source of adventure.
- Dilettantes discover that a family heirloom has a more interesting history than originally thought.
- A friend is in trouble. While trying to help, it becomes apparent that helping will be more trouble than the team initially bargained for.

This theme relies more on the characters' **Plot Hooks** than any other theme.

Examples:
- *Spirou* (comic)
- *Tintin* (comic)
- *Franka* (comic)
- *Yoko Tsuno* (comic)

SLEUTHS

In the tradition of Sherlock Holmes, the characters are trying to solve crimes. Often, they are freelancers, only loosely affiliated with the law and not constrained by intelligence or police organisations. In fact, depending on how many rules the characters break in order to solve crimes, they may have almost as many problems with the law as with the villains.

- Someone's wife or husband has disappeared.
- A family heirloom is stolen.
- A character witnesses a crime.
- Someone, perhaps even one of the characters, is accused of a crime they did not commit.

This theme relies on player participation and willingness to solve mysteries.

Examples:
- *Gil Jourdan* (comic)
- *The Saint* (television show and books)

AGENTS

The characters are tied to a possibly secret organisation. Their boss sends them on assignments, and it's the characters' job to accomplish whatever goals they are given.

- An intelligence agency sends them on missions to thwart plots against the state.
- A special branch of the police fights a war against the criminal underworld, sometimes with the aid of private consultants.
- A secret organisation has vowed to bring Nazi war criminals to justice.
- A university department is looking for curious (and dangerous) artifacts from history.

This theme does not use **Plot Hooks** that much. Although they may stumble on a case from time to time, it's more common for the characters to be assigned a mission.

Examples:
- *Valérian & Laureline* (comic)
- *Clifton* (comic)
- *The Man from UNCLE* (television show and movie)
- *James Bond* (movies and books)
- *Mission: Impossible* (television show, the old one)

HEISTS

The characters are actually crooks, with the goal of stealing from the rich to give to – well, mostly themselves. This means that they will be hunted by law enforcement and rival gangs. A theme like this works best if the characters are "gentleman thieves". It also leaves the planning of the heists to the characters: they will basically make their own adventures, and the Director's job is mainly to insert danger and Complications into the characters' plans.

- An ex-wife of a ridiculously wealthy nobleman asks the characters to steal a Fabergé egg.
- A girl asks the characters to kidnap her to expose her abusive parents.
- A contact needs a microfilm stolen from a weapons manufacturer. The microfilm is stored in a vault, together with warrants and bonds worth millions.

This theme relies very much on player participation and uses the **Story Point** economy. **Plot Hooks** are useful, but the theme works best if the players themselves come up with ideas for heists.

Examples:
- *Lupin III* (anime and manga)
- *The Rogues* (television show)
- *Carmen Sandiego* (2019 animated show)

We like the Director's idea, and after some discussion we go for a Curious Adventurers theme mixed with Heists. We want a mixed group with different specialties. My player goes for a mad scientist of some kind.

My player has the idea of a cat burglar and ex-French Resistance character, not quite as gentlemanly as The Saint.

My player wants to play a secret agent, and proposes that governments may join forces with the anti-Octopus underworld.

My player thinks that the campaign needs fast cars, and goes for a no-nonsense rally driver.

As I'm going to play a female secret agent, it might be fun if we consider making an all female team.

I'm a bit uncomfortable playing a character of the opposite gender.

That's okay. Pick whatever you think will be the most fun for you. It's important to be comfortable playing your character.

ROLES WITHIN THE TEAM

Here are some examples of roles within the team:

The Doer: The Doer is the person that gets things done. She is often a leader and has a clear view of the problem and what needs to be done. It's not necessary that she do things herself. Delegating tasks is a big part of her role in the team. She frequently owns or controls some key asset for the team, such as their base of operations.

The Investigator: The Investigator is the person that digs up the clues and tries to put them together to form a coherent picture. This is a smart and attentive person, often a bit obsessive about order and details.

The Muscle: The Muscle is often thought of as dumb. Their job is to dish out and take hits, so that the others can do their jobs. However, if they want to stay alive, they have to be smart about it. In *The Troubleshooters*, being the Muscle has one more obstacle: these are not the highways of days past, and there is law enforcement and a justice system to contend with. Taking and dealing hits in a way that doesn't attract attention from the police, or getting away before they arrive, means that the Muscle has to be smarter than most give them credit for.

The Fixer: The Fixer is the one with the contacts. Often a charmer and a cosmopolitan person, the Fixer has been everywhere, knows everyone and ensures the group gets jobs, has a base camp ready, and has access to the proper equipment and leads. Even if jobs find the team, the Fixer's contacts are vitally important for everything else.

The Specialist: Even the Specialist is actually a jack-of-all-trades. They're just better at one special thing, be it driving, flying, sneaking past security systems, repairing stuff and so on.

I'm a real secret agent, and an officer, so I will probably take the Doer role.

I'm more of a Fixer. I know everyone, but they probably aren't as savvy as Frida would prefer.

I'm probably a bit of the Muscle type. I do physical stuff, not just driving cars, but also punching people. And kicking them in the groin.

I'm a pure Specialist. My role is to create gadgets. I will probably investigate gadgets too, and I will know things, so I'll probably take the Investigator role.

LOCATION

When you create the team, you should also decide on where the characters usually stay. It's better if they are pretty close to one another, so agree on a city or town, preferably in Europe.

Some things to think about:

- Where do you live?
- Where do you work?
- Where do you have lunch?

We will use Paris as a starting point for many of our adventures.

We decided on Paris because of the location and importance as a communications hub all over the world, and because it is a beautiful capital city with a rich history.

One key asset in our adventures will be the fictional newspaper *La République*, located at Avenue Claude Vellefaux in X$^\text{e}$ arrondissement. The newspaper is social-democratic but unaffiliated to any regional or national French party.

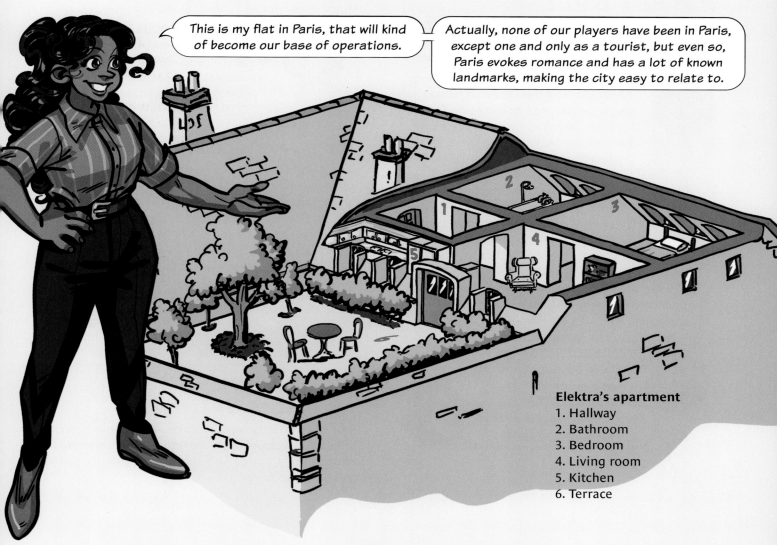

This is my flat in Paris, that will kind of become our base of operations.

Actually, none of our players have been in Paris, except one and only as a tourist, but even so, Paris evokes romance and has a lot of known landmarks, making the city easy to relate to.

Elektra's apartment
1. Hallway
2. Bathroom
3. Bedroom
4. Living room
5. Kitchen
6. Terrace

CREATING A CHARACTER

The process of creating a character consists of 10 steps:

1 Pick a Template
2 Set Skills
3 Pick two Abilities and a Complication
4 Determine **Max Vitality**
5 Pick languages
6 Select 5 gear kits
7 Choose **Plot Hooks**
8 Optional: customise
9 Design your character
10 Decide how you met

At least the steps *Choose Plot Hooks* and *Decide How You Met* have to be done together with the other players. It is also very useful to pick Templates together as a group, and setting Skills and customising Skills together allows you to cover each other's bases. It's also more fun to make characters together.

STEP 1: PICK A TEMPLATE

On page 40, there is a number of Templates to choose from. Pick one. Each Template has a bullet list of instructions that you follow as you create the character.

My player has the idea of a female mad scientist, but finds the Aspiring Student Template. She decides to go for a young technical genius rather than the older professor type.

This spawns a fun idea: maybe I inherited my genius from one of my parents. My player floats the idea that I have a French mother and an unknown German mad inventor father – a bit like having Doctor Frankenstein as my dad.

I like the idea! It has lots of opportunities in my Octopus-based campaign. Who knows which of my minions is the father of, uh...

Éloïse Giraud. That's my name.

Sheez! That name is almost impossible to type!

STEP 2: SET SKILLS ACCORDING TO THE TEMPLATE

Each Template has a set of 11 Skills, with set Skill values. The spearhead Skill has the Skill value 75%. The four core Skills have a Skill value of 65%, and the six complementary Skills have a Skill value of 45%. Any Skills which do not have a specified Skill value get set to 15%.

*According to the Aspiring Student Template, I get 75% in **Investigation**, 65% in **Engineering**, **Electronics**, **Humanities** and **Search**, and 45% in **Contacts**, **Languages**, **Medicine**, **Melee**, **Science** and **Willpower**. All other Skills are at 15%. It's a good mix, but needs some tweaking.*

STEP 3: PICK TWO ABILITIES

Each Template has a list of Abilities. Read up on what they do on page 62 and onwards, and then pick two. You get those regardless of whether you meet the prerequisites or not.

Of course I have the Abilities Tech Wiz and Young. still in school, but somewhat of a genius already – I get it from my unknown father.

STEP 3 ½: PICK ONE COMPLICATION

Your Template has a list of three Complications. Pick one of them.

Try to pick one that will lead to interesting situations, not one that you think will never happen to your character. The Complication is one way of gaining **Story Points**, so you want it to be active as often as possible. Since it is supposed to come into play a lot, you might as well make it fun and interesting.

Since I am still a school student, I should obviously have the Underage Complication.

STEP 4: DETERMINE MAX VITALITY

Your **Max Vitality** score is set on the Template. Technically, **Vitality** depends on the **Agility** Skill value and the value of one Combat Skill, but these Skills are already preset on the Template.

If you customise your character and change those Skills, your **Max Vitality** score may also change. See *Customise your character* on page 34.

> My **Vitality** is 5. Not abysmally bad, but it is rather meh.

STEP 5: PICK LANGUAGES

From the start, your character can speak, read and write at least English and French.

- If your character is from an English-speaking country, English is your native tongue and French is a second language.
- If your character is from a French-speaking country, French is your native tongue and English is a second language.
- If your character is not from a French or English-speaking country, English and French are second languages, and your country's language is your native tongue.

The Template indicates if you get additional language picks. How many depends on your **Languages** Skill value, so if you customise your character and the Skill value of **Languages** changes, the number of languages may change also. See *Customise your character* on page 34.

Some Abilities grant additional languages as well.

> I'm French but with a German father, but I don't have the Double Nationality Ability. I speak French as my native language, English as a second language, and can pick German as an extra language from the Template. But I want to cheat a little and make German a native language too, besides French.

> Rules-wise, there's no difference between a native language and a second language, so I will allow it. It fits the background you thought up, and in game terms, it doesn't actually matter, so it's a small concession.

STEP 6: SELECT GEAR KITS

You get three gear kits from your Template. You get these whether you meet the prerequisites or not. You can make one of these into a **Signature Gadget** if you want (see page 113).

In addition, you can pick two more gear kits, if you meet any prerequisites they have.

> I get an Electronics toolbox, a Chemistry lab set, and a Bicycle from the Template. I also pick a Walkie-talkie and Ski gear for the other two slots. And the Electronics toolbox is my **Signature Gadget**. It's not a toolbox per se, but I have tools and components in just about every pocket I have and a soldering iron in the school bag.

STEP 7: CHOOSE TWO PLOT HOOKS

Each Template has a list of suggested **Plot Hooks**. Each character should have one or two (preferably two) unique **Plot Hooks** that no other character has. To make sure that your character's **Plot Hooks** are unique, you have to talk to the other players, and you may have to compromise and pick a **Plot Hook** from the master list.

Plot Hooks will be used to kick off adventures. The Director will generally pick two **Plot Hooks** and use them to get the characters involved and introduce the plot.

- If one of your **Plot Hooks** is chosen by the Director, try to get things started and kick off the adventure.
- If none of your **Plot Hooks** are chosen by the Director, it is a great idea to have your character be the sidekick to the **Plot Hook** characters and try to make them be the main characters of the adventure. Try to not steal the limelight, but support the **Plot Hook** characters and help them excel! Don't worry: it will be your turn to be the hero in another adventure.

> As we discuss the **Plot Hooks**, I discover that the only **Plot Hook** that is easily available from my Template for me without causing serious trouble for the others is I **Owe You**. So I pick that.

> **Exile, Looking for a Case** and **Arch-Enemy: The Octopus** are free, so I could pick one of those as a second **Plot Hook**, even if they are not on my Template's list, or I could skip a second **Plot Hook** entirely.

> Because of my secret mad inventor dad, **Arch-Enemy: The Octopus** fits, in a quirky way. Perhaps dad deserted his family and joined the Octopus, and now I hate him for it?

OPTIONAL STEP 8: CUSTOMISE YOUR CHARACTER

Here are some ways you can customise your character, with the Director's permission.

Get other Skills: Replace one or two Skills you have in your list with Skills not on the list. The values remain the same.

Swap Skills around: Decrease one Skill by 10 to increase another Skill by 10. You can do this up to twice. You can combine the swaps if you want, and decrease two Skills by 10 each and increase one by 20, decrease one Skill by 20 to increase two Skills by 10 each, or decrease one Skill by 20 to increase another Skill by 20. The only limit is that no Skill can have a starting value higher than 85.

Check Vitality: **Vitality** is 4 by default. If **Agility** or one weapon Skill is 45, set **Vitality** to 5; If **Agility** or one weapon Skill is 65+, set **Vitality** to 6. If both **Agility** and one weapon Skill are 65+, set **Vitality** to 7.

Check Languages: Pick one extra language if Language is 45. Pick two extra languages if **Languages** is 65+.

Another Ability: Replace one of the Ability picks with an Ability that is not on the Template's list. If it is a tier 0 or tier 1 Ability, you don't have to fulfil any requirements. You can only pick Abilities on tier 2 or higher if you fulfil the requirements.

Another Complication: Pick a Complication not on the Template's list.

Make things more complicated: If you want, you can pick a third Ability, not limited to the Template's list, but only if you also pick a second Complication. As above, you don't have to fulfil any requirements of tier 0 or 1 Abilities, but you can only pick Abilities on tier 2 or higher if you fulfil the requirements.

Change gear: Replace one gear pick with one other gear kit not on the Template's list.

Time for the tweaks I was talking about. I lower **Humanities** by 20 to 45%, and instead increase **Science** to 65%. That feels more in line with a teenage genius. I decide to swap **Humanities** for **Security**, so now I have **Humanities** 15% and **Security** 45%. I also swap **Medicine** for **Engineering**.

My final Skill list is 75% in **Investigation**, 65% in **Electronics, Science, Medicine** and **Search**, and 45% in **Contacts, Languages, Engineering, Melee, Security** and **Willpower**. All other Skills are at 15%.

I also decide to take the Ability Mad Inventor to amplify my mad scientist heritage, and balance it with the Complication Sleepy.

And as a final touch, I swap my Bicycle gear kit from the Template for a Scooter, and decide that it is a mint coloured Vespa.

STEP 9: DESIGN YOUR CHARACTER

The next step is to think about your appearance. In the comics that inspired *The Troubleshooters*, all characters are made to be distinguishable – from Tintin's quiff and Spirou's concierge uniform to Yoko Tsuno's headband and bangs. You can immediately see which character is in the scene, even if they dress differently or are in a crowd.

Aim for a similar description of your character: first find one or two prominent features that distinguish your character. Think like a character designer: you want to make your character stand out from all the others drawn in the same panel. Once you have the distinguishing details figured out, build the rest of the appearance around that.

If you need inspiration, pick two or three items from the Design Ideas table as a starting point, or roll a **d%** on the table two or three times. If the result of a roll doesn't fit your idea, roll again or pick something else.

At this stage, you should also have reached a decision on everything else about your character: name, description and so on. Fill in the appropriate fields in the Passport.

I already have the idea that I'm in school somewhere, probably a Catholic boarding school. That means that the artist would have to draw me in a Catholic school uniform.

That doesn't make me stand out in a boarding school environment, so I roll on the Design Ideas table, and get the results Wild hair, High cheeks and Bushy Moustache.

Seriously?!! The 'stache is right out, and I replace it with a scarf instead.

Now there are some other personal details to fill out in the Passport, like birth place and such. I stay at the boarding school most of the time, but officially i live with my mother in Montparnasse in Paris. I am 154 cm tall and weigh 51 kg. I was born in Phalsbourg in the Lorraine region in the east of France. I have red hair and blue eyes from my mother, and lots of freckles, especially in summer.

Table: Design Ideas

d%	Design idea						
1	Arm rings	26	Freckles	51	Narrow face	76	Something green
2	Athletic	27	Frilly skirt	52	Neck tie	77	Square face
3	Baggy trousers	28	Full beard	53	Nylon stockings	78	Square glasses
4	Bald	29	Greasy hair	54	Overweight	79	Stetson
5	Bandana	30	Habit	55	Parasol	80	Straw hat
6	Beret	31	Hairband	56	Pearl necklace	81	Sun hat
7	Big bosom	32	Hairpins	57	Pince-nez	82	Tall
8	Big earrings	33	Handbag	58	Pin-stripe jacket	83	Tie-dyed dress
9	Boat shoes	34	Handlebar moustache	59	Pointy beard	84	Tie-dyed shirt
10	Bomber jacket	35	Headcloth	60	Pointy face	85	Thigh-high socks
11	Bowler hat	36	High cheeks	61	Pointy nose	86	Thin moustache
12	Bow tie	37	High heels	62	Round face	87	Thin trousers
13	Braided hair	38	Hiking boots	63	Round glasses	88	Top hat
14	Bun	39	Hooked nose	64	Sandals	89	Trainers
15	Bushy moustache	40	Knee-high socks	65	Scarf	90	Trench coat
16	Business suit	41	Knitted dress	66	Scrawny	91	Turtleneck
17	Chic dress	42	Knitted pullover	67	Short	92	Umbrella
18	Chubby	43	Loafers	68	Short hair	93	Uniform
19	Denim jacket	44	Long nose	69	Short skirt	94	Waistcoat
20	Denim trousers	45	Long skirt	70	Shorts	95	Walrus moustache
21	Dress shoes	46	Messy hair	71	Small nose	96	Wide-brimmed hat
22	Fedora	47	Military boots	72	Sneakers	97	Wide-rimmed glasses
23	Flat face	48	Military cap	73	Something blue	98	Wide skirt
24	Flower-printed blouse	49	Monocle	74	Something red	99	Windbreaker
25	Formal dress	50	Muscular	75	Something yellow	100	Wild hair

Comic book aging

Don't worry too much about your character's age, and worry even less about aging. Even if you set your age at 15, it won't affect you unless you specifically pick the Ability Young or the Complication Underage.

The game is like that on purpose. It's said that when Hergé was asked how old Tintin was, he had two standard answers. If the asker had stated their age and was a child, Hergé always matched the asker's age. If the asker was 13, then Tintin was 13. If that was not the case, his standard reply was that Tintin was 14 in the first album, *Tintin in the land of the Soviets* (published 1930), and had then aged about *"three or four years in forty years"*.

We will assume that your character ages in about the same way.

STEP 10: DECIDE HOW YOU MET

One thing you should discuss is how you met and became friends with all the other characters. To start the discussion, use the Meetup Location Table.

- Select one player. That player rolls on the table to determine a location where the player's character met someone.
- The player selects one other character, and then spins a tale about how they met at that location, based on the earlier discussion about the team.
- The other player then rolls on the table and determines a new location.
- The other player selects a third character in the same way, and tells how the first two characters met the third.
- The third character's player then rolls on the location table, selects a fourth character, and tells how the first three characters met the fourth at that location, in the same way as before.
- Repeat until all characters have met.

The last player will not get to roll on the table (sorry).

> Who will have the honour of starting?

> I'll start. I roll 97, which means **Zell am See, Austria**. I think it was February 1963, when Paul and I broke into the same hotel room.

> I was trying to find evidence that an Italian jet setter was actually a Soviet spy, while Paul was only out to get his mistress' jewellery. We joined forces, and succeeded.

> Sounds like an excellent story about how the gentleman cat burglar met the Swedish intelligence officer.

> My turn. 41, Lillehammer, Norway. There seems to be a winter resort theme in our meetups. That was around Christmas 1963, I think. We met Éloïse and her mother there, with her mother's current fling, a German skier. And he proved to be an East German spy, and we caught him with the help of the teenage mad scientist and handed him over to the authorities. I don't think Éloïse's mother has forgiven us.

> Haha! Good one, and no, she has not forgiven you. That's why I am at this Catholic boarding school, to keep me away from you. Not that it works.

> Uh, I roll a 92, which means **Venice, Italy**. Oooh! I know. Mom was really angry at me for being involved in getting Erich arrested as a spy, so I ran away a month later and met this crazy Greek rally driver. Then I joined her as she toured northern Italy by car. Paul and Frida went after me to get me back, and finally met us in Venice, just in time for the Carnival when the secret Octopus organisation was about to test, uh, mind control drugs on the participants.

> But of course we were.

> And that's how we got together and started investigating the Octopus and generally being a monkey wrench in their machinery – in between all the things we normally do.

> And that's the last introduction. Since I am the last character in our group, I don't get to roll.

BRING IT ALL TOGETHER

Now that you have a team and created your characters, all you need to do is record all the information in your passports and flesh out the background a bit. Don't overdo it: you want some expansion room for the future. Directors also are not interested in reading pages upon pages of character background.

Table: Meetup Location

d%	Location	d%	Location	d%	Location	d%	Location
1	Addis Ababa, Ethiopia	26	Geneva, Switzerland	51	Matterhorn, Italy/Switzerland	76	Split, Yugoslavia
2	Amman, Jordan	27	Giza plateau, Egypt	52	McMurdo Station, Antarctica	77	Stockholm, Sweden
3	Amsterdam, The Netherlands	28	Helsinki, Finland	53	Melbourne, Australia	78	Strasbourg, France
4	Angkor Wat, Cambodia	29	Honolulu, Hawaii, USA	54	Miami, Florida, USA	79	Sydney, Australia
5	Ankara, Turkey	30	Istanbul, Turkey	55	Monaco, Monaco	80	Tehran, Iran
6	Aswan, Egypt	31	Jericho, Israel	56	Moscow, Soviet Union	81	Tel Aviv, Israel
7	Baghdad, Iraq	32	Jerusalem, Israel	57	Munich, Germany	82	Tenerife, Canary Islands, Spain
8	Barcelona, Spain	33	Kiev, Soviet Union	58	New Orleans, Louisiana, USA	83	Tenochtitlan, Mexico
9	Beijing, China	34	Kiruna, Sweden	59	New York, New York, USA	84	Teotihuacan, Mexico
10	Belgrade, Yugoslavia	35	Kisumu, Lake Victoria, Kenya	60	Oslo, Norway	85	Tijuana, Mexico
11	Boston, Massachusetts, USA	36	Kourou, French Guiana	61	Paris, France	86	Tokyo, Japan
12	Brighton, United Kingdom	37	Kyoto, Japan	62	Petra, Jordan	87	Ulaanbaatar, Mongolia
13	Brussels, Belgium	38	La Rochelle, France	63	Ponta Delgada, Azores, Portugal	88	Vancouver, Canada
14	Cairo, Egypt	39	Las Vegas, Nevada, USA	64	Port-au-Prince, Haiti	89	Val-d'Isère, France
15	Cardiff, United Kingdom	40	Leningrad, Soviet Union	65	Prague, Czechoslovakia	90	Valletta, Malta
16	Casablanca, Morocco	41	Lillehammer, Norway	66	Pripyat, Soviet Union	91	Vatican City, enclave in Rome, Italy
17	Chicago, Illinois, USA	42	Lisbon, Portugal	67	Reykjavik, Iceland	92	Venice, Italy
18	Colombo, Sri Lanka	43	London, United Kingdom	68	Rio de Janeiro, Brazil	93	Vienna, Austria
19	Copenhagen, Denmark	44	Longyearbyen, Svalbard, Norway	69	Rome, Italy	94	Vladivostok, Soviet Union
20	Cusco, Peru	45	Los Angeles, California, USA	70	San Francisco, California, USA	95	Warsaw, Poland
21	Delhi, India	46	Lübeck, Germany	71	Salzburg, Austria	96	West Berlin, West German enclave in East Germany
22	Dublin, Ireland	47	Machu Picchu, Peru	72	Serengeti, Tanzania	97	Zell am See, Austria
23	Dubrovnik, Yugoslavia	48	Madrid, Spain	73	Skara Brae, United Kingdom	98	Zürich, Switzerland
24	East Berlin, East Germany	49	Malmö, Sweden	74	Smolensk, Soviet Union	99	Östersund, Sweden
25	Edinburgh, United Kingdom	50	Marseille, France	75	Sofia, Bulgaria	100	Soviet Budushcheye-1 space station, Low Earth Orbit

TEMPLATES

WHAT'S IN A TEMPLATE

To help you get into the game quickly, there are a number of Templates provided to speed up the character creation process. Templates are nearly finished characters that require very little extra work to flesh out. Templates provide inspiration to get you started and kick off your imagination: a blank sheet of paper can easily be a mind-blocker.

The Templates in this book also show the kinds of characters that fit within the world of *The Troubleshooters* and future adventure books.

A Template consists of the following:

- A list of 11 Skills with Skill values
- A list of 5 Abilities (choose two)
- A list of 3 Complications (choose one)
- **Vitality**
- Extra languages
- A list of 3 gear kits
- A list of **Plot Hook** suggestions

You will find that there aren't many pure combat-oriented Templates, even if many of them have a moderate level in at least one Combat Skill. Completely combat-oriented characters are not common to the genre, but on the other hand, characters should be competent enough to participate in a fight scene.

MAKING TEMPLATES

Use the following as an outline for making Templates:

Skills: Set Skill percentages at: a 75, b 65, c 65, d 65, e 65, f 45, g 45, h 45, i 45, j 45, k 45. Set all other Skills to 15.

Abilities: Pick two of the following Abilities: a, b, c, d, e

Complications: Pick one of the following Complications: a, b, c

Vitality: 4 (5 if **Agility** or one weapon Skill is 45; 6 if **Agility** or one weapon Skill is 65+; 7 if both **Agility** and one weapon Skill are 65+)

Languages: — ("Pick one extra language" if **Languages** is 45; "Pick two extra languages" if **Languages** is 65+)

Gear: You have an a, b and c. Select one of them as your **Signature Gadget**. Pick up to two more gear kits of your choice.

Suggested Plot Hooks: Pick one or preferably two **Plot Hooks**, for instance one or two of these: a, b, c, d

Things to think about while making Templates:

- Consider having at least one Combat Skill at 45% or higher. That way the character isn't completely useless if a fight breaks out.
- Do not pick any Abilities of tier 2 or above. This would force the player to pick the tier 1 prerequisite first, making the Template less flexible.
- You can make a gear kit pick into a choice of two or more gear kits. Try to make such choices mutually exclusive, so that you will need one or the other but not both.

MAKING TEMPLATE-LESS CHARACTERS

You could build a character without a Template. Just follow this procedure:

- Allocate the Skill values 75, 65, 65, 65, 65 (4 Skills with the value 65), 45, 45, 45, 45, 45, 45 (6 Skills with the value 45) among 11 Skills. Set all other Skills to 15.
- Pick two Abilities. You can pick tier 0 or 1 Abilities without worrying about prerequisites, but at tier 2 or higher, you must fulfil the prerequisites.
- Pick one Complication.
- Pick five gear kits. Select one of them as your **Signature Gadget**.
- Pick two **Plot Hooks** that no other character has.
- Customise your character according to the guidelines on page 34.
- Set **Vitality** and pick extra languages according to the same guidelines.

Yes, it's that simple.

There is no fitting Template for an intelligence officer, so my player created a Template-less character.

I chose Ranged Combat for the 75% slot, Alertness, Subterfuge, Vehicles and Endurance for the 65% slots, and Agility, Melee, Red Tape, Strength, Investigation and Charm for the 45% slots.

I have the idea of being a fighter pilot, so I chose Pilot and Military Rank as her Abilities and Code of Honour as a Complication. To become a fighter pilot, I would need the Fighter Pilot Ability. That is a tier 2 Ability, requiring both Pilot and Military Rank, which I have already picked. But to get the Fighter Pilot Ability, I also need a second Complication according to the customisation rules. I choose Patriot, since I do things for king and country.

As for gear, I choose a Dinner Jacket, but rename it Parade Uniform instead and adjust the list of stuff in the gear kit. I also choose a Handgun, a Pocket Pistol and a Radio Set. There is no Fighter Jet gear kit, but I could possibly make one.

Just a moment, my dear. A fighter jet is not something that everyone has. It's military stuff, requiring military personnel for maintenance and preparation.

Second, I don't have any plans for air combat in my adventures, so the fighter jet will probably just sit unused in its hangar in Sweden somewhere.

I propose that you pick something more useful, like a Bicycle, and if there is a need for a fighter jet in an adventure, it will probably be mission equipment or available for **Story Points**.

Okay, that makes sense. When the group discusses **Plot Hooks**, I pick **Secret Service** as I am an intelligence officer.

Yurika has already taken **Foreign**, so I can't take that, even if I'm a foreigner in France. With one weapon Skill at 65+ and **Agility** at 45+, my **Vitality** is set to 6.

And being Swedish means I speak Swedish as my native language, and French and English as second languages.

TEMPLATE DESCRIPTIONS

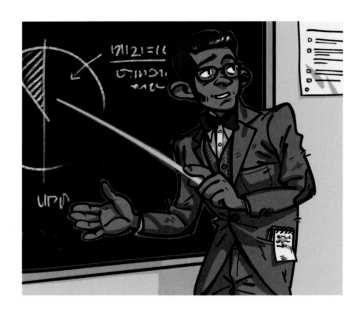

ADVENTUROUS SCHOLAR

As a scholar, your true place is in the field, not locked up in a library with moldy old books or a classroom with pesky students asking stupid questions.

The past is not found in a textbook. Such tomes are merely deposited in libraries, to be referenced in the future by people seeking simple explanations of the past. History is found in the field, in tunnels and tombs not yet explored, hills not yet excavated, languages not yet decoded.

Skills: Set the following Skills: **Humanities** 75, **Contacts** 65, **Investigation** 65, **Languages** 65, **Science** 65, **Medicine** 45, **Melee** 45, **Search** 45, **Status** 45, **Vehicles** 45, **Willpower** 45. Set all other Skills to 15.
Abilities: Pick two of the following Abilities: Good Reputation, Licensed Professional, Polyglot, Swordsman, Teacher
Complications: Pick one of the following Complications: Honest, Memorable, Phobia
Vitality: 5
Languages: Pick two extra languages
Gear: You have a Forensics kit, a Compact car, and an Archaeologist kit. Select one of them as your **Signature Gadget**. Pick up to two more gear kits of your choice.
Suggested Plot Hooks: Pick one or preferably two **Plot Hooks**, for instance one or two of these: **Foreign, Arch-Enemy: The Octopus, Friends in High Places, Looking for the Past**

May we all return to our alma maters again.
– Professor Vincent, Adventurous Scholar

ASPIRING STUDENT

This is the best time of your life, the fleeting period between childhood and adulthood. The first step towards independence and a career is acquiring an education. This is where you are: the time of freedom between the obligations of your parents' home and the obligations of your professional career, where you grow to face the future. All doors are open and the future looks bright!

Except the test next week, which you really ought to study for.

Skills: Set the following Skills: **Investigation** 75, **Engineering** 65, **Electronics** 65, **Humanities** 65, **Search** 65, **Contacts** 45, **Languages** 45, **Medicine** 45, **Melee** 45, **Science** 45, **Willpower** 45. Set all other Skills to 15.
Abilities: Pick two of the following Abilities: Cheerful, Curious, Focused, Tech Wiz, Young. Ignore any requirements on these Abilities.
Complications: Pick one of the following Complications: Drunkard, Crude, Underage
Vitality: 5
Languages: Pick one extra language
Gear: You have an **Electronics** toolbox, a Bicycle and a Chemistry lab set. Select one of them as your **Signature Gadget**. Pick up to two more gear kits of your choice.
Suggested Plot Hooks: Pick one or preferably two **Plot Hooks**, for instance one or two of these: **Do-Gooder, I Owe You, Foreign, Looking for the Past**

I don't have time to be captured!
I have an exam tomorrow!
– Éloïse Giraud, Aspiring Student

CARING VETERINARIAN

Animals get hurt and ill too. They feel pain, just like we do, but they cannot tell you where and how. They can only show you their distress. There are thousands of nurses and doctors caring for us, but almost nobody to care for animals. It is your job – no, your passion – to help them when they are in need.

After all, we are judged by how we treat the most helpless.

Skills: Set the following Skills: **Medicine** 75, **Endurance** 65, **Investigation** 65, **Science** 65, **Search** 65, **Agility** 45, **Charm** 45, **Contacts** 45, **Ranged Combat** 45, **Survival** 45, **Vehicles** 45. Set all other Skills to 15.

Abilities: Pick two of the following Abilities: Animal Friend, Focused, Licensed Professional, Pet, Sixth Sense. Ignore any requirements on these Abilities.

Complications: Pick one of the following Complications: Code of Honour, Honest, Combat Paralysis

Vitality: 5

Languages: —

Gear: You have a Van, a First aid kit, and a Medical kit. Select one of them as your **Signature Gadget**. Pick up to two more gear kits of your choice.

Suggested Plot Hooks: Pick one or preferably two **Plot Hooks,** for instance one or two of these: **Do-Gooder, I Owe You, Friends in High Places, Looking for a Case**

Poor creature! Did that hurt, sweetums? – I wasn't talking to you, you big oaf, I was talking to Fifi!
– Angeline Cuinard, Caring Veterinarian

CAT BURGLAR

Without hate, without violence, but certainly illegal, that's the life of a Cat Burglar. But it's also exciting to break into secure sites and come out with small but invaluable stuff without anyone knowing – if you hadn't left a calling card.

You can't leave without signing your masterworks, after all.

Skills: Set the following Skills: **Security** 75, **Agility** 65, **Prestidigitation** 65, **Search** 65, **Sneak** 65, **Alertness** 45, **Charm** 45, **Investigation** 45, **Melee** 45, **Subterfuge** 45, **Vehicles** 45. Set all other Skills to 15.

Abilities: Pick two of the following Abilities: Acrobat, Allure, Famous, Lock-Picker, Sixth Sense. Ignore any requirements on these Abilities.

Complications: Pick one of the following Complications: Amorous, Bad Reputation, Overconfident

Vitality: 6

Languages: —

Gear: You have Lockpicks, a Flashlight, and Binoculars. Select one of them as your **Signature Gadget**. Pick up to two more gear kits of your choice.

Suggested Plot Hooks: Pick one or preferably two **Plot Hooks,** for instance one or two of these: **Do-Gooder, I Owe You, Looking for an Adventure, Arch-Enemy: The Octopus**

I never steal from honest people. I only take out long-term loans from people that deserve to have their fortune reduced a bit.
– Paul Marchand, Cat Burglar

COSMOPOLITAN DILETTANTE

Having been everywhere and knowing very important people is enough for some careers, even if you don't have any actual skills or qualifications. You're one of these people. You go places, you meet people, you know someone who knows someone else. And although you don't necessarily do something on your own, knowing the right person and being at the right place at the right time can change the world.

Skills: Set the following Skills: **Credit** 75, **Charm** 65, **Contacts** 65, **Status** 65, **Subterfuge** 65, **Alertness** 45, **Entertainment** 45, **Languages** 45, **Ranged Combat** 45, **Vehicles** 45, **Willpower** 45. Set all other Skills to 15.

Abilities: Pick two of the following Abilities: Famous, Good Reputation, Nouveau Riche, Old Money, Peerage. Ignore any requirements on these Abilities.

Complications: Pick one of the following Complications: Drunkard, Amorous, Prejudiced

Vitality: 4

Languages: Pick one extra language.

Gear: You have an Evening Dress or Dinner Jacket, Luxury Car or Sports car, and Wad of Cash. Select one of them as your **Signature Gadget**. Pick up to two more gear kits of your choice.

Suggested Plot Hooks: Pick one or preferably two **Plot Hooks,** for instance one or two of these: **Do-Gooder, Media Darling, Exile, Looking for an Adventure**

I demand to see the manager!
– Chance Stirling, Shipping Magnate

CURIOUS ENGINEER

Machines are wonderful. They do things! But the best thing is not the machine itself – the machine is just a source of pride representing a job well done. But creating a machine, or understanding it, that's the real challenge, and it's the reason that you chose your job.

Skills: Set the following Skills: **Engineering** 75, **Electronics** 65, **Machinery** 65, **Science** 65, **Search** 65, **Contacts** 45, **Security** 45, **Investigation** 45, **Melee** 45, **Vehicles** 45, **Willpower** 45. Set all other Skills to 15.
Abilities: Pick two of the following Abilities: Cheerful, Curious, Focused, Licensed Professional, Tech Wiz. Ignore any requirements on these Abilities.
Complications: Pick one of the following Complications: Combat Paralysis, Crude, Unlucky
Vitality: 5
Languages: —
Gear: You have a Mechanic's toolbox, **Electronics** toolbox and a Ham radio set. Select one of them as your **Signature Gadget**. Pick up to two more gear kits of your choice.
Suggested Plot Hooks: Pick one or preferably two **Plot Hooks**, for instance one or two of these: **Exile**, **Looking for an Adventure**, **Friends in High Places**, **I Owe You**

Hello, my little friend! What kind of device are you, and what are you doing in my engine?
– Matti Kivisto, Curious Engineer

DIPLOMAT

Diplomacy is often described as the ability to tell someone to go to Hell and make him look forward to the journey. That's not true: diplomacy is much more nefarious than that. But it is a part of the Big Game between nations, and you are playing it. You need to be devious on the highest arena there is.

Skills: Set the following Skills: **Status** 75, **Charm** 65, **Contacts** 65, **Languages** 65, **Red Tape** 65, **Alertness** 45, **Credit** 45, **Investigation** 45, **Search** 45, **Subterfuge** 45, **Willpower** 45. Set all other Skills to 15.
Abilities: Pick two of the following Abilities: Diplomatic Immunity, Good Reputation, Famous, Military Rank, Tough Liver. Ignore any requirements on these Abilities.
Complications: Pick one of the following Complications: Code of Honour, Memorable, Overconfident
Vitality: 4
Languages: Pick two extra languages.
Gear: You have an Evening dress or Dinner jacket, an Overnight bag, and a Tape recorder. Select one of them as your **Signature Gadget**. Pick up to two more gear kits of your choice.
Suggested Plot Hooks: Pick one or preferably two **Plot Hooks**, for instance one or two of these: **Secret Service**, **Friends in High Places**, **Arch-Enemy: The Octopus**, **I Owe You**

I believe that we are close to a breakthrough in these negotiations, don't you think?
– Colonel Bennet, Diplomat

Endurance 45, **Humanities** 45, **Melee** 45, **Survival** 45, **Vehicles** 45. Set all other Skills to 15.

Abilities: Pick two of the following Abilities: Been Everywhere, Curious, Double Nationality, Empathy, Good Reputation. Ignore any requirements on these Abilities.

Complications: Pick one of the following Complications: Amorous, Bad Reputation, Memorable

Vitality: 5

Languages: Pick two extra languages.

Gear: You have an Overnight bag, Hiking gear and a Camera. Select one of them as your **Signature Gadget**. Pick up to two more gear kits of your choice.

Suggested Plot Hooks: Pick one or preferably two **Plot Hooks**, for instance one or two of these: **Media Darling, Looking for an Adventure, Secret Service, Do-Gooder**

Sitomeyang is not a place where I have been. Let's go there!

— Harry Fitzroy, Globetrotter

INQUISITIVE JOURNALIST

The public deserves the truth! You are going to give it to them, but it requires some serious digging. You will not make friends, you will probably not be rich, but you will be famous, and the truth will come out!

Skills: Set the following Skills: **Contacts** 75, **Alertness** 65, **Investigation** 65, **Search** 65, **Subterfuge** 65, **Charm** 45, **Languages** 45, **Melee** 45, **Prestidigitation** 45, **Status** 45, **Vehicles** 45. Set all other Skills to 15.

Abilities: Pick two of the following Abilities: Been Everywhere, Empathy, Good Reputation, Investigator, Press Credentials. Ignore any requirements on these Abilities.

Complications: Pick one of the following Complications: Bad Reputation, Code of Honour, Honest

Vitality: 5

Languages: Pick one extra language

Gear: You have a Camera, a Forensics kit or a Tape recorder, and a Compact car or a Scooter. Select one of them as your **Signature Gadget**. Pick up to two more gear kits of your choice.

Suggested Plot Hooks: Pick one or preferably two **Plot Hooks**, for instance one or two of these: **Looking for an Adventure, Foreign, Do-Gooder, I Owe You**

Monsieur Reynault? Yurika Mishida, Senjogahara Shinbun! Is it true that you have paid over ninety thousand francs to cover up the investigation of your mistress?

— Yurika Mishida, Inquisitive Journalist

ELITE ATHLETE

Your mind is ready and your heart is on fire. Out there, on the field or in the ring, you're taking hold of every moment. In your mind, you have already won the game.

Skills: Set the following Skills: **Willpower** 75, **Agility** 65, **Endurance** 65, **Melee** 65, **Strength** 65, **Alertness** 45, **Status** 45, **Credit** 45, **Medicine** 45, **Ranged Combat** 45, **Survival** 45. Set all other Skills to 15.

Abilities: Pick two of the following Abilities: Acrobat, Athlete, Judo Black Belt, Mean Left Hook, Young. Ignore any requirements on these Abilities.

Complications: Pick one of the following Complications: Crude, Greedy, Honest

Vitality: 7

Languages: —

Gear: You have a Bicycle or Ski gear, a Compact car, and a Film camera. Select one of them as your **Signature Gadget**. Pick up to two more gear kits of your choice.

Suggested Plot Hooks: Pick one or preferably two **Plot Hooks**, for instance one or two of these: **Media Darling, Looking for an Adventure, Exile, I Owe You**

There's just one thing better than winning, and that is winning.

— Avery Johns, Elite Athlete

GLOBETROTTER

There's one thing that you are the master of: travelling the world with basically no money. You know people everywhere, and you're familiar with secret travel routes and sites to explore off the typical tourist paths.

Skills: Set the following Skills: **Charm** 75, **Contacts** 65, **Credit** 65, **Languages** 65, **Willpower** 65, **Alertness** 45,

INTREPID EXPLORER

To be the first person at a site, that's something. To challenge nature, defeat the undefeatable, climb the highest mountain, cross the desert or the icy wastes – that's what drives you.

Skills: Set the following Skills: **Survival** 75, **Agility** 65, **Endurance** 65, **Vehicles** 65, **Willpower** 65, **Alertness** 45, **Contacts** 45, **Languages** 45, **Machinery** 45, **Ranged Combat** 45, **Search** 45. Set all other Skills to 15.

Abilities: Pick two of the following Abilities: Diver, Been Everywhere, Bushman, Peerage, Polyglot. Ignore any requirements on these Abilities.

Complications: Pick one of the following Complications: Overconfident, Honest, Phobia

Vitality: 6

Languages: Pick one extra language.

Gear: You have Hiking gear, **Survival** gear, and a Hunting rifle or a Camera. Select one of them as your **Signature Gadget**. Pick up to two more gear kits of your choice.

Suggested Plot Hooks: Pick one or preferably two **Plot Hooks**, for instance one or two of these: **Looking for an Adventure, Exile, Looking for the Past, Media Darling**

Why climb the highest mountain?
Because it's there, of course! Why else?
– Allen Pitzer, Intrepid Explorer

PLAINCLOTHES POLICE

You are the last line of defence for the law, the ones who are called in when someone went too far, and someone has to investigate a crime. You inspect crime sites, interrogate suspects and witnesses, and figure out what happened. And with a little luck, a lot of cooperation and even more tenacity, you may eventually put the perp behind bars.

Skills: Set the following Skills: **Investigation** 75, **Alertness** 65, **Ranged Combat** 65, **Red Tape** 65, **Search** 65, **Medicine** 45, **Melee** 45, **Science** 45, **Subterfuge** 45, **Vehicles** 45, **Willpower** 45. Set all other Skills to 15.

Abilities: Pick two of the following Abilities: Focused, Forensics, Gunman, Investigator, Police Badge. Ignore any requirements on these Abilities.

Complications: Pick one of the following Complications: Drunkard, Overconfident, Memorable

Vitality: 6

Languages: —

Gear: You have a Handgun, a Sedan and a Forensics kit. Select one of them as your **Signature Gadget**. Pick up to two more gear kits of your choice.

Suggested Plot Hooks: Pick one or preferably two **Plot Hooks**, for instance one or two of these: **Looking for a Case, Do-Gooder, Secret Service, Arch-Enemy: The Octopus**

Marchand! I will arrest you this time!
– Claudia Stuckart, Plainclothes Police

RACING DRIVER

You have high-octane petrol in your blood, and the world is too slow. Only on the race track, with engines howling in your ears and the smoke of burning rubber in your nose, is the world up to speed. That's where you compete, with the best of the best. That's where you truly live!

Skills: Set the following Skills: **Vehicles** 75, **Alertness** 65, **Engineering** 65, **Endurance** 65, **Willpower** 65, **Credit** 45, **Machinery** 45, **Melee** 45, **Search** 45, **Status** 45, **Strength** 45. Set all other Skills to 15.

Abilities: Pick two of the following Abilities: Been Everywhere, Born Behind the Wheel, Good Reputation, Sixth Sense, Tech Wiz. Ignore any requirements on these Abilities.

Complications: Pick one of the following Complications: Bad Reputation, Crude, Overconfident

Vitality: 5

Languages: —

Gear: You have a Racing car, a Film camera and a Mechanic's toolbox. Select one of them as your **Signature Gadget**. Pick up to two more gear kits of your choice.

Suggested Plot Hooks: Pick one or preferably two **Plot Hooks**, for instance one or two of these: **I Owe You**, **Media Darling**, **Looking for an Adventure**, **Foreign**

Hold on! That car is not getting away from me!
— Elektra Ambrosia, Racing Driver

SUFFERING ARTIST

Your spoken words cannot express who you are. There's a soul inside that can't reach out, except through art. It is a painful process to express your soul, but it would be even more painful to lock it up, hide who you really are and pretend to be just like all the others that surround you.

Skills: Set the following Skills: **Prestidigitation** 75, **Charm** 65, **Entertainment** 65, **Languages** 65, **Status** 65, **Agility** 45, **Humanities** 45, **Melee** 45, **Search** 45, **Vehicles** 45, **Willpower** 45. Set all other Skills to 15.

Abilities: Pick two of the following Abilities: Actor, Artist, Empathy, Famous, Tough Liver. Ignore any requirements on these Abilities.

Complications: Pick one of the following Complications: Drunkard, Combat Paralysis, Sensitive

Vitality: 5

Languages: Pick two extra languages

Gear: You have a Camera, a Musical instrument or Painting gear or a Typewriter, and a Scooter. Select one of them as your **Signature Gadget**. Pick up to two more gear kits of your choice.

Suggested Plot Hooks: Pick one or preferably two **Plot Hooks**, for instance one or two of these: **I Owe You**, **Looking for the Past**, **Do-Gooder**, **Media Darling**.

What do you know! The Fallen Madonna with the Big Boobies by van Clomp! Lost in France during the Nazi occupation of Normandy! ... I don't like it.
— Sir Howard, earl of Haribo, Suffering Artist

VIGILANTE LAWYER

You are the last hope of those that the law forgot. You give them a chance before the courts, to overcome the legal hurdles that ordinary people never have a hope of fighting. Your opponents are formidable, and if you have to cheat a little to shift the odds in your favour during your personal David-against-Goliath moment, then so be it.

Skills: Set the following Skills: **Investigation** 75, **Charm** 65, **Prestidigitation** 65, **Red Tape** 65, **Search** 65, **Alertness** 45, **Contacts** 45, **Entertainment** 45, **Melee** 45, **Vehicles** 45, **Willpower** 45. Set all other Skills to 15.

Abilities: Pick two of the following Abilities: Called to the Bar, Curious, Good Reputation, Investigator, Mean Left Hook. Ignore any requirements on these Abilities.

Complications: Pick one of the following Complications: Code of Honour, Overconfident, Unlucky

Vitality: 5

Languages: —

Gear: You have a Forensics kit, a Tape recorder and a Camera or Film camera. Select one of them as your **Signature Gadget**. Pick up to two more gear kits of your choice.

Suggested Plot Hooks: Pick one or preferably two **Plot Hooks**, for instance one or two of these: **Looking for a Case**, **Do-Gooder**, **Friends in High Places**, **I Owe You**.

Objection, your honour!
The prosecution is leading the witness!
— Jacques Miranda, Vigilante Lawyer

PLOT HOOKS

"I hear the snow is great in Lipiçe"

"That was last week. Now it has rained."

"But rain can be beautiful too."

Happy to meet you. What do you have?

There's trouble brewing in Athens. Another agency has increased its activity in the area. Here are the details, cover story and plane ticket. And remember, we never met. Good luck.

WHAT IS A PLOT HOOK?

The purpose of **Plot Hooks** is to get characters into the adventure. Each character should have one or two unique **Plot Hooks** out of a list of just 11. No character should have the same **Plot Hooks** as another character.

In adventure books, there will be startup handouts for four to six of the **Plot Hooks**. To start the adventure, the Director picks one or two **Plot Hooks**, each matching a different character. These two characters are referred to as "*Plot Hook characters*". Their job is to drag the other characters into the adventure.

Because there are so few **Plot Hooks**, it is all but guaranteed that in a regular team of troubleshooters, there should be at least one possible **Plot Hook** character in each adventure. This way, it is easy to get adventures started.

The other players could consider the **Plot Hook** characters to be the main characters of that particular adventure.

CHOOSING PLOT HOOKS

Discussing and choosing **Plot Hooks** for the characters is a group effort: all team members should participate when choosing **Plot Hooks** at character creation. The goal is for all players to have relevant **Plot Hooks**, while no **Plot Hooks** should feel out of place.

If new players join the group, or if characters die or retire and are replaced by new characters, you may need to have a new **Plot Hook** discussion to allow good **Plot Hooks** for the new characters. In this discussion, existing characters may drop **Plot Hooks** or swap **Plot Hooks** around, to make a good mix for the team as a whole.

It is actually good to have a **Plot Hook** discussion every now and then, even if new characters have not joined the team, just to make sure that the **Plot Hooks** are all still relevant.

PLOT HOOK DESCRIPTIONS

There are only 11 **Plot Hooks**. It may seem like too few, but the low number is intentional: to make sure that there is a guaranteed overlap between the **Plot Hooks** of the characters and the startup handouts in adventure books.

All 11 **Plot Hooks** are described below.

ARCH-ENEMY: THE OCTOPUS

The Octopus is something of an umbrella organisation for organised crime, a terror organisation, and a conspiracy for world domination all rolled into one. They strive for control through any means necessary, both directly through nefarious plots or indirectly as a shadow government. Like the octopus, it has arms everywhere, and if you cut off one, there are still plenty more. The Octopus doesn't like attention. You have been on their radar for some time.

DO-GOODER

You can't help it! You just have to help others, especially those that nobody else will. You don't have to help everyone, but sometimes there is nobody else there to offer assistance, except you.

EXILE

You left your homeland long ago, but still maintain ties to wherever it is you hail from. On top of that, your former homeland's security services are still looking for you. Sometimes they urge you to come back. Sometimes they use force. And sometimes there are others with a similar fate to yours.

FRIENDS IN HIGH PLACES

Having friends in high places is nice. It opens a lot of doors. But friendship is a double-edged sword – sometimes they bring their problems to you.

FOREIGN

You're not from here, but from another place with a distinctly different culture. But that doesn't stop you – you find everything in your new homeland quite exciting! It's so weird! This has a tendency to land you in more adventurous situations than you bargained for.

I OWE YOU

You owe someone a big favour. One day, that someone – or someone they know – will call it in. And that will undoubtedly lead to new and exciting adventures.

LOOKING FOR A CASE

Some people make a living by solving other people's troubles. Some people make a living reporting on other people's troubles. Some people are just nosy busybodies.

LOOKING FOR AN ADVENTURE

A mundane life is not for you. You want to push the boundaries, press into the unknown. You are the type that sails solo around the world, climbs the highest peaks, treks across the wildest wilderness, skis to the poles, whatever isn't part of modern, civilised, boring everyday life.

LOOKING FOR THE PAST

Europe – and the world – has a long history that sometimes resurfaces. You have an interest in the past, and sometimes the past has an interest in you. Whichever the case, it can unexpectedly lead to adventures.

MEDIA DARLING

You're constantly in the limelight. This not only means constant coverage in magazines and the news, but also that you often know reporters and journalists.

SECRET SERVICE

Europe is a hotbed for spies. Everyone spies on everybody – including allies like the Americans, the Germans, the British, heck, even the Scandinavians spy. You are an agent in secret government service. Most of the time, you just report and try to recruit people, but sometimes your masters give you other assignments...

STARTING ADVENTURES

Adventure books have at least four startup handouts, each for a different **Plot Hook**. If the group has at least four players and each character has two unique **Plot Hooks**, at least one startup handout will match at least one of the characters' **Plot Hooks**.

When starting the adventure, pick one or two startup handouts that fit the characters, and deal them to these players. These are the **Plot Hook** characters. The Director may have to adapt the **Plot Hooks** and provide some background to them. Also, try to pick **Plot Hooks** for characters that were not **Plot Hook** characters in the last adventure.

If you are writing your own adventures, you use **Plot Hooks** in a similar fashion. The difference is that you pick two **Plot Hooks** from two characters, and then create startup handouts for just these two. They become the **Plot Hook** characters.

I am planning to run *The U-boat Mystery*, which has startup handouts for the **Media Darling**, **Looking for a Case**, **Arch-Enemy: The Octopus**, and **Do-Gooder** Plot Hooks.

Elektra has the **Media Darling** Plot Hook, and Éloïse has the **Arch-Enemy: The Octopus** Plot Hook. I could also pick Paul, who has the **Do-Gooder** Plot Hook, or Yurika who has the **Looking for a Case** Plot Hook – if the player shows up tonight. Frida has the **Plot Hook Secret Service**, and Harry has **Friends in High Places** and **Looking for the Past**, so I can't use them.

I decide to make Elektra and Éloïse the **Plot Hook** characters of the adventure, and give them the respective handouts.

EXPANDING STARTUP HANDOUTS

Instead of just distributing the startup handouts amongst the players, you can easily expand one or more into full scenes, and play them in the game. Although there is a risk that players will go off script, you can deal with it by ending the scene as soon as the point is made.

Another option, and maybe a better one, is to encourage the **Plot Hook** characters' players to adapt the content of their startup handout and tell you and the other players what happened. This option gives players control of the startup, making them more invested in the story, and customises the startup to their character, without the risk of running off script.

PLOT HOOK CHARACTERS

Plot Hooks are not only used to start adventures. They are also used during the game. In a sense, the **Plot Hook** characters become the main characters for the adventure.

In printed adventures, there will often be events and clues specifically for the **Plot Hook** characters. It's a good idea to incorporate similar clues and events into your adventures for the **Plot Hook** characters.

If your character is one of the **Plot Hook** characters, try to get things started and pull the other characters into the adventure.

If your character isn't one of the **Plot Hook** characters, instead have your character be the sidekick to the **Plot Hook** characters and try to make them be the main characters of the adventure. Try not to steal the limelight. Instead, support the **Plot Hook** characters, help them stand out and just generally make them seem awesome!

Try to use different **Plot Hook** characters for each adventure, thus shifting the limelight around.

What? Did the director use Arch-Enemy: The Octopus as the Plot Hook? Geez! And I have an exam in two weeks.

Anyway, I have this handout about a contact, Nena Wallhaus, the wife of an Octopus defector, who was shot in the back as she was about to meet me in Paris, and as she laid bleeding, she handed me a strange map. It looks like a sea chart, and it was very important to her. She is in intensive care right now, but will likely survive. Her husband has disappeared, though.

Since she and her husband have both tried helping me find my father in the past, I feel that I owe her some help with...whatever it is that this map has to do with. Since it is a sea chart of a strait on the other side of the world in a place called Sitomeyang, I guess that Frida and Harry are the people to call.

I have a different story. It says on my handout that I had an interview with a journalist and fan, Pierre Martin, and just as we walked off from the interview, a van stopped beside us and three thugs grabbed Martin and pushed him into the van.

I tried to stop them, but one of the thugs was completely ungentlemanly and, well, punched me hard. Now, all I have is the registration number of the van, Martin's bag with a tape recorder and an art catalogue, and a black eye.

I can't let a fan down like that. I think this is either secret agent or underworld stuff, so I call Frida and Paul.

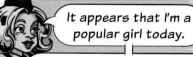

It appears that I'm a popular girl today.

Alright, let's meet up at my place. These two events were close to one another, which may mean that they're connected. It's likely not a coincidence.

Of course it's a coincidence! Would I have any ulterior motives with these handouts?

SKILLS

Can you hurry up, please? I don't want to be caught red-handed.

That's what makes this exciting! Don't worry, I'm the best safecracker in Paris, I'll have this thing open in no time. Just keep watching my back!

I'm not questioning your skill, I'm just worried that there are guards here that are as good at spotting as you are at cracking safes.

Then keep your voice down and let me work in peace, so I can get it open faster!

HOW SKILLS WORK

Skills are written as a percentage that roughly grades your expertise in that area and the probability of success if you attempt an action that relates to it. The lowest Skill value you can have is 15, while the highest is 106, but Skill values rarely go over 100. The highest starting value is 85. When making a task check, you try to roll lower than or equal to the Skill value in order to succeed.

There are five kinds of Skills.

- **Background Skills** describe your basic capabilities.
- **Social Skills** describe your interaction with others.
- **Investigation Skills** are used to gather clues to solve mysteries.
- **Action Skills** are mainly used to resolve physical feats.
- **Combat Skills** are like Action Skills, but for combat.

Skills are used in the following two ways:

- In task checks to determine success or failure, in order to drive the plot forward.
- As a guideline to what the character is good at.

After the description of the Skill, the entry "Use when" tells you when and how to use the Skill in task checks or challenges; and "If the task check fails" lists possible consequences of a failed task check.

HOW GOOD IS GOOD?

Skills measure how good you are in certain fields. The lowest possible Skill value is 15%. The highest is 106%. But what do the values in between mean?

- If you have a Skill value around 65%, you are competent enough to work as a professional in that field.
- If the Skill value is in the 80% region, you belong to the elite in that field.
- If the Skill value is close to 100%, you are a legend in that field.

> Through extensive and often (for the subject) painful scientific experiments, I have found that Skill values around 66% are most fun.

> They are the golden spot in a way. It is all subjective: because of how players perceive the outcomes of random task checks, two thirds chance of success often feels about 50–50, so you need to be at least that good to not feel like a total klutz. On the other hand, a higher chance of success means that there is no perceived challenge, or room for growth.

> This is only valid for what players think of their spearhead Skills. The perception of other Skills is more forgiving.

> That is why the system is designed so that characters have a small number of spearhead Skills at about 65% or higher, and about twice as many support Skills at 45%.

(Not) creating new Skills

Since creating new Skills often leads to Skill inflation, we recommend that you try to avoid this whenever possible. House-ruled Skills are often too narrow, too broad, build on already existing Skills, or supersede other Skills. In most cases, it is better to do any of the following rather than creating a new Skill:

- Is it a narrow field of an existing Skill? Use that Skill instead.
- Is it a field that spans over multiple Skills? Make a challenge of it instead, or create an Ability.
- Is it a narrow field of a Skill that doesn't exist? Create an Ability instead.
- Is it an advanced sub-topic of a Skill? Create an Ability instead, or several tiered Abilities to give the sub-topic depth.

Only create a new Skill after attempting all other avenues of adding the topic by other means. Try to make it roughly as broad as the other Skills.

Table: Skill List

Skill	Type	Situation
Agility	Background	Jumping, climbing, running fast
Alertness	Background	Noting things before they happen
Charm	Social	Charming, seducing, making a good impression
Contacts	Social	Knowing people, getting in touch, getting favours
Credit	Background	Purchases, loans, bribes, having cash on hand
Electronics	Investigation	Examining, repairing, and building electronic devices, knowledge about electronics
Endurance	Background	Enduring physical hardships, doing things for an extended period
Engineering	Investigation	Examining, repairing, and building machines, knowledge about engineering
Entertainment	Social	Singing, playing instruments, telling stories, acting
Humanities	Investigation	Knowledge about art, history, linguistics, anthropology
Investigation	Investigation	Retrieving, documenting, examining evidence and drawing conclusions from it
Languages	Social	Speaking well, linguistics, express yourself
Machinery	Action	Operating machines
Medicine	Investigation	Knowledge about medicine, treating trauma, disease, or poisoning
Melee	Combat	Boxing, wrestling, fighting with melee weapons
Prestidigitation	Background	Magic tricks, lockpicking, pickpocketing, legerdemain
Ranged Combat	Combat	Rifles, handguns, crossbows, bow and arrow, thrown weapons
Red Tape	Investigation	Bureaucracy, law, tracing documents
Science	Investigation	Understanding and practicing physics, chemistry, biology, genetics, toxicology, mathematics etc
Search	Investigation	Actively looking for clues, hidden items or people trying to hide
Security	Action	Understanding, implementing and defeating security system such as CCTV, alarms, sensors, patrol schedules, guard animals, electronic locks etc
Sneak	Action	Hiding, moving silently
Status	Social	Impressing or intimidating people, making people do you a favour, high society
Strength	Background	Strength feats like pushing, lifting, or throwing
Subterfuge	Social	Trickery, bluffing, cheating
Survival	Action	Bushcraft, handling yourself in the wilderness, setting up camp, foraging, navigating in the wilderness
Vehicles	Action	Driving and maintaining vehicles
Willpower	Background	Resist temptation or mind control, withstand pain, not give up when faced with difficulty

SKILL DESCRIPTIONS

AGILITY
Background Skill

Agility is about movement and flexibility of the body. Whenever you run, swim, climb or jump, **Agility** is a good Skill to use.

Agility is not used for dodging in combat. Use Unarmed **Melee** for this purpose.

Agility is used with a Combat Skill to determine **Max Vitality**.

Use when: Climbing, running, swimming, and other physical tasks. You can use the Skill in challenges together with others such as **Endurance**, **Strength** and perhaps Performing arts. You can use **Agility** for defence checks against ranged attacks if you are in cover.

If the task check fails: You do not accomplish your task, or you accomplish it too late.

ALERTNESS
Background Skill

Alertness is about being aware of one's surroundings and noticing if things are out of place. It's not about actively searching for something, or collating information to come to a conclusion. The former falls more under the **Search** Skill, and the latter under **Investigation**.

Use when: **Alertness** is often in opposed checks against Director characters' **Sneak** or as a part of a Challenge to find clues. In an ambush, **Alertness** is often used to determine if you are **Surprised** or not.

If the task check fails: You missed it. You miss a vital clue, you don't notice anything suspicious, you notice something too late, or you just have a feeling of something being wrong but you can't put your finger on what it is. In ambush situations, you may get the **Surprised** Condition.

CHARM
Social Skill

Charm is the magnetic quality of personality or appearance, combined with a sophisticated and sometimes flattering way of communication, in order to reach out and persuade. Character, poise, clothes, conversational skills, finesse and elegance are all part of **Charm**.

Of course, behaviour is a part of **Charm**: your '68 behaviour may work fine on campus, but won't sit well at all with the European elite. Etiquette is formal – a set of rules that you are expected to follow. You have to speak properly, dress properly, use the right form of address – in the right order – eat properly, sit properly, even complain properly.

Rhetoric, the old art of speaking well is a must in classical education, and is also included in **Charm**.

Use when: Bluffing, seducing, charming, making a good impression, wooing, persuading a group of people, striking up a conversation, and so on. Make simple task checks when trying to understand what the diplomat or the Prince's valet is telling you.

You can use **Charm** In challenges with for instance **Contacts**, **Status** and **Credit** to gain access to Very Important People.

If the task check fails: Your charms don't help you to get the result you wanted. It doesn't mean that you're repulsive or uncharming.

Or you could make a faux-pas. That's simply not how it is done. Everyone will be too polite to tell you directly, but their glances should tell you that they are not amused.

CONTACTS
Social Skill

To get somewhere in the modern society, you need contacts that can introduce you to someone, open doors, speak well about you and recommend you, that can tell you something you need to know or put you in touch with that someone.

Use when: **Contacts** is often used in challenges to get access to gadgets or as a part of an investigation.

If the task check fails: Your contact can't help you, don't want to help you, or there's a heavy price attached.

CREDIT
Background Skill

Credit measures your wealth and economic status, not just by means of cash on hand, but other assets as well: property, art, stock, bonds, and so on.

Skill value		
15%	Poor	You barely make ends meet, and a lunch out is a luxury.
35%	Middle class	You get by, but a house, a car or a college education is a major investment for you, and probably require a loan or saving for some time.
55%	Well off	Although not rich, money is not an everyday issue for you.
75%	Rich	You don't have to worry about money.

Use when: When you want to get gadgets or buy something, you can either just assess from the Skill value whether it is affordable, or make a roll. Apply modifications if the purchase is expensive for you.

You can also use **Credit** to get access to certain contacts, especially in the financial and political world.

If the task check fails: You cannot afford that purchase right now, or you have to take a loan (future **Credit check**s gets a Down modifier) to finance it. You are denied access to contacts right now.

ELECTRONICS
Investigation Skill

Electronics is quickly entering every appliance in the modern world, replacing electromechanical and mechanical applications. This Skill is for understanding how electronics work, design electronic applications, get equipment and parts, and analysing and modifying existing applications.

Use when: Make a task check whenever you want to rewire something electronic, modify or hack something, understand what an unknown appliance does, or something similar. Make a task check when you need to get or have tools and parts. The Skill is often used as a part of a challenge to accomplish something, for instance in

combination with **Security**, **Search** and **Investigation** to bypass electronic security systems.

If the task check fails: You can't find the parts or the specs, the modification doesn't work, you can't identify what the appliance do, your design doesn't work.

ENDURANCE
Background Skill

This is a Skill that you pay for in sweat! It's about enduring pain, physical strain and other physical hardships. The Skill is not about physical strength – that falls under **Strength** – or mental endurance – that's **Willpower**.

Use when: **Endurance** is often used in challenges for physical tasks, like mountaineering, diving, hikes and marches, or in survival situations. It can also be used in sports.

If the task check fails: The hike takes longer time than planned. You have to quit the marathon race. You don't get there in time. You simply don't have the energy to go on from this stop.

ENGINEERING
Investigation Skill

Engineering is about designing, analysing, repairing and understanding constructions, including machinery.

Use when: If you want to repair your car, figure out the load-bearing walls of a house, understand a locomotive's control panel, or something similar, you can use the **Engineering** Skill.

The Skill is often used in challenges for repair, modification and sometimes even demolition, and in simple task checks to figure out what stuff do.

If the task check fails: You can't repair the machine or get your modification to work. The project just confounds you. You can't figure out which pillars to knock down to make the house collapse.

ENTERTAINMENT
Social Skill

The **Entertainment** Skill covers singing, stand-up comedy, playing instruments, acting, dancing, and other performing art forms.

A common use for this Skill is to behave like someone else, or to not give an impression that you're lying. It is often used to distract someone, or even a crowd, such as when one character draws attention with a performance while the other characters do something shady. The most common use is probably as pure colour: to tell the Director and your fellow players that your character is a bit of an artist.

Use when: **Entertainment** is often used in a challenge with **Subterfuge** and **Charm** to act like someone else. If used as a distraction, combine **Entertainment** with **Subterfuge**, **Sneak**, and **Security**. Sometimes, it is used to impress audiences. You can also use it to assess the performance of other artists.

If the task check fails: Use the Skill value rather than a task check to assess the quality of your performance. If your Skill value is low, you show that you're a beginner. If your Skill value is high, you didn't impress the audience. In any case, they are not entertained.

HUMANITIES
Investigation Skill

This Skill is about the study of aspects of human society and culture: history, anthropology, theology, literature, philosophy, visual arts and much more.

Some fields, like languages (**Languages** Skill), law (**Red Tape**) and performing arts (**Entertainment**), are handled by those Skills, and only a general background is included in this Skill.

Sometimes, it's only used to indicate that your character has had a classical education.

Use when: **Humanities** is often used in challenges and task checks for the research of subjects covered by this Skill. It can also be used to gain access to contacts in universities in Europe.

If the task check fails: You can't find the information you're looking for, you're missing out on a crucial detail, Professor Durand is on vacation and won't be back until the next semester.

INVESTIGATION
Investigation Skill

Investigation is the methodical gathering and collating of information and facts to come to a conclusion. The Skill overlaps somewhat with **Search**, in that you use it to find clues. The difference is context: if you are just looking for something at a location, you use **Search**. If you are documenting a scene to analyse later, looking in archives, or investigating multiple locations, it's part of **Investigation**.

Use when: When carrying out a crime scene investigation, the Skill is used to put together all the evidence and understand it. It's often used with **Search** and other Skills.

If the task check fails: There is information missing. You can't come to a conclusion, there are several competing hypotheses, or you can't prove your hypothesis.

LANGUAGES
Social Skill

Languages is about being able to understand others while making yourself understood, along with knowing how to express yourself clearly. The Skill also determines how many extra languages you are fluent in from the start. If the Skill value increases, you do not automatically become fluent in more languages.

Simply put, this Skill is about comprehending and communicating in different languages.

Use when: Whenever you want to understand something in a language in which you don't have fluency, make a **Languages task check**. The more distant the language is from any you are fluent in, the more difficult the task check. If you succeed, you understand at least the context and general meaning, even if you miss a lot of details.

The Skill is also used for expressing yourself in the languages you know.

Languages

In *The Troubleshooters*, all characters speak French and English. The reason is that we don't want language to be a barrier between the characters, meaning it's more convenient if they are able to interact with the locals in most places.

Language barriers are instead used as a pacing mechanism for clues in your adventures. A document could be written in Medieval Latin, which either requires one of the characters to know Latin or forces them to find someone who can translate the document for them. You can use a **Languages task check** to get the general gist of the document and motivate the players to engage in further research. You then use the quest to find someone who can translate the clue.

Locations may have a language table, similar to the one below, where the most spoken languages are listed along with the chance of anyone random knowing them:

Languages in Strasbourg	Chance (%)
French	100
Alsatian or German	65
English	35

When the characters meet a random person in the world, and there is a language table for that location, roll once for each language on the table to see if the random person understands that language.

Lingua franca

Due to the British Empire's wide reach, English has been the language of international trade, and can often be used all over the globe. Since the War and American dominance, English has become the lingua franca in many parts of the world.

But English is not the only international language. Other useful international languages are:

Arabic: Arabic is not only the majority language on the Arabian Peninsula, northern Africa and the African horn; it is also used by the clergy in other Muslim countries, where it is often a second language. You can always find an imam who can speak Arabic.

French: Used in parts of Africa, the Caribbean, Canada, Indochina and the Pacific, and traditionally a language of diplomacy and culture.

German: Used as a scientific language, especially in physics, chemistry and anthropology. Its popularity has fallen since the War.

Hindi: Hindi is spoken by a great many people, but its use is not widespread outside India. Even in India, it is a native language to the Hindustan region, and a second language elsewhere.

Latin: Wherever you find the Catholic Church, there will almost certainly be a priest who can speak Latin.

Mandarin: Mandarin is not spoken much outside China, but 700 million Chinese know it. Even if they don't, they can still read hanzi, the written form.

Portuguese: Used in Brazil, Macau, Angola and Mozambique.

Russian: A second language in most of the Warsaw Pact countries.

Spanish: Used in most of Latin America, except Brazil and some French and British colonies.

MACHINERY

Action Skill

The **Machinery** Skill is less about creating technology and more about understanding and using it. You could see it as the ability to read the manual and figure out how a thing is supposed to work, from scuba gear to harbour cranes, when you have never seen that sort of thing before.

The Skill is not for using handguns, manipulating security systems, building or repairing machines and electronic devices, operating vehicles, or figuring out the secrets of the universe. There are other Skills for those things. This Skill is for figuring out what buttons to push and levers to pull, and then pushing and pulling them to achieve the desired result.

Use when: **Machinery** is used whenever you need to operate an existing machine that is not a weapon,

vehicle or computer. It can be part of a Skill challenge, but more often it is used as a task check. Apply modifications depending on how intuitive or unintuitive the machine's controls are, and how much skill you need to operate the machine.

If the task check fails: If a task check fails, you often do the wrong thing in an amusing way with the machine. You swing the crane left instead of right, you start the wrong assembly line in the factory, or you lower the boom but do not open the bridge, and so on.

MEDICINE

Investigation Skill

Medicine is a broad Skill, ranging from general practice to specialist areas such as pharmacology and surgery.

In *The Troubleshooters*, **Medicine** is mostly an investigative Skill. You don't need it to restore your **Vitality**, but you may need it to provide Tender Loving Care to speed up healing of the **Wounded** Condition (see page 95).

The Skill does not automatically allow you to practice **Medicine**. In addition to being able, you must also be licensed, which is what the Ability Licensed Professional is about.

Use when: **Medicine** is often a part of an investigation challenge.

You can use **Medicine** to treat the **Wounded** Condition in order to not count that Condition in the next scene. The **Wounded** Conditions are not healed and not dropped: you just don't count them in the next scene.

If the task check fails: You don't find the information you're looking for, or can't make a definite diagnosis. Your bedside manner slips a bit. If you use the Skill to disregard the **Wounded** Condition, it is still in effect.

MELEE

Combat Skill

Melee is more common in sports such as boxing, wrestling, karate, judo, fencing or kendo than as an actual Combat Skill. Some people train in armed martial arts as well, but this is even less common than sport fencing.

Although most armies have close combat systems, it's mostly limited to bayonets or knife fighting, and kept very basic. Special forces members sometimes train in unarmed systems like krav maga or sambo.

Thrown weapons are included as well. Kids often throw spears, knives and even axes and are frustrated by how bad they are at it. Adults mostly use thrown weapons on the athletics field in forms specialised for sports. Some special forces members train to use thrown weapons as a backup, and a ninja wouldn't be a ninja without a supply of shurikens.

Use when: Outside combat, use the Skill to assess the price and craftsmanship of melee weapons, the skill of other combatants, and to contact other martial artists and weapon makers.

In combat, use **Melee** for attack and defence checks. You can use **Melee** for defence against ranged attacks if the attacker is in the same zone, but you can't use the Skill for defence against ranged attacks from outside the same zone.

One Combat Skill is used with **Agility** to determine **Vitality**, if you customise your Template or build a new Template from scratch.

If the task check fails: In combat, you miss your attack. Outside combat, you do not get the information you are looking for.

PRESTIDIGITATION
Background Skill

Prestidigitation is the art of having quick and nimble fingers. It's a common Skill among pickpockets, stage magicians, escape artists, lockpickers, card cheaters and the like.

Use when: Make a **Prestidigitation task check** when you want to pick someone's pocket, perform a card trick, juggle crystal balls in your fingers and palms, pick a lock, and so on.

If the target is alert and prepared, make an opposed check against **Alertness**.

Prestidigitation is often used in challenges with for instance **Engineering**, **Search** and **Investigation** to break into secure sites.

If the task check fails: You can't do what you wanted to do. The lock is too hard, the pocket is closed, you drop the crystal ball, et cetera. If you're picking pockets, you're not discovered. Being discovered happens when you get **Bad Karma**.

RANGED COMBAT
Combat Skill

Ranged Combat encompasses the use of handguns, submachine guns, machine guns, rifles, and even bows and crossbows.

Using handguns is a bit of an oddity in Europe. Most conscripts in Europe get to fire a handgun a few times, but are not trained to use them. It's mostly for police officers and guards, athletes, and a few enthusiasts.

Rifles are much more common, both for hunting and sport, and of course for national defence: conscripted soldiers are trained in the use of rifles, and in many national militias the soldiers keep their rifle in their home.

Archery is a curiosity these days, its practice mostly restricted to athletes, movie stars, reenactors and a few traditionalists.

Use when: Outside combat, use the Skill to assess wounds, the price and craftsmanship of ranged weapons, the skill of other shooters, and to contact other shooters, gunsmiths and bowmakers.

In combat, use **Ranged Combat** for attack checks with handguns, rifles, machine guns, bows, crossbows and the like. You can't use the Skill for defence.

One Combat Skill is used with **Agility** to determine **Vitality**, if you customise your Template or build a new Template from scratch.

If the task check fails: In combat, you miss your attack. Outside combat, you do not get the information you are looking for.

RED TAPE
Investigation Skill

Cutting through red tape and navigating the tangled maze of bureaucracy is not easy, but it can be done. It requires an equal measure of know-how, know-who, social flexibility, and an understanding of rules, regulations, jurisdictions and procedures. But if there is anything a sleuth must know, it's bureaucracy and law. After all, sleuthing is about finding those that break the law and doing the paperwork to prove their guilt.

Being allowed to practice law is another thing. Knowledge about the law and even having a law degree is not enough. You also have to have the Called to the Bar Ability to be licenced to practice law.

Use when: You want to navigate bureaucracy smoothly, you're building a case before court, negotiating business deals, et cetera. You may also use **Red Tape** as part of a challenge or during an investigation.

If the task check fails: You cannot find a precedent to support the case, the law is unclear or contradictory on a matter, you're stuck in the labyrinth of regulations, or it's beyond your field of expertise.

SCIENCE
Investigation Skill

The Troubleshooters is set in the age of rocketry and atomics and the emerging science of computers and robots. This Skill reflects the science behind all those advancements and more. It's about astronomy, chemistry, astrophysics, quantum physics, materials science, and much more.

Use when: **Science** is often used for investigation in a challenge, or as a task check to understand what Professor Mikhailov is talking about. Conceivably, the Skill could be used to control a nuclear reactor or plot an orbit for a space shuttle or space capsule. Together with **Engineering** and **Electronics**, it could be used in a challenge to construct gadgets.

If the task check fails: Huh?

SEARCH
Investigation Skill

The difference between **Search** and **Investigation** is that **Investigation** is used to methodically gather evidence to get to a conclusion, while **Search** is used to just find something. There isn't a particularly clear line between the two, and they overlap somewhat. You could use **Investigation** to try to find the weapon at a murder scene and put it in its context; you could use **Search** as well to just find the weapon that you are missing; and of course you can use them both as part of a challenge for a criminal investigation.

Search is not used for noticing something, looking for someone stalking you, or just being aware. You use **Alertness** for that.

Use when: Whenever you are looking for something at a location.

If the task check fails: You don't find it.

If at first you don't succeed – too bad!
Contrary to the old saying, if your **Search task check** fails, you *don't* get to try and try again. Your friends don't get to try either: the failed task check means that whatever you're looking for is too well hidden for you and your friends.

This goes for just about any Skill, by the way, not just **Search**. If you fail, you don't get a second chance unless the situation has changed to a significant degree, such as when an entirely new scene begins.

If you want to mitigate the risk of failure, ask for a challenge instead. That way, the quality of your searching depends on the total number of successes in the challenge, rather than one single task check.

Another method is to hand out a basic clue whenever someone searches, and have a successful **Search task check** result in more, better and in-depth clues. For instance, instead of a failed **Search check** meaning that the characters don't find the hidden door, they automatically find the hidden door if they search for one, but a failed task check means they don't find the opening mechanism.

SECURITY
Action Skill

Security is the ultimate Skill for spies and cat burglars. This Skill is about security systems, including physical barriers like fences, locks and doors, monitoring systems like CCTV and sensors, and security protocols like patrol routes, shift changes, and identification checks.

It's also about beating said systems and protocols.

Use when: Characters won't use the Skill very often to design a security system, although that is certainly possible. Then it could be used as an opposed check for Director character thieves to beat, or as a challenge with opposed rolls.

Security is more commonly used to break into secure sites, often in a challenge together with **Sneak**, **Alertness**, **Electronics** and **Subterfuge**.

If the task check fails: You set off an alarm, you can't beat a lock, or you miss a security system somewhere. You may not be in trouble now, but soon.

SNEAK
Action Skill

This is a mandatory Skill for every private eye, spy, ninja or cat burglar. The Skill is all about evading detection, both by sight and sound. To some extent it also includes sensors like cameras, and also camouflage.

Use when: **Sneak** is often used in opposed checks against **Alertness** or **Search**. **Sneak** can also be used in a challenge together with **Alertness**, **Security**, **Subterfuge** and **Electronics** to break into secure sites.

If the task check fails: You're discovered, either at once or after some delay from traces you leave. You're not captured or cornered – yet.

STATUS
Social Skill

In the modern world, status is a little more fluid than in the past. You can rise to stardom and make a fortune, and although it's still a factor, heritage is not as important as it once was. This Skill reflects both status and fame, earned and inherited, but not wealth or contacts.

Use when: On social occasions, **Status** may be used to gain access to important people. **Status** is often used in challenges, together with at least Etiquette, **Credit** and **Contacts**, to get in touch with important people – especially the "Old Boys network" – and get favours from them.

If the task check fails: Your status may be high enough, but there are still obstacles, and the "Old Boys network" is not homogeneous. There may be bad blood somewhere, lingering rumours, skeletons in the closet, or they consider you uppity – especially if you're nouveau riche or just a media star.

STRENGTH
Background Skill

Like **Endurance**, **Strength** is a Skill that you pay for in sweat! **Strength** is about lifting, pushing, pulling and other tasks that involve raw muscle power.

The Skill is not about enduring hardships, mentally or physically. Use **Willpower** or **Endurance** in those cases.

Use when: **Strength** is used for physical feats: lifting, pulling, pushing, tearing, throwing and similar actions. The Skill is also used in challenges, often with **Endurance** and **Willpower**, especially if the action takes so long to complete that doing so might conceivably wear the character down. It can also be used in sports.

If the task check fails: You have to let go. You can't hold the door open or push it closed. You don't throw the object far enough. You can't lift it high enough. You can't break it.

SUBTERFUGE
Social Skill

Subterfuge is about trickery and deceit – an important Skill in any con artist's toolbox. It involves the art of disguise, bluffing, trickery, acting and even cheating.

Subterfuge is about looking and behaving like someone else. It's as much about theatre as it is about just making the disguise. Sometimes the forgery of documents is included.

Subterfuge is also important for gambling – not necessarily for cheating, but being a good gambler means deceiving your opponents into thinking that your hand isn't what it is.

Use when: If you want to appear as someone else or avoid being recognised. It's often used in opposed checks against someone else's **Search**, **Investigation** or **Alertness**.

You can also use the Skill for gambling as a challenge together with **Alertness**, **Charm** and **Willpower**. If you want to cheat, add **Prestidigitation**.

If the task check fails: You're caught bluffing. They see through your forgery. Your disguise raises suspicion, and sooner or later someone will check up on you if they don't do it immediately. You're not caught or cornered, yet – unless you had **Bad Karma** as well. But even if you didn't have **Bad Karma**, expect trouble, and soon.

SURVIVAL
Action Skill

Nature is harsh and indiscriminate. Most of us live comfortably in communities so we don't have to face it head on. There are exceptions, though: adventurers that enjoy the challenge or rangers that must be able to survive on their own behind enemy lives. Boy scouts and girl scouts do it in a limited sense, as do hunters, campers and hikers.

Use when: **Survival** is often used in Skill challenges together with **Alertness**, **Willpower** and **Endurance** for treks in the wilderness. It can also be used for simple campsite construction – lavatory pits, tripods etc. The Skill is also used for map reading and navigation off the beaten path.

If the task check fails: You could get the **Exhausted** Condition, or maybe even a **Wounded** Condition, if it is used in a Skill challenge or an actual survival situation.

VEHICLES
Action Skill

As we all know, most drivers can't drive, but somehow they manage to get from home to the office and back every day without a major incident.

The Skill **Vehicles** is not for these situations. It's for races, car chases, precision driving, and to some extent technical knowledge about the car. Other vehicles besides cars can also be operated with **Vehicles**, including boats, submarines and airplanes.

Use when: In a vehicle chase, or when attempting a stunt with a vehicle. In an aircraft, use **Vehicles** when in a dogfight. You can also use it for assessing the skill of other drivers, for basic maintenance and repair, and for geeking out on vehicle facts. You can also use **Vehicles** to find a good route when driving or operating the vehicle.

If the task check fails: If you use the Skill in an opposed check, the opponent wins. In a car stunt or aerobatic one, you're forced to abort or don't impress the audience. You don't crash – though that could happen if you get **Bad Karma**.

WILLPOWER
Background Skill

This Skill is about iron will. It's about strength of the mind, mental endurance, the will to survive and the power to not give up. This Skill is not about physical ability – that would be **Strength** and **Endurance**.

Use when: **Willpower** is often used in challenges in hard conditions like survival situations or endurance sports. In combat, it has the specific use of clearing your mind to drop the **Stunned** Condition.

If the task check fails: You don't get a grip. You're confused or dazed. You're ready to give up, you can't resist pressure or temptation.

ABILITIES

Éloïse, what ... what are you doing?!!

I'm remotely electrifying my Vespa, of course, by modulating high frequency energy!

Can you do that?

Of course I can! Everyone can learn science, but it takes a special mind to turn theory into practice. A spark of genius! Give me a Tesla coil and a particle accelerator, and I will beam unlimited power straight to my Vespa! I am invincible!

Éloïse, please stop! You scare me!

HOW ABILITIES WORK

Abilities are special rules that enable you to do things most people can't. They are the things that allow you to drive a car like a pro or wield a sword like a master.

Abilities have several effects, sometimes with stipulations attached. The most common is that it will cost **Story Points** to activate the Ability. In other cases, the stipulations allow for activation only in some specific situation.

Abilities are described in a common format.

- After the name of the Ability, there is a header with tier, prerequisites if any, and what Skills you use for learning and the number of ticks you need to learn it.
- Each Ability has a short description that helps you act out the Ability.
- Finally, there are the crunchy bits, detailing the actual rules involved with using the Ability. The most common structure for an Ability is to **spend Story Points** for a particular effect, often flips or rerolls.

PREREQUISITES AND TIERS

Each Ability has a tier, depending on its prerequisites (if any).

- A tier 0 Ability has no prerequisites at all.
- A tier 1 Ability only requires that you have a minimum Skill value in one or more Skills.
- A tier 2 Ability requires that you have one or more specified tier 0 or tier 1 Abilities.
- A tier 3 Ability requires that you have one or more specified tier 2 Abilities, and so on.

Abilities in the Core Book range from tier 0 to 2. Future expansions may list more Abilities, including those at tier 3 and above.

When creating a character, you can pick a tier 1 Ability even if your Skill level is not high enough. For tier 2 Abilities or higher, you must fulfil the requirements even at character generation, and if you want to learn a tier 1 Ability later in the Debriefing phase, you must fulfil its requirements as well.

CREATING YOUR OWN ABILITIES

To make your own Ability, it is often easiest to start with a name and what it is supposed to do rules-wise. Then add the flavour text if necessary, and set prerequisites and the number of ticks needed to learn the Ability.

- **Prerequisites:** Many Abilities do not have any prerequisites. If they do, it's often a Skill value, usually 65% or higher; or another Ability. Prerequisites can be used to balance more powerful Abilities, especially by requiring another Ability. You can use Ability prerequisites in tiers to build a progression path or progression tree, which can create a sense of unlocking secret knowledge, for instance about mysticism or martial arts.
- **Learning:** All Abilities must have at least one Skill you can roll for to learn it. If there is more than one Skill listed, it means it is easier to get – a useful way to balance weak Abilities. Ignore Learning if you use the optional experience point system.
- **Cost:** Cost indicates how many ticks you must collect on an Ability to learn it. The average Ability requires 5 ticks, but it could be as low as 3 or as high as 8. Use the cost to balance out what you can't balance with **Story Point** cost and prerequisites.
- **Task checks:** Certain very specific task checks may get a modification, usually **+2 pips**.
- **Story Points:** A good guideline is that spending **1 Story Point** can flip task checks for specific Skills or

specific kinds of task checks, and spending **2 Story Points** can reroll a task check. **Story Points** could also have narrative influence effects, like Acrobat allowing you to find a thing to grab and stop your fall. It is even plausible to increase damage, as with Mean Left Hook. Be creative, but set a **Story Point** cost that reflects the effect.
- **Other effects:** Some Abilities may have other in-world effects as well, like the *Rank* effect of Military Rank, or the *Landed* effect of Old Money. Be creative: Abilities with other effects stand out more and are more fun to play. Make sure the other effects are named properly.

If you are a player and have a great idea for an Ability, feel free to write it down according to these guidelines, but remember to clear it with the Director before using it with your character.

CUSTOMISE ABILITIES

A simple way of customising the Abilities is to simply change their name. If you rename Boxer to Karate Black Belt, Boxing Champion to Karate Master and Mean Left Hook to Mean Left Foot, you have immediately changed the tone of the Abilities to fit a karate fighter rather than a boxer.

ABILITY DESCRIPTIONS

ACROBAT

Tier 1: Requires **Agility** 65%
Learning: Agility
Cost: 7

You are a trained acrobat or gymnast, able to accomplish the most incredible feats of acrobatics.

Task checks: Movement task checks are at **+2 pips**. You can add acrobatic flavour when describing how you move to the next zone.

Story Points: Spend 1 Story Point to flip an **Agility** or Defence task check.

Spend 2 Story Points to stop a fall without being harmed by finding something to grab. The existence of something to grab has to be plausible. You end up hanging from whatever you grabbed.

ACTOR

Tier 1: Requires **Entertainment** 65%
Learning: Subterfuge or **Entertainment**
Cost: 5

You are a natural actor. It's almost easier for you to live other people's lives than your own.

Be someone else: You can take on the role of someone else, provided you have a script, wardrobe and make-up. A thorough background check and detailed files may count as a script, but will require a **Charm, Entertainment, Investigation, Subterfuge** and **Willpower** challenge.

Story Points: Spend 1 Story Point to flip a **Subterfuge task check** when pretending to be someone else.

Spend 2 Story Points to make a new task check for **Entertainment** or **Charm**, and keep the new roll.

ALLURE

Tier 1: Requires **Charm** 65%
Learning: Charm
Cost: 5

There is something about you that makes you particularly attractive. It's not limited to beauty, but more about impression and personality.

Past lovers: You may have a history of past lovers. You can introduce them if you want to, and the Director may use past lovers you introduce to further complicate the plot.

Story Points: Spend 1 Story Point to get the attention of anyone in the scene and make them less attentive to anything else. Their task checks to notice something are at **–2 pips**; task checks for trying to evade their attention are at **+2 pips**.

Spend 1 Story Point to flip a **Charm task check**.

Spend 4 Story Points to make a Director character a past lover that still has feelings for you. The Director may veto this use, in which case the **Story Points** are returned.

ANIMAL FRIEND

Tier 0
Learning: Charm
Cost: 5

Suddenly you find yourself in a pile of two cuddling cats, a dog with its head in you lap and a parakeet on your head. That's your thing: animals like you. And it's not limited to domesticated animals: even wolves think you're just a member of the pack.

Story Points: Spend 1 Story Point to not be attacked by one domesticated animal, or calm down a panic-stricken domesticated animal, such as a watchdog, horse, camel or bull, as long as you do not attack the animal.

Spend 2 Story Points to not be attacked by one wild mammal or bird, or calm down a panic-stricken wild mammal or bird.

Spend **4 Story Points** to have any wild animal of sufficient size carry you away from the scene and leave you unharmed. If there is no wild animal of sufficient size present, one appears. If it is not plausible in the scene, the Director will give you the **Story Points** back.

ARCHER

Tier 1: Requires **Ranged Combat** 45%
Learning: Ranged Combat
Cost: 5

You are specialised in the ancient art of fighting with bows.

Story Points: Spend 1 Story Point to flip an attack check if you are shooting a bow.

Spend 2 Story Points to reroll an attack check with a bow, and keep the new roll.

ARTIST

Tier 0
Learning: Charm
Cost: 5

You can express yourself in the form of art.

Live for the art: Pick one art form that you are proficient in, for instance Musician, Painter, Photographer, Poet, Singer, Writer

Make art: Spend a scene putting on a public performance of your art. In a future scene for the same crowd, social task checks are at **+2 pips**.

Story Points: Spend 1 Story Point to flip a **Charm** or **Status task check** as a result of your art.

Spend 2 Story Points to reroll a **Charm** or **Status task check** related to your art, and keep the new roll.

ATHLETE

Tier 1: Requires **Endurance** 65%
Learning: Endurance
Cost: 5

You are a professional athlete.

Sport: Select one team or single sport, for instance football, rugby, horse polo, sprint, biathlon etc. Decide which Skill is primary for the sport. It is usually **Agility** or **Endurance**, but **Melee** could be allowed by the Director for fencing, kendo, boxing, judo or karate. Be restrictive with **Ranged Combat**, even if archery or other forms of target shooting exist as sports.

Story Points: Spend 1 Story Point to flip a task check for the primary Skill for the sport.

Spend 1 Story Point to use the primary Skill for the sport instead of **Contacts** to get in touch with a

fan that could help you in return for an autographed memento.

At a sporting event, **spend 1 Story Point** to be surrounded by a small group of fans.

BEEN EVERYWHERE

Tier 0
Learning: Credit, Contacts, Humanities or **Survival**
Cost: 5

Taj Mahal? The Great Wall? Machu Picchu? Boring and mainstream. You have already been there. In fact, you have been everywhere, met everyone, and got the t-shirt.

Story Points: Spend 1 Story Point to know someone at the location.

Spend 1 Story Point to flip a **Contacts** or **Red Tape task check** when not in your home country.

Spend 1 Story Point to flip a **Languages task check** for modern languages.

BORN BEHIND THE WHEEL

Tier 1: Requires Drive 65%
Learning: Drive
Cost: 5

You are one with the vehicle and the road.

Story Points: Spend 1 Story Point to flip a task check to handle a vehicle.

Spend 2 Story Points to reroll any task check you make to handle a vehicle.

Spend 2 Story Points to make a car stunt possible in the scene – driving on two wheels, jumping over obstacles etc.

BOXER

Tier 1: Requires **Melee** 65%
Learning: Melee
Cost: 5

You are a trained boxing fighter, perhaps dreaming of the day when you stand in the ring for real, fighting for the championship.

Stamina: If an unarmed defence check has **Good Karma**, make the Recovery roll at **2dP** instead of **1dP**.

Story Points: Spend 1 Story Point to flip an attack check if you are fighting unarmed.

Spend 1 Story Point to focus and make a **1dP** Recovery roll as a side action.

If an attack check against a *Mook* is successful, **spend 1 Story Point** to give him a solid shot and make him **Out Cold**, regardless of the Damage roll.

Spend 2 Story Points to reroll the attack check.

BOXING CHAMPION

Tier 2: Requires Boxer
Learning: Melee
Cost: 5

You're a prize fighter. You're up there in the ring, paying for the affection of the audience with sweat, pain and blood.

Story Points: Spend 1 Story Point to flip a **Status task check.**

Spend 2 Story Points if you get a Lieutenant character's **Vitality** to 0 to force the character to go **Out Cold** and not get the **Wounded** Condition.

Spend 2 Story Points to reroll a Damage roll and keep the new one.

BUSHMAN

Tier 1: Requires **Survival** 65%
Learning: Endurance or **Survival**
Cost: 5

You know all the secret tricks of hiking in the outback and surviving on bush food.

Walked five hundred miles: In a hiking or other outback travel Skill challenge, your roll is at **+2 pips.**

Walked five hundred more: Given time, you can make a primitive shelter and get a fire going from almost nothing.

Story Points: Spend 1 Story Point to flip a **Survival** or **Endurance task check.**

CALLED TO THE BAR

Tier 1: Requires **Red Tape** 65%
Learning: Humanities, Investigation or **Red Tape**
Cost: 5

As a certified lawyer, you are allowed to argue in court on behalf of another party.

Dear colleagues: Use **Red Tape** instead of **Contacts** to get in touch with colleagues in law: barristers, advocates, solicitors, judges and lawyers.

Here's my card: Task checks for **Status** are at **+2 pips** in situations where your knowledge of the law could impress other people.

Story Points: Spend 1 Story Point to flip a task check for **Red Tape.**

Spend 2 Story Points to find a witness.

CHEERFUL

Tier 0
Learning: Charm
Cost: 3

There are no worries at all in the world. The sun shines, and if it doesn't, it shines somewhere else. Not that you are affected by the sun not shining on you: you would happily sing in the rain too.

Story Points: Spend 1 Story Point to flip a **Charm** or **Willpower task check.**

Spend 2 Story Points to cheer someone else up and have them reroll one non-combat task check.

CRAFTER

Tier 0
Learning: Endurance, Prestidigitation or **Willpower**
Cost: 5

Not everyone creates things according to science. You create them by hand, in a tradition passed down for generations from master to student.

A typical Skill challenge for crafting things would use **Alertness, Endurance, Prestidigitation** and/or **Willpower** to make things, and **Contacts, Credit** or **Red Tape** to get the perfect material you are looking for.

Ancient wisdom: You can craft things that are considered Ancient Wisdom at downtime between sessions.

Story Points: Spend 1 Story Point to flip any task check while crafting.

CURIOUS

Tier 0
Learning: Alertness, Investigation or **Search**
Cost: 5

There is always a mystery. Not one of those criminal mysteries, or ancient mysteries, but rather mundane everyday mysteries, like what's in this box? Where does this door lead to? How many 7400N TTL chips do you need to build an arithmetic unit? Is that really a gun?

Curiosity killed the cat: Your curiosity can get you into trouble. Change a successful **Sneak, Security** or **Investigation task check** to a failure to get the unwanted attention of the security detail. Doing so puts you in a world of trouble and gets you **3 Story Points.**

Story Points: Spend 1 Story Point to flip an **Alertness, Investigation** or **Search task check.**

Spend 2 Story Points to reroll an **Alertness, Investigation** or **Search task check** and keep the new roll.

DIPLOMATIC IMMUNITY

Tier 0
Learning: **Contacts**, **Red Tape** or **Status**
Cost: 8

The Vienna convention codifying diplomatic relations is actually rather recent, but the custom goes back millennia. You are one of those accredited with a diplomatic passport. It's not a carte blanche to do whatever you want, and not everyone cares about your diplomatic immunity. But you are somewhat immune: you are granted safe passage, and you cannot be prosecuted or sued in the host country. However, you can be detained, your home can be searched, and you can be expelled and forbidden to return.

Story Points: Spend 1 Story Point to not have your personal belongings searched by law enforcement if detained.

Spend 1 Story Point to be released immediately if detained by law enforcement.

DIVEMASTER

Tier 2: Requires Diver
Learning: **Alertness**, **Endurance** or **Machinery**
Cost: 5

You are an experienced diver and capable of training or supervising untrained divers. You can also handle technical dives at depths below 30 metres, including air mixtures for those depths and using multiple air bottles.

Supervisor: If another diver under your supervision is in trouble during the dive, the Director should tell you first.

Story Points: Spend 1 Story Point to have another diver under your supervision reroll a task check while diving and keep the new roll.

DIVER

Tier 0
Learning: **Alertness**, **Endurance** or **Machinery**
Cost: 5

You are a trained and licensed SCUBA diver, able to dive on your own without professional supervision. You can plan the dive, including air mixture, bottom time, ascending time, etc. You also have the licence to show when you want to rent SCUBA gear, to prove that you can handle it.

Hand signals: You can communicate basic instructions and information with other characters with the Diver Ability using hand signals, allowing you as the player to talk freely about what you want to communicate.

Story Points: Spend 1 Story Point to flip an Endurance or **Agility task check** when diving.

Spend 2 Story Points to reroll an **Endurance** or **Agility task check** when diving, and keep the new roll.

DOUBLE NATIONALITY

Tier 0
Learning: **Investigation** or **Red Tape**
Cost: 4

Your parents come from two distinctly different cultures. You speak both languages, and you have citizenship (and a passport) in both your parents' countries.

Languages: When creating the character, pick an additional native language.

My other country: If your nationality gets you into trouble with the immigration office or customs, you can use your other nationality to get out of trouble (unless that nationality also puts you in trouble).

Story Points: Spend 1 Story Point to flip a **Charm** or **Status task check** by the sheer exoticism of your other nationality.

Spend 1 Story Point to flip a **Contacts** or **Credit task check** thanks to knowing someone from the other nationality.

DUELLIST

Tier 2: Requires Swordsman
Learning: **Melee** or **Status**
Cost: 4

The sad thing about the modern world is that the honourable one-on-one duel has all but disappeared. You keep the tradition alive.

En garde!: Challenge a target in a fight scene. If accepted, you engage in a one-on-one duel. Neither of you may attack anyone besides the other duelist, except as a counter-attack if interfered with.

Ranged attacks on any target in a duel may hit either one of you (roll **1d6**: you are hit on 1–3, the opponent is hit on 4–6). If anyone else makes a melee attack against any target in a duel, the target may flip the defence check for free.

On **Good Karma** on a defence check against an attack from outside the duel, the duelist may immediately make a counter-attack against the attacker (this is the only case where a duelist may attack someone outside the duel) instead of making a Recovery roll.

You may stop the duel by giving up, by mutual agreement, or when either one of you is **Out Cold**. If either party is **Wounded**, the opponent must give them the chance to give up.

EMPATHY

Tier 0
Learning: **Charm**
Cost: 4

You understand other people, and see what makes them tick.

Story Points: Spend 1 Story Point to flip a **Charm** or **Subterfuge task check.**

Spend 2 Story Points to reroll a **Charm** or **Subterfuge task check.**

Spend 2 Story Points to have a Director character tell you about their problem, if they have a reason to trust you. If they don't, the Director may veto this use, in which case the **Story Points** are returned.

EXTRA GADGET

Tier 0
Learning: **Credit**, **Contacts**, **Status** or **Willpower**
Cost: 3

One gear kit is so synonymous with you that it is part of your persona. To see you without it is nearly unthinkable.

There are many like it but this one is mine: One additional gear kit is considered to be a **Signature Gadget** (see page 113). Describe what your **Signature Gadget** is, and why it is special to you.

You can't stop with one: You can get this Ability more than once, each time making one additional gear kit into **Signature Gadget.**

Story Points: Gain 3 Story Points if your **Signature Gadget** is lost, destroyed or not available for a big part of the adventure. The **Signature Gadget** is restored at the start of the next session at the latest.

FAMOUS

Tier 0
Learning: **Status**
Cost: 5

You are famous. Everyone knows your name! Your face is on magazine covers, movie posters, or television.

Story Points: Spend 1 Story Point to be recognised and surrounded by a small crowd of fans and journalists.

Spend 2 Story Points to slip away from a crowd of fans unnoticed or to persuade them that you are not you.

Spend 1 Story Point to flip a **Contacts** or **Credit task check** to get in touch with your greatest fan.

FIGHTER PILOT

Tier 2: Requires Pilot and Military Rank
Learning: **Engineering**, **Ranged Combat** or **Vehicles**
Cost: 5

Military fighter planes are a different kind of beast than even a small private jet. They're immensely powerful and nimble, and of course they're also armed with missiles, bombs, rockets and cannons. They're complex machines, with radar systems, jamming systems and flares. Some of them can even land vertically. They're also restricted: you have to be trusted to fly these expensive and dangerous airplanes.

Story Points: In a dogfight, **spend 1 Story Point** to flip an attack check with the fighter plane's weapons.

Spend 2 Story Points to take your turn in a dogfight now.

FOCUSED

Tier 0
Learning: **Willpower**
Cost: 5

You have the rare ability to cut out all distractions and remain focused on the task ahead.

Story Points: Spend 1 Story Point to reroll a failed task check, but for **Willpower** at **+2 pips** instead. If successful, you succeed in your task by sheer focus and tenacity.

Spend 2 Story Points to get someone else to focus and reroll a failed task check but for **Willpower** at **+2 pips** instead. If successful, they manage to pull through.

FORENSICS

Tier 0
Learning: **Medicine**, **Investigation** or **Science**
Cost: 5

You are a trained forensics analyst. Using a Forensics kit, you can lift fingerprints, semen, blood, fibres, hair and other evidence for analysis in a lab and as evidence in a court of law.

Chain of evidence: Your treatment of evidence is impeccable. Any use of the Skill **Red Tape** using your evidence to convict or expose a criminal is at **+2 pips**. The task check for **Red Tape** doesn't have to be yours, but the evidence must link the criminal to the scene.

Story Points: Spend 1 Story Point to flip an **Investigation** or **Search task check** if you are taking part in a forensic crime scene investigation.

Spend 2 Story Points if you have a Forensics kit to reroll an **Investigation** or **Search task check**, and keep the new roll.

GUNSLINGER

Tier 2: Requires Gunman
Learning: Agility, Ranged Combat or **Status**
Cost: 5

You are a legendary gunslinger. Nobody in their right mind would mess with you.

Trick shot: Use a main action and make a successful task check for **Ranged Combat** to do any of the following:

- Cut a wire or rope
- Plug a firearm's barrel with your bullet, making it unusable
- Flip a switch
- Disarm someone by shooting the gun out of their hands

Story Points: Spend 1 Story Point to take your turn now, before someone else's turn.

Spend 1 Story Point to make an extra attack against another target in the same zone as the first as a bonus action.

INTIMIDATING

Tier 0
Learning: Status, Strength, Subterfuge or **Willpower**
Cost: 5

You have a threatening look or air about you. You look or feel like someone who means trouble if crossed. It doesn't necessarily mean that you are an ugly brute, instead you might be steely-eyed, cold or have a perpetual, no-nonsense scowl.

Story Points: Spend 1 Story Point to flip a task check for persuading someone. If you succeed this way, the target will obey you and be scared of you.

If a fight has not yet started, **spend 2 Story Points** and make an opposed check for **Status, Strength, Subterfuge** or **Willpower** against the Mooks' **Willpower** (the Mooks roll collectively). If successful, **1d6** Mooks run away.

GOOD REPUTATION

Tier 0
Learning: Charm or **Status**
Cost: 5

Your reputation precedes you, and in a good way.

Story Points: Spend 1 Story Point to have someone introduce you with some kind words in a social situation.

Spend 2 Story Points to have someone's good words give you a modification of **+2 pips** in a social situation.

Spend 4 Story Points to have someone vouch for you to you get you out of trouble, at least momentarily and only if it's not a serious crime that you are accused of. The Director may veto this use, in which case the **Story Points** are returned.

GUNMAN

Tier 1: Requires **Ranged Combat** 45%
Learning: Agility or **Ranged Combat**
Cost: 5

You are a great marksman with handguns.

Story Points: Spend 1 Story Point to flip an attack check if you are shooting with a handgun.

Spend 1 Story Point to reload a handgun as a free action rather than as a main action.

INVESTIGATOR

Tier 0
Learning: Alertness, Investigation, Red Tape, Science or **Willpower**
Cost: 5

You have an eye for minute details and the ability to instinctively discern their meaning.

Story Points: Spend 1 Story Point to flip a task check for **Search** or **Investigation**.

Spend 2 Story Points to make a failed task check for **Search** or **Investigation** into a success instead.

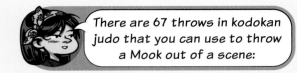

There are 67 throws in kodokan judo that you can use to throw a Mook out of a scene:

Hand throwing techniques
- *Ippon seoinage* (一本背負い投げ): Single-handed back throw
- *Kata guruma* (肩車): Shoulder wheel
- *Kibisu gaeshi* (踵返): One-hand reversal
- *Morote gari* (双手刈): Two-hand reap
- *Obi otoshi* (帯落): Belt drop
- *Seoi nage* (背負い投げ): Back throw
- *Seoi otoshi* (背負落): Back drop
- *Sukui nage* (掬投): Scoop throw
- *Sumi otoshi* (隅落): Corner drop
- *Tai otoshi* (體落): Body drop
- *Uchi mata sukashi* (内股透): Inner thigh void throw
- *Uki otoshi* (浮落): Floating drop
- *Yama arashi* (山嵐): Mountain storm
- *Kouchi gaeshi* (小内返): Small inner reap reversal
- *Kuchiki taoshi* (朽木倒): Single leg takedown

Hip throwing techniques
- *Daki age* (抱上): Hugging high lift*
- *Hane goshi* (跳腰): Spring hip throw
- *Harai goshi* (払腰): Sweeping hip throw
- *Koshi guruma* (腰車): Hip wheel
- *O goshi* (大腰): Full hip throw
- *Sode tsurikomi goshi* (袖釣込腰): Sleeve lifting and pulling hip throw
- *Tsuri goshi* (釣腰): Lifting hip throw
- *Tsurikomi goshi* (釣込腰): Lifting and pulling hip throw
- *Uki goshi* (浮腰): Floating half-hip throw
- *Ushiro goshi* (後腰): Rear throw
- *Utsuri goshi* (移腰): Hip shift

Foot throwing techniques
- *Ashi guruma* (足車): Leg wheel
- *De Ashi Harai* (出足払): Advanced foot sweep
- *Hane goshi gaeshi* (跳腰返): Hip spring counter
- *Harai goshi gaeshi* (払腰返): Hip sweep counter
- *Harai tsurikomi ashi* (払釣込足): Lift-pull foot sweep
- *Hiza guruma* (膝車): Knee wheel
- *Kosoto gake* (小外掛): Small outer hook
- *Kosoto gari* (小外刈): Small outer reap
- *Kouchi gari* (小内刈): Small inner reap
- *O guruma* (大車): Large wheel
- *Okuri Ashi Harai* (送足払): Sliding foot sweep
- *Osoto gaeshi* (大外返): Big outer reap counter
- *Osoto gari* (大外刈): Big outer reap
- *Osoto guruma* (大外車): Big outer wheel
- *Osoto otoshi* (大外落): Big outer drop
- *Ouchi gaeshi* (大内返): Big inner reap counter
- *Ouchi gari* (大内刈): Big inner reap

- *Sasae tsurikomi ashi* (支釣込足): Propping and drawing ankle throw
- *Tsubame gaeshi* (燕返): Swallow counter
- *Uchi mata* (内股): Inner-thigh
- *Uchi mata gaeshi* (内股返): Inner-thigh counter

Forward sacrifice techniques
- *Hikikomi gaeshi* (引込返): Pulling in reversal
- *Sumi gaeshi* (隅返): Corner reversal
- *Tawara gaeshi* (俵返): Rice bag reversal throw
- *Tomoe nage* (巴投): Circle throw
- *Ura nage* (裏投): Rear throw

Side sacrifice techniques
- *Daki wakare* (抱分): High separation
- *Hane makikomi* (跳巻込): Springing wraparound
- *Harai makikomi* (払巻込): Hip sweep wraparound
- *Kani basami* (蟹挟): Crab or scissors throw*
- *Kawazu gake* (河津掛): One-leg entanglement*
- *Osoto makikomi* (大外巻込): Big outer wraparound
- *Soto makikomi* (外巻込): Outer wraparound
- *Tani otoshi* (谷落): Valley drop
- *Uchi makikomi* (内巻込): Inner wraparound
- *Uchi mata makikomi* (内股巻込): Inner thigh wraparound
- *Uki waza* (浮技): Floating technique
- *Yoko gake* (横掛): Side prop
- *Yoko guruma* (横車): Side wheel
- *Yoko otoshi* (横落): Side drop
- *Yoko wakare* (横分): Side separation

* These techniques are forbidden in competitions.

Technically, German Suplex is not a legal judo technique, but...

JUDO BLACK BELT

Tier 1: Requires **Melee** 45%
Learning: Melee
Cost: 5

You are an expert in judo, aikido, or a similar martial art.

Story Points: Spend 1 Story Point and yell the name of an aikido or judo technique to flip a Whump! melee throw or grapple attack check.

If an attack check against a *Mook* is successful, **spend 1 Story Point** and yell the name of an aikido or judo technique to remove that *Mook* from the fight – out through the window, into a cupboard, down the laundry chute, or any other way of your choice suitable to the scene.

JUDO MASTER

Tier 2: Requires Judo Black Belt
Learning: Melee or **Status**
Cost: 5

You are a master in judo, aikido or a similar martial art.

Master Dodger: You can use **Melee** for defence checks against ranged attacks, whether or not the attacker is in the same zone, as long as you are aware of the attacker.

Zen: Checks to resist terror or frights, to downgrade **Terrified**, and to drop **Frightened**, are at **+2 pips. Spend 2 Story Points** to downgrade **Terrified** or drop **Frightened** as a bonus action.

Story Points: Spend 2 Story Points to make an attack check a success, no matter what you rolled. If it is an opposed check, your roll equals what you rolled.

LICENSED PROFESSIONAL

Tier 0
Learning: Status or **Willpower**
Cost: 5

Some professions require you to have a license. Exactly which professions require a licence varies from country to country, but generally it will be those that may cause a large negative impact on individuals, such as lawyers, police officers or physicians. Other professions such as teachers, plumbers, electricians and even taxi drivers may require a license as well.

Some of these are covered by the Abilities Called to the Bar, Pilot, Military Rank and Police Badge. This Ability is for the other protected professions.

Field of expertise: Pick one field in which you are a licensed professional: physician (**Medicine**), electrician (**Electronics** or **Engineering**), plumber (**Engineering**), taxi driver (**Vehicles**). You are allowed to practice professionally within that field. The Skill noted next to each entry above is the primary Skill for that field of expertise.

Dear colleagues: Use your primary Skill instead of **Contacts** to get in touch with colleagues in your field of expertise.

I'm a pro: Task checks for **Status** are at **+2 pips** in situations where your field of expertise could impress other people.

Stand back: In a fitting emergency situation, **spend 1 Story Point** to yell "*Stand back, I'm a professional!*" and have the crowd stand back to let you do your job. You can also command the crowd to do simple things, like bring you an object or call someone.

Story Points: Spend 1 Story Point to flip a task check for the primary Skill of your expertise.

LOCK-PICKER

Tier 1: Requires **Prestidigitation** 45%
Learning: Prestidigitation
Cost: 3

Not every lock-picker is a thief. Some actually do it as part of their job. For others it is merely a hobby. Either way, this is the specific Ability you need to quickly pick a lock.

Story Points: Spend 1 Story Point to flip a task check for **Prestidigitation** or **Engineering** when picking a lock or cracking a safe.

MAD INVENTOR

Tier 1: Requires **Science** 65% and **Engineering** 65%
Learning: Science or **Engineering**
Cost: 5

You have the Spark, the gene that allows mad science to become reality. You master it all, from Zvyerdlov manifolds of space-time to reverse encephalography to the complete genetic sequence of fungi. With that knowledge, you will soon invent a machine that will allow you to claim dominion over the world!

...or make ice cream. Either works.

Mwahahaha!: Once per session, and if you have a dangerous-looking device with impressive special effects, you can activate it or wave it around while laughing maniacally, which will scare away **1d6** Mooks.

Furious inventing!: One of the downtime periods between sessions counts as two downtime periods for the purpose of crafting.

Beyond cutting edge: You can invent spy tech and weird science in downtime periods between sessions, as well as jury-rig the device in a planning scene.

Story Points: Spend 1 Story Point to flip a task check for **Electronics, Engineering** or **Science**.

MEAN LEFT HOOK

Tier 1: Requires **Melee** 65%
Learning: Melee or **Strength**
Cost: 5

Your fists are murder! You can beat a grown man to a pulp using nothing more than your fists.

Fists of iron: You inflict an additional **+1dX** damage when fighting unarmed.

Story Points: Spend 1 Story Point to inflict another **+2dX** extra damage in one hit when fighting unarmed. You may activate this Ability and pay the **Story Points** after you have rolled the initial damage.

MILITARY RANK

Tier 0
Learning: Status
Cost: 5

You are a commissioned or non-commissioned officer in the armed forces.

Rank: Decide on your rank. The higher your rank, the less likely it is that you will be sent on field missions. The least problematic ranks are the non-commissioned ranks (corporals, sergeants) and company officers (subaltern, lieutenant and captain ranks), although field officers (major, commander, lieutenant colonel or colonel) could work fine, especially for fighter pilots or intelligence officers. Flag or general ranks (admirals and generals) are problematic, unless you're retired.

Duty: If you are an active officer, you may be sent on missions at any time. Your superiors could be used as a Patron.

Story Points: Spend 1 Story Point to get any soldier with the rank of private who belongs to the same armed forces as a uniform you are wearing to obey your orders, regardless of whether they are in your chain of command or not.

Spend 4 Story Points to get any officer from the same armed forces as your uniform to obey your orders, regardless of whether they are in your chain of command or not.

Note that you could use the Ability this way on enemy soldiers if you wear their uniform and speak their language, but the Director may also ask for a **Subterfuge task check.**

NATURAL LEADER

Tier 0
Learning: Charm, Status or **Willpower**
Cost: 5

Being a leader means that you have the rare ability to make other people want to follow you. You are responsible for the group, not just a looming authority figure. And that's why they follow you.

Listen up: You can invoke your leadership to get parts of a crowd of non-hostile Director characters to stop and listen to what you are saying. Unless provoked or attacked, you have their undivided attention, and they will ignore disturbances in the vicinity. Use **Charm** to persuade them at **+2 pips** if needed.

Story Points: Spend 1 Story Point to flip a **Charm** or **Status task check** when commanding a crowd.

Spend 2 Story Points to calm down a crowd.

NOUVEAU RICHE

Tier 1: Requires **Credit** 65%
Learning: Credit
Cost: 6

You're among the filthy rich, and you made your money on your own. You have an expensive flat in the city centre. Although many people think you have done well, a lot (especially others who are well-off) think that you are less than them because you didn't start as upper-class.

Posh place: You have a posh place downtown, a big flat or house near the city centre or a floor in a skyscraper. The place includes some staff and services: garage, concierge, cleaning service etc. They will never join you on an adventure.

Money: You have a lot of wealth. This may not be reflected in the **Credit** Skill rating. In that case, the **Credit** Skill reflects how much cash you have on hand, not your total fortune which could consist of non-liquid assets such as stock shares, bonds, art, property, and similar investments that you can't liquidate easily. Still, the Director should be very liberal with **Credit task check**s and allow them to just succeed.

Story Points: Spend 1 Story Point to flip a **Credit** or **Contacts task check**.

Spend 2 Story Points to reroll a **Credit** or **Contacts task check**.

OLD MONEY

Tier 1: Requires **Credit** 65% and **Status** 65%
Learning: Investigation or **Status**
Cost: 8

You have inherited a great fortune, including a mansion or a chateau outside the city.

Landed: You have a mansion or chateau with a huge estate. The estate may include some basic staff, such as an administrator, cook, maids, and keeper of the grounds. They will never join you on adventures.

Butler: You employ a butler. He may join you on your adventures and will take care of menial tasks so that you can have an adventure in style.

Money: You have a lot of wealth. This may not be reflected in the **Credit** Skill rating. In that case, the **Credit** Skill does not reflect your total fortune which could consist of estates, stock shares, bonds, funds, art and other inherited resources. Instead, the **Credit** Skill is your liquid assets – cash on hand – and how fast you can liquidate your other assets.

Story Points: Spend 1 Story Point to flip a **Credit** or **Status task check**.

Spend 2 Story Points to have the butler take a hit if present in a scene. The butler works a bit like body armour with **4dP** protection each time he is used, but then the butler is **Out Cold** for the rest of the adventure.

PEERAGE

Tier 1: Requires **Status** 65%
Learning: Investigation or **Status**
Cost: 6

You have aristocratic ancestry.

Noble title: Pick a noble title for your character. Here are some examples: *Prince/Princess, Marquess/Marchioness, Margrave/Margravine, Earl or Count/Countess, Viscount/Viscountess, Baron/Baroness, Baronet/Baronetess, Knight/Dame, Esquire.*

If you gain this Ability in-game, it is usually a knighthood, but rules-wise it's possible to get any title. Just come up with a good explanation: maybe you're an unknown descendant of an old family, you kept it secret until now, or you married into nobility.

Story Points: Spend 1 Story Point to flip a **Charm** or **Subterfuge task check**.

PET

Tier 0
Learning: Credit or **Charm**
Cost: 5

You have a special pet which in itself is a side character in the story. Not necessarily "special" as in a pet tiger or wolf, but more likely a cat, dog or parrot. It loves you, adores you and frequently causes you trouble.

Fetch: Your pet can get non-vital things for you.

What did you find there?: If you **spend Story Points** to receive a clue, your pet could find it for you. With the Director's permission, the cost of the clue could be reduced by 1.

Story Points: Spend 1 Story Point to have the pet escape capture when you are captured. With the Director's permission, you can act as your pet while your character is captured.

Spend 1 Story Points to have the pet wake you up in the following scene if you are **Out Cold**, usually by licking you in the face or biting your toes.

Spend 2 Story Points to fetch you a vital thing, like the keys to the cell door, a clue.

Spend 1 Story Point to flip a **Charm** or **Subterfuge task check** when the pet can charm or distract people.

PILOT

Tier 0
Learning: Engineering or **Vehicles**
Cost: 5

Gone are the days when anyone could just jump into an airplane and zoom to the sky. These days, you need a licence to legally fly an airplane.

I can fly: You know how to fly an airplane and the proper procedures to follow, how to make and file a flight plan, how to communicate with air traffic controllers and so on.

Story Points: Spend 1 Story Point to flip a **Status task check** related to being a pilot.

Spend 1 Story Point to flip any task checks for social interactions with pilots, air traffic controllers or other airport or airplane personnel.

POLICE BADGE

Tier 0
Learning: **Investigation**, **Red Tape** or **Security**
Cost: 5

You are an officer of the city's finest, and you have the badge to prove it.

Dear colleagues: Use **Red Tape** instead of **Contacts** to get in touch with colleagues in the police corps.

I'm from the police: Task checks for social interactions are at **+2 pips** within your jurisdiction if you show your police badge.

Story Points: Spend 1 Story Point to flip a task check for **Red Tape** or **Investigation**.

Spend 1 Story Point to commandeer a vehicle and chase after the villain.

POLYGLOT

Tier 0
Learning: **Humanities** or **Languages**
Cost: 5

You have a talent for languages.

Story Points: Spend 1 Story Point to flip a **Languages**, **Investigation** or **Humanities task check** related to speaking or understanding languages.

Languages: Pick one extra language when you create the character. Learning new languages only requires four ticks, not five.

PRESS CREDENTIALS

Tier 0
Learning: **Investigation** or **Willpower**
Cost: 5

You are officially recognised as a journalist for some news source. It does not give you any rights as such, but it opens some doors (and closes others). It also gives you access to a lot of news stories across the world.

Can I quote you?: When your press credential would be advantageous, you get a **+2 pip modifier** to gain access to someone.

Get that out of my face: Similarly, if someone is not on friendly terms with the press, get a **–2 pips modifier** when you try to gain access to that person.

Story Points: Spend 2 Story Points to gain access to a press conference (establish that there is one) with an important and relevant Director character, such as a police chief, mayor, corporate official, government official or something similar. If you attend, the conference is a scene in which you can get clues that the Director character would know about.

Spend 2 Story Points to gain access to a news publisher that you are not employed by or another competing reporter, with which you can exchange information and clues.

RIFLEMAN

Tier 1: Requires **Ranged Combat** 45%
Learning: **Ranged Combat**
Cost: 5

You are trained in the use of rifles, submachine guns and assault rifles.

Story Points: Spend 1 Story Point to flip an attack check if you are shooting with a rifle, submachine gun, or assault rifle.

Spend 1 Story Point to reload the rifle as a free action rather than as a main action.

SIXTH SENSE

Tier 0
Learning: **Alertness**
Cost: 5

Intuition, sixth sense, eyes in the back of your head – whatever you call it, you have it.

Story Points: Spend 1 Story Point to drop the **Surprised** Condition and act as normal.

Spend 1 Story Point to flip an **Investigation task check**.

Spend 2 Story Points to note something important in a scene. The Director will either notify you of one important thing, or return the **Story Points**.

SWORDSMAN

Tier 1: Requires **Melee** 45%
Learning: **Melee**
Cost: 5

There are those that keep the old martial ways alive. Even in the modern world, the sword has its place in society – usually not as a weapon on the battlefield, but for ceremony, culture, tradition and competition.

Story Points: Spend 1 Story Point to flip an attack check if you are fighting with a sword or sword-like object.

Spend 1 Story Point to not do any damage after a successful attack check, but instead disarm your opponent.

SWORDSMASTER

Tier 2: Requires Swordsman
Learning: Melee or **Status**
Cost: 6

Just as a good sword is a work of art – an art form almost lost to history – mastery of the weapon itself is an art, also almost lost. You keep the old forms alive and seek to perfect them.

Quick draw: If you have your weapon at your side, you do not have to spend a side action to draw your sword. You can draw your sword as part of a defence check or as part of the main action.

Bullet cutting: You can use your weapon for defence against ranged weapons, even if you are in another zone than the shooter.

Story Points: At anytime in a round, **spend 1 Story Point** if you have not yet taken your turn to act before the next character takes their first action in their turn, or directly after the current character has finished their turn.

TEACHER

Tier 0
Learning: Status or **Willpower**
Cost: 5

There's no self-purpose to knowledge. It's about the next generation. They need the guidance to learn what is necessary to build their own future. You will provide that guidance.

This will be on the test: When you get **Good Karma** on a task check, you can lecture one other character present in the scene. That other character also gets an experience tick for the Skill you just used. If you use the point-based system, you can give one reward point for the Skill you got **Good Karma** on. You can do this once per character and session.

Story Points: Spend 1 Story Point to flip a task check about scholarly knowledge.

Spend 1 Story Point to flip a **Status task check**.

TECH WIZ

Tier 1: Requires **Engineering** 65% and **Electronics** 65%
Learning: Engineering or **Electronics**
Cost: 3

If you think that a computer is a highly complex device that requires a production facility or an army of engineers, think again: all it takes is a basement, lots of TTL chips, a soldering iron, a tech wiz and patience. Your tech wizardry is not limited to computers, by the way. We could also be talking about phreaking the phone system using whistles from breakfast cereal boxes; building an improvised incendiary device from a pine cone, pine resin, rags and a lighter; or shorting out a security camera with a paper clip You are the kind of kid that does that for fun, and sometimes profit.

MacGyver it: Jury-rig a gadget in a regular action scene outside a planning scene. It must be reasonable to create the device using the tools and materials at hand. After that, the device breaks down. You may have to **spend Story Points** for materials and tools to be at hand, at the Director's discretion.

Beyond cutting edge: You can invent spy tech and weird science in downtime periods between sessions, as well as jury-rig devices in a planning scene.

Story Points: Spend 1 Story Point to flip a task check for **Electronics**, **Engineering** or **Machinery**.

Spend 2 Story Points to reroll a task check for **Electronics**, **Engineering** or **Machinery**.

TOUGH LIVER

Tier 0
Learning: Endurance
Cost: 4

You handle alcohol better than most. Although you get as drunk as anyone else, you sober up faster and your hangovers aren't as severe. The rest of the world envies you.

Story Points: Spend 2 Story Points to improve the result of an intoxication check one step as a side action.

Spend 4 Story Points to drop the **Intoxicated** Condition as a side action.

YOUNG

Tier 0
Learning: Contacts or **Red Tape**
Cost: 5

Not being an adult is a mixed blessing. On one hand, society is usually more lenient towards your transgressions. On the other hand, your age means a certain prejudice against your alleged lack of experience.

Story Points: Spend 1 Story Point to be ignored by adults in the scene, unless you do something violent or alarming.

Spend 4 Story Points when you take the **Wounded** Condition to get a royal scolding from a villain instead. The scolding works exactly as the **Wounded** Condition until after the fight scene, when it is dropped. The only thing hurt is your pride.

COMPLICATIONS

Paul Marchand. International man of mystery, former Resistance, burglar – I suppose you want to call yourself "gentleman burglar", but I don't.

And by whom do I have the honour of being so accused?

Inspector Burgess of Scotland Yard. I know who you are, Marchand. Don't try any funny stuff.

Charmant, inspecteur. Am I suspected of anything?

If there is anyone more suspicious here, I would be surprised. I don't have anything to tie you to the crime... yet! Don't leave town.

HOW TO USE COMPLICATIONS

There are four primary uses for Complications:

- As a guide for the player on how to act in character.
- As a source of inspiration for trouble that the Director can inject into the plot.
- As a guideline for interpreting the rules when Complications make life more difficult for the character.
- As a source of **Story Points** for the player.

STORY POINTS AND COMPLICATIONS

After the general description of each Complication, there's a header that lists possible ways of using it to **gain Story Points**. These should be initiated by the player, not by the Director: Complications are the player's way of getting more **Story Points**.

Story Points are gained in two different amounts:

- 3 points for making a task check in a scene more difficult, or for failing a successful task, or taking a Condition.
- 6 points if you write yourself out of a scene altogether.

They are both connected to the Complication in question, but they should not be limited to the Skills or situations listed. As long as you can come up with a plausible reason for why a task is harder for you (before you roll), why a successful task check failed, or why you are not in the scene due to the Complication, you should get **Story Points**.

COMPLICATIONS MUST MATTER!

The general rule is that the Complication must involve some consequence for the character in order to **gain Story Points** for bringing it into play.

I think those two are stalking us.

Who? Oh, those two.

Merde! Now you've done it! They're running off! Come on, people, we have to stop them!

"Alleheah aimuhi, onne humma hehohianhoweah!"

What?

Well, I had a glass too many on the flight, and a couple more in the hotel bar, so I'm bloody wasted at this time. I get three **Story Points** if I take the **Intoxicated** Condition.

Oh la la!

It could be worse. I could have collapsed at the bar and not been in the scene at all. That'd be worth six **Story Points**.

But it only works because it's the beginning of a chase scene. If you had taken a day off, your happy hour would have happened between scenes and not had any consequences, and then you would not get any **Story Points**.

hic

COMPLICATION DESCRIPTIONS

AMOROUS

It's great to be in love, and you're a shameless flirt! It's not that you're a creepy stalker or anything – you just love flirting.

Story Points: Gain 3 Story Points to be distracted by your emotions and get a **–2 pips** modification to any task checks that don't involve your sensual interests.

Gain 3 Story Points if your romantic moment causes you trouble.

Gain 6 Story Points if a date or romantic moment prevents you from participating in an important scene.

BAD REPUTATION

Your reputation precedes you, and not in a good way. You're the person that everyone talks about, and it will get you into trouble.

Story Points: Gain 3 Story Points to take **–2 pips** on task checks for **Charm**, **Contacts**, or **Status** in a scene.

Gain 6 Story Points to get thrown out of a scene because they don't want your kind around.

CODE OF HONOUR

There are things that you simply do not do. It's not just a matter of upbringing or politeness, it's a matter of principles, of honour. Yes, it may limit your options, sometimes severely, but if it distinguishes the civilised world from the brutes and barbarians, then so be it.

Story Points: Gain 3 Story Points when a villain gets away because of your code of honour.

Gain 3 Story Points for taking a **–2 pips** modification on actions that go against your code of honour.

Gain 6 Story Points when someone betrays your code of honour.

COMBAT PARALYSIS

It's not necessarily that you're a coward. It could be that harming another human being or using violence goes against your core principles. Whatever it is, sometimes it stops you from taking action when blows are being dealt.

Story Points: Gain 3 Story Point for forfeiting at least one round in a combat scene. During the forfeited round, you cannot take a Move or Main action.

Gain 6 Story Points for forfeiting all rounds in a combat scene. You cannot take a Move or Main action during the entire scene.

CRIMINAL BACKGROUND

You are or have been a crook. You're known by the authorities, and if anything unruly happens, you will be the first one they blame, or at least suspect. Whether you see this as a badge of honour or a blemish on your reputation, the fact remains that justified or not, the police are always on your heels.

Story Points: Gain 3 Story Points for having the police turn up at the most inopportune moment (with the Director's approval). **Gain 3 Story Points** for taking a **–2 pips** modification on social task checks in a scene.

Gain 6 Story Points for being detained by the police for one scene – you will be released later.

CRUDE

You and etiquette are not the best of friends. It's not that you're rude – though you could be. You're just… crude. Rough around the edges. You may be working class crude, rural crude, or just foreign and not good at handling this country's social situations.

Story Points: Gain 3 Story Points when you make a fool of yourself with your crude manners.

Gain 6 Story Points to be ignored for the scene when you attempt social actions, and thrown out if you do something dangerous or threatening.

DRUNKARD

You are an alcoholic. If your addiction to alcohol is not satisfied, there will be a withdrawal effect. Balancing your alcoholism with a normal work life will be a challenge, and even if you go clean, any lapse will drag you back down the hole.

Story Points: Gain 3 Story Points if you are affected by your alcoholism or the withdrawal and take the **Intoxicated** Condition.

Gain 3 Story Points if your alcoholism puts you in a difficult spot with the authorities.

Gain 6 Story Points if your alcoholism prevents you from participating in an important scene altogether.

GREEDY

You want it all. You may be jealous as well, but the important thing is that you want your share and then some. It may upset some people, but you're entitled to it. It should be yours!

Story Points: Gain 3 Story Points for taking a **–2 pips** modification on social interactions in a scene as a result of your greed.

Gain 6 Story Points when your greed gets you in trouble with the law or a powerful Director character in such a way that you cannot participate in an important scene.

Gain 6 Story Points when your greed makes a powerful Director character your enemy.

HONEST

Honesty is at the very core of a civilised society. You dislike falsehoods and lying. It goes against your very core and it makes you uncomfortable.

Story Points: Gain 3 Story Points for taking a **–2 pips** modification on task checks for any task checks for bluffing in a scene.

Gain 6 Story Points when your honesty gets you in trouble with the law or a powerful Director character in such a way that you cannot participate in an important scene.

Gain 6 Story Points when your honesty makes a powerful Director character your enemy.

MEMORABLE

There is something about you that makes people remember you. It may be your appearance, your voice, they way you dress or the way you move. No matter what it is, once they see you, they will never forget you.

Story Points: Gain 3 Story Points for taking a **–2 pips** modification on a **Subterfuge** or **Sneak task check**.

Gain 6 Story Points when an old adventure gets you into trouble because of you being so memorable.

NO SENSE OF DIRECTION

You constantly get lost. Your sense of direction is so bad that you could not navigate your way out of a closet. You're often late to appointments because you could not find the office or even the room, and you should never enter any Egyptian pyramids or Minoan labyrinths without a guide.

Story Points: Gain 3 Story Points for taking a **–2 pips** modification on a task check associated with travel and transportation.

Gain 6 Story Points if you get so lost that you can't be present in a scene.

OVERCONFIDENT

You can do it all. And if you don't succeed, it's because you didn't really want to anyway, or maybe you just felt like letting someone else win for a change. In the long run, you can't fail!

Story Points: Gain 3 Story Points for taking a **–2 pips** modification on one of your Skills with a value of 65% or higher. Decide before you roll. Keep the modification for the entire scene.

PATRIOT

There's nothing wrong with loving your country, but sometimes it can cloud your judgement.

Story Points: Gain 3 Story Points for failing a successful **Investigation** or **Subterfuge task check** and coming to the wrong conclusion, if the wrong conclusion is based on your patriotism.

Gain 6 Story Points to take a hit for king and country, when an attack check actually missed or was deflected.

PHOBIA

You have an irrational fear of something that sometimes incapacitates you and makes you freeze up. On a conscious level, you know that it is silly, but your subconscious doesn't agree.

Select the source of your phobia, for instance dirt, open spaces, dogs, spiders, snakes etc. Be aware that a very uncommon phobia will not come into effect in the game and will not give you any **Story Points**.

Story Points: Gain 3 Story Points for taking a **–2 pips** modification in a scene where you are faced with the target of your phobia.

Gain 6 Story Points for forfeiting all rounds in a combat scene because of your phobia. You cannot take a Move or Main action during the entire scene.

Gain 6 Story Points if your phobia prevents you from participating in an important scene.

PREJUDICED

You don't like a group of people. You struggle to hide your disdain – in fact, you would rather be open about it, but society apparently thinks it is a bad thing to dislike those people. But sometimes – or maybe quite often – you slip.

Select something to be prejudiced about, for instance the opposite gender, another nationality, the working class, the bourgeoisie etc.

Story Points: Gain 3 Story Points for taking a **–2 pips** modification in a scene where you act out your prejudice.

SLEEPY

You are not really a morning person. Not an evening person either, for that matter, and a mid-day and afternoon nap would be rather nice now that you think of it. It's not that you're lazy, it's just that you need to sleep more than most.

Maybe you're actually a cat?

Story Points: Gain 3 Story Points for taking a **–2 pips** modification on an **Alertness**, **Endurance** or Initiative task check due to yawning at a critical moment.

Gain 6 Story Points if you miss a scene due to oversleeping or falling asleep prior to the scene.

UNDERAGE

Being young is not always desirable. Sometimes it means that your age keeps you from taking part in certain activities.

Legal implications: You cannot buy booze, drive a car, own a firearm, or enter certain premises if you are underage. Depending on how young you are, you may not be allowed to have sex. For a lot of other actions, you need the permission of a parent or legal guardian.

Story Points: Gain 3 Story Points for failing a successful **Charm** or **Subterfuge task check** after the fact when your arguments are dismissed because of your age.

Gain 6 Story Points for being unable to participate in a scene because your age prevents you from entering wherever it takes place.

UNLUCKY

Fortune does not favour some people. You are one of them.

Story Points: The Director can flip any task check you make. Each time the Director does, you **gain 3 Story Points**.

ACTION

> I am the best rally driver in the world! It shouldn't be a problem for me to outrun that crazy MI6 agent, not even if he's in an Aston Martin DB5.

> I wouldn't count on it. After all, nobody does it better than him, not even a Greek rally princess, and he has a four-litre straight six in his DB5 with three side-draught Weber carburettors!

> Wanna bet? I don't care how many technical gizmos he has in his car, he is not going to overtake Elektra Ambrosia!

RESOLVING ACTIONS

The Troubleshooters is played as a dialogue between the players and the Director. The Director usually sets the scene and describes it. The players describe how their characters act or react. The situation then develops as is reasonable or by using and interpreting the rules. Other things happen as a result. This way, you create a story together.

Sometimes, the outcome of an action is not that clear. You may need some structure to progress through a scene, or you may want a way of resolving actions that everyone agrees is "fair". That's when you use task resolution.

The most basic rule of *The Troubleshooters* is this:

> When you want to do something, describe what you do and how. If the desired outcome is reasonably likely but not guaranteed, find a fitting Skill, roll percentile dice and compare the outcome to the Skill value.

This is a *task check*: an attempt to perform an action when there is some uncertainty regarding the outcome, that uses dice to determine what happens.

WHEN TO USE THE DICE

Use dice when…

● Success or failure is not assured one way or the other.
● You are trying to do something daring, challenging or dangerous, that might have serious consequences.
● You want to resist, challenge or stop someone else.
● You want to use your Skills to show off.
● Whenever you find it interesting.

Don't use dice when…

● The outcome is not interesting or relevant to the story.
● There is no risk, danger or challenge.
● The only outcome of a success or failure is that nothing happens.
● There is nothing stopping your character.
● Someone else has already made a task check to accomplish the same thing and failed. If you want to try and help them, say so before they roll in order to make their task check easier.
● The character can't affect the situation in any way.

SETTING THE SCENE

Usually, we're not interested in every little detail of the story. Some parts we skip, because it's not important to know when your character is using the loo (unless an Octopus agent has planted a bomb there – then the loo visit becomes very interesting).

Most of the time, we focus on the more engaging events by using scenes, framed situations where something interesting happens, and skipping uneventful parts of the story.

There are three main types of scenes:

Transitional scenes: Use transitional scenes when you need to move on to the next part of the story. Travel is often involved. If there are any actions in the scene, sum them up, make the dice rolls to see how it goes, do a little bookkeeping, and then move on.

A special type of of transitional scene is the **planning scene**. In a planning scene, players pour over clues, decide what to do next, and get equipment. The Director is rarely involved in a planning scene, except when players ask if they can get the stuff they need. When all participants are in consensus that they're done, It's often followed by travel to the location.

Detailed scenes: Detailed scenes are used when you need a better overview of the location and tighter interaction that is not easy to sum up. When the cast characters are infiltrating the Octopus base, looking for evidence in Dr Nephario's lab, or mingling at a Monte Carlo casino, then you use a detailed scene. Detailed scenes are not summed up. Instead, you deal with what happens, action for action, line for line.

Action scenes: A special type of detailed scene is when action happens. Not only do you need to resolve actions, but you also need to determine their order and immediate consequences. All fight scenes are action scenes, but not all action scenes are fight scenes.

FRAMING A SCENE

When setting the scene, you determine the following things:

● **Where?** Where are you when something happens? On the road? In the hotel bar? In a lost temple in the Cambodian jungle? What does the place look like?
● **What?** What happens? Are villains chasing the characters? Is it a party or a fist fight?
● **Who?** Who is involved, not counting the characters?

In a transitional scene, you really don't have to spend much time on describing the scene. Explaining that the characters are at a crowded airport near Paris may be enough. When you switch to a detailed scene or action scene, there's need for more specific information, but you don't have to outline it all at once.

It's not that important to classify the different kinds of scenes or to set up rules for them. The important thing is to know how they work.

You don't need to determine that this is a transitional scene, this is a detailed scene and so on. You will notice what kind of scene it is, and play it out as required. Sometimes you will set scenes without even being aware of it.

A scene is over when it is over. Often a scene is done as you set a new scene, but sometimes it is just over.

TASK CHECKS

A task check is a **d%** roll that is compared against a modifier and a Skill value to determine whether a task succeeds or not.

THE STANDARD TASK CHECK

The standard task check compares a **d%** roll to the Skill value only.

- If the roll is lower than or equal to the Skill value, the task *succeeds*.
- If the roll is higher than the Skill value, the task *fails*.

MODIFIERS

Modifiers measure circumstances beyond your personal aptitude that affect the chance of success. Equipment may make a task easier, bad weather conditions may make it harder – these are typical kinds of modifiers. Up modifiers makes a task easier and Down modifiers make them harder. Both are measured in "pips".

If a check has a modifier, you first compare the **Ones** of the **d%** roll to the modifier. This takes precedence over the comparison to the Skill value.

Up modifiers: When a task is easier than normal, you apply an Up modifier, written as "**+X pips**".

- Check if the **Ones** of the **d%** roll is between 1 and X. If so, the task *succeeds*, regardless of the rest of the outcome.
- If the **Ones** is not between 1 and X, check if the outcome is equal to or lower than the Skill value as usual.

Elektra and I are trying to stop a secret agent from reaching Vienna. Our primary goal is to get to the border before the secret agent so we can have the border guards close it. But there's something wrong with Elektra's Lancia, and I'm trying to fix it.

Luckily, I have a Mechanic's Toolbox, which gives me a **+2 pips modifier** when repairing something.

I have **Engineering 45%**. I roll 81. The task check is a success even if 81 is higher than 45, because the **Ones** of my roll (1) is within 1 and 2 from the **+2 pips** modifier. I quickly identify the problem as loose tube clamps at the cooler, fix them and fill up the cooler with water.

Down modifiers: When a task is harder than normal, you apply a Down modifier, written as "**–X pips**".

- Check if the **Ones** of the **d%** roll is between 1 and X. If so, the task *fails*, regardless of the rest of the outcome.
- If the **Ones** is not between 1 and X, check if the outcome is equal to or lower than the Skill value as usual.

Thanks to Éloïse's quick fix, we're still able to get to the border before that secret agent, but the stop costs us valuable time. I need to make a **Vehicles task check** at **–2 pips**. Not a problem: I have **Vehicles 75%**.

But my roll is 12! The **Ones** of my roll is 2, which is within 1 and 2 from the **–2 pips** modifier, so the task check fails. That means that the agent slips away.

You can use the following guideline for determining the modifier based on a task's difficulty.

Difficulty level	Modifier
Very easy	+5 pips
Easy	+2 pips
Challenging (most task checks)	—
Hard	–2 pips
Very hard	–5 pips

STACKING MODIFIERS

You can stack modifiers as long as they are from different categories. The categories are:

- Difficulty
- Circumstances
- Gear kits
- Abilities

You can only use one modifier from each category. Up and Down modifiers cancel one another pip by pip.

Note that no matter how many pips the modifier is, 0 on the **Ones** is not affected.

You can mitigate the risk by creating a challenge instead. Then the overall quality of your attempt depends on the total number of successes in the challenge.

Just failing is boring and stops the action. "Fail forward" is a philosophy that drives the action forward by having something else happening on top of the desired outcome not happening. If not in a fight scene, the Director could consider that one of the following happens:

- Separate the characters.
- Unwanted attention.
- Change the scene or zone.
- Take their stuff.

Instead of not making it to the border in time, I have a better idea. You catch up with him right at the border as he and his car are being subjected to a customs inspection. The both of you jump out to try to get the border guards to arrest the agent. But as you do, he grabs Éloïse...

Eeep!

...and pulls her at gunpoint into his car. Using Éloïse as a hostage, he forces himself across the border into Austria. What do you do now?

Not that it matters now that I actually made the task check, but could I theoretically use the electrical tape from the Electronics Toolbox gear kit to make sure that the tube is fixed at the right position and doesn't fall off again, and get +2 pips from that gear kit too?

No. You can only use the modifier from one gear kit, and you are already using the Mechanic's Toolbox. As the modifier is the same from either, it doesn't matter which you use, but you can only use one.

IF YOU SUCCEED

If the task check succeeds, you get the desired result.

IF YOU FAIL

In most cases, a failed task check means that the task has failed.

You don't get to try again. Not even your friends get to try. You need to significantly change the circumstances to get to roll again: for instance, it must be another scene, and you may need to get proper equipment or additional assistance.

EXPERIENCE TICKS

If you use the regular experience system, you get an experience tick whenever you use a Skill in a meaningful way (i.e. the plot progresses because of it) for the first time during a session. There's a small checkbox for it next to the Skill value. You can only have one tick per Skill.

You don't need to make an actual task check for the Skill. You just have to use a Skill in a way that progresses the plot. You should not abuse the system and use a Skill to just get the tick: that doesn't progress the plot, and the Director may (and should) veto the experience tick if you do. Here are some situations that may be vetoed:

- Someone else has already made a task check and failed.
- There is no risk, danger or challenge involved.
- The action is not important to the story.

After each session, during the Debriefing phase, you use experience ticks to improve Skills.

If you use the optional point-based experience system, ignore experience ticks altogether.

So I'm the hostage of a womanising, psychopathic secret agent. Well, at least I got a tick in **Engineering** from repairing the cooling tube.

My **Vehicles** Skill is already ticked, so I don't get another one.

OPPOSED CHECKS

Opposed checks happen when you pit your capabilities against those of another person.

- Both participants make a task check.
- If both participants fail, the opposed check results in a stalemate. Neither side wins or loses.
- If one participant succeeds while the other fails, the successful participant wins the opposed check.
- If both participants succeed, the participant with the highest roll wins the opposed check.
- If both participants succeed and the rolls are tied, the opposed check results in a stalemate. Neither side wins or loses.

When attacking and defending, the last point is important: the attacker only inflicts damage if the attacker wins the opposed check. If both the attacker and defender succeed, but there is a tie, the defender "wins" on a technicality.

FLIPPING CHECKS

Under certain circumstances, you can flip a task check. This can save your bacon and turn a failed task check into a success. You can flip a task check if you spend two **Story Points**, or if an Ability allows you to flip a task check. Flipping checks with Abilities is either conditional, can be done a limited number of times per session, or will cost you one **Story Point** but is limited to a small set of Skills or situations.

When you want to flip a task check:

- Tell the Director how you flip the check: by spending **Story Points**, what Ability you are using and so on.
- Switch places between the **Ones** and **Tens**. A roll of 73 now counts as 37, a roll of 29 counts as 92, and so on. A roll of 100 is still 100.

This way, you can snatch victory from the jaws of defeat.

Wait a minute. I'm in the passenger seat of a secret spy's car. There has to be about a million gadgets that I could use to at least signal where I am. I try to plug in a feedback circuit from my Electronics Toolbox to the car's satellite tracker in the centre panel, to make it broadcast our position. That's an **Electronics task check.**

Right, but you're next to the guy who kidnapped you, and he may notice what you're doing, so it will be an opposed check. I roll 49 for his **Alertness check.** If you succeed but don't beat that, he will notice.

You're evil. But here goes. I have **Electronics** 65%. Crap! I roll 28. But I can spend a **Story Point** and activate Tech Wiz to flip that roll to 82, and beat him thanks to the +2 modifier from the electronics toolbox.

Rgntudjuuuu!!
Stop foiling my plans!

KARMA

If you roll the same number on both dice for a **d%** task check, e.g. 11, 22, etc. you gain **Karma** and a **Story Point**. If the roll succeeds, you gain **Good Karma**. If the roll fails, you gain **Bad Karma**.

Good Karma means something positive happens, as agreed upon by you and the Director. Some situations provide specific rules for **Good Karma**. Here are two basic fallback suggestions, but be sure to describe what happened:

- The next task check you make in the scene is at **+2 pips**.
- The next task check your opponent makes in the scene is at **–2 pips**.

Bad Karma means something bad happens. As with **Good Karma**, some situations provide rules for determining the outcome. Here are two simple fallback suggestions:

- Enemy reinforcements arrive.
- Your next task check is at **–2 pips**.

I jump into my car and go after the secret agent who just kidnapped Éloïse!

You need a **Vehicles check** to get away before they lower the boom barrier.

Right. I roll 55, so success and Good **Karma**! Does that mean I go so fast that I catch up?

No, but it means that something nice happens. How about that the Austrian border guard joins you in the car chase, so if you manage to stop the secret agent, you will have some reinforcements?

Yeah! He won't get away this time!

CHALLENGES

Challenges are used in situations that require cooperation, take time, or involve multiple Skills (between 3 and 5 Skills).

Challenges can use simple or opposed task checks. A challenge will have an outcome, depending on how many of the task checks succeeded or in the case of opposed challenges, who won.

When written, challenges specify what Skills are to be used and why; a list of modifiers (optional); and a list of outcomes and what they mean. If there are more modifiers than Skills, they generally can stack at the Director's discretion.

OUTCOME

There are five possible outcomes of a challenge.

- **Great outcome:** The desired result of the challenge, but even better. There could be a bonus effect, improved quality that adds a good tag to a project, Up modifiers to future rolls etc.
- **Good outcome:** This is the desired result of the challenge.

- **Limited outcome:** The desired result of the challenge, but with an additional bad effect, a hard choice, a flaw that adds a bad tag, Down modifiers to future rolls, etc.
- **Bad outcome:** You do not get the desired result. The project fails, you do not reach the destination etc. You do get a "consolation prize", however – you can reuse the material, or you may learn something and get a future Up modifier.
- **Abysmal outcome:** Everything that could go wrong went wrong, and probably something that could not go wrong went wrong anyway.

RUNNING A CHALLENGE

When running a challenge, tell the players what Skills are involved. Have the players distribute the task checks as evenly as possible among the characters in the scene. Every character in the scene should have at least one task check.

Then the players make the task checks. Keep track of how many checks succeed (and which ones). Depending on how many checks there are in total for the challenge, and how many of them succeed, you get an outcome.

| | # Successful/won task checks | | | | | |
#Task checks	0	1	2	3	4	5
3	Abysmal	Limited	Good	Great	—	—
4	Abysmal	Bad	Limited	Good	Great	—
5	Abysmal	Bad	Limited	Limited	Good	Great

CREATING CHALLENGES

Many challenges are defined in adventures. There are also many suggestions to be found under How to resolve situations below. If you need to create a challenge from scratch, here's how you do it.

- Start by listing three to five Skills for the challenge.
- Decide on a **Good outcome**, based on the desired result.
- Decide what happens if you don't get the desired result. Often, it's just that: you don't get it. That's the **Bad outcome**.
- Decide the worst thing that can happen. That's your **Abysmal outcome**.
- Add something even better for the **Great outcome** and some setback or hard choice for the **Limited outcome**. You can do that as it comes up.

You can find an example for challenges in chapter 12, when Éloïse tries to make her Vespa able to fly.

DUELS

A special kind of challenge is the Duel. It is often used for chases, games, and even actual duels – any case where two sides challenge one another to some kind of competition that involves more than one Skill or takes time. Each side of the duel may consist of one or more participants.

In the duel, you try to be the first to win a number of opposed task checks. You don't set the Skills for the task checks in advance, but make them up as you go.

- At the start of the duel, the Director sets up a target number, usually 3. Whomever wins that many task checks first wins the challenge.
- Both parties decide on what they want from the challenge, or what they hope the outcome of the duel will be.
- The participant who initiates the duel goes first and calls an opposed task check for any Skill that suits the purpose of the duel, narrate the action and provide reasoning for the Skill choice.
- Then both parties make an opposed task check for that Skill.
- Note who won the task check. The winner narrates the outcome of that task check. If nobody won (because both failed, or because both succeeded but the rolls are tied) then the score stands and the participant who called for the task check narrates the outcome.
- Then the other party does the same: call an opposed task check, provide reasoning for it, and make the task check
- Repeat until one side has won as many task checks as the target number and wins the duel. The winner narrates how they reached the desired outcome.

Sometimes it may not make sense for both sides to use the same Skill in an opposed task check. In that case, agree on a more sensible pair of opposed Skills, and make an opposed task check for those.

When calling a Skill that has been used before in the duel, you – the caller, not your opponent – get a **–2 pips modifier** on your task check for each time beyond the first that the Skill was called.

DIRECTOR CHARACTERS AND DUELS

Director characters often have very few Skills beyond the **Specialist** and **Basic** Skills. That means that you may have to treat them differently than characters.

- When a character calls a Skill that the Director character doesn't have, use the best applicable Skill. If no

Skill is applicable, use **Specialist** if it is within the Director character's expertise, and **Basic** if it isn't.
- When the Director character picks a Skill, pick one from the Skill list on page 52. Then follow the same procedure as above.

Catching up with the secret agent is a Duel. Let's go for a Target Number of 3. Since you have initiated the chase, you go first. His goal is to get away from you. What's your goal?

My goal is to catch up with him and stop him. I think I'll keep my **Vehicles** to be my ace in the hole, so I start with **Alertness** to see which way he goes. A success at 49.

Right. The agent fails with a roll of 81.

Right, he zooms off in the night, and I burn rubber to get after him. As I have my headlights down, he doesn't notice me at first, but I can clearly see the red rear lights of his car. Your turn.

The agent assumes that he will be pursued, so he will still try to trick any pursuers by taking an alternate route and hiding in front of a lorry, with, uh, **Sneak**?

And I should roll for **Sneak** as well? That's weird. Doesn't **Search** work better?

Go for that.

Doesn't my electrical tracking device sabotage count?

Well, it counts. Elektra, you get **+2 pips** on your task check. The agent is a sneaky bastard with 65%, and ... I roll 67 which is a fail.

I have 45, and fail with a roll of 59. I can't even flip that and the **+2 pips** didn't help.

So we're still at one-nothing in wins. You saw him get off on that alternate route, and you can still see the rear lights now and then in front of the truck. Your turn.

 Okay, I think it's time for some serious driving. As we approach Graz, I step on the accelerator and overtake the lorry and catch up with him. So that's **Vehicles**, and I think I should have **+2 pips** from the Lancia. Ha! 82! Beat that!

He tries to keep you at bay with a roll of 69, but that's less than your 82, so it's a second win for you.

 Right, suddenly I zoom by the lorry, headlights glaring in the night and come up side by side with him, right in front of a surprised lorry driver honking his horn like a madman!

Right, he reacts violently, and as you pass the city limit of Graz, he pulls his gun and shoots at you. It's a hit of 36. You may oppose his **Ranged Combat** with **Agility** if you want.

 Ow, I have 15 in Agility. I can't even beat that.

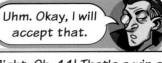 I'm still here. Can I yank his arm with **Melee** instead?

Uhm. Okay, I will accept that.

 Right. Oh, 44! That's a win and a **Good Karma** as well. As he pulls his gun and aims across the passenger seat, I grab his arm and pull it down so that he only shoots the inside of the car. I bite him in the arm for good measure.

 Haha! Three wins! As Éloïse yanks his arm and bites him, he loses control of his car and slams right into a bus stop!

Poor car.

HOW TO RESOLVE SITUATIONS

Using task checks, opposed checks and challenges, you can resolve most situations. Here are some examples of how to use these mechanics:

Act in a role: Subterfuge task check; opposed **Subterfuge** against **Alertness task check**; **Alertness, Charm, Languages, Subterfuge, Willpower** challenge
Aerobatic stunt: Vehicles task check
Appraising art: Humanities task check
Appraising ranged weapons: Ranged Combat task check
Art research: Contacts, Investigation, Humanities, Search challenge
Archive search: Investigation task check; **Contacts, Investigation, Red Tape/Science/Humanities, Search** challenge
Ask around for clues: Charm, Contacts, Investigation, Red Tape challenge
Assess nature of wounds: Medicine, Melee or **Ranged Combat task check**
Assess security system: Security task check
Bluffing: Charm or **Subterfuge task check**
Buying expensive things: Credit task check
Bypass a security system: Electronics, Engineering, Prestidigitation, Security challenge
Car chase: Duel
Car stunt: Vehicles task check
Card trick: Prestidigitation task check
Chasing after someone on foot: Duel
Climbing a cliff face: Agility, Alertness, Endurance, Strength challenge
Constructing a gadget: Credit, Electronics, Engineering, Science challenge
Crime scene analysis: Alertness, Investigation, Search challenge
Cryptanalysis: Investigation, Languages, Science, Security challenge
Dogfight: Duel
Downgrade Terrified to Frightened: Willpower check
Drop Frightened Condition: Willpower check
Drop Out Cold Condition in the next scene: Medicine task check by someone else.
Drop Stunned Condition: Willpower task check
Duel: Duel
Figure out a mechanical device: Machinery task check
Figure out an electronic device: Electronics task check
Frisk a person: Opposed **Search** against **Subterfuge** or **Prestidigitation task check**
Gain someone's trust: Opposed **Charm** or **Subterfuge** against **Willpower task check**
Gambling: Duel

Getting in touch with someone: Contacts, Credit, Red Tape or **Status task check**; **Contacts, Credit, Red Tape, Status** challenge
Getting restricted items: Charm, Contacts, Credit, Red Tape/Subterfuge challenge
Getting up a ladder in time: Agility task check
Hiking: Alertness, Endurance, Strength, Survival, Willpower challenge
History knowledge: Humanities task check
History research: Contacts, Investigation, Humanities, Search challenge
Identify drugs: Medicine or **Science task check**
Identify spoken or written language: Languages task check
Juggling: Prestidigitation task check
Knowledge regarding law and bureaucracy: Red Tape task check
Lifting something heavy: Strength task check
Making a good first impression: Charm, Status or **Subterfuge task check**
Mountaineering: Alertness, Agility, Endurance, Survival, Willpower challenge
Modify an electronic device: Electronics task check
Not being Surprised: Alertness task check
Operate a harbour crane: Machinery task check
Picking pockets: Prestidigitation task check; opposed **Prestidigitation** against **Alertness task check**
Picking locks: Prestidigitation or **Security task check**
Resist hypnotic effects: Willpower task check
Rewire something electronic: Electronics task check
Scuba diving: Agility, Alertness, Endurance, Machinery, Willpower challenge
Seduction: Opposed **Charm** against **Willpower task check**
Searching a scene: Search task check
Sneaking as a group: Sneak × number of participants challenge; **Alertness, Search, Security, Sneak** challenge
Sneaking up on someone: Sneak task check; opposed **Sneak** against **Alertness task check**
Spotting a sneaking person: Opposed **Alertness** against **Sneak task check**
Swimming turbulent waters: Agility task check; **Agility, Endurance, Willpower** challenge
Treat the Wounded Condition: Contacts, Credit or **Medicine task check** (see *Healing* on page 99)
Wounded Condition has no effect for one scene: Medicine task check by someone else
Understanding blueprints: Electronics, Engineering, Investigation, Science challenge
Understanding scientific scribbles: Science task check
Understanding the gist of an unknown language: Languages task check

FIGHTS AND COMBAT

CONTEXT OF FIGHTS

In *The Troubleshooters*, there will be danger and challenges, fisticuffs and shootouts – even massive explosions! Despite that, *The Troubleshooters* isn't deadly or gritty. In this game, your character may be knocked unconscious, or disappear from the scene, or be taken prisoner – a staple of the genre – but your character will not die unless that's want you want or you do something really stupid.

But we still want fights to be fair. After all, if you are to capture or even kill the characters, you better do it by the book, even if you are the Director.

Just fighting is boring. When you plan a fight, give it context and meaning. Make sure there's a reason for the conflict that gets the players invested in the scene.

CONSEQUENCES OF FIGHTS

Although fights in *The Troubleshooters* do not lead to the death of characters (unless the player wants that to happen), there are still consequences.

- **In the short term**, fights attract attention. Gunshots will result in armed police showing up at the location very fast. Even fistfights in public may make people call the police.
- **In the long term**, wounds need care. Professionals will also call the police if the characters walk into the ER with bullet wounds. And even if you can get a shady doctor to treat your wounds, recuperation is slow.

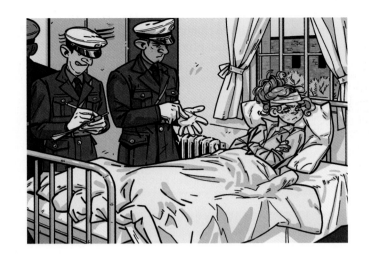

STARTING FIGHTS

When the fight starts, set up the scene's zones and then determine initiative order.

What is the natural reaction when someone points a gun at you?

I don't know about you, but I would just raise my hands and give up. Most sensible people are the same, including the main characters in the comics that this game is inspired by. If they fight, it's often a bit later, when the villain is distracted.

Similarly, I would wait for the opportune moment. I also have an extra incentive to not fight: if I give up and am captured, I will get nine **Story Points**.

So even before the guns come out or the fists start to fly, and regardless of whether you are a player or the Director, consider all your options before you start a fight.

Clever girl!

If you or your group are seasoned role-players, it will probably be near-instinctive to start a fight, and then fight to the death, but *The Troubleshooters* isn't that kind of game.

Speaking strategically, it is very easy to be **Out Cold**, and you can only take the **Wounded** Condition once (unless you make a point of recuperating and wasting time during the adventure). You may want to save that for the showdown at the end.

So chances are that if a fight starts, the characters will be captured if the opposition is somewhat competent. And if you are to be captured, why not be awake and aware as I tell you my evil plans?

But this is by design: it is very easy to get captured, but also very easy to escape thanks to all the **Story Points** you get. And you will know about my evil plans and be inside my secret base.

ZONES

The basic unit of space in a fight is the zone. A zone is an area that is distinct and somewhat homogeneous. It doesn't matter exactly where in the zone you are: it is assumed that you are constantly moving about, and that when you do something or when something happens to you, you happen to be at the appropriate location in the zone.

Moving between zones is an action, however. Often it just requires you to use the Move action, but sometimes the Move action requires a task check.

Zones are not intended to be used to measure distance, but to make terrain interesting and to make tactical movement easy without a grid.

If an area is so huge that it would be silly to not have some distance involved, plan the zones accordingly. Set up objects that restrict movement into certain zones and give zones different properties.

> If I plan a showdown in an open square, I better not make it just a single open square zone. It is boring. If I divide the empty space into several zones, I can track distance, but it is still boring.

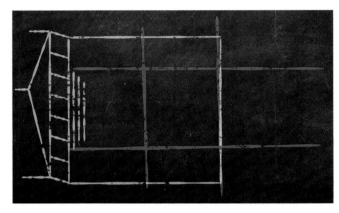

> Instead, I could set up a street, a sidewalk, and the rest of the square as three zones. I add a fountain in the middle of the square with some benches left and right, and trees to the side. That way I split the square zone into four.

> On top of that, I place the bus stop in the middle of the sidewalk and split the sidewalk into two zones, and also add Agent X's spy car and Elektra's car to the street, and I make the area between them into a zone, which splits the street zone into three. It's a bit difficult to get in and out of that zone, because of the blocking cars. Technically, inside the cars are also zones, both of which are difficult to get into or out of.

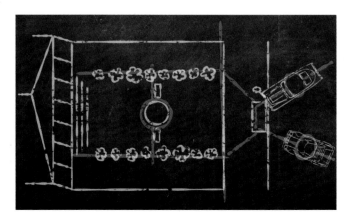

> This way, the seemingly boring empty square becomes a more interesting place to stage a fight. It's really simple: if the terrain is boring, add more zones, and don"t be afraid to put things into those zones to make them more interesting.

> This is the scene when the fight starts. Elektra is in the Lancia, and Agent X and Éloïse are in the Aston Martin. Austrian border police may be on the way, but that's unknown for now.

> Roll for initiative!

INITIATIVE

The initiative roll is a task check for **Alertness** (or the **Basic** Skill for Director characters that do not have **Alertness**).

- On **Bad Karma**, your initiative is 0.
- If the check fails, your initiative is the **Ones** of the roll.
- If the check succeeds, your initiative is the **Tens** plus the **Ones** of the roll.
- On **Good Karma**, add 10 to your initiative.

Many Director characters have preset initiative numbers, especially Underlings and Mooks. The Director then doesn't have to roll for their initiative.

In descending order of initiative (highest to lowest), each character then takes one turn. Each character can only take one turn during a round, even if their initiative drops during the turn.

On a tie, player characters take their turn first. Tied player characters act in any order the players agree on. Tied Director characters act in the order the Director deems fit.

> I have **Alertness** 65%. I roll a 57 for the initiative check – a success!

> My Initiative is 5+7=12.

> I have **Alertness** 15%. I roll a 40 for the initiative check and fail.

> My initiative is 0.

Agent X does not have an Alertness value, but Basic 45.

I roll 72, a failure, so the Agent's initiative is 2.

The order of initiative is thus Elektra first, then Agent X, and finally Éloïse. If anyone else arrives, we'll see what initiative they have.

Initiative can drop during the scene, from activating Abilities or from the *...pam! Aimed shot* option. Initiative can never drop below 0. If something causes your initiative to drop below 0, it becomes 0 instead. If an Ability or option requires you to lower initiative, and you have **initiative 0**, you cannot activate that Ability or option.

If new characters arrive to the fight and get involved, have them roll initiative at the start of the turn after they arrived.

ON YOUR TURN

The basic unit of time in a fight is the round. A round is not a fixed amount of time, but the time it takes for everyone in the scene to do their thing. In a round, everyone involved gets to take one turn in descending order of initiative.

Each turn consists of three phases:

- Start of turn
- Actions
- End of turn

These phases are mostly for clarity. Some effects from Conditions and tags apply at the Start of turn and End of turn, but if you don't have any such effects, you just take your actions and hand things over to the next character in initiative order.

HUFF HUFF HUFF

START OF TURN

At the start of the turn, there may be things happening. For instance, some Conditions are dropped at the start of your turn. This does not count as an action.

ACTIONS

On your turn, you can take three actions. You can do them in any order you like.

- One Move action.
- One Free action.
- One Main action.

In some cases, you may get a fourth action, a *Bonus action*. This happens directly after the Main action.

Some actions happens outside of your turn.

- **Delayed actions:** If you delay your main action, it may be triggered outside your turn.
- **Defence:** When you are attacked, you may in some cases defend yourself.
- **Counter-attacks:** Some Director characters can make a counter-attack if attacked. The counter-attack happens immediately after the attack, before any other action including bonus actions.

MOVE ACTIONS

There's only one move action, namely "Move". It has its own category so that you do not have to choose between moving and doing stuff.

Move: You may move to an available adjacent zone.

Some zones may be *Restricted* and require a task check to move into or out of. If the task check fails, the move action is forfeited.

FREE ACTIONS

Free actions are short actions that happen concurrently with another action.

Say something: You have the time to say something short – a command, a short instruction, a statement, about a sentence long that is not too complex.

Other people may respond quickly, even if it is not their turn.

Pick up something: If something is in the same zone, clearly visible and can be carried by hand, then you can pick it up.

Drop something: If you have something in your hands or in a strap over the shoulder, you can drop it as a free action.

Ready a weapon: You draw a weapon from its sheath or holster. You can cock it if you want.

Change weapon: If you hold one weapon in your hands and have another weapon readily available, you can drop the current weapon and draw the other one. If you also have an empty holster or sheath easily accessible, you can sheath one weapon and draw the other.

Break cover: You may pop out of cover to start taking Move actions, but you are no longer in cover.

Fall Prone: You drop to the ground and are now **Prone**.

MAIN ACTIONS

Main actions are what you attempt to achieve during the round.

Sprint: Take an extra move action. Some zones may be *Restricted* and require a task check to move into or out of. If the task check fails, the move action is forfeited.

Attack: Attack someone. They may get to defend themselves. See the Attacks and defence heading for more information.

Catch your breath: Take a moment to catch your breath, and make a **2dP** Recovery roll.

Reload: If your weapon is empty (see the *Reload* tag), you take an action to reload. If the conditions are hard, or the weapon has the *Tough Reload* tag, a successful Skill check for an appropriate Combat Skill is required.

Take cover: You duck behind something (define what). You can now make Defence checks against ranged attacks from another zone. You cannot take a Move action until you break cover.

Survey: You survey the situation to get an overview of what is happening. Reroll your initiative.

Delaying your main action: You wait for the right moment. Set a specific condition and a response, in the format of "if–then": "if he moves, I'll shoot"; "if he draws his weapon, I'll hit him". If the condition triggers, you immediately take your main action at the same time as the triggering action. If the condition doesn't trigger before your next turn starts, you don't get to take your main action.

BONUS ACTIONS

You may take one bonus action directly after your main action if there is a condition or Ability that allows for one. You can only take one bonus action per round. You must do it directly after the main action, before you take your next action.

If you attack a character with the *Counter-Attack* tag, the counter-attack happens directly after the attack but before the bonus action, so don't forget the bonus action after the counter if you have it.

END OF TURN

Like at the start of the turn, there may be things happening at the end of the turn. Again, dropping Conditions may be one example, and again, these do not count as actions.

As soon as you are done, say that you are done. Then the next character in initiative order starts their turn. Once your turn ends, you normally are not allowed to backtrack and change what you did.

ATTACKS AND DEFENCE

An Attack check is a task check against a Combat Skill. The check may be a simple task check for an appropriate Combat Skill, or if the target takes a defence action, an opposed check of the attacker's Combat Skill against that of the target. If the Attack checks wins, (or just succeeds, if not opposed by a Defence check), you hit your target and inflict damage.

THE BASIC ATTACK

An attack action rarely consists of *one* shot or *one* swing – you hit the target several times trying to get through its defences, or fire a salvo or burst of shots in rapid succession. (The exception is when a ranged weapon only allows for one shot, for instance if it is a musket, a crossbow or a javelin – which really are exceptions in the modern era – or carefully aimed ranged shots.)

These multiple swings and shots are abstracted into the basic attack.

The basic attack uses this procedure:

- Select a valid target.
- Make an Attack check. It may be opposed by a Defence check.
- On a successful attack, roll for Damage.
- Handle the *Reload (X)*, *Single Shot* or *Thrown* tags.
  - **Reload (X):** X is a range, often between 9–0, but sometimes just 0 or 8–0. If the ones of the Attack check is within the listed range of X, the weapon needs to be reloaded if you want to use it again. If you have **Bad Karma** and the weapon is empty, then the weapon is jammed and has to be fixed in a later scene.
  - **Single Shot:** The weapon needs to be reloaded.
  - **Thrown:** You are no longer in possession of the weapon. Use a free action to swap to another weapon before the next attack, or attack unarmed.

VALID TARGETS

- **In melee**, you can only attack targets in the same zone (unless you or the target's zone specifies something else).
- **In ranged combat**, you can attack targets in your own zone, or any zone that does not have a Blocked line of sight and is in range.

LINE OF SIGHT

You don't need a grid to determine line of sight. Just look at the zone layout, and decide whether the line of sight is Clear, Hindered or Blocked.

- **Clear:** You can see the target's entire zone from the attacker's zone.
- **Hindered:** You can see parts of the target's zone from the attacker's zone. Maybe there's a doorway that only allows you to see some of the zone, obstacles in between, one zone in between has the *Restricted* tag, and so on. If the line of sight is Hindered, Attack checks are at **–2 pips** per zone that hinders line of sight.
- **Blocked:** You can't see the target's zone from the attacker's zone, in any way. It may be around a corner, on another level, the doors are closed, doorways don't line up, et cetera. If the line of sight is Blocked, the target is not valid.

RANGE

A few ranged weapons – mainly throwing weapons – have the *Short Range (X)* tag. This means the weapon can only be fired at a target that is X zones or less away from the attacker. The zone currently occupied by the attacker is not counted.

ATTACK OPTIONS

When you attack, you have some options available to you. If you don't pick one, you use the **Basic** attack.

WHUMP! – MELEE THROW OR GRAPPLE

If you try to grapple or throw someone, make an Attack check. If successful, choose two of the following:

- You inflict **1dX** damage
- The target is **Restrained**
- The target is **Prone**

...PAM! – AIMED SHOT

Requires: Initiative 1+

Using the aimed shot option, you fire one carefully aimed shot or make one carefully aimed attack with a thrown weapon. You don't have to worry about the *Reload (X)* tag (but *Single Shot* and *Thrown* work as usual). All three of the following apply when making an aimed shot:

- Make an Attack check at **+2 pips**.
- If you hit, you inflict **+1dX** Damage.
- Your initiative drops by 2.

The Defence check is opposed to the Attack check, so the attacker not only has to roll lower than or equal to their Combat Skill, but also higher than the defender's Defence check.

You can make a Defence check in the following situations:

Situation	Cast character Defence check	Director character Defence check
You are the target of a melee attack	**Melee**	Defence score
You are the target of a ranged attack and the attacker is in the same zone	**Melee**	Defence score
You are the target of a ranged attack from another zone and you are in cover	**Agility**	Defence score

If you don't get to make a Defence check, you will still defend yourself, but the defence is part of the uncertainty of the Attack check.

RATATATAT! — RANGED ATTACK, EMPTY YOUR WEAPON

Requires: *Reload (X)* tag

Using a semi-automatic or automatic firearm, you can also pour it on the enemy until the weapon is empty.

- Either make Attack checks against all targets in one zone, or make an Attack check against one target and inflict **+2dX** extra Damage on that target.
- Your weapon is automatically empty and you need to reload.

This option requires the *Reload (X)* tag. You cannot use this option if your weapon has the *Single Shot* tag.

DEFENCE

A Defence check is a task check for the **Melee** Skill, or for the Defence score for Director characters.

- If a Director character doesn't have a Defence score, they don't get to make a Defence check.
- If a Director character has a Defence score, and the situation allows for a Defence check, they may make one when they are the target of an attack.
- If a cast character is attacked, and the situation allows for a Defence check, they may make one when they are the target of an attack.

Cast characters can also use **Agility** against ranged attacks if they are in cover.

(Lack of) defence for director characters

The Defence score of Director characters is usually a bit lower than the attack value, and a bit higher than the **Basic** Skill. The reason is that with a high Defence score, combat tends to drag out a bit and become boring.

Some Director characters – Underlings and Mooks generally – don't have a Defence score at all. This is by intent. Their defence is the characters' chance to miss – static defence, in other words. That, and the Mooks' low **Vitality**, usually means that they drop like flies.

DID YOU HIT?

You hit the target if:

- The Attack check succeeds and the target doesn't make a Defence check.
- The Attack check succeeds and wins over the Defence check. If the Attack check is tied with the Defence check, the attack fails to hit.

KARMA IN COMBAT

In combat, **Karma** has specific effects.

- **Attack check has Good Karma:** Underlings and Mooks are **Out Cold**. You may discard the Damage roll, even after it is exploded, and make a new Damage roll. You have to keep the new result.
- **Attack check has Bad Karma:** Something bad happens that complicates things for the character. The character's next check is at **–2 pips**.

- **Defence check has Good Karma:** Make a **1dP** Recovery roll after Damage has been resolved.
- **Defence check has Bad Karma:** You are knocked down by the attack and are **Prone**.

Don't forget that a **Karma** result on a task check gives you **1 Story Point**.

DAMAGE, VITALITY AND WOUNDS

If the attacker hits, the attacker rolls Damage. Damage rolls (**dX**) explode: for each 6 you get, roll another die. If any of those is a 6, roll another die, and so on, until you no longer roll any 6s. For each 4–6 you end up with, the defender loses 1 point of **Vitality**.

If the defender has some kind of body armour or other form of light protection, the defender makes a Soak roll. For each 4–6 in the Soak roll, reduce the **Vitality** loss by 1.

Pro tip: Push any 4–6 dice to the side. That way, you don't have to worry that they may tumble over while rolling more dice. If there is a Soak roll, you can then remove that number of dice from the pile, and count the rest.

- If **Vitality** loss is zero or less, nothing happens.
- If **Vitality** loss is at least 1, reduce the target's current **Vitality** by that much.
- If **Vitality** ever reaches zero, you're **Out Cold**.
- Player characters (and some Director characters) can take the **Wounded** or **Mortal Peril** Conditions instead of **Vitality** loss.

Out Cold means that you're no longer in the fight. You're usually unconscious, but you might have been thrown off a cliff into the sea or out a window, fallen down a trapdoor, or something similar that removes you from the fight and stops you from returning.

Player characters can take **Wounded** and **Mortal Peril**. Unimportant Director characters can not: Mooks

and Underlings are **Out Cold** when **Vitality** runs out. Lieutenant Director characters can take the **Wounded** Condition.

Boss Director characters can take the **Mortal Peril** Condition. They don't have to: just like characters, they may be taken prisoner and wait for an opportune moment to try and escape. Even if jailed, they are often sprung between adventures to appear in the next.

WOUNDED

Player characters and Bosses and Lieutenant Director characters can take the **Wounded** Condition instead of **Vitality** loss. They don't have to, but they can choose to if they want to avoid getting **Out Cold**. Being **Wounded** has consequences later, though, and it sticks for some time. After the fight, you remain **Wounded**, and when the fight scene is over, all your task checks are at **–2 pips** until the wound heals (see *Healing* on page 99):

You can only have one **Wounded** at a time. If you are already **Wounded**, you cannot take **Wounded** again.

> Note that even if someone shoots you with a gun and inflicts lots of **Vitality** loss, there's no harm, wounds or blood unless you take the **Wounded** Condition. This is important!

MORTAL PERIL

Player characters and Boss Director characters can take the **Mortal Peril** Condition instead of **Vitality** loss. Again, this is not mandatory, but they can choose to if they want to avoid getting **Out Cold** and want to risk everything.

If you take the **Mortal Peril** Condition, you can flip attack checks at will for the remainder of the scene. But it comes at a cost: if you are in **Mortal Peril** and you run out of **Vitality**, you're not **Out Cold**. You're dead!

	Wounded	Mortal Peril
Player characters	✔	✔
Mooks, Underlings	—	—
Lieutenants	✔	—
Bosses	✔	✔

DYING

In *The Troubleshooters*, by default cast characters don't die. More often, you're **Out Cold** instead. Even Director characters die rarely, if at all. There are three exceptions:

- **Abuse rules or goodwill:** When you are abusing the rules or the Director's goodwill and do silly things, you may actually die. "Since I can't die, I wrestle with the bear" – "Right, the bear eats you. You are dead." Don't mess with the Director and don't abuse the "no cast character death" rule.
- **Sacrifice:** The Director may set death as an option in a situation where the ultimate choice is up to you: "you may save baroness Zonda and have her rethink her evil ways by putting yourself between her and the saw blade, but you will die", or "if you continue to hold Graf von Zadrith inside the burning warehouse, you will both die". The Director should not use this option lightly, saving it for when it creates great drama. If you then choose that option, your character is dead. You may describe your untimely end if you want and the Director agrees.
- **Mortal Peril:** When you take the **Mortal Peril** Condition and run out of **Vitality**, your character dies. You may get to say a few last words to your friends, but you are a goner.

KILLING

The Troubleshooters is not a game where you kill indiscriminately, or even in cold blood.

Even Unimportant Director characters are rarely killed. Instead, enemies are knocked out, thrown out of the scene, or disarmed and forced to surrender when they are **Out Cold**.

Bosses can die, but mostly only when it's dramatically appropriate. They use the same rules as player characters, so they can die from taking the **Mortal Peril** Condition. Most of the time, they escape before that, or are taken prisoner.

Resolving the adventure without unnecessary bloodshed, and instead taking the villains prisoner, is rewarded with three free improvement ticks.

You do not kill Director characters who give up. If you are tired of the arch-enemy always escaping from jail to appear in the next adventure, talk to the Director instead, and ask for the arch-enemy to be put away for good and use a new threat instead. But do not kill the villain. That's just not the way things work in these kinds of stories!

> If the players still want to kill Director characters in cold blood, consider not giving them any free improvement ticks at all for this session.
>
> Also, remove all **Story Points** from a character that kills in cold blood, plus half from those characters that could have stopped the act but didn't.

COMBAT EXAMPLE

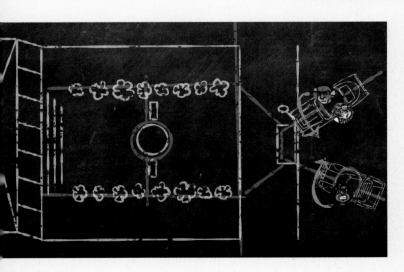

As I said, the order of initiative is Elektra first, then Agent X, and finally Éloïse. Elektra starts in her car, Éloïse and Agent X in his car. Elektra, you go first.

I get out of the car and into the middle zone. Can I get directly into it?

It will take as long to get over to the passenger side as getting out on the left side and running around.

You need to make a Very Difficult **Agility check** to get out there as a Move action, or an Easy **Agility check** to get out on the left side and into the middle as a Move and a Main action. If you fail the Very Difficult check, you're stuck in the car for this round, and if you make the Easy check, you're out of the car but not in the middle.

Very Difficult? You must be kidding me. Okay, I get out and around the car. Hah! I roll a 22! Because it's an Easy check, I make it and get Good karma and a **Story Point**! Must be my lucky day!

So something good happens. How about his gun has fallen to the floor somewhere, so he can't shoot you?

Oh, I forgot that. As a Free action, I pick up a wrench to have something to hit the agent with.

Okay. The agent's turn. He tries to open the door on the driver's side, but it's jammed. That's the Free action.

So he makes that Very Difficult check to get over Éloïse and out as his Move action. When he's out, he realises he has to get rid of Elektra. "I apologise" he says, "I usually don't hit ladies". Then he attacks with his Super Secret Martial Art and hits with a roll of 26.

I defend myself with, uh, I don't defend myself with a roll of 97.

Right, so he hits you for 1 point of **Vitality** loss.

Ow.

His gun is somewhere under the seat, right? I search for it.

That's your Main action, then? Make a **Search check**.

52, I find it.

Great, you now have a 9 mm Beretta and no license. That's the end of the round. At the start of round five, the border police will arrive. Now, next round. Elektra?

"Too bad for you that Greek women aren't opposed to hitting horrible men" I say and whack him with the wrench. 46, a hit!

He fails his defence at 77, so he's knocked **Prone**.

Serves him right, I inflict 4 points of vitality loss.

He's down on the ground, gets up on all fours, and says "I think I have to take the "lady" part back. You won't get away with this, bloody Greek harpy!"

"And you won't get away with kidnapping my friend, stupid British bulldog!" I'm done.

Well, it's his turn anyway, and he sweeps with his feet trying to trip you with an Attack check of 59.

Drat! 92!

So he trips you, you are on the ground and **Prone**, and he gets on top you and twists your arm in an armlock so that you are **Restrained** too.

Does he get up?

No.

Good. Then I shoot him. 21. I could flip that for two **Story Points** to 12 – I do that.

Right, and he defends himself...

 No, he doesn't. He's in another zone. So I hit and I inflict, uh, 3 points of **Vitality** loss.

 That would make him **Out Cold**, but he's a Boss and takes the **Wounded Condition** instead of the **Vitality** loss. Éloïse shoots him with his own pistol, making a hole and a red messy stain in his otherwise impeccable suit.

 I have 2 on the **Ones**, and the pistol has like Reload (9–0) or something, so I'm good to continue shooting.

 But that's for later. Round two is over, now it's round three. Elektra?

 I hit him in the head with my wrench. 33! Give me a **Story Point**! Does he defend himself?

 He does, but with a roll of 03.

 Right. Damage is not good: 1 point. That doesn't make him **Out Cold**, right?

 No, he still has one **Vitality** left.

 But since I had Good karma, I can discard that roll and reroll my damage. That's better. A lot better! 6!

 Wham! He's **Out Cold**, and he doesn't take **Mortal Peril** because the two of you will fricking kill him.

 I'm not **Restrained** anymore, I guess, so last in my turn I get up. "And that's what happens when you kidnap Elektra Ambrosia's friends!"

 Okay, there's deafening silence on the square as the fighting and shooting stops.

 I think I'm crying from shock right now.

 Indeed you are, and seconds later, the silence is broken by sirens from the border police plus the regular police as they roar into the square before the Opera House.

HEALING

As soon as the fight scene is over, two things happen:

- If you have the Condition **Mortal Peril**, drop that Condition now.
- Restore your current **Vitality** to **Max Vitality**.

OUT COLD

If you have the Condition **Out Cold**, you eventually lose the Condition.

- As soon as the fight scene is over, one other character that is not **Out Cold** can make a **Medicine task check**. If it succeeds, you lose the Condition, and can act immediately. If the task check fails, you're still **Out Cold** until the scene following that. Basically, someone else has to make a successful **Medicine check**, or you have to skip a scene.
- If all characters are **Out Cold**, or if some characters are **Out Cold** while the others made a tactical retreat, they're at the Director's mercy. They will still lose the Condition eventually, but they may do so while tied to a chair or locked in a cell. All is not lost, however: they will **gain 9 Story Points** each for being captured (see *Gaining Story Points* on page 104).

WOUNDED

The **Wounded** Condition remains for some time. There are two ways to drop the **Wounded** Condition:

- Spend a scene healing the wound. The scene must contain two days of recuperation *and* either a hospital scene (awkward questions from the police), a successful **Credit** or **Contacts task check** and doctor's visit with an appropriate bribe to keep quiet, or a successful task check for **Medicine**.
- Spend downtime between adventures on recuperating.

You can ignore the effects of the **Wounded** Condition for one scene, if someone else patches you up with a successful **Medicine task check**. If successful, you still have the **Wounded** Condition and cannot take another **Wounded** Condition – you only ignore the **–2 pips** modification for one scene.

 The fight is over. Elektra, you get your Vitality back.

 The agent won't die, will he?

 No, he's just Wounded. He's Out Cold too.

 I want to wake him. I suck at Medicine, but I need to know where he hid the secret microfilm.

 Okay, make a Medicine check.

 31 and my Medicine is just 15. But I can spend two Story Points and flip it to 13. So, eh, I find a half-empty bottle of soda and pour it over him.

 Is that Greek first aid?

 No, Greek first aid would have been ouzo.

 Hahaha! Anyway, he's awake. You have time for one question before the border police arrive.

CONDITIONS

Most Conditions are binary: you have a Condition, or you don't. If you have that Condition, it affects you.

Some Conditions stack. Stacking Conditions are Conditions that you can have more than one of. Each of them adds its effect to the others.

Conditions are eventually dropped. Stacking Conditions are dropped one at a time, not all at once.

BLINDED

All checks to notice something by sight automatically fail. All checks for **Search** and **Investigation**, and all Attack checks and Defence checks are at **–5 pips**. Many actions, like reading, are impossible.

If the cause of the blindness is due to darkness, drop the **Blinded** Condition when light is restored.

If the cause of the blindness is temporary, drop the **Blinded** Condition after the scene.

DEAF

All checks to notice something by hearing automatically fail. Checks for **Charm**, **Languages**, **Entertainment** and even **Contacts** and **Sneak** can be at **–2** or **–5 pips**.

If the cause of the deafness is a sudden loud sound, drop the **Deaf** Condition after the scene.

EXHAUSTED (stacks)

Temporarily halve your **Max Vitality**. If your vitality exceeds the temporary **Max Vitality**, your current **Vitality** is equal to your temporary **Max Vitality**.

Exhausted Conditions stack.

Drop one **Exhausted** Condition after eating, rehydrating and having a good night's sleep.

FRIGHTENED

You cannot enter the same zone as the source of your fright. Attack checks are at **–2 pips**.

Drop the **Frightened** Condition by making a successful **Willpower task check** as your main action.

INTOXICATED (stacks)

All task checks are at **–2 pips**. You can't take defence actions at all. You **gain 1d6** Protection.

The **Intoxicated** Condition stacks up to three times. You don't get a fourth **Intoxicated** Condition, but instead collapse and fall unconscious (counts as **Out Cold**).

Drop one **Intoxicated** Condition the next morning, and then another at each six-hour interval thereafter.

MORTAL PERIL

Take the **Mortal Peril** Condition instead of **Vitality** loss. You can only take the **Mortal Peril** Condition if you do not already have the **Mortal Peril** Condition.

- Flip any Attack check for the remainder of the fight.
- If **Vitality** runs out in the current fight, you die, unconditionally.

You choose when to take the **Mortal Peril** Condition; you never have to. The reasons for taking the **Mortal Peril** Condition are usually to prevent yourself from going **Out Cold** when **Wounded**, if you want the ability to Flip attack checks in a critical fight, or if you want to make a statement that this fight is important to you.

Drop the **Mortal Peril** Condition once the fight scene is over.

ON FIRE

At the start of your turn, take **1dX** Damage. If you are **Out Cold** at the start of your turn and still **On Fire**, take one **Wounded** Condition.

You can take a Main action to try to put out the fire if you are in a zone that is not on fire. Make an **Agility task check**. If successful, drop the **On Fire** Condition.

Someone else can also put out the fire in the same way on their turn.

If you have a blanket or other fire-extinguishing tool, the task check is at **+2 pips** or more.

OUT COLD

When **Vitality** runs out, you're **Out Cold** and you are no longer in the fight.

Drop the **Out Cold** Condition at the start of the next scene if another character makes a successful **Medicine task check**. Drop the Condition at the start of the scene after that if the task check failed or if there was no **Medicine task check**.

OVERBURDENED

When **Overburdened**, movement and attack checks are at **–2 pips**.

Drop the **Overburdened** Condition as a Free action if you can put down or drop the items that make you **Overburdened**.

Drop the **Overburdened** Condition as a main action if you have to wriggle out of a harness to put down the items that make you **Overburdened**.

PARALYSED

You can't take any actions on your turn.

At the end of your turn, make an **Endurance task check**. If successful, "unlock" one kind of action (Free, Move, Main or Bonus) for the rest of the scene. Depending on the reason for the paralysis, there may be a modifier on the task check.

Drop the **Paralysed** Condition when the source of the paralysis says it should be dropped.

PRONE

You can't take a Move action. You can take a Sprint action, but it requires an **Agility task check**. Ranged Attack checks made against you from another zone are at **–2 pips**. Your Defence checks against melee attacks or ranged attacks from the same zone are at **–2 pips**.

At the end of your turn, you may get up and drop the **Prone** Condition as a bonus action.

RESTRAINED

You cannot take a Move action or Sprint action.

Drop the **Restrained** Condition by making a successful Unarmed **Melee**, **Strength** or **Agility task check** as your Main action. The check is opposed if another character is holding you. If the check fails, or if you lose, you're still **Restrained**.

STUNNED

Attack checks are at **–5 pips**. Sprint or Move actions that normally require a task check are also at **–5 pips**. Regular Sprint or Move actions now require a task check.

Other task checks are at **–2 pips**.

Unless being **Stunned** is the result of poison or illness, you can often use your Main action to make a **Willpower task check**. If successful, drop the **Stunned** Condition.

Drop the **Stunned** Condition at the start of the next scene if it is still in effect.

SURPRISED

Whenever you are surprised, caught unprepared, or otherwise not ready for action, you get the **Surprised** Condition.

You can only take a Free action on your turn.

Drop the **Surprised** Condition at the end of your turn.

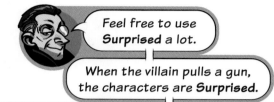

Feel free to use Surprised a lot.

When the villain pulls a gun, the characters are Surprised.

You can amplify it with a delayed action: if the characters do something, the villain shoots.

That should put the characters in a really bad situation if they start a fight, so that being captured is the preferred option.

TERRIFIED

All checks are at **–2 pips**. Attack checks against the source of your terror are at **–5 pips**. You cannot move closer to the source of your terror. At the start of your turn, if you are in the same zone as the source of your terror, make a **Willpower task check** as a Free action. If it fails, you must move out of the zone before doing anything else.

Replace the **Terrified** Condition with the **Frightened** Condition by making a successful **Willpower task check** as your Main action.

WOUNDED

Take the **Wounded** Condition instead of **Vitality** loss. You don't have to take the **Wounded** Condition if you don't want to. You can only take the **Wounded** Condition if you do not already have the **Wounded** Condition.

Once the fight ends, all further task checks are at **–2 pips** until the **Wounded** Condition heals. Ignore the effects of the **Wounded** Condition for one scene if someone else makes a successful **Medicine task check**.

Drop the **Wounded** Condition after a two-day recuperating scene and a successful **Medicine**, **Credits** or **Contacts task check** (and possibly some uncomfortable questions from the police), or by spending downtime on Mend and Recuperate.

OTHER WAYS TO GET HURT

Being beat up by my brutes is not the only way that characters can be hurt. Falling is a particular favourite of mine, because it takes them some time before they hit the ground, and I love the look of dread on their faces when they realise what is about to happen. Explosions are also a crowd-pleaser. Let's be honest: who doesn't love a good explosion?

Device	Damage	Trigger
Hand grenade	6dX	First in the next round
Stick of dynamite	8dX	First in a specified round depending on the fuse
Trap bomb	8dX	When the triggering action or situation occurs
Rocket-propelled grenade	9dX	Attack action
Timed bomb	8–12dX	First in a specified round

DROWNING

If you are submersed or otherwise unable to breathe, you have to make an **Endurance task check** at the start of your turn. If you are **Surprised** when it happens, the task check is at **–2 pips**. If you have time to prepare for it, the task check is at **+2 pips**. If the task check fails, you take **1dX** damage at the start of your turn.

EXPLOSIONS

Any explosive device inflicts damage to everyone in the zone when it goes off. Roll damage individually for cast characters, lieutenants and bosses. Underlings and Mooks can be handled as a group. The zone may also be **On Fire** afterwards.

Everyone in adjacent zones takes half damage (round the damage down to full dice). Roll damage individually for cast characters, Lieutenants and Bosses.

If it is a very powerful explosive device (you have at least **5dX** damage left after halving the damage), halve the damage again for zones adjacent to adjacent zones, and continue repeating this process to simulate the blast spreading outwards. Stop when the damage was less than **5dX**.

- Hand grenades and similar devices will explode in the next round after pulling the pin. The device will go off first in that round.
- Some explosive devices – bazooka rockets etc – will explode in the same action they are fired.
- Some explosive devices have a timer or a fuse. Set a time when the device will detonate, for instance "in round four, the bomb will go off". The device will go off first in that round.
- A few devices are traps, triggered by a specific action or situation. "If someone opens the safe", "if someone walks down the stairs and does not check for trip wires" and so on. Mines are typical examples. As soon as the action or situation occurs, the device detonates.

FIRE

If a zone is **On Fire**, you take **1dX** damage at the start of your turn and have to make an **Agility task check**. If you have thick clothing or wet clothes, the task check is at **+2 pips**. If the task check fails, you get the **On Fire** Condition.

FALLING

If you fall more than 1 metre or deliberately jump from more than 2 metres, make an **Agility task check**, modified by **–1 pip** per extra meter. If the task check fails, you're **Wounded**. If you already have the **Wounded** Condition when you fall or jump, you're **Out Cold**.

POISON

Poison has a strength that works as a Skill. 50 is a weak poison or a small dose, and 75 is a strong poison or a strong dose. If you are poisoned, make an opposed task check for **Endurance** against the poison.

- If the poison fails, it has no effect.
- If the poison's task check succeeds, but you win the opposed check, you only get the initial effect.
- If the **Endurance task check** succeeds, but you lose the opposed check, you get the initial effect and the prolonged effect for the duration.
- If the **Endurance task check** fails and the poison's check succeeds, you get the initial effect and the prolonged effect for double the duration.

Table: Poison Types

Poison	Strength	Initial effect	Prolonged effect	Duration
Sleeping gas	75	**Stunned** for **1d6** rounds	Asleep, cannot be awakened	**1d6** hours
Paralysing poison	75	**Stunned** for **1d6** rounds	**Paralysed**, cannot move	**1d6** hours
Deadly poison	65	**1d6** damage	**1dX** damage at the end of turn for the duration	**1d6** rounds
Hallucinogenic poison	50	Everything is blurry, **Stunned** for **1d6** rounds	Cannot discern reality from hallucinations, **Stunned** and **Intoxicated**	**1d6** hours

SNIPING/ATTACKED FROM BEHIND

It's not fun being killed from an ambush or by a sniper.

If a cast character is attacked by a sniper or from behind, have them make an **Alertness task check**.

- If the task check has **Bad Karma**, simply declare that the character is **Out Cold** and possibly also **Wounded**.
- If the task check only fails, make a Damage roll for the attack with **+4dX** Damage and give the character the **Surprised** Condition.
- If the task check succeeds, make a normal Damage roll for the attack. The character is not **Surprised**.
- If the task check has **Good Karma**, the attack is noticed in time and the character can make a Defence check if applicable. The character is not **Surprised**.

If a Director character is sniped by the characters, have the attacking characters make **Sneak task checks**.

- If the task check has **Bad Karma**, the target is alerted in time and can defend themselves. They are not **Surprised**.
- If the task check fails, the target becomes aware of the attack, but not in time. The character makes a normal Attack check. The target is not **Surprised**.
- If the task check succeeds, the character makes an Attack check at **+2 pips**. If successful, the damage roll is at **+2dX**. The target is **Surprised**.
- If the Attack check has **Good Karma**, the player decides if the target is just **Out Cold**, or **Out Cold** and **Wounded**.

Then make initiative checks, if you haven't already, and let the fight proceed as normal.

STORY POINTS

 And whose idea was this again?

The situation was untenable. Given the circumstances, it was inevitable. Just be happy that nobody is seriously hurt.

 That's not the problem. The problem is that we're being marched off by the goon squad here.

Silence! Resistance is futile! Keep walking.

 As they say across the pond, 'it ain't over 'til it's over'.

Ah-haha-haha! You stupid fools! It's over!

  And a new opportunity arises!

GAINING STORY POINTS

Story Points are a kind of currency that cast characters can spend to influence the plot.

- You can have up to **12 Story Points** – the **Story Point** limit.
- You start each session with **4 Story Points** in your **Story Point** pool, unless the Director says otherwise. For instance, the Director may say that you start with the amount that you had at the end of the previous session, if the previous session ended in a cliffhanger.

You can use beads, chips, coins or other tokens to keep track of the current number of **Story Points** you have, or keep track of them in your passport.

The main principle is that you get **Story Points** for introducing twists in the story that are not to your advantage. This encourages players to play on their characters' weaknesses, which adds to the story and makes it more fun.

The Director can also award players for making the game more fun, but this is often forgotten in the heat of the action. Please remind him.

KARMA: 1 point

Every time you get **Good Karma** or **Bad Karma** (i.e. when the **Ones** and **Tens** in a task check are equal), you get **1 Story Point**.

GETTING CAPTURED: 9 points

The best way of gaining **Story Points** is to get captured – give up when the villain points their guns at you, or get knocked **Out Cold** in a fight and dragged off to captivity. If you are captured, you **gain 9 Story Points**.

FAIL A TASK CHECK TO PUT YOURSELF IN A BIND: 2 points

You can change a successful task check to a failure that gets you into a troublesome situation. Tell the Director what the outcome would be from the failed task check. If the Director agrees, you get **2 Story Points**.

- "Wouldn't it be fun if I fail this **Sneak task check** instead, and just as I sneak past that door, it opens and two guards pop out?"
- "I need **Story Points** for later. This door actually has an electronic code lock, rather than the key lock that I can pick, so I fail this **Security task check**."

Sometimes, there may be some negotiation for the **Story Points** if the proposed consequence of making a successful check into a failed check is not severe enough.

- "Can I fail this Drive task check and run over a, uh, flower stand to get **Story Points**?"

"Well, okay, but then you have to come to a dead halt, and the villains get away. And there's an angry shopkeeper yelling at you."

ACTIVATE A COMPLICATION: varies

Another source of **Story Points** is your Complications. If you activate one, you get **Story Points** if there are some consequences for the character. Otherwise, the character won't get any **Story Points** for activating Complications. If you activate Addiction and get dead drunk during downtime or on a day where nothing happens, you won't get any **Story Points**.

Complications generally give **Story Points** in two amounts:

- The lowest amount gives you **3 Story Points**. This is for either making a successful task check into a failure, taking a **–2 pips** modification on task checks in the scene, or taking a Condition. Note that you get more **Story Points** for failing a task check because of a Complication than just failing.
- The highest amount gives you **6 Story Points**. This is for removing yourself from a scene altogether.

ENTERTAIN THE TABLE: 1 point

If an action entertains the table, the Director can award you **1 Story Point**. Any player can at any time suggest that another player should be awarded **1 Story Point** for entertaining the table, in case the Director forgets it.

Don't overuse this option. It's not entertaining to hog the limelight all the time. It's often at least as entertaining to push the other characters into the spotlight.

USING STORY POINTS

Story Points allow you to influence the story, open new avenues of action, and fuel your Abilities.

ACTIVATE AN ABILITY: varies

Most Abilities have effects that cost **Story Points** to activate. The economy of Abilities looks like this:

- For **1 Story Point**, you can flip a task check for certain Skills.
- For **2 Story Points**, you can change a failed task check for certain Skills into a success.
- For **4 Story Points**, you can activate a major special effect, unique for that Ability.

GETTING GADGETS: varies

The five gear kits you start with may not be the ones you need for the adventure. To gain access to other gear kits, you may have to **spend Story Points**.

FLIP A CHECK: 2 points

If you have no matching Ability, you can still flip a check for **2 Story Points**.

GET A CLUE: 1–4 points

Spend a number of **Story Points**, and the Director will give you a clue. Most clues cost **1 Story Point**. The Director may set a higher cost, or have you make a relevant task check to get the clue.

This option is great to use while captured by the villain. Spend up to **4 Story Points** to have Graf von Zadrith gloat about his evil plan, if he doesn't do it on his own.

ADD SOMETHING MINOR: 2 points

Spend two **Story Points** to add something minor to a scene. "Something minor" could be:

- There's a gun that someone dropped just over there.
- That big red button on the control panel is the fire alarm.
- You have a hair pin or lapel pin which you can use to pick the lock.
- Your chest attracts the attention of every villain of the opposite sex in the area, distracting them and allowing someone else to do something.
- One of the villains is an old lover.

The Director may say no if the addition is too ridiculous or too unbelievable, but generally, adding something minor is not a problem.

ADD SOMETHING MAJOR: 6 points

Spend six **Story Points** to add something major to a scene. "Something major" is usually a twist that takes the story in an entirely new direction.

- The old lover will help the characters escape.
- A Director character shows up to save the character's bacon.
- The damage done in an earlier scene causes a wall to collapse so that the characters can escape.

"Something major" often needs some reworking of the adventure, so don't be surprised if the Director denies it or suggest a modification.

ADDING TOO MUCH

Sometimes, the Director may think that the suggested addition doesn't work. In those cases, the Director should offer up a different idea that will fit the overall plan for the adventure, but is inspired by the suggestion. If the player accepts, then that happens. This may include downgrading something major to something minor, in which case the Director hands some of the **Story Points** back.

If the player doesn't accept, hand all of the **Story Points** back.

It is also possible to just reject the player's suggestion and hand all of the **Story Points** back, but players' suggestions should only rarely be rejected outright. It is better to modify the suggestion.

I have finally captured the pesky heroes! They are escorted to the central control room in my Octopus base, where I can gloat about their puny efforts to stop my ingenious plan for world domination.

"A-haha-haha! So you think you could beat the Octopus! You have failed! Now it is too late, and you will witness..."

Since I now have an almost full pool of **Story Points** after being captured, I interrupt and hand over six of the beads that we use for **Story Points** to the Director.

"Dad! Stop it. You're embarrassing me with your B-movie villainy!"

"Pumpkin? What ... what are you doing here? It's so good to see you! How have you been?"

"I have been captured by my megalomaniac dad. How do you think I would feel? You better release all of us or Mom will never talk to you again!"

"Keep quiet, rebellious girl! I have more important things to do than concern myself with your mother's feelings."

I'm in a dilemma here. Rules-wise, this is perfectly legal, but there would not be an adventure. So I suggest that the revelation of my identity is actually a minor thing worth two **Story Points**, but it will make it easier to escape now that it is established that Éloïse is my daughter.

I guess that's fair. So the reunion doesn't go well, like this:

"You never had time for your family! You only cared about yourself! You never could face the responsibility, and that's why you ran off to play a parody of a Bond villain!"

"That's it! Go to your room! Without dinner!"

And then you're marched off under guard to Éloïse's childhood room where you are locked in, without dinner. Here are four of your six **Story Points** back. Oh, and here is an additional point for entertaining the table!

At least my room is better than a cell, even if it is twice as embarrassing with all the pink and fluff. I better make a note of trying to get the Peerage Ability in the future to match the von Zadrith legacy.

LOSING STORY POINTS

In some cases, you may lose **Story Points**. The most common reason is to act against the genre conventions, in particular killing in cold blood. But first, let's talk about what you shouldn't remove **Story Points** for.

- **Never remove Story Points for acting against your plans:** This only teaches the players to satisfy your interests, rather than to have fun and act as their characters. Instead, admit that they players outwitted you, were not motivated to follow your lead, or found something more interesting to do. Then save what you can and play along.
- **Never remove Story Points to punish a player for behaving bad in real life:** Removing **Story Points** is for in-game breaches of genre conventions, not real life transgressions. In that case, take a timeout and talk to the player instead. Tell them that you do not enjoy obnoxious behaviour, that it hurts the entire group, and that it makes it difficult or downright impossible to enjoy the game. Ask them to reconsider

what they are doing. In the worst case, consider not inviting that player to your game.

KILL UNNECESSARILY OR IN COLD BLOOD: All Story Points (+ half of other players' Story Points)

The contract of no killing goes both ways. It's hard to kill player characters unless the player wants to let it happen, but it should go the other way as well. Self defence may be justified, but killing needlessly? No.

- If a player character kills any character in cold blood or when they really don't have to, feel free to remove all **Story Points** from that character.
- If the killing is exceptionally cruel, also remove half the **Story Points** (round up) from the other player characters for not stopping the act.

And that's on top of the story consequences. It's pretty likely that the character is now wanted for murder.

EQUIPMENT

We won't get to Gare de Lyon in this traffic, Élo-chan. The roads are completely congested.

With this vespa, we don't need roads.

But... it is illegal to drive on the sidewalk.

Yurika, you're a brilliant woman, but you clearly exhibit two-dimensional thinking. Now watch this.

Wha... UWAAAA! WE'RE FLYING! LET ME DOWN! LET ME DOWN!

Not until Gare de Lyon. Wee!

EQUIPMENT AND PROPERTY

Property and money are not particularly important in *The Troubleshooters*. You don't have to keep track of exactly how much money or food you have. Money and property are abstracted into the **Credit** Skill and Abilities like Old Money, and a lot of non-interesting property is just hand-waved away.

Gear kits, on the other hand, are more important. Gear kits are the things that enable you to have fantastic adventures. At character creation, you get five gear kits. The Template gives you three of the kits. Two kits are freely chosen by you, so long as you fulfil any requirements of the kits.

Your character probably owns a lot more things than the gear kits. Your character's property is what can be expected for her lifestyle and is within reason: a place to live, a means of transportation, clothes for different occasions, equipment to work with and those kinds of things.

This depends to a great extent on your character's Abilities. For instance, the Old Money Ability allows your character to have a mansion or chateau. Nouveau Riche allows your character to have a fancy place to live in the city centre, like a floor in a downtown skyscraper.

If there is ever any doubt whether your character owns a particular object or can buy it, make a task check for the **Credit** Skill, with a proper modifier depending on how expensive it would be. Sometimes you can use a Skill associated with the equipment for this check.

> Despite having the **Plot Hook Media Darling**, I'm not the kind of girl who would be seen at a gala evening. If I am to attend such an occasion, I would have to get a gala dress.

> What I have to do to get a gala dress depends on how I get it. If I rent it, that's most likely it: no task check required, but on the other hand, I don't get any advantages from it.

> If I want a gala dress that would make an impression on people, I would have to buy one and have it fixed for me by a tailor. That would merit a **Credit task check**, or maybe **Contacts** or even **Charm**, depending on how I get it (and with the Director's approval, of course). Such a dress would make people talk and smile, but I would not have any advantages in game terms.

> If I want a gala dress that is perfect for me and gives me advantages in game terms, it could be a gear kit, and I would have to use **Story Points**. Which is another thing entirely.

The concept of money

The concept of money is rather complex in the modern world. At the simplest level, you get your salary, and then you pay your rent, insurance, fees, subscriptions and your taxes. Then you live on the rest until you get the next salary cheque. That assumes that you live in an apartment and have a fixed job, which often is not very permitting for those who run around taking part in adventures.

If you go on adventures, things get more complicated. First of all, you can rarely have an ordinary nine-to-five job. Second, adventures are expensive, which realistically would require you to have either ridiculous personal wealth or financial backing from some outside source. Outside financial backing means that you are using someone else's money, which means that the funding is limited, requires oversight and application, or both. Ridiculous personal wealth is often bound to real estate, inventory, the stock market or other assets, which in turn means that it is a complicated process to liquidate your wealth and use it to fund your adventure.

All that is boring as heck! (At least, that is what we think!) This game is about comic book adventures, not accounting!

Instead, we use the **Credit** Skill, **Story Points**, gear kits and some Abilities to abstract away all problems with money, and just assume that your exciting adventures are funded one way or another.

GEAR KITS

Gear kits are defined as a collection of things (each kit may consist of several items) that potentially are important for the story. They also often have rules effects, mostly in the form of tags. Gear kits can also define the character and be a part of their persona.

Each character has five slots for gear kits. Each gear kit lists a number of effects, and may also have a requirement, either a Skill value or an Ability. The gear kit also lists a number of items. This list is a suggestion, intended to give you an impression of what the kit is about and to quantify the gear kit in game terms. If you think that the gear kit should have more items, or want to swap an item for another, discuss it with the Director.

The important thing is not the content of the gear kit, but the complete kit.

You can *own* more than five gear kits, but you can only *slot* five gear kits at the same time. Swapping one gear kit for another can be done in a planning scene, or at startup.

But what about realism?

Stuff realism! This is a game about comic book adventures! The reason we use gear kits and slots is for game balance and for planning scenes, not to simulate reality.

GETTING GEAR KITS

You get gear kits during a planning scene, never during the action. If you didn't get the gear kit before the action starts, it's too late.

In a planning scene, you decide what you need to do and what gear you need for it. Note that there are still only five slots available to each character, so the characters may have to swap gear kits out and plan who carries what kit. Some kits may be offered to the characters by employers if they are considered mission-critical. The characters may opt to get other kits on their own initiative.

There are three ways to get gear kits:

Mission-critical equipment: Some gadgets are handed to the characters as a part of the mission. For the duration of the mission (or a part of it), the characters have access to that gear kit. This way of getting gear kits depends on the mission planning of the Director. This is most common if the characters have an employer for a mission or belong to an organisation, but could also happen if they have a patron that can provide gadgets.

> I and my friends have accepted a mission from the British intelligence service to search for a hidden Octopus base somewhere in the Greek archipelago.

> Our "employer" Olivia Mansfield–Cumming has made a yacht available from the British detachment on Cyprus, fitted with a secret compartment in which there are handgun gear kits (one each) and submachine gun gear kits (2 in total) that we can use. Since this is mission-critical equipment, we don't have to pay any **Story Points** for the gear kits. We have to shuffle around our gear kits to make slots available: Harry made space for the Yacht gear kit, for instance.

Use Story Points: Gear kits have a **Story Point** cost attached to them. They may also have requirements.

- You must fulfil the requirements of the gear kit.
- Pay the cost in **Story Points** for the gear kit.
- The gear kit is automatically returned at the end of the story if not lost before.

> As cool as the yacht is, I feel that we will occasionally need something faster and more flexible. So when planning for the mission, I call in a favour from the Greek Army to get access to an Aerospatiale Gazelle helicopter. It will cost me **2 Story Points**.

> Pretty please, can the yacht have a helicopter landing platform?

> Well, okay, since you ask so nicely.

Jury-rigging gear: Sometimes there's the option of creating a gadget. If you create one in an adventure, it is always a single-use scrounged devices that will be unreliable at best. You usually need a planning scene to make the gadget, but the Tech Wiz Ability allows you to create a gadget even outside the planning scene.

- Define the gadget, including desired tags.
- The Director defines a Skill challenge.
- Make the task checks. Other characters could help with getting parts and funding.
- When all task checks are complete, you hopefully have a working device.

> In another adventure, The Octopus has set up a REP projector, a kind of area effect mind control device, at the top of the Eiffel tower, pacifying Paris and the French government. We can't even come near it without being affected.

> But I could jury-rig a counter-field projector from a walkie-talkie, a television set, a car battery, and a wheelbarrow, using the theory of phase delay and cancelling.

> My original idea was that a simple tin foil hat could isolate the brain from the field, but don't tell Éloïse! I define a Skill challenge using **Electronics, Engineering, Science** and **Search** (to find the parts), but at **−5 pips** since it is weird science.

> Merde! The checks for **Search** and **Engineering** fail, which means a **Limited** outcome.

110

A-haha-haha! My evil plan cannot be stopped! The device works but with limited range, and the wheelbarrow will not fit in the elevator in the Eiffel tower. Now, success is all but guaranteed!

A jury-rigged device will only work once (maybe twice if the outcome is Great) before going "poof!".

Crafting gear: If you want a permanent gadget, you have to craft it as a project in downtime. You usually need the Crafter, Inventor or Tech Wiz Ability to create a permanent new gadget, but it's up to the Director to allow it.

- Define the gadget, including desired tags.
- The Director defines a Skill challenge.
- For each downtime period, you can make one task check from the challenge.
- When all task checks are done, the project is complete and you hopefully have a new gadget as a gear kit.

If you want to modify a gadget or gear kit by adding a tag or swapping one tag for another you do the same as if crafting gear, but you make two task checks for each downtime period. The gear kit is not available from the start of the project to the end of it.

Do you know what is cooler than a vespa? A flying vespa!

So I have undertaken a summer project of making my vespa fly, using the same technology the Octopus uses in their octopods.

In game terms, it already has Impression and Moving in heavy traffic, and I want to add Flying to it.

In the challenge to create the flying Vespa from my regular Vespa, I will use **Credit** 15%, **Electronics** 65%, **Engineering** 45%, **Science** 65%, and either **Search** 65% or **Contacts** 45%. Of course I choose to use **Search**.

Having three tags means that three task checks in the Skill challenge will be at −2 pips. Since I am modifying an existing gadget, one task check will be at +2 pips. All task checks will be at −5 pips because it is weird science.

Since it is a modification, I can make two task checks in each downtime period, but I decide to be careful and only make one task check in each downtime period, but at +2 pips on each.

Now it's just a matter of optimising the outcome of the challenge. Thanks to the extra time, but also because of the weird science, all task checks are at −3 pips.

Since I'm dirt poor with **Credits** 15%, and not that good at **Engineering** at 45%, I will stack as much bad stuff as I can on **Credits** but buff **Engineering**. I place one of the −2 pips modifications from the three tags to **Credits**, for an end modification of −5 pips (meaning that this task check can only succeed if I roll 6–10).

The +2 pips for modifying an existing gear kit go to **Engineering** for a total of −1 pips. I place a −2 pips modification on **Search**, for a total of −5 pips. The final −2 pips modification could be on **Electronics** or **Science**. I decide to put it on **Electronics**, since I could use my **Electronics** toolbox to cancel it.

So the final Skill challenge will be **Electronics** 65% at −3 pips, **Science** 65% at −3 pips, **Search** 65% at −5 pips, **Engineering** 45% at −1 pip, and **Credit** 15% at −5 pips

For **Electronics**, I roll 30 which is a success. **Science** fails at 86. **Search** is a success with a roll of 47, and so is **Engineering** with a roll of 20. **Credit** fails with a roll of 42. That means that I failed **Science** and **Credit**, for a **Limited** outcome.

A **Limited outcome** means that I can remove a tag or add a bad tag. It would fit the outcome if I removed the Impression tag, since it would then be created from scrounged parts and be ugly as heck, but I could also add an Unreliable (9–0) tag. I think the latter is the most fun.

I should also note that the task requires five downtime periods, and until finished, you can't use your Vespa. Five downtime periods will likely need at least the downtime after this and the next adventure, and possibly as much as five adventures. This is no summer project, but more like a year-long project, if not longer.

Sample Challenge: Building a gadget

Credit, for funding.
Electronics, for control systems.
Engineering, for figuring out how to build the thing.
Science, for getting the calculations right.
Search or **Contacts**, for getting the parts.

Modifiers

–2 pips on one task check per enabler tag you want the gadget to have.

–2 pips on all task checks if the gadget is spy tech or ancient wisdom.

–5 pips on all task checks if the gadget is weird science or lost wisdom.

+2 pips on one task check per limiter tag you add to the gadget.

+2 pips on one task check if you build a new gadget and take two downtime periods instead of one for that task check. You can do this for each task check.

+2 pips on one task check if you modify an existing gadget and only make one task check for one downtime period. You can do this for each task check.

+2 pips on one task check if it is a modification of an existing gear kit.

Ambiguous tags counts as enablers for creating a gadget, but not for modifying a gadget or if they are default.

Outcomes

Great outcome: You create the gadget, and it will work twice or have an additional tag.

Good outcome: You create the gadget with the desired tags.

Limited outcome: You create the gadget, but with a flaw that adds a limiter tag or removes an enabler tag of the Director's choice.

Bad outcome: The gadget doesn't work. Sorry.

Abysmal outcome: Something goes spectacularly wrong: the gadget could for instance explode in your face, blow up something else, affect everyone in the vicinity, and so on. You won't know until you use it, though.

SPY TECH AND ANCIENT WISDOM

Some gadgets are clearly beyond the norm. We divide those into four categories:

- **Spy tech** is extreme high tech beyond the market's most cutting edge technology. It is usually only available to governments or possibly the richest corporations. If it is available in the real world today, but not in the 1960s, it's probably spy tech. Mainframe computers are not spy tech, only very very expensive and non-portable. Hand-held computers with wireless networking (i.e smartphones) would be spy tech. Spy tech also includes gadgets depicted in spy movies from the era – laser cutters, wire shooters, radio tracers, listening devices, holograms, and so on. Spy tech would require the Mad Inventor or Tech Wiz Abilities.

- **Weird science** is anything beyond us today, either because it is too advanced or just comic book technology. This includes human-like robots, anti-gravity, mind control projectors, clones, ray guns and so on. Weird science would require the Mad Inventor Ability.

- **Ancient wisdom** is knowledge from the past that is not common in the modern world and is borderline mystic. Damascus sword forging, Japanese sword forging, herbal medicine and so on would qualify as ancient wisdom. Ancient wisdom could be available to characters with the Ability Crafter.

- **Lost wisdom** is definitely mystical in nature, unexplained by science and bordering on magic. It is generally not available to player characters.

Spy tech, weird science and ancient wisdom can rarely be jury-rigged. Use the jury-rig option sparingly and only with the Director's approval. Lost wisdom should never be jury-rigged.

What is the difference between Elektra's Lancia and my Citroën 2CV? It's actually very simple: Elektra's Lancia is a **Signature Gadget** that defines Elektra's character.

My Citroën 2CV isn't. It's just an affordable mode of transportation that is represented as the compact car gear kit.

Should I decide that the 2CV is an important part of my character, I can get the **Signature Gadget** Ability. But as long as I don't, it's just a car that will get me to the next scene – if it is available.

SIGNATURE GADGETS

At character creation, you may appoint one piece of equipment in a gear kit to be a **Signature Gadget**. This piece of equipment is as much a part of your persona as it is a personalised object. The **Signature Gadget** is available to you at most times and doesn't require a scene to get it. If you want to make another gear kit into a **Signature Gadget**, you have to get the Extra Gadget Ability.

A **Signature Gadget** must have a description. It can't be a generic vehicle or a generic gun: it must at least be a specific brand, and should preferably also have a description and maybe even a name.

My Lancia Stratos is not just any Lancia: It's mine! It is bright yellow with two white stripes across the hood and the roof, extra headlights, a big spoiler at the rear, and big white roundels with the starting number "14" on the doors and the hood, at least for this season. I aim to have starting number "1" in the next.

The Director should avoid removing **Signature Gadgets** from play, except as a plot point for a mission. There may be points in the story where the **Signature Gadget** is not directly available, such as a car indoors or a gun on an airplane, but this is just temporary.

If a **Signature Gadget** is not available to the player for a big part of the adventure (as a result of being left behind, destroyed or stolen) the character gains **3 Story Points**.

If removed, there should be a way of getting the **Signature Gadget** back, and even if that fails, it is still restored when the mission is over. Even if a **Signature Gadget** is stolen, lost or destroyed, it is replaced later, at the session following the end of the mission at the latest.

COLLECTING STUFF

Sometimes, you may collect and keep things that you stumble on in your adventures. Collected items are stored somewhere, such as the display room at a chateaux, in the attic, or the garage, and not active.

If you want to use them during an adventure, you assign them to one of your gear kit slots at the start-up of the adventure or in a planning scene later. You may have to unslot an existing gear kit. You don't have to explain how you get the item – you already have it.

Anything to declare?

In the Passport, there is a section dedicated to "dangerous items", where you can list your weapons and protective gear. Other gear kits can also be listed there, on one of the Visa stamp pages, or on a separate paper.

You can also get Gear Card decks, and use the cards to keep track of your gear. The cards fit nicely in your Passport.

WEAPONS

RANGED WEAPONS

The guns in the weapon list are grouped by "typical calibers", not exact calibers. If your favourite handgun caliber is not on the list, pick one that is somewhat similar. Or make your own stats!

Weapon	Skill	Damage	Tags
Handgun, .25 ACP	Ranged Combat	4dX	Short Range, Reload (7–0), Concealable
Handgun, 7.62 mm	Ranged Combat	4dX	Loud, Short Range, Reload (9–0)
Handgun, 9 mm or .45	Ranged Combat	5dX	Loud, Short Range, Reload (9–0)
Handgun, .357 Magnum	Ranged Combat	6dX	Loud, Short Range, Reload (8–0)
Shotgun, 12 gauge	Ranged Combat	7dX	Loud, Short Range, Reload (7–0)
Hunting rifle, .30-30	Ranged Combat	7dX	Loud, Single Shot
Assault rifle, 7.62 mm	Ranged Combat	7dX	Loud, Reload (8–0)
Assault rifle, 5,56 mm	Ranged Combat	6dX	Loud, Reload (9–0)
Submachine gun	Ranged Combat	5dX	Loud, Reload (9–0)
Light machine gun	Ranged Combat	7dX	Loud, Reload (0), Unwieldy
Crossbow	Ranged Combat	5dX	Single Shot
Longbow	Ranged Combat	5dX	Single Shot, Swift Reload
Throwing knife	Ranged Combat	4dX	Thrown, Silent, Short Range
Shuriken	Ranged Combat	4dX	Thrown, Silent, Short Range, Concealable
Molotov cocktail	Ranged Combat	3dX	Incendiary (5–6), Thrown, Short Range

MELEE WEAPONS

Weapon	Skill	Damage	Tags
Arming sword	Melee	5dX	Chopping
Dagger	Melee	4dX	Precise
Improvised weapon	Melee	3dX	Brittle
Halberd	Melee	4dx	Chopping, Long Reach, Cumbersome
Katana	Melee	5dX	Cutting
Longsword	Melee	5dX	Chopping, Cumbersome
Quarter-staff	Melee	3dX	Long Reach, Tripping
Rapier	Melee	5dX	Precise
Sabre	Melee	5dX	Cutting
Spear	Melee	4dX	Long Reach, Cumbersome
Truncheon	Melee	3dX	Non-lethal
Unarmed	Melee	2dX	—

TAGS

Brittle: The weapon breaks and is unusable after an attack or defence check with **Karma** (good or bad). If it was an attack check, apply damage first.

Chopping: On a hit, reduce protection by **–1dP** to a minimum of **0dP**.

Concealable: Hiding the weapon is at **+2 pips**.

Cumbersome: The weapon is always in the way, and you have the Condition **Overburdened** when carried but not when you fight with it.

Cutting: If the opponent fails the defence check or doesn't make one, add **+1dX** to damage.

Incendiary (X): The weapon can set flammable items, for instance cloth or petrochemicals, ablaze. Roll 1D6: if it is within the range X, the item is on fire. If the item is very flammable, add +1 to the die roll.

Long Reach: Initiative is increased by 2 when making an Initiative check or setting Initiative.

Loud: Using the weapon will be heard in the Vicinity.

Non-lethal: The target cannot take the **Mortal Peril** Condition.

Paralytic: The target cannot take the **Wounded** or **Mortal Peril** Conditions. The target can take the **Stunned** Condition instead of **Wounded**, and **Paralysed** instead of **Mortal Peril**.

Precise: A hit with **Good Karma** adds +2dX to damage.

Reload (X): If the **Ones** of an Attack check is within the range X, the weapon is empty after the attack and needs to be reloaded (see page 92). If you have **Bad Karma** and the **Ones** fall within the range X, then the weapon is jammed and has to be fixed in a later scene.

Short Range: You can attack targets in your zone or one adjacent to it. You can attack targets one zone beyond an adjacent zone at **–2 pips**. Beyond that, the target is out of practical range.

Single Shot: After an attack, the weapon needs to be reloaded (see page 92).

Silent: Use of the weapon can only be heard with a successful **Alertness check**, and only in the same zone.

Snaring: The target cannot take the **Wounded** or **Mortal Peril** Conditions. The target can take the **Restrained** Condition instead of **Wounded**.

Swift Reload: Reloading the weapon is a Free action.

Thrown: You can only use the *Single Shot* attack option. Afterwards, you need to draw another weapon, or spend an action to recover the weapon. You can only recover the weapon if you are in the same zone as the target.

Tripping: Using the weapon for the *Whump! – melee throw or grapple attack* option is at **+2 pips**.

Unwieldy: You automatically have the Condition **Overburdened** if you carry or use a weapon with this tag, unless you can use the weapon with support. With support, attacks at targets in a different zone from the previous attack is at **–2 pips**.

Worn: The weapon is worn rather than held, and allows the use of your hands for other things.

A note on firearms

In *The Troubleshooters*, the use of firearms is strongly discouraged.

- **Firearms are loud!** If they are used, someone will call the police, who will respond quickly. You will end up in trouble, especially if someone is hurt. So you don't want to escalate to the point where firearms are used.

- **Firearms are dangerous!** Chances are that you will be **Out Cold** if someone shoots at you and gets one or two hits.

- **Firearms are restricted!** You will need a licence to have one, and to get a licence you need a reason. And personal protection doesn't count. Sporting or hunting may count. If you need one for your job (for instance as a police officer), the weapon is only available on duty.

TAGS

Tags are very flexible and can be invented on the spot. Most tags are of the type that give you a modifier on a task check in certain circumstances, or that enable or limit your ability to do something. The Director makes the call whether the tag is applicable or not.

Some tags – especially weapon tags or Director character tags – have specific rules effects attached to them. These are more clear-cut and don't need much adjudication. Take, for instance, the *Reload (9–0)* tag: either the **Ones** of the task roll is 9 or 0 which activates the tag; or it isn't and the tag is not activated.

ENABLERS

Enablers are tags that enable the character to do something using the gadget. Basically, enablers are advantages of the gear kit or gadget. All gear kits have at least one enabler. An enabler could for instance be any of the following:

- Situations with Up modifiers. In that situation, the modifier is applied. A +2 modifier counts as one tag, a +5 modifier counts as three tags. Example: Mountaineering **+2 pips**.
- Something that you normally cannot do. Example: Flight. If you also add an Up modifier to it, it counts as three tags.
- The following specific weapon tags:
  - *Concealable*
  - *Silent*
  - *Worn*
  - *Paralytic*
  - *Snaring*
  - *Unwieldy*
  - *Precise*
  - *Swift Reload*
  - *Reload (0)*
  - *Tripping*
- Extra damage or protection is treated as an enabler tag, one per extra **+1dX** damage or **+1dP** protection.

LIMITERS

Limiters are tags that limit the characters if they use the gadget or gear kit. They usually indicate some weakness in the gadget, typically because of:

- Situations with Down modifiers. In the specified situation, the modifier is applied. Example: Peripheral vision –2.
- Something that stops you from doing something you would normally be able to do. Example: No running.
- The following specific weapon tags:
  - *Brittle*
  - *Loud*
  - *Single Shot*
  - *Chopping*
  - *Non-lethal*
  - *Thrown*
  - *Cumbersome*
  - *Reload (8–0 or lower)*
  - *Unwieldy*
  - *Cutting*
  - *Incendiary*
  - *Short Range*
- Less damage is treated as a limiter tag, one per **–1dX** damage.

When characters create gadgets, the Director can add any of the above tags to the gadgets on Limited results. You can also use the following specific tags:

Unreliable (X): if the **Ones** of a task check involving the gadget falls within the range X, the gadget stops working and has to be repaired. The range X is usually 9–0.

Illegal: Using this gadget may lead to legal trouble, ending in fines, jail time and confiscation of the gadget when the authorities find out.

Smoky: The gadget spews out a cloud of black toxic smoke, making everyone in your zone **Blinded** and **Stunned** until they can crawl out of the zone or vent the smoke.

Noisy: Using the gadget leaves everyone in the zone **Deaf** for at least **1d6** hours, and makes everyone in the Vicinity aware of the gadget.

Dangerous (X, YdX): If the **Ones** of a task check involving the gadget falls within the range X, it will cause Y **dX** damage to the user. The range X is usually 9–0 and the damage Y is usually **4dX**. The gadget still works.

Really Dangerous (X, YdX): If the **Ones** of a task check involving the gadget falls within the range X, it will cause **YdX** explosion damage to everyone in the same zone as the gadget, as per the explosion rules (page 102). The range X is usually 0 and the damage Y is usually **8dX**. The explosion is also heard in the Vicinity, and those in the zone are also **Deaf**. The gadget is no more.

Tiring: Using the gadget gives you the **Exhausted** Condition.

AMBIGUOUS TAGS

Some tags are both enablers and limiters. Some tags are neither enablers nor limiters, but just replace one effect with another. Some tags are the default behaviour that needs to be classified. We call these tags "ambiguous tags".

The following specific weapon tags are ambiguous:

- *Paralytic* (replaces damage)
- *Reload (9–0)* (default behaviour on firearms)
- *Snaring* (replaces damage)

Outside these specific tags, ambiguous tags are actually pretty rare. Most tags are either limiters or enablers.

A weapon's damage of **5dX** is considered the default behaviour of a weapon and thus an ambiguous tag. A damage of **3dX** would then be regarded as two limiter tags for the purpose of gadget creation, and a damage of **6dX** would be regarded as one enabler tag.

LIST OF GEAR KITS

ALPINIST GEAR

Story Points: 1

Contents: Hammer, spikes, cramps, line, hooks, crampons

Tags: Mountaineering: **+2 pips**

ARCHAEOLOGIST KIT

Story Points: 1

Contents: Shovel, pickaxe, trowel, brushes, dust pan, sculpting tools, dentist's tools, tape measure, compass, nylon string, scale arrow, pens and notepads, an assortment of paper and ziplock plastic bags.

Tags: Archaeology or excavation: **+2 pips**

ARCTIC GEAR

Story Points: 1

Contents: Fleece underclothes, down trousers, fur trimmed down coat with hood, warm gloves or mittens, warm boots, crampons, protective goggles.

Tags: **Survival**, arctic: **+2 pips**

ASSAULT RIFLE

Story Points: 2

Contents: Assault rifle (typically 7.62 mm), strap, 4 magazines, bag or pouches for magazines

Tags: Assault rifle: **Ranged Combat**, Damage **7dX**, *Loud*, *Reload (8–0)*

AUTOGYRO

Story Points: 2

Contents: Small single-seat or double-seat aircraft with propeller and auto-rotating rotary wing, crash helmet

Tags: Flight

BEACHWEAR

Story Points: 1

Contents: Swimsuit or swimming trunks, sandals, summer dress or shorts and polo shirt, sunglasses, elegant hat, beach towel, parasol

Tags: Impression on the Riviera: **+2 pips**

BICYCLE

Story Points: 1

Contents: Bicycle, repair kit, pump, basket, lock

Tags: Short distance or heavy traffic travel: **+2 pips**

BINOCULARS

Story Points: 1

Contents: Binoculars, strap, carrying case

Tags: Spotting at a distance: **+2 pips**

CAMERA

Story Points: 1

Contents: 35 mm camera, lenses, rolls of film, padded bag

Tags: Documentation and location analysis: **+2 pips**

CAMPING GEAR

Story Points: 1

Contents: Backpack, tent, tarp, sleeping bag, blanket, freeze-dried rations, simple knife, roll of string, pot, pan, matches, camping stove, lightweight folding chair

Tags: **Survival** and camping: **+2 pips**

CHEMISTRY LAB SET

Story Points: 1

Contents: Microscope, glass slides, slide covers, test tubes, erlenmeyer flasks, pipettes, glass tubes, catalyzers, reactants, alcohol burner, alcohol, distilled water, protection mask, cotton swabs and wipes, case.

Tags: Chemistry analysis or investigation: **+2 pips**

COMPACT CAR

Story Points: 1
Contents: Four seats, steering wheel
Tags: Road travel

COMPETITION BOW

Story Points: 2
Contents: Modern recurved balanced bow for competitions, carrying case, 12 arrows, quiver, armguard, finger tab
Tags: Competition bow: **Ranged Combat**, Damage **5dX**, *Single Shot*, *Precise*

CRYPTO MACHINE

Story Points: 2
Contents: Crypto machine, code book, notepad, pen, batteries, case for carrying
Tags: Encryption/decryption

DAGGER

Story Points: 1
Contents: Dagger, sheath
Tags: Survival knife: **Melee**, Damage **4dX**, *Precise*

DINNER JACKET

Story Points: 1
Contents: Black, midnight blue or white suit, black or white waistcoat, white dress shirt, link cuffs, black bow tie, black leather dress shoes
Tags: Impression at formal occasions: **+2 pips**

DISGUISE KIT

Story Points: 1
Contents: Wig, make-up, lenses, cotton pads
Tags: Disguises and acting: **+2 pips**

DIVING GEAR

Story Points: 1
Contents: Face mask, wetsuit, flippers, snorkel
Tags: Surface diving and swimming: **+2 pips**

DOUBLE-BARRELED SHOTGUN

Story Points: 2
Contents: Breech-loaded shotgun (typically 10 or 12 gauge), strap, hunting vest, hat, 6 reloads
Tags: Shotgun: **Ranged Combat**, Damage **7dX**, *Short Range*, *Reload (6–0)*, *Loud*

ELECTRONICS TOOLBOX

Story Points: 2
Contents: Soldering iron, solder, solder removal pump, solder wire, multimeter, magnifying glass, clamps, leads, jumper wires, an assortment of components
Tags: Jury-rigging, creating, or repairing electronics: **+2 pips**

EVENING DRESS

Story Points: 1
Contents: Dress, matching handbag, make-up, perfume, matching shoes.
Tags: Impression at formal occasions: **+2 pips**

FILM CAMERA

Story Points: 1
Contents: 8 mm or 16 mm moving film camera, film cassettes, padded bag
Tags: Documentation and event analysis: **+2 pips**

FIRST AID KIT

Story Points: 1
Contents: Dressings, bandages, compresses, antiseptic wipes, plasters, scissors, tweezers, mild painkillers (aspirin or paracetamol)
Tags: First aid: **+2 pips**

FLASHLIGHT

Story Points: 1

Contents: Flashlight with batteries

Tags: Spotting things in the dark: **+2 pips**

FLOATPLANE

Story Points: 2

Contents: Single engine propeller aircraft with pontoons, six seats and limited cargo space

Tags: Wilderness transport: **+2 pips**

Requires: Pilot

FORENSICS KIT

Story Points: 1

Contents: Fingerprints duster, tape, cotton swabs, measuring tape, indicator strips, ziplock bags, paper bags, latex gloves, tweezers, magnifying glass

Tags: Forensics investigation and documentation: **+2 pips**

HAM RADIO

Story Points: 1

Contents: Transceiver, handset, Morse key, power supply, antenna

Tags: Radio communication, very long range

HANDGUN

Story Points: 1

Contents: Handgun (typically caliber 9 mm Parabellum), holster, 5 extra magazines, bag or pouches for magazines

Tags: Handgun: **Ranged Combat**, Damage **5dX**, *Loud, Short Range, Reload (9–0)*

HANG GLIDER

Story Points: 1

Contents: Folding cloth wing, carrying bag

Tags: Unpowered flight

HEAVY HANDGUN

Story Points: 2

Contents: Handgun (typically caliber .45), holster, 3 extra magazines, bag or pouches for magazines

Tags: Heavy Handgun: **Ranged Combat**, Damage **6dX**, *Loud, Short Range, Reload (8–0)*

HEAVY REVOLVER

Story Points: 2

Contents: Revolver (typically caliber .357 Magnum), holster, 4 reloads, cartridge belt

Tags: Heavy revolver: **Ranged Combat**, Damage **6dX**, *Loud, Short Range, Reload (8–0)*

HELICOPTER

Story Points: 2

Contents: Light single-engine helicopter, optional floats, hangar space, radio

Tags: Versatile air transport: **+2 pips**

Requires: Pilot

HIKING GEAR

Story Points: 1

Contents: Comfortable boots, warm and durable clothes, mittens, walking stick

Tags: Hiking and long marches: **+2 pips**

HORSE

Story Points: 1

Contents: Horse, saddle, saddle blankets, bridle, brush, farrier's paring knife, stable

Tags: Wilderness travel: **+2 pips**

HUNTING CROSSBOW

Story Points: 2

Contents: Modern steel crossbow with rifle stock, carrying case, 12 bolts, quiver

Tags: Crossbow: **Ranged Combat**, Damage **5dX**, *Single Shot*

HUNTING GEAR

Story Points: 1

Contents: Comfortable boots, warm and durable clothes, poncho, warm mittens, knife, harness, tarp, fancy hat

Tags: **Survival** and hunting: **+2 pips**

HUNTING RIFLE

Story Points: 1

Contents: Rifle (typically caliber .250), strap, scope, protecting sleeve, 4 reloads, ammunition pouches

Tags: Hunting rifle: **Ranged Combat**, Damage **7dX**, *Loud, Single Shot*

JETPACK

Story Points: 2

Contents: Big backpack-sized rocket, flight suit, helmet, ear protectors, 30 seconds flight time

Tags: Flight

LIGHT AIRCRAFT

Story Points: 2

Contents: Single-engine two-seater aircraft, hangar space, radio

Tags: Flight

LOCKPICKS

Story Points: 1

Contents: Lockpicks, case

Tags: Picking locks: **+2 pips**

LONGBOW

Story Points: 2

Contents: Ash or yew tree longbow, carrying case, 12 arrows, quiver, armguard, finger tab

Tags: Longbow: **Ranged Combat**, **5dX**, *Single Shot*, *Swift Reload*

LUNCH BASKET

Story Points: 1

Contents: Basket with lid, blanket, food, wine, plates, forks, knives, cups, corkscrew

Tags: **Charm**ing picnic: **+2 pips**

LUXURY CAR

Story Points: 2

Contents: Very comfortable car with soundproof interior, champagne, private driver.

Tags: Impression: **+2 pips**

Requires: Old Money or Nouveau Riche.

MECHANIC'S TOOLBOX

Story Points: 1

Contents: Assorted screwdrivers, torque wrench with bits, adjustable wrench, spanner, hammer, pliers, cutters

Tags: Jury-rigging, creating or repairing machines: **+2 pips**

MEDICAL KIT

Story Points: 1

Contents: Sutures, stethoscope, blood pressure cuff, surgical tape, scissors, tweezers, assorted medical drugs, syringes and needles, in a doctor's bag.

Tags: Treating Wounds, illnesses and poisoning: **+2 pips**

MOTORCYCLE

Story Points: 1

Contents: Motorcycle, boots, chaps, jacket, gloves, helmet

Tags: Heavy traffic: **+2 pips**

MUSICAL INSTRUMENT

Story Points: 1

Contents: Portable musical instrument, carrying case with strap or handle, musical notes, tuning fork

Tags: Musical performance: **+2 pips**

OFF-ROAD VEHICLE

Story Points: 1

Contents: Four seats, steering wheel, roomy luggage compartment, rear hatch

Tags: Road travel, Off-road travel: **+2 pips**

OVERNIGHT BAG

Story Points: 1

Contents: Underwear changes, extra clothes, extra shoes, hygiene articles, make-up (optional), bag

Tags: Comfortable overnight travel: **+2 pips**

PAINTING GEAR

Story Points: 1

Contents: Portable easel, canvases, carrying bag, oil or acrylic paint, sponges, paint brushes, palette, palette knives, sketch pad, coals or pencils, bottle of cleaning solution for brushes

Tags: Painting and artistry: **+2 pips**

PARACHUTE

Story Points: 1

Contents: Parachute, reserve chute, harness, windproof jumpsuit, protective goggles, altimeter wristwatch

Tags: Parachuting

PET

Story Points: 1

Contents: Pet, leash or harness

Tags: Tricks and trouble *(9–0)*

PICKUP TRUCK

Story Points: 1

Contents: Three seats, steering wheel, cargo area with low sides and tailgate

Tags: Road travel, Off-road travel, Huge loads

POCKET PISTOL

Story Points: 2

Contents: Small pistol (typically caliber .25 ACP), holster, strap, 6 reloads

Tags: Pocket pistol: **Ranged Combat**, Damage **4dX**, *Short Range*, *Reload (7–0)*, *Concealable*

PRIVATE JET

Story Points: 2

Contents: 8 or 12-seat jet, champagne, wine, flight attendant, hangar space, pilot, radio, radio telephone

Tags: Luxury air transport: **+2 pips**

Requires: Nouveau Riche or Old Money.

PUMP-ACTION SHOTGUN

Story Points: 2

Contents: Shotgun (typically 12 gauge), strap, bandolier, 2 reloads

Tags: Shotgun: **Ranged Combat**, Damage **7dX**, *Short Range*, *Reload (7–0)*, *Loud*

RACING CAR

Story Points: 2

Contents: One or two seats, steering wheel, no trunk, roll cage

Tags: Car chases or races: **+2 pips**

RAPIER

Story Points: 1

Contents: Rapier, sheath, sharpening stone, cleaning cloth

Tags: Rapier: **Melee**, Damage **5dX**

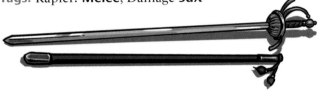

REVOLVER

Story Points: 2

Contents: Revolver (typically caliber .38 Special), holster, 6 reloads, ammunition belt

Tags: Revolver: **Ranged Combat**, Damage **5dX**, *Loud*, *Short Range*, *Reload (9–0)*

SAMURAI SWORD

Story Points: 1

Contents: Sword, sheath, uchiko powder ball, oil flask, cotton cloth

Tags: Katana: **Melee**, Damage **5dX**, *Cutting*

SCOOTER

Story Points: 1

Contents: Chic scooter, helmet, lock

Tags: Impression: **+2 pips**, Travel in heavy traffic: **+2 pips**

SCUBA TANK

Story Points: 1

Contents: Tank, regulator, pressure gauge, harness, depth gauge

Tags: Scuba diving

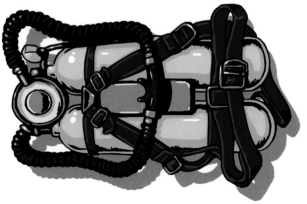

SEDAN

Story Points: 1

Contents: Four seats, steering wheel, trunk

Tags: Road travel

SHORTWAVE RADIO SET

Story Points: 1

Contents: Transceiver, handset, batteries, antenna, backpack, case

Tags: Radio communication, long range

SILENCER

Story Points: 1

Contents: Removable silencer for pistols and rifles

Tags: Removes *Loud* tag from firearms

SKI GEAR

Story Points: 1

Contents: Skis (downhill or cross-country), ski boots, ski poles

Tags: Travel on snow: **+2 pips**

SNIPER RIFLE

Story Points: 2

Contents: Rifle (typically 7.62 mm NATO), strap, scope, protecting sleeve, 4 clips, bag or pouches for clips

Tags: Sniper rifle: **Ranged Combat**, Damage **7dX**, *Loud*, *Single Shot*, *Precise*

SNOWMOBILE
Story Points: 2
Contents: Space for 2, can pull a sleigh
Tags: Travel on snow: **+5 pips**

SPORTS CAR
Story Points: 1
Contents: Two seats, steering wheel, minimal trunk
Tags: Car chases, travel in style: **+2 pips**

STATION WAGON
Story Points: 1
Contents: Four seats, steering wheel, roomy luggage compartment, rear hatch
Tags: Road travel

SUBMACHINE GUN
Story Points: 2
Contents: Submachine gun, strap, 4 magazines, bag or pouches for magazines
Tags: Submachine gun: **Ranged Combat**, Damage **5dX**, *Loud*, *Reload (9–0)*

SURVIVAL GEAR
Story Points: 1
Contents: Knife, compass, string, matches, flint and steel, tinder, mylar blanket, fishing hook, fishing line, scalpel, water cleaning tablets, and two flares, packed in a watertight box
Tags: **Survival**: **+2 pips**; **Survival** knife: **Melee**, Damage **4dX**, *Precise*

TAPE RECORDER
Story Points: 1
Contents: Compact cassette, microcassette or reel-to-reel recorder, microphone, extra tape reels or cassettes
Tags: Sound recording

ULTRALIGHT AIRPLANE
Story Points: 2
Contents: Small single-seat or double-seat aircraft with propeller and foldable cloth wing, crash helmet
Tags: Flight: **+2 pips**

VAN
Story Points: 1
Contents: Three seats, steering wheel, huge luggage compartment
Tags: Road travel with huge load

WAD OF CASH
Story Points: 1
Contents: Bank notes, rubber band
Tags: Purchase: **+2 pips**, No questions asked: **+2 pips**

WALKIE-TALKIE
Story Points: 1
Contents: Handset, batteries, microphone, belt strap
Tags: Short-range radio communication

WEIRD TECH

These items are considered either weird science or spy tech. They are beyond the normal technological level of the 1960s, only available to governments, mad scientists, or aliens from other planets (not that there are any on Earth – officially).

ADVANCED JETPACK

Story Points: 4
Contents: Big backpack-sized rocket, flight suit, helmet, ear protectors, 5 minutes flight time
Tags: Personal flight
Requires: Pilot

NIGHT VISION GOGGLES

Story Points: 4
Contents: Goggles that amplify light, allowing the wearer to see in darkness.
Tags: Night vision

DISNEURO RAY

Story Points: 6
Contents: Paralytic ray projector, cable, pocket battery pack, extra battery pack
Tags: Disneuro ray: **Ranged Combat**, **4dX**, Paralytic, *Reload (0)*

HOMEMADE COMPUTER

Story Points: 1
Contents: Main unit, tape storage, teletype terminal
Tags: **Science** and calculations: **+2 pips**

JET FIGHTER

Story Points: 6
Contents: Single-seat or double-seat jet fighter, hangar space, radio, radar
Tags: Air-to-air missile *(4)*: **Ranged Combat**, Damage **6dX**, *Loud*, *Single Shot*, *Fighter scale*
Cannon: **Ranged Combat**, Damage **6dX**, *Short Range*, *Reload (9–0)*, *Fighter scale*
Requires: Pilot, Fighter Pilot

LEVITATION BELT

Story Points: 4
Contents: A belt that allows one person to levitate and carry the equivalent of one adult. Has to be shut down after two minutes, or it will overheat and stop working.
Tags: Personal flight

MAINFRAME COMPUTER

Story Points: 4
Contents: Huge main unit, tape and disk storage, teletype terminal, ticker tape printer, advanced networking, voice control. Can calculate anything.
Tags: **Science** and calculations: **+5 pips**

MASK PRINTER

Story Points: 4
Contents: Prints a lifelike rubber mask from a photo. You will need a matching wig (and possibly a false moustache/beard).
Tags: Disguise: **+5 pips**

MINI SUBMARINE

Story Points: 4
Contents: One-man submarine. The operator needs scuba gear.
Tags: Underwater travel: **+5 pips**

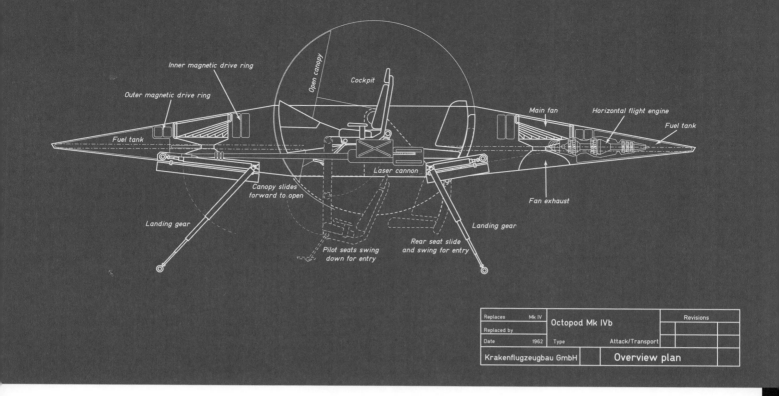

Replaces	Mk IV	Octopod Mk IVb		Revisions	
Replaced by					
Date	1962	Type	Attack/Transport		
Krakenflugzeugbau GmbH		Overview plan			

Labels on diagram: Inner magnetic drive ring; Outer magnetic drive ring; Open canopy; Cockpit; Main fan; Horizontal flight engine; Fuel tank; Fuel tank; Laser cannon; Canopy slides forward to open; Landing gear; Pilot seats swing down for entry; Rear seat slide and swing for entry; Fan exhaust; Landing gear

NET SHOOTER

Story Points: 2

Contents: Rifle that shoots a 2×2 meter net, ensnaring the target. 12 net cartridges, bandolier

Tags: Net shooter: **Ranged Combat**, **4dX**, *Snaring, Single Shot*

NINJA GEAR

Story Points: 2

Contents: Black gi with hood, soft boots, ninja sword, 6 shurikens, climbing claws

Tags: Ninja sword: **Melee**, Damage **5dX**

Climbing claws: **Melee**, Unarmed melee, Damage **4dX**, Worn

Shuriken: **Melee**, Damage **3dX**, *Thrown, Silent, Short Range*

OCTOPOD

Story Points: 4

Contents: Small Octopus flying saucer with two seats and limited cargo space.

Tags: Versatile air transport: **+5 pips**

Requires: Pilot

RAY GUN

Story Points: 6

Contents: Ray gun, holster, 2 extra battery packs, belt pouch for battery packs.

Tags: Ray gun: **Ranged Combat**, **5dX**, *Short Range, Reload (0)*

REP PROTECTORS

Story Points: 2

Contents: Earplugs that protect the wearer from Reverse Encephalography fields (and from loud noises)

Tags: Ignore REP effects

REVERSE ENCEPHALOGRAPHY PROJECTOR

Story Points: 4

Contents: Projector, tripod, carry bag with strap, battery pack

Tags: Giving commands or persuade: **+2 pips**

ROBOT ASSISTANT

Story Points: 4

Contents: Humanoid biped or wheeled robot with voice control. Can obey simple commands and answer simple questions. Stupid as a brick, though.

Tags: Serving tea and accomplishing simple tasks: **+2 pips**

SPACE MOBILITY SUIT

Story Points: 2

Contents: A skintight space suit that uses mechanical pressure rather than air pressure. Lightweight and flexible, but does not protect against radiation or micrometeorites. Or ray guns.

Tags: Space walks: **+2 pips**

AFTER THE ADVENTURE

Why can't I have some wine?

You're not of age.

What's the problem? The adventure ended happily this time. We got away, we blew up that secret Octopus base, you got reunited with your dad...

Who proved to be a parody of a villain in a James Bond movie...

...and we stopped his evil plans. I think that calls for a little celebration. What harm can a glass make?

No!

THE POST-SESSION PHASE

After each game session, there's a post-session phase in which you try to raise Skills or learn languages or Abilities. The post-session phase looks like this:

1   For each tick in the experience checkbox next to a Skill, either make an Experience check for that Skill, a tick for a language if the Skill with the tick is **Languages**, or a tick for an Ability associated with the Skill.
2   Get free improvement ticks (1 to 5).
3   For each improvement ticks, either make an Experience check for that Skill, a tick for a language if the Skill with the tick is **Languages**, or a tick for an Ability associated with the Skill. You may not use more than one improvement tick for any one single Skill – you must use them for different Skills.
4   Get Reward checks after the adventure.
5   Recalculate **Vitality** if necessary.
6   Determine downtime.

126

EXPERIENCE TICKS

Each time you use a Skill in a significant way, you get to tick the experience checkbox next to the Skill value. You don't even have to make a successful task check for the Skill, or indeed even make a check at all, as long as the Skill is used in a significant way.

On the other hand, if you misuse this rule, and just do something inconsequential to get the tick, the Director may override it so that you won't actually get to tick the box.

You can only have one tick per Skill.

After the session, you can use each tick to do one of the following for that Skill:

● Make an Experience check for that Skill.
● Put a tick towards learning a language.
● Put a tick towards gaining an Ability.

FREE IMPROVEMENT TICKS

After each session, the characters get a number of free improvement ticks.

● All present characters get one free improvement tick.
● If the players interacted with Director characters in a significant way beyond just Skill checks, the characters get one additional free improvement tick each.
● If the players interacted with each other in a significant way, the characters get one additional free improvement tick each.
● If the **Plot Hook** characters dragged the others into the adventure, the **Plot Hook** characters get one free improvement tick.
● If the other players worked to make the **Plot Hook** characters the main characters of the adventure, they get one free improvement tick.
● At the end of the adventure, if the players resolved the adventure without unnecessary bloodshed and instead put the villains behind bars, they get three (3) free improvement ticks.
● **Any character that kills any Director character in cold blood forfeits some or all their free improvement ticks this session!**

You can use the free improvement ticks just like you would use a tick in the experience checkbox.

● Make an Experience check for any Skill that you have not used a free improvement tick for.
● Put a tick to learn a language.
● Put a tick to learn an Ability.

You can only use one free improvement tick per Skill, and you can only use one free improvement tick per Ability or language, for a total of two ticks per Skill, Ability or language in each debriefing phase.

EXPERIENCE CHECKS

Experience checks represent an attempt to improve a Skill. When you use an experience tick or a free improvement tick this way:

● Roll **d%** and compare the result with the Skill value. You cannot use **Story Points** to flip this check.
● If the result is equal to or greater than the Skill value, the Skill increases by **1d6**. Erase the old Skill value and write the new value next to the Skill.
● If the result is lower than the Skill value, the Skill is not increased.
● Either way, remove the tick in the checkbox.

I have a tick in **Agility** since the last session. My current Skill level is 63. I roll 73, so I roll a d6 to see how much it increases. The d6 ends up as 5, so I raise my **Agility** from 63 to 68.

I also have **Ranged Combat** 83% and a tick there. I roll 42, so **Ranged Combat** does not increase. It's hard to get better when you're the best.

The best of the best

The highest possible Skill value for a cast character is 106. There is only one path to get this Skill value:

○ Get exactly 100% in a Skill.
○ Roll 100 on the Experience check.
○ Roll 6 on the Skill increase roll.

We never said that it was easy.

LEARNING LANGUAGES

An experience tick for **Languages** can be used to learn a language instead of improving the Skill. You can also use one free improvement tick to learn a language per session, so at each debriefing phase, you can put two ticks at the language.

- Write down the language under **Languages** in the Passport, if you haven't already. Put the language in parentheses to show that you are not fluent yet.
- Put a tick next to the language you want to learn.
- If you used an experience tick for the Skill **Languages**, remove the experience tick from the checkbox next to the Skill.
- When you have five ticks next to the language you want to learn, you become fluent in that language. Remove the parentheses.

Until you have learned a language, you must still make Language task checks to understand the language. However, the task checks are at **+1 pip** for each tick next to the language.

GAINING ABILITIES

Gaining Abilities works in much the same way as learning languages. Each Ability has a cost and one or more associated Skills. Abilities may also have requirements of Skill levels and other Abilities. If you do not fulfil the requirements, you cannot gain the Ability.

You may use one free improvement tick to make a tick for an Ability you want to learn. You may also use one experience tick for one of the associated Skills to make a Gain Ability check. So at each debriefing phase, you have up to two chances per Ability to learn it.

- Check that you fulfil the requirements of the Ability. If you do not fulfil the requirements, you cannot gain the Ability.
- Write down the Ability under Abilities in the Passport, if you haven't already. Put the Ability in parentheses to show that you don't have that Ability yet. Write the cost of the Ability in the box next to it, but make space for the ticks.

- Put a tick next to the Ability.
- If you used an experience tick for one of the associated Skills, remove that tick.
- When you have as many ticks as the cost of the Ability, you have gained the Ability and can use it in future sessions. Remove the parentheses and the cost.

I want to get the Peerage Ability, now that it is official that Graf von Zadrith is my father. Unfortunately, it has the requirement **Status** 65%, and my **Status** is currently 15%. I spend one free improvement tick to make an Experience check. I roll 39, so it goes up by a **d6** roll of 2 to 17.

I want to go for the Ability Judo Master. Its prerequisite is Judo Black Belt, which I already have.

The cost is 5, and I can use **Melee** or **Status**. I have a tick in both, but I can only use one of them since you're only allowed to use one experience tick. I decide to use the one for **Melee** to learn Judo Master, and use the other one to increase **Status** since **Melee** is higher, at 65%. That way, I optimize my chances for both raising **Status** and getting a tick for Judo Master.

I have **Status** 45%, and I roll 28. No gain there – it stays at 45, since I didn't roll 45 or higher. Then I put a tick towards gaining Judo Master. I decide to spend a free improvement tick to put another tick towards gaining Judo Master I spend another free improvement tick on **Status**, and I roll 96 this time. **Status** increases with a **d6** roll of 4 to 49.

I have a third free improvement tick. I decide to use that one on **Melee**. Even if I have used the **Melee** experience tick to get Judo Master, using a free improvement tick is still allowed. This time, I roll 88, so **Melee** increases with a **d6** roll of 3 to 68%. **Karma** doesn't count.

REWARD CHECKS

After an adventure, you can reward the characters with additional reward checks. Reward checks should be tied to particular goals of the adventure and they only get the checks if they fulfil the "victory conditions" of the adventure. Three to five victory conditions is usually about right.

Reward checks are also tied to particular Skills. Typically, Skills like **Status** (fame and glory), **Credit** (monetary rewards) and **Contacts** (new friends) are subject to such reward checks. Depending on the victory conditions you set up, there can be more than one reward check per Skill.

Reward checks work just like any experience tick: they can be used for experience checks, or for learning languages or gaining abilities. Reward checks go beyond the normal "two ticks per Skill, Ability or language" rules.

CHECK IF VITALITY IMPROVES

After all experience is handled, check whether your **Vitality** increases. Your **Vitality** will increase if **Agility** or your highest Combat Skill value increases over certain thresholds.

- **Vitality** is 4 by default.
- If **Agility** or one Combat Skill is 45–64, set **Vitality** to 5.
- If **Agility** or one Combat Skill is 65+, set **Vitality** to 6.

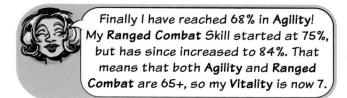

Finally I have reached 68% in Agility! My *Ranged Combat* Skill started at 75%, but has since increased to 84%. That means that both Agility and *Ranged Combat* are 65+, so my Vitality is now 7.

- If *both* **Agility** *and* one Combat Skill are 65+, set **Vitality** to 7.

DOWNTIME

Downtime happens if the end of the session coincides with the end of an adventure. Until the next session, when the next adventure starts, your character can do whatever she wants.

Unless the next adventure starts the next day, you get one or more downtime periods until the next adventure. You can use this table as a guideline.

Table: Very rough guideline to downtime periods

Time to next adventure	# downtime periods
About a week	1
About a month	2
About half a year	3
A year or more	4

Don't worry if you don't know how long it will be until the next adventure starts. You can give the characters one downtime period now, and the rest at the start of the next session.

You can do one of the following downtime activities in each downtime period.

CRAFT

Make one task check for a crafting project (see *Getting gear kits* on page 110). When all task checks in the Skill challenge are done, you will hopefully have crafted the gear and gained access to it.

You can still only have 5 gear kits slotted, but as long as you're near your home or can send for it, you don't have to pay **Story Points** to slot the gear kit in a planning scene during adventures.

MEND AND RECUPERATE

You're on sick leave for at least some time, possibly in the hospital or on vacation, to allow your wounds to heal.

If you spend a downtime period to Mend and Recuperate, drop the **Wounded** Condition.

SHOP

You spend some time to save up or liquidate some of your assets to invest in something that you need. Get one more gear kit, with the Director's approval. Generally, weird science is not available.

You can own more than 5 gear kits, but you can only have 5 gear kits slotted. You can slot the gear kits as you see fit at the start of an adventure. As long as you're near your home or can send for it, you don't have to pay **Story Points** to re-slot your gear kits in a planning scene during adventures.

SOCIALISE

You meet someone that you establish a relationship with (not necessarily a romantic one).

Invent a Director character that you can turn to, and give the Director a short brief on the character (no longer than half a page). Make it an interesting character that the Director wants to use in adventures. Even if the Director doesn't use the character, you can still visit them and use them as a contact to provide you with information, aid, support, or just a relaxing time.

Additionally, start the next episode with 2 extra **Story Points**.

TRAIN

One downtime period allows you to make one extra Improvement check for a Skill, one Learn Language check, or one Learn Ability check. You can still only make two checks for the same Skill, Ability or language during each debriefing phase.

TRAVEL

You travel to some other place and establish a connection there.

Invent a place where you are welcome, and give the Director a short brief on the place (no longer than half a page and a map). Make it an interesting place that motivates the Director to place an adventure in the area.

Additionally, start the next session with 2 extra **Story Points**.

> It's the end of the adventure. The next adventure will take place in the summer of 1965, about four months from now. You get three Downtime periods each until then.

> Arigato! I spend the first Downtime period recuperating so I get rid of the **Wounded** Condition.

> In the second period, I'll travel and make a trip back home to Japan. During the trip, I visit an inn with an onsen hot spring in Fujiyoshida near Mount Fuji together with my parents. At the inn, I get to hear a lot of strange stories involving foxes, ghosts and gods, and recently even flying saucers.

> I write roughly half a page about the inn, list the proprietor and some of the personnel, and also draw a floorplan of the inn to give to the Director. I don't know if the Director will use my story and floorplan – I included the flying saucers and the floorplan just to bait him – but I will start the next session with **6 Story Points** instead of just 4.

> I'll go shopping for the third period! As nice as the Honda moped is, it limits me to the Paris area and its immediate surroundings, so I will get a car instead. I'm thinking a nice Italian sports car, for instance an Alfa Romeo Giulietta Spider.

THE DIRECTOR AND DOWNTIME

Players use Craft, Travel and Socialise to signal to you that they want those objects, places and people to be in future adventures, investing time to create something that advances their character development. They want to use that gadget, go to that place, meet that person, because that's what they feel their character is about.

You should use these resources in your adventures – not at once or even in the next adventure, but in the near future. Doing so has several advantages: not only is it one less resource for you to create, but it is also a resource that the players already care about.

If you have no intention of using anything that the players create in Craft, Travel and Socialise downtime, be honest about it and tell the players. Then they can make an informed decision to use their Downtime that way or not.

Table: Raising Skills

Skill value	Raise Skill by
15–65	**1d6**
66–85	**1d6**/2 (round up)
86–95	**1d6**/3 (round up)
96–100	1

ALTERNATIVE RULE: POINT-BASED EXPERIENCE

If you want more predictability and control over the characters' progression, you can use this optional point-based system instead. Everyone in the group should use the same system, so discuss which one you prefer.

The main difference with the point-based system is that you don't tick Skills when you use them, and you don't get any free improvement ticks. Instead you get Experience Points, which you use to buy Skill raises, Ability ticks and language ticks.

With this system, the post-session phase is a bit different.

1 The Director hands out experience points every session.
2 Use Experience Points to increase Skills or learn Abilities or languages. You can only use one experience point per Skill, Ability or language.
3 After the conclusion of an adventure, the Director hands out reward points tied to specific Skills.
4 Use reward points to increase those specific Skills. If the Skill is at 85% or higher, you can use that reward point to learn an Ability or language. You can only use one reward point per Ability or language.
5 Recalculate **Vitality** if necessary.
6 Determine what you do in the downtime to the next adventure.

GETTING EXPERIENCE POINTS

At the end of the session, the Director hands out experience points, which you can use to increase Skills or learn Abilities and languages. Just like free improvement ticks, you get experience points for:

● Being present.
● Interacting with Director characters
● Interacting with the cast characters
● **Plot Hook** characters dragging other characters into the adventure
● Other characters pushing **Plot Hook** characters into the spotlight
● Resolving an adventure without unnecessary bloodshed (3 points)

Any character that kills a Director character in cold blood forfeits some or all their experience points from the session.

RAISE A SKILL

Refer to the table on the left to see how much your Skill is raised by when you spend one Experience Point. Remember that you can only raise a Skill once per session.

LEARN A LANGUAGE

Use an experience point to learn a language. You can only use one experience point per language.

● Write down the language under **Languages** in the Passport, if you haven't already. Put the language in parentheses to show that you are not fluent in the language yet.
● Put a tick next to the language you want to learn.
● When you have five ticks, you have learned the language.

Until you have learned a language, you must still make Language task checks to understand the language. However, the task checks are at **+1 pip** for each tick next to the language.

GAIN AN ABILITY

Gaining Abilities works in much the same way as learning languages. Each Ability has a cost, and may also have requirements of Skill values or other Abilities. If you do not fulfil the requirements, you cannot gain the Ability.

You may use one experience point to gain an Ability. You can only use one experience point per Ability.

● Check that you fulfil the requirements of the Ability. If you do not fulfil the requirements, you cannot gain the Ability.
● Write down the Ability under Abilities in the Passport, if you haven't already. Put the Ability in parentheses to show that you don't have that Ability yet. Write the cost of the Ability in the box next to it, but make space for the ticks.
● Put a tick next to the Ability.
● When you have as many ticks as the cost of the Ability, you have gained the Ability and can use it in future sessions. Remove the parentheses and the cost.

REWARD POINTS

Instead of Reward checks, you award characters reward points. Reward points are tied to a Skill, just like Reward checks. You can only raise that Skill using that point. See the *Raising Skills table*.

If the Skill is at 85 or higher, you can choose to use that reward point to learn a language or Ability instead of raising a Skill. You can only use one reward point per language or Ability this way.

THE WORLD OF
THE TROUBLESHOOTERS

Do you remember where you were when Monsieur Renard landed on the Moon?

So desu ne... I was at Tanegashima, covering the event for Senjogahara Shinbun. It was just after lunch, and everyone was starving because we did not dare to miss the event. You?

I was in the dining hall at school. We were supposed to be sleeping, but just about everyone of us snuck out of the dormitories and watched the event on television. Paul, where were you?

Oh, ehm, I missed it. There was this safe in Marseille, and the security guards were nailed to the television, so... you know, when opportunity rises...

THE DAY THAT
CHANGED THE WORLD

March 19th, 1964, was not a Thursday like any other. Worldwide, people were glued to their television sets, or flocked to home appliance stores, even if it was in the middle of the night in Europe, to watch the first Moon landing.

At 04:50 Greenwich Mean Time, a joint Japanese-French project reached its climax as the giant atomic rocket *Kaguyahime*, the Moon Princess – affectionately called Monsieur Renard ("Mister Fox") in France because of its orange-red paint job – gently touched down in Mare Nectaris. Just under two hours later, Commander Toyomi Ichi and Captain Yvette Collard stepped off the elevator and onto the Moon's surface.

Distorted by the long distance from the Moon, the first words from the lunar surface echoed around the globe in broken English: "*We make this step together, not as conquerors, not as representatives of Japan and France, but as humans from the planet Earth, and as explorers of a new world.*"

Most people in Europe were late for work that day.

Welcome to the world of *The Troubleshooters*.

A note about history

In this chapter, you will find the Moon landing is not the only discrepancy between "real" history and what is presented in the game world. This is often by intent – we want to evoke a romantic and adventurous world, and sometimes events happen earlier, later, not at all, or not in the way our history books say.

The consequence for you is that you don't have to know the 1960s in detail. Go with what sounds like the 1960s and will be the most fun.

THE WORLD OF THE TROUBLESHOOTERS

The Troubleshooters is set between the latter half of the 1960s and the first half of the 1970s. The official start date is 1965 and adventures will have a suggested start date in release order, but the exact date is not that important.

History in *The Troubleshooters* is similar to what we are all familiar with, but it has some differences. We are not interested in simulating history, and we don't want to constrain you by a fixed history that you can't change. Most important, we don't require you to study history to play the game. We want you to have the freedom to be wrong without being bothered or hampered by know-it-alls.

One of the best ways to tell people that it's okay to be wrong in a historical setting is to use an alternative timeline with some demonstrable differences. That way, nobody can complain about you being wrong – because in this timeline, you are right. The showcase event in *The Troubleshooters* is the Franco-Japanese Moon landing in March 1964, before the timeline of the game started. The joint Japanese-French mission launched from Tanegashima Island in Japan using a huge single-stage atomic rocket. The rocket (without its atomic reactor, and with the surrounding structures replaced and decontaminated) is currently on display next to Tokyo Tower. Standing almost 100 meters tall, it is just under a third of the height of the Tokyo tower.

For the most part, the history in *The Troubleshooters* is not that different from the real world. It is a fact in *The Troubleshooters* that the World Wars happened, and that Europe is divided into a Western bloc and an Eastern bloc.

Fantasy tourism

It is sometimes said that roleplaying games are *fantasy shopping*. You go through the lists of skills, abilities, magic items and whatnot, you plan what you should get and how you can get it, and then you act on that plan. It's not that much different from shopping for clothes, furniture or construction supplies.

While there are such elements in *The Troubleshooters*, there is another element: *The Troubleshooters* is also *fantasy tourism*. It is about visiting exotic places without ever having to leave the room.

This fits well into the tradition that *The Troubleshooters* is inspired by. Do you know what Carl Barks, Hergé and Hal Foster have in common, other than making comics? Many of their adventures were inspired by National Geographic. Even though they rarely left their hometowns, they still managed to portray stories that took place across the entire globe thanks to this inspiration, and they brought us along for the ride.

This chapter is a bit like a tourist guide for the exact same reason: to enable you to take part in this fantasy tourism.

THE ZEITGEIST OF THE TROUBLESHOOTERS

If you have to pick two words to describe the zeitgeist of *The Troubleshooters*, then it is probably "progress" and "optimism". The Second World War has ended and Europe has been freed from the yoke of National Socialism. Europe has largely recovered and rebuilt, and science and technology promises a better future for everyone, no matter which side of the Iron Curtain they live on.

Even though Europe is divided between the Capitalist Western Europe and the Communist Eastern Europe, and things can get tense and even hostile, both sides avoid direct confrontation and even work together in secret against common enemies.

Through music and mass media, a youth culture is emerging and counter-culture and anti-establishment views are in the air. The conflict in Indochina, although low-key, is catalysing a peace and anti-war movement. And in the homes and on university campuses, women have found their voices and taken their place in society.

NOT YOUR GRANDMOTHER'S EUROPE

Just as there isn't a fixed timeline in *The Troubleshooters*, there isn't a fixed geography either. If we had a detailed map of the world of *The Troubleshooters*, you would find some countries that don't exist in the real world.

But we don't have a detailed map, and that's on purpose. We have left the world generally like our own, but with lots of blank spaces for new countries should you need one.

Nine glorious countries that don't exist

- **Al-Ansur:** The small desert kingdom in Arabia is right in the transition between the traditional Arabic society and the modern world. There is still a thriving nomadic Bedouin culture in the country, while the capital is a modern shining beacon in the desert. Al-Ansur's greatest natural resource is not oil (although that exists), but water: there is an underground aquifer which makes Al-Ansur into an oasis the size of a small country, leading to a tradition of water management that stretches into antiquity. Al-Ansur's best defence is the desert, and the second best defence is a military alliance with France, allowing France to have an air force base in the middle of the Middle East.
- **Arenwald:** Formerly a part of the Austro-Hungarian Empire, this alpine principality is squeezed in between Hungary, Sylveria and Yugoslavia, as a West European sliver driven into the Eastern bloc. Its greatest claim to fame is that the Arlberg Orient Express line from London to Athens goes right through Arenwald and its capital Gleichen, and that it has some of the best ski slopes in Europe available to tourists in

Western Europe. Being surrounded by three Eastern bloc powers and a popular tourist attraction, it is an ideal entry point for spies from the Communist bloc coming into the West.
- **Bukhustan:** On the plains in the shadow of the Tengri massif, east of the Urals, lies this little socialist republic that nobody has tried to conquer, because there is not much to conquer. Recently, deposits of rare earth metals have been found, which has opened up the country for trade with China and the Soviet Union, its most powerful neighbours. The Bukhustani government in the capital Tengrigrad is on somewhat friendly terms with both, despite China and the Soviet Union not being friendly to one another at all.
- **Katsutori:** Katsutori is a pacific archipelago southwest of Guam, formerly a British, German and Japanese colony in that order. It was made a UN protectorate after the war, but has recently gained its independence. Katsutori is a principality whose Princess Regent is distantly related to the Japanese imperial family. It is a tropical paradise which is quickly becoming popular and more accessible with the advent of the jetliner. There are many left-over bunkers and pillboxes from the war, along with unexplored underground passageways built by the Japanese during the same period. Despite the heavy fortifications, the islands never became a target. The islands were a bit out of the way and as the Japanese empire collapsed they no longer held any strategic interest to anyone, beyond tying down a substantial part of the Japanese army.
- **Montecasciano:** In the Pennines, the small city republic of Montecasciano remains independent from the rest of Italy, but has a passport and currency union with Italy. It is mostly known for producing flower decorations for some events in Europe, and for its wine production. Casciano wines are rather heavy and strong and are very popular with red meat or on their own. Montecasciano used to be a water resort, but that ended with the passing of the last century. It is still a place for the jet set elite to get away to, on a rather strict "invite-only" basis: you have to know someone in Montecasciano to be accepted. It's not easy, but once it happens, it's a good place to stay if you do not want to be haunted by paparazzi all the time and don't mind the rustic setting. Your host usually has a shotgun loaded with rock salt and a good aim.
- **San Ariel:** The people of the island San Ariel in the Caribbean suffer under a ruthless dictator. The island republic has not had general elections since the coup in 1949 and the courts are almost comically corrupt, more resembling an auction for the judge's favour than a trial. San Ariel is pretty much the dictionary

definition of "banana republic", rife with corruption and nepotism. Bananas are even the main export. As long as American fruit companies continue to bribe General Auguste and lobby the US government, there's no real chance for change.

- **Sitomeyang:** Between Indonesia and Australia, on a chain of about 1,000 mostly volcanic islands, lies the small kingdom of Sitomeyang. It is a cultural melting pot: the main population is Javanese, but there are also large Malay, French, Chinese and English minorities. The kingdom has never been a colony, but in the past some islands have been rented or occupied by the English, French and Chinese. After the Second World War, most of the islands were returned except for some of those in the north that ended up as part of Indonesia. There's still a border dispute about those islands. The capital, Selangit, has a distinct colonial style to it, but is rapidly being developed into a modern city.

- **Sylveria:** The Socialist Republic of Sylveria, formerly the other half of the principality Arenwald, is now an independent republic and aligned to the Eastern bloc. At the end of the Second World War, about a third of Sylveria was occupied by the Soviet army, and became a country of its own. The Communist Sylverian government in Arenesti has stated that its goal is the reunification of the country under Communist control, by whatever means necessary. Arenwald, on the other hand, has not given up its claim to "Sylverian Arenwald", and refuses to recognise its neighbour. Sylveria's main exports are iron, lead, zinc and copper to the Soviet Union, and spies to the West.

- **Zewange:** The East African republic Zewange is split between a developed and democratic coastal region with the capital Undure and an underdeveloped and tribal inland. President Chiedza Dziike is currently the only female president in Africa, and she is not looked on favourably by the tribal leaders of the inland regions, even if she is desperately trying to modernise Zewange's education system and agricultural and fishing industries. There has so far been four attempts on her life, including one notorious duel of science versus "voodoo magic" that actually proved to be an attempted poisoning by one of her aides.

A WORLD DIVIDED

One of the things that *did* happen was the Second World War. It ended with the Allied forces defeating those of the Axis on two fronts, the Soviet Union taking Berlin in late April 1945 and the United States dropping two atomic bombs on Japan in August the same year.

But there were already cracks in the Allied front as the war ended: the Capitalist Western allies and the Communist Soviet Union were too different. As a result, the world was divided. An iron curtain descended across Europe, and across the world, the two systems now face one another by proxy.

So far, the two blocs have avoided direct confrontation with one another. The closest they came to an outright exchange was the Cuban missile crisis in 1962, and since those thirteen days, both blocs have gone to great lengths to normalise their relations and create a spirit of detente.

A WORLD UNITED

The technological marvels of the jetliner and the car, the appearance of an urban middle class, and the expanding economy have all led to something new: travel abroad. Both professionally and on vacation, ordinary people visit foreign countries and experience other cultures. The effort to open the borders between countries in Western Europe for trade and travel has brought an unprecedented unity to Europe.

The growing popularity of media forms like music, movies and television also exposes people to foreign cultures. Magazines and the press contribute as well. Photo magazines provide a window into other cultures through glossy, high-quality, four-colour prints, and every major newspaper worthy of its name must have a foreign correspondent in at least the capitol city of most countries.

You don't have to travel to experience foreign cultures. They come to you. All you have to do is keep an open mind and greet the strangers who visit your country.

RELIGION

Even if Europe has freedom of religion, Europe has been dominated by Christianity for a very long time. Some countries have a Protestant state church, some adhere to Catholicism, and still some, particularly in Eastern Europe, have no state church at all. Other religions are at least tolerated, although there is often some bias against them.

Religion is generally respected and well-perceived if it is traditional and low-key, but it is by no means safe from satire and criticism. It is quite common to make fun of the Catholic church in particular, with a certain level of loving irreverence, and the most ardent brimstone-and-fire Protestants are just plain ridiculed.

Religion in your adventures

Kick upwards: Religion is a sensitive matter. At most, poke fun at the subject, but there's rarely a need to vilify a particular religion unless it somehow serves the plot. And always make sure that all the player's are okay with doing so beforehand.

Clues: Churches, temples and mosques are often full of interesting clues that you can use in your adventures. Use altar paintings, statues, hidden scribbles, old religious texts and so on, and make them clues in your adventures. Like most clues, give the basic clue to the players "for free", and add deeper clues for story points or successful task checks.

Help: One thing that religious institutions often do is help people, through charities and direct action. Characters can get care, rest, refuge, and often expert help at a church, temple or monastery.

Mythology: Be inspired by the mythology of present religions and ancient ones for mystic adventures. Make sure that they are kept ambiguous, and could be interpreted in multiple ways.

THINGS THAT DON'T (OR ALMOST DON'T) EXIST

The era of *The Troubleshooters* is different from the world of today. The world is more analogue, more mechanical, more electrical, and nowhere as digital as today.

- **CDs:** Music is either broadcast on radio, or sold on vinyl. You can also find a compact cassette player in many cars, and battery-powered record players are common. There are a few other strange, mostly tape, formats. CDs and streaming media are out – and no Spotify. Sorry.
- **Cell phones:** There aren't any cell phones. There are radio telephones at best: they use VHF or UHF to connect to the regular wired telephone network at a receiving station. Radio telephones are not only expensive, but also heavy. Most of them are built into vehicles.

  The majority of people only have a landline connected to a single telephone in the home, usually in the hall of the house. In older apartment buildings, there is one line to the doorkeeper's desk, which tenants can use for a fee. Companies have several landlines connected to a switchboard, where receptionists connect incoming calls to the right recipient.
- **Computers:** Computers do exist. They're just huge and consume a lot of power, or are very limited. At best, you control the computer by typing commands on a keyboard. Many computers are programmed using punch cards or magnetic tape, and the few home models that are commercially available (and that you have to assemble yourself) are programmed using switches.
- **EU:** The European Union hasn't been formed yet. There is the European Economic Community (EEC), established in 1958 as the successor to the Coal & Steel Union, but it is still more of an economic trade agreement than a political union, and it only has six members. The European Free Trade Area (EFTA) is an even looser free-trade association comprising Great Britain, the Nordic countries, and Switzerland.

- **Fast food franchises:** Fast food does exist. However, it's mostly in the form of diners, pubs, kiosks or stands. Fast food franchises are mostly an American phenomenon, so don't expect double golden arches on the horizon in every city in Europe.
- **Home video:** There's no Netflix, no DVD or bluray, not even VHS. If you want to watch a movie, you go to the cinema. If you're lucky, you can get some movies on film which you can play back using a projector.
- **The internet:** The idea of linking computers together is primitive at best. It is done by the military to link radar sites to command centres, and by airline companies to book tickets and hotel rooms. It is certainly not an open information or communications network. If you want to reach someone, you don't use email or social media: you call them, visit them or send a telegram or letter. If you want to look up something, you don't google it: you visit a library.

THINGS THAT DO EXIST!

- **Cigarettes:** It is not yet seen as dangerous or wrong to smoke, so everyone smokes (about 40% of adults). Even Éloïse probably smokes as well, but in secret so that the nuns at the school don't notice.
- **Housing:** It is pretty easy to get an apartment. It will probably not be luxurious or big, the toilet is in the yard, and there is a communal washing room – and the landlady will not accept visitors of the opposite sex. You have to use her telephone if you want to call someone, or the phone box on the corner. But it is your own home, and the rent is cheap.
- **Jobs:** It is possible to get an unqualified or even semi-qualified job the day you graduate. Just walk to the local factory or store and ask for the manager, show your grades and an introduction letter from Dad, and presto! you have a job. Fifty years later, you get a gold fob and a pension, probably from the same place. Changing employer is not that common yet – you are expected to make your career within the company.
- **Long distance telephone calls:** With the slow decline of telegraph services, long distance telephone calls are becoming more commonplace. You can instantly recognise them by the low hiss on the line. The easiest way to place a long distance call is by the use of the operator of the telephone company, who will do the routing to the destination. Long distance calls are often expensive.
- **Longwave radio:** One cool thing you can do with an ordinary radio is to set it to the longwave band and turn the dial until you find a transmitter half a continent away. The sound quality will not be fantastic, but you will be able to listen to the greatest hits from the other side of the Iron Curtain.
- **Space stations:** Well, there are two: the US *Aurora*, and the Soviet *Budushcheye-1*. *Aurora* is a science platform, consisting of cylindrical sections joined in a cross-like pattern. It is strictly off limits to non-US Air Force and Strategic Air Command personnel,

causing many to speculate that it is a secret weapons platform.

The toroidal *Budushcheye-1* was similarly off-limits to non-Soviet citizens, but its focus was on reaching the Moon – which the Japanese-French team did at least two years earlier. That limit has been formally lifted, so in theory, it would be possible for a non-Soviet astronaut to visit *Budushcheye-1*.

- **Steam trains:** There are actually still steam trains running, even in Europe, although steam locomotives are being replaced by their diesel and electric counterparts. In Britain, there are a few remaining steam services, including the Fifteen Guinea Special between Liverpool and Manchester and the Flying Scotsman on the London-Edinburgh service.

In other corners of our planet, particularly in the undeveloped world, steam trains are also still chugging along. Many narrow-gauge rail lines take locals, goods and adventurers into forests, jungles and mountains.

- **Telegrams:** Although you can place international telephone calls, it is still often easier and cheaper to send a telegram if you want to reach someone on the other side of the planet. In the big cities, telegrams are generally delivered within the hour. Telegrams are paid for per word, usually by the sender.
- **Youth culture:** Until recently, you were a child, and then you were an adult. Starting some time after the war, the youth began to be seen as something of their own, unique group – to a great extent because they are an attractive market. As an example, portable record players are not aimed at the adult population, but at youths who want to take their music with them, and the pop and rock'n'roll music they play is specifically aimed at them. But this goes both ways: youth are starting to influence culture directly. The Japanese edition of Time Magazine has even listed school girls collectively among the 100 most influential Japanese persons in history.

THE COLD WAR

At the end of the Second World War, tension was already building between the Western allies and the Soviet Union. After the war, the tension resulted in a Europe divided in two by the "Iron Curtain", dominated by the two superpowers, the United States of America and the Union of Soviet Socialist Republics.

The superpowers' intelligence organizations, such as the CIA, KGB, and MI6, are active all over the world "to block our enemies' war-mongering plots". They are involved in everything from espionage via assassinations and gun-running to coup-d'états – even proxy wars happen.

Nine shady intelligence organisations

- **CIA:** The United States' foreign intelligence service has a bit of a tainted reputation. It is very good at intelligence analysis, but some of its covert actions abroad have backfired quite a lot.
- **DST:** The *Direction de la Surveillance du Territoire* ("Directorate of Territorial Surveillance") is responsible for counter-intelligence, counter-terrorism, and the general security of France.
- **GRU:** The Soviet Union's other security agency is the GRU, the Main Intelligence Directorate (*Glavnoye razvedyvatel'noye upravleniye*). It handles military intelligence and signals intelligence, and is attached to the Soviet Army's general staff.
- **KGB:** The Soviet Union's security agency, KGB (short for *Komitet Gosudarstvennoy Bezopasnosti*, or "the Committee for State Security") handles both internal security, border security, along with the intelligence agency and the secret police. It is vast and powerful, with its own army and air force.
- **MI5:** The Security Service, more commonly known as Military Intelligence Section 5 or MI5 since 1914, is the security and counter-intelligence organisation of the United Kingdom. Its main focus is on breaking Soviet spy rings.
- **MI6:** Like MI5, "MI6" is not the actual name of the Secret Intelligence Service, the foreign service of British intelligence. They are very good at turning high officials in the Eastern bloc into valuable intelligence assets.
- **Mossad:** One of the most gutsy intelligence agencies, this Israeli agency has undertaken operations all over the world, including kidnapping Nazi leader Adolf Eichmann and smuggling him to Israel to stand trial.
- **SDECE:** The French intelligence service SDECE (*Service de Documentation Extérieure et de Contre-Espionnage*, or "External Documentation and Counter-Espionage Service") has a reputation for some bizarre operations, ranging from stealing Soviet fuel to analysing anti-freeze additives to kidnapping and drugging Soviet agents on the Orient Express.
- **Stasi:** The main task of the East German Ministry for State Security is to spy on its own people, through a network of informants. Stasi also conducts operations and espionage in foreign countries.

SPIES IN YOUR ADVENTURES

Of course there will be spies in your adventures. If your characters aren't spies, they will meet definitely meet some.

Enemies: The things spies do are by definition illegal in the country where they are acting. That makes them obvious enemies to your characters.

Allies: Quite often, spies try to save the world – especially when they are trying to stop the Octopus or terrorists. Characters may find themselves side by side with elite spies from other countries working towards the same goal.

Resources: Sometimes, spy agencies can provide resources to the characters – intelligence, weapons, explosives, tools, vehicles. The characters should be wary, though. The aid often comes at a price.

Masters: If the characters are spies themselves, the agencies will give them an assignment from time to time, which kicks off an entirely new adventure!

MONEY

Money is weird: money has a value because people believe money has a value. As long as enough people agree on that, money can be used to make trade easier. That's also the reason for financial crises: people stop believing money (or another important commodity) has value anymore.

Money is issued by a country's central bank. In some cases, money is tied to gold (the United States still has a gold standard), and some currencies are fixed to another currency or a basket of currencies. Some currencies are only based on the value people think they have.

Salary: A blue-collar male worker is paid on average about 1500 francs/month, while a female blue-collar worker is paid around 1250 francs/month. White collar jobs are better paid: even a janitor, store clerk or technical assistant will have a salary comparable to blue collar workers, but the higher the position, the higher the wages. Managers can earn up to 5000 francs per month, and directors and board members can earn even more.

In most cases, you get paid every second Friday, on the 25th of every month, or the last Friday of the month. The salary is often paid in cash or as a cheque from the boss or staff office, or from the local bank office which gets the payment list from the company. Expect long queue lines both at the staff office and the bank on payday. People not only have a salary to collect, but also utility bills, rent and mortgages to pay. Rent is not that big a problem, as you often pay the landlord directly in cash.

Cheques: Speaking of cheques, almost everyone has a cheque book. In essence, a cheque is a form telling the bank "pay the person holding this form this much money, and deduct it from my account". Most people only accept cheques from people they know and trust, because there's nothing that prevents anyone from writing a bad cheque which will bounce.

Savings: There are lot of local "mutual savings banks", small bank offices that accept their customers' deposits and pay interest in return for being able to invest the deposited money. You need a bankbook to keep track of deposits and withdrawals. Most of the time you have to visit the physical bank where you save your money, although some larger brands can wire money from one office to another.

Credit cards: Credit cards are mostly an American thing, Diner's Club being among the first. Do not expect them to be accepted in Europe. Some international hotel chains or larger hotels might be able to accept a credit card, but in general, expect to pay in cash.

Traveller's cheques: Instead of credit cards, traveller's cheques are common ways of carrying money to foreign countries without risking losing actual money.

You purchase traveller's cheques in different denominations and then cash them in at offices in other countries.

Living costs: While we're talking about this boring economic stuff, it is quite possible to support a family on a single income, and still put aside a little for the children. Here is a rough outline of average living costs in francs/month.

	Single household	Family with children
Housing	100	160
Food	200	400
Clothing	51	131
House furnishings	37	107
Medical care and hygiene	23	57
Recreation	106	146
Transportation and vehicle	110	116
Miscellaneous	53	103
Total living costs	680	1220

139

CURRENCIES

In 1960, the new franc or *nouveau franc* was introduced in France, worth 100 old francs, thus revaluating the currency and boosting the economy. People still use old francs to describe large sums.

You buy foreign currency at the bank or at a currency exchange. The rate changes daily, and sometimes even more often.

Country	Currency	Exchange rate
France	French francs	1.00
United States	US dollar	0.20
Switzerland	Swiss franc	0.88
China	Chinese yuan renminbi	0.50
Japan	Japanese yen	73.5
United Kingdom	British pound	0.073
West Germany	German deutsche mark	0.81
Sweden	Swedish krona	1.04
Hong Kong	Hong Kong dollar	1.17
Australia	Australian dollar	0.18
Spain	Spanish peseta	12.2
Italy	Italian lira	127.5
Greece	Greek drachma	6.12
Belgium	Belgian francs	10.1
Soviet Union	Soviet rubles	0.18
East Germany	East German mark	0.81*
Poland	Polish zloty	0.33
Turkey	Turkish lira	1997
Portugal	Portuguese escudo	26.6
—	Gold (per troy ounce)	175.6

* The official exchange rate is at parity with deutsche marks. On the black market, you get about 5–10 East German marks for 1 deutsche mark.

Multiply the amount of francs with the exchange rate to get the equivalent amount in the target currency. *Divide the amount of foreign currency* with the exchange rate to get the equivalent amount in French francs.

LIVING

In the city, you don't have much choice: you have to live in an apartment. Most are owned by private landlords. The landlord or the caretaker often lives on the first floor and in many cases owns the only telephone in the house.

Often, there's also a laundry shed in the yard or the basement, and sometimes even a common toilet and washing room. If there is an emergency, you have to do it in the potty and then carry it out in the morning. However, there's a water closet and sometimes even a bathtub in most apartments, due to the hygiene offensive in the 1950s where many apartments were reconditioned with modern closets.

SERVICE AND TIPPING

Automation and self-service is not yet a thing. Hotels have a concierge who takes care of the guests' needs and expectations. Bell-boys carry the luggage to the rooms. Ocean liners and jetliners have stewards and stewardesses who cater to the whims of the passengers. Apartment buildings often have a portier to help guests and tenants, and tend to the building.

Speaking of service, this is an era where tipping is still a thing in Europe. Tipping is not mandatory, but a reward for good service. if the service was good, it's rude to not tip. In most situations – porters, bell boys and so on – it's usually whatever loose change you have in your pockets.

MONEY IN YOUR ADVENTURES

The currency table is useful if you should find price information from 1965 but not in French francs, to give you a sense of what things cost back then. For instance, if you have the list price for a Ford Mustang of $2279, you get that it is equivalent to 2279/0.20 = 11,395 francs, which for a blue-collar worker with a family would be about 7.5 months salary, or almost 30 months surplus from their budget. So in that way, you get a sense of plausible prices of the era and what they mean to the average François.

You can also use the currency table as flavour when travelling around the world.

But that's just understanding the value of money at the time. As *The Troubleshooters* employs a more abstract system using the **Credit** Skill and Abilities, you don't have to worry about money, cost of living or currency conversion in the game.

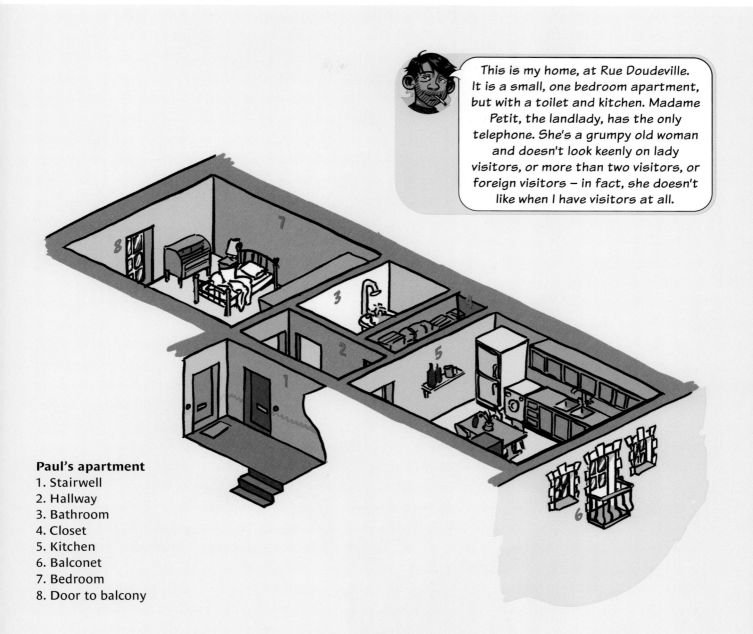

This is my home, at Rue Doudeville. It is a small, one bedroom apartment, but with a toilet and kitchen. Madame Petit, the landlady, has the only telephone. She's a grumpy old woman and doesn't look keenly on lady visitors, or more than two visitors, or foreign visitors – in fact, she doesn't like when I have visitors at all.

Paul's apartment
1. Stairwell
2. Hallway
3. Bathroom
4. Closet
5. Kitchen
6. Balconet
7. Bedroom
8. Door to balcony

Don't worry too much about the characters' homes. Of course they live somewhere. If they draw maps of their apartments, so much the better – that makes them invested in the world.

Try to resist the temptation of having a fight break out in their homes. Rather, respect that a character's home is meant to be a place of peace, where they can rest between adventures. If you have to have a fight at the character's home, don't overdo it and do it rarely.

AIR MAJESTIQUE

Service aérien affilié   Affiliated airline service
Service régulier   Regular service
Service Concorde   Concorde service

TRAINS, PLANES AND AUTOMOBILES

The world is getting smaller. Airplanes, ships and railways allow you to get to more places faster, and telephones connect every little corner of the Earth.

AIR TRAVEL

Air travel has a flair of its own. The world is connected in a way it has never been before. The two revolutions of the era are the Jumbo Jet, a jet plane so huge that it has two floors; and the Supersonic Jet, that makes the hop over the Atlantic in five hours or less.

The supersonic Concorde, Boeing SST and Tupolev Tu-144 made the world smaller. Not everyone can afford to ride them, but for those in a rush and with the money to spend, supersonic jets are the way to go!

Other modes of flying are not cheap either. With purchase and operating costs, there's no room for budget air travel, and even a relatively modest flight in a Jumbo Jet is a once in a lifetime event for many working-class families. But on the other hand, there's luxury and service in air travel. Even when flying economy, you get decent service.

At the other end of the spectrum are the bush hoppers: small planes taking off and landing on primitive grass or gravel air strips, or sea planes using lakes and rivers.

Air Majestique – "Travel like a King"

Fictional airlines like Air Majestique are a good way to offer air travel without the Director having to get bogged down in research. (The other way is to not give a damn about research and just wing it – pun intended.)

Air Majestique is a French private airline with routes all over the world. Most of the routes go to and from France and the majority of routes are in Europe.

Air Majestique is the first private airline and the first airline outside British Overseas Air Corporation and Air France to get the Aérospatiale/BAC Concorde. Their seven Concordes fly daily to and from New York, bi-weekly to and from Tokyo by way of Miami, Los Angeles and Honolulu as well as Sydney by way of Bombay and Hong Kong, and weekly to Buenos Aires and Rio de Janeiro. Other routes are served by Boeing 707s, 737s and DC-10s.

Service on board is good, even splendid, especially on the Concorde flights where they truly live up to their slogan.

Nine glorious airplanes

- **Aérospatiale/BAC Concorde:** The first supersonic jetliner has just entered service for the BOAC, Air France and Air Majestique in the world of *The Troubleshooters*. Pan Am, Qantas and JAL are next to receive the first of their ordered planes.
- **Antonov An-2:** The biggest biplane in the world, this rugged old workhorse still flies for many bush airlines and private pilots. Its simple design means that it can be fixed using the same toolkit as you would a car, and its big balloon wheels can land on just about any moderately flat surface.
- **Boeing 707:** One of the most successful commercial jetliners in service, this four-engine plane is used everywhere. It isn't luxurious, but it does its job on mid-range lines.
- **Boeing 747:** A newcomer on the market and a giant, this airplane gives the term "jumbo jet" its meaning. It has two decks, the upper deck with a lounge, and typically more than 360 seats. It is a true long-distance liner, making the world smaller even for average people. Not every airport can accommodate this giant.
- **De Havilland Comet:** The Comet was the first jetliner in the world, with its maiden flight in 1949. Sadly, there were a few early disasters with the plane, and other manufacturers came to dominate the market. But the Comet still flies.
- **Douglas DC-3:** Based on the C-47 Skytrain that served the Allies in the Second World War, this old workhorse still flies, mostly in third-world countries, because of its ruggedness and easy maintenance.
- **Douglas DC-8:** This four-engine mid-range jetliner is in service with just about every airline in the world. It's not the most modern jetliner, but it has a proven track record.
- **Lake Buccaneer:** A four-seat amphibious airplane, capable of landing on rough runways as well as on water. It has a pusher propeller in a nacelle over the wing. The plane is rather popular among bush pilots in northern climates.
- **Saunders-Roe SR.45 Princess:** One of the last flying boats in service, this luxury giant has an uncertain future. It still flies between Southampton and New York, carrying about a hundred passengers in luxury and comfort, but it is likely to be overtaken by the Boeing 747 and Concorde and retired within a few years.

Challenge: Unnecessary complications

The logistics of air travel in 1965 is not as developed as present day, which means that displaced luggage, delays, and other mishaps often associated with air travel are even more common. Use this challenge if you want to risk some farcical sidetracks when going by air. Don't use it if such sidetracks would risk derailing the adventure.

Credit, because service costs
Red Tape, to navigate air travel bureaucracy
Status, because the famous get better service
Willpower, to not give up

Modifications:
–2 pips on all task checks if the journey ends, starts or makes a stop in a country with a bit too much mañana.
–2 pips on one task check per change of flights.

Outcome:
Great outcome: Superb service. The luggage is waiting for the characters on a cart when they arrive.
Good outcome: As expected. The characters have to wait for their luggage at the luggage track, but nothing is lost and there are no unexpected delays.
Limited outcome: Choose one of the following: one bag with one gear kit is misplaced and arrives a day later (your choice); the group misses a connecting flight, delaying you for **2d6** hours; one character is fined in customs for a minor infringement and get **–2 pips** on the next **Credit task check**.
Bad outcome: One flight is cancelled for mechanical reasons. A replacement flight is available the next day, but the characters have to stay at the airport hotel for the night. Have them make a **Red Tape task check:** if successful, the stay is at no cost. If failed, the next **Credit task check** for all characters is at **–2 pips**.
Abysmal outcome: The luggage is lost. All gear kits not in the carry-on baggage are not available until the end of the adventure. The characters get **Story Points** for the lost luggage.

BY CAR

The road network in Europe is mostly old with meandering two-lane roads, or even single-lane roads, crossing the countryside on the same paths since time immemorial. Motorways are not as common in Europe compared to the United States, but generally of good quality.

The European road network, plus narrow city streets and tight corners, means that European customers and car manufacturers generally prefer better handling and turning over speed. Even European supercars like the new Lamborghini Miura have a handling to match the narrow roads and city streets.

Nine glorious cars

- **Alfa Romeo Giulietta:** The name of this series of cars is a play on Shakespeare's Romeo and Juliet. It is a beautiful car with a romantic flair. The four-seater models are popular family cars, but there are also two-seater sport models, including a spider. It has even had some success as a racing car.
- **Citroën DS:** A technological marvel, the DS set new standards in ride comfort, handling and braking. It is a large, expensive executive car, but nonetheless it is one of the most successful cars ever, and certainly one of the most beautiful.
- **Ford Mustang:** The recent launch of the Ford Mustang, the archetypal American muscle car, is probably the most successful launch since the Model A. Relatively affordable with a list price of $2,368, it was an instant hit in the United States. Quite a few have even reached Europe.
- **Isetta:** After the Second World War, microcars became popular in Europe as demand for motorised transport increased but fuel prices rose and metal was sparse. The egg-shaped Isetta is one of them. It was designed in Italy by Iso Autoveicoli, but licensed to many companies all over Europe, the BMW Isetta being the most well-known and most produced. In France, where it is known as the "yogurt pot", the Isetta is produced by VELAM.
- **Land Rover:** After the War, the Rover Company's line of luxury cars were no longer in demand, and resources were limited. Instead, the company came up with a light utility vehicle, like the Willys Jeep but mainly for agricultural use, just to get the cash flowing. Instead, it proved to be a big hit. It is almost as ubiquitous as it is indestructible: the company claims that about 70% of all Land Rovers built are still in use.
- **Mercedes-Benz 300 SL:** The 300 SL was built for racing. The choice of a tubular frame for the chassis of the 300 SL not only gave the car exceptionally low mass and high stability, but also resulted in deep side panels and high instep. For this reason, Mercedes could not use regular doors, but instead had to make the eye-catching "gullwing" doors.

- **Morris Mini-Minor:** To some extent, the Mini is the response to microcars like the Isetta: the British Motor Corporation decided to design a "proper miniature car". Being a smidgen over 3 metres long and under 1.4 metres wide and tall, the Mini is not just a miniature car, but also a proper car with a surprisingly roomy interior. The Cooper S variant has had great success in racing and rally.
- **Moskvitch-408:** From the other side of the Iron Curtain comes the Moskvitch-408. It's a no-nonsense saloon car, "more worth than its price" according to the sales slogan, and does what it is supposed to do with no frills. It sells well in the Eastern bloc, but half of the production is for export. In France, the car is known as the Moskvitch 1300.
- **Volvo P1800:** This list lacks a touring car, and for that purpose, Volvo P1800 is a good choice. Based on the Volvo Amazon but with a more powerful dual carburettor engine and with a body developed under the tutelage of designer Pietro Frua, the P1800 is a touring car for the stars.

BY TRAIN

Unlike the United States, the invention of the motorway has not led to the demise of railway travel. On the contrary, countries in Europe have spent huge sums of money on electrification, expansion and harmonisation of the railway system. Commuter trains bring workers from the suburbs to the city centre, and express trains connect the cities of Europe.

The cost of bringing railway travel to the future is that it has become a mass transit system. With some exceptions, railway travel no longer has the romance of the past.

As with everything else since the War, the Iron Curtain also divides rail travel. Even going from West Germany to West Berlin means going through a closely watched railway corridor with stern-faced East German border guards making inspections. The divide put a halt to the classical Orient Express after the war, but the relations have improved enough for the lines to open again. But expect frequent inspections and delays once you cross the Iron Curtain.

Nine glorious train services

- **20th Century Limited:** Running from Grand Central Terminal in New York to LaSalle Street Station in Chicago, this express train is the ultimate passenger conveyance on the ground, and offers exclusivity and sophistication to its passengers. It is the origin of the phrase "red-carpet treatment", because of the red carpet that passengers walk on when entering the train.
- **The Flying Scotsman:** The Flying Scotsman express service has only recently stopped being hauled by steam locomotives, and is now hauled by diesel locomotives. The express train makes the route from London to Edinburgh in just under six hours, with a single stop in Newcastle.
- **The Ghan:** In this age of moon rockets and jet planes, the Ghan is a bit of an anachronism. Twice every week, this train crosses the Australian desert between Port Augusta at the coast and Alice Springs almost in the middle of the continent on a narrow-gauge track still pulled by steam locomotives. The service is notorious for delays: it has a flatbed car behind the locomotive with sleepers and tools to repair the track if it is washed away by a sudden spring flood.
- **Glacier Express:** If you want to cross Switzerland in style, do it on the "slowest express train in the world". The Glacier Express traffics a narrow-gauge railway between Zermatt and St Moritz through the centre of the Swiss Alps. It is only "express" in the sense that the train stops at a very limited number of stations, and it takes about eight hours to reach its destination.

- **Golden Arrow:** The original Golden Arrow, *La Flèche d'Or*, is an all first-class lounge car service between Paris and Calais. Soon after its introduction, a similar British service from Dover to London started, with a ferry across the channel. The entire trip, including the channel crossing, takes six hours. It is no longer exclusively a lounge car service, but also has regular first and third class cars.

- **Orient Express:** The Orient Express has a reputation for comfort, luxury and murder mysteries. There are actually several Orient Expresses: The original line is from Paris to Istanbul over Strasbourg, Munich, Vienna and Bucharest. The *Simplon Orient Express* goes from Paris to Istanbul over Milan, Venice, Belgrade and Sofia. The *Arlberg Orient Express* goes from London to Athens over Calais, Paris, Zürich, Innsbruck, Vienna, Budapest, Gleichen, Belgrade and Athens. Sadly, both lines to Istanbul will probably soon close due to financial reasons.

- **Semmeringbahn:** The Semmeringbahn is only 41 km, but passes through 14 tunnels, 16 viaducts, 11 iron bridges and more than 100 stone bridges in a stunning Austrian alpine landscape. It is often named as the most beautiful train line in the world. Built between 1848 and 1854, the line is now operated by the Austrian Federal Railway and a part of its rail network.

- **Tōkaidō Shinkansen:** The Tōkaidō New Trunk Line, or "shinkansen" in Japanese, is better known as the Bullet Train in the rest of the world due to the trains' bullet-shaped streamlined front. The trains almost fly along the tracks at an incredible 220 km/h, cutting the journey from Tōkyō to Ōsaka in half, from six hours forty minutes to three hours ten minutes.

- **Trans-Siberian Railway:** With a length of 9,289 km, not including the spur line to Pyongyang, the Trans-Siberian Railway is the longest railway line in the world. It takes almost a week to make the journey from Moscow to Vladivostok.

BY SEA

Atlantic crossing by ship is still a thing. There are several transatlantic passenger lines, of which many are a matter of national pride. But truth be told, passenger shipping is on the decline as air travel becomes more affordable. Still, going to the Americas by ship is far more romantic than flying, even on one of the new Jumbo jets.

Ocean liners are not the only means of oceanic travel. You can rent a cabin on many cargo ships, which is a lot cheaper, not particularly luxurious or romantic, and a lot slower than an ocean liner, but it can also get you to places the ocean liners don't go.

Sometimes, a short trip in a boat is necessary. At many places, a ferry is the only way to cross a body of water. It may be too expensive or difficult to build a bridge. Car and personnel ferries are very common in archipelagos and other brown-water environments, where it is often the only way to get from island to island. Tickets on these ferries are often cheap, but you have to wait for the scheduled department, which can be everything from once every ten or fifteen minutes to a few tours per day.

Nine glorious ocean liners

- **Alexandr Pushkin:** Sailing for the Baltic Sea Shipping Company, *Alexandr Pushkin* is the pride of the Soviet Union, trafficking the Leningrad-Montreal route. The ship has greater hull strength than most other ocean liners in order to navigate through broken ice. Customs inspections in both Leningrad and Montreal are rigorous.

- **SS Atlantis:** The flagship of the mysterious Celestia Line launched in 1963, the *Atlantis* has been named the most luxurious ocean liner in the world. She usually traffics the Le Havre-New York route in summer and the San Francisco-Honolulu-Tokyo route at other times of the year. There are rumours that it carries a small submarine in a hidden dock in the bow section of the ship.

- **SS France:** The longest passenger ship in the world and the pride of France, *France* was built to function both as a liner and as a cruise ship. *France* has had some of the most famous passengers in the world, including the Mona Lisa, Leonardo da Vinci's famous painting, for its American tour.

- **Hurtigruten:** *Hurtigruten*, the Norwegian coastal express, isn't a ship but a route from Bergen to Kirkenes. It is known as the world's most beautiful sea voyage. The round trip takes 11 days and stops at some 40 ports along Norway's stunning coastline.

- **Queen Anna Maria:** Formerly *RMS Empress of Britain*, this Greek ocean liner serves the Piraeus-Naples-New York route. It is a second lease on life for this classic Cunard ocean liner, and it has a special place in the hearts of many Greek-Americans.

- **Queen Elizabeth 2:** *Queen Elizabeth 2* is not yet in service. The keel has just been laid down in Clydebank in Scotland. If all goes well, she will be launched in 1967, and enter service for the Cunard line in 1969 after outfitting and sea trials.

- **SS Shalom:** Recently badly damaged in a collision, *SS Shalom* has just returned to service the route between Haifa and New York. To accommodate a wider clientele, the ship has two kitchens, one kosher and one non-kosher, which has stirred up controversy in the religious community in Israel.

- **SS United States:** The world's fastest ocean liner, *United States* broke the transatlantic speed record on her maiden voyage, making the journey in 3 days, 10 hours and 40 minutes, for an average speed of 35.59

knots. Her actual top speed is considered a military secret, as she can easily be converted to a troop ship.

- **MS Wangaratta:** The great ocean liners don't go everywhere. If you want to go to somewhere outside the regular routes, one possibility is to rent a cabin on a freighter which is going in the right direction. *MS Wangaratta* is such a freighter, owned by the Swedish shipping company Rederi AB Transatlantic. The harbour office is the right place to find a suitable ship, but you have to negotiate with the skipper or the shipping line for cabin passage.

TRAVEL IN YOUR ADVENTURES

The characters will travel a lot. Here's how to handle it:

To get somewhere: The characters arrive. If they want to go in style, someone will need to have **Credit** 65+ or the Abilities Nouveau Riche or Old Money, or make a successful **Credit task check**. If the task check fails, they have to travel like the peons.

Under time constraints: Have the characters make an appropriate task check, or make a challenge. If the task check fails or the outcome is Low or Abysmal, the characters arrive too late.

Challenging wilderness journey: Make a challenge. If the outcome is Low, the characters arrive but **Exhausted**. If the outcome is Abysmal, they may even be **Wounded** when they arrive.

Chasing someone, or being chased: Make a challenge. If the outcome is Low or Abysmal, the other party arrives first or catches up with you.

Long travel: If the characters go by ship or train and the journey is long, you could have an adventure on the train or ship.

WHAT A WONDERFUL WORLD!

There are many exciting places around the world. To cover them all would be almost impossible, but here is a selection of interesting locations and what you can do there.

BERLIN

> ### Berlin in a nutshell
> **Foundation:** ca 1163 CE
> **Population:** 3,232,000
> **Area:** 891 km²
> **Elevation:** 34 m
> **Climate:** Oceanic/continental
> **Notable landmarks:** Brandenburg Tor/"Checkpoint Charlie", Siegessäule victory column, Unter den Linden, Tempelhof airport, The Wall

On August 13, 1961, Berliners found themselves in a divided city. Soviet troops had surrounded the British, French and American zones with barbed wire, and soon after, the wall was built.

Not only does the city straddle the river Spree, it is also cut in two by the Berlin Wall, built only a few years ago to isolate the French, American and British occupation zones from the Soviet occupation zone. The eastern part of the city is the capital of the German Democratic Republic – more commonly known as East Germany – while the western part is an enclave and part of the Federal Republic of Germany, "West Germany".

West Berlin is a showcase of the West, a cosmopolitan city enclave with two million inhabitants, and a centre of education, research and culture. It is heavily subsidised, though, and can only exist as an enclave with aid from its Western allies.

The glitz of the western half of the city contrasts with the highly politicised culture of East Germany. Heavily controlled by the government, but constantly competing with the "Klassenfeind" (class enemy) to the west, East Germany has developed a distinct "socialist consumerism" culture, and nowhere is it more apparent than in East Berlin.

Being the focal point of the east-west divide, Berlin is the city of spies. Here, Western intelligence agencies spy on their Eastern counterparts, and being the home of French, US and British garrisons and one of the most massive and elaborate intelligence operations, West Berlin is equally a target for Eastern spies.

Languages in Berlin

As Berlin is in part an occupied city with British, American and French armed forces present in the west and those of the Soviet Union in the east, it is quite common for foreign languages to be spoken. Many officials and service members in the western parts of the city have a passing knowledge of English and some also of French. In East Berlin, Russian is the most spoken second language.

Languages in West Berlin	Chance (%)
German	95%
English	55%
French	45%

Languages in East Berlin	Chance (%)
German	95%
Russian	55%
English	35%
French	15%

Money in Berlin

West Berlin uses Deutsche Marks as currency, while East Berlin uses the East German mark, officially known as Mark der Deutschen Notenbank. US dollars are also commonly accepted, especially in East Berlin.

Officially, West and East German money are at a 1:1 exchange rate; unofficially, you can often get 5–10 East German marks per Deutsche Mark.

HOW TO GET TO WEST BERLIN

Being an enclave, it is a bit tricky to get to West Berlin. Flying to West Berlin and its airports Tegel and Tempelhof (IATA codes "TXL" and "THF" respectively) is no different than flying to any other airport. Assuming you have the proper paperwork in order, the worst that can happen is getting through customs. There is also RAF Gatow, a military air base in the British sector operated by the Royal Air Force. It is usually off-limits to civilians, though.

There are interzonal trains run by Deutsche Reichsbahn, the East German rail service, from Hanover, Nuremberg, Hamburg and Frankfurt to Berlin. These trains do not stop between the East German border and West Berlin except for passport and visa checks. The *de facto* central station of West Berlin is Zoologische Garten.

There are four dedicated transit routes leading from West Germany to West Berlin. To use them, you need a transit visa (5 DM), and there is also a road tax of 10 Ostmark (payable in DM as well on a 1:1 exchange rate). It is illegal for transit passengers to meet with East Germans, so border guards calculate how long the journey should take and regularly check to see if any transit goes over this time.

If you are from the Eastern bloc and want to visit West Berlin, you not only need a visa from West Germany, but also travel permission from your home country, no matter what mode of transportation you plan on taking. When applying for a travel permit, you will be subjected to an extensive background check and interviews by security officers.

HOW TO GET TO EAST BERLIN

Getting to East Berlin depends on where you come from. Periodically, West Berliners are banned from entering East Berlin, depending on the tension between the Western and Eastern bloc and whether East Germany has a political point to make.

If you're from East Germany, it is generally very easy. For everyone else, you must apply for a visa, and

paradoxically it is harder for non-East German people from the Eastern bloc to get the necessary papers to go to East Berlin than for someone from the Western bloc to get a visa.

The cheapest way to get to East Berlin for Eastern bloc citizens is by train.

If you go by plane, Schönefeld Airport (IATA code "SXF") serves East Berlin. Air travel is generally not affordable for Eastern bloc citizens, although it is within reach for Western bloc citizens.

Two lines of the U-bahn (underground) of West Berlin take a turn inside East Berlin through about a dozen stations in the centre, but the trains never stop. They just pass through the abandoned stations.

There are eight transit points between East and West Berlin. The most famous, "Checkpoint Charlie", is in the American sector at Friedrichstraße.

Challenge: Getting to East Berlin

The challenge should be used when it is appropriate. If the characters are really bad at the Skills noted, or if you want to be sure that the characters can enter East Berlin, either don't use this challenge, or modify the Bad and **Abysmal outcomes** so that the characters are allowed entry but there are later consequences for the characters while in East Berlin.

Credit, to afford the trip
Red Tape, to navigate the bureaucracy
Status, because life's not fair
Contacts, because it is a lot easier if you know the right person

Modifiers
West German citizen: +2 pips on one check
Non-German Eastern bloc citizen: –2 pips on all checks

Outcome
Great outcome: Travel permit and visa application accepted after **1d6** hours.
Good outcome: Travel permit and visa application accepted after **2d6** days.
Limited outcome: Your visa is accepted after **3d6** days. Choose one of the following: going through customs takes **2d6** hours and they will confiscate one gear kit of the Director's choice; you are now on the watchlist of Stasi or the KGB; or you have to wait **1d6**+1 months for your visa application to be accepted.
Bad outcome: Visa denied.
Abysmal outcome: Visa denied, and you are now on the watchlist of Stasi, the KGB, or both.

"I am a jelly donut"
Following the division of Berlin, President Kennedy visited the city to show solidarity with the beleaguered people of West Berlin. On June 26 1963, in the middle of the 1963 crisis, he ended one of his best speeches ever with the now immortal "*Ich bin ein Berliner*".

Many people have made fun of the ending, remarking that by using the indefinite article "ein", "Berliner" would refer to a pastry similar to a jelly donut.

However, in the context of Kennedy's speech, using "ein" is perfectly good German, and the Berliner pastry is not called "Berliner" in Berlin, but "Pfannkuchen" (literally "pancake").

Nobody listening to the President's speech assumed that he said that he was a jelly donut, and the President's visit and speech greatly boosted the moral of those in West Berlin.

WHERE TO STAY

- **Hotel Adlon (Mitte district, East Berlin):** Most of the classic hotel Adlon was heavily damaged in the war. The surviving part of the former luxury hotel on Unter den Linden has recently reopened after a lengthy renovation.
- **Savoy Hotel (Charlottenburg district, West Berlin):** The Savoy survived the war practically unscathed, and was used as the British headquarters after the war but was then restored as a hotel. Its Times Bar is a classic in the bar scene in Berlin, with its own library and a wide range of Cuban cigars.
- **Schlosshotel Gehrhus (Grunewald district, West Berlin):** Pannwitz Palace escaped being plundered by Soviet troops thanks to a cunning maid hoisting the Yugoslav flag. Thanks to her, the fantastic interior in Italian Renaissance style survived. Since 1951, Pannwitz Palace has been used as a castle hotel, and everyone who is someone stays here. The exterior is extensively used in movies.
- **Hotel Berlin (Tiergarten district, West Berlin):** One of the largest hotels in Berlin, Hotel Berlin at Lützowplatz is an elegant post-war modernist hotel, often used for conferences.
- **Hotel de France (Wedding, West Berlin):** Centre Français de Berlin combines a hotel, a French cultural centre, the headquarters of the French occupation force, and the French restaurant Pastis, all in the same building. There's a miniature replica of the Eiffel tower just outside.
- **At your aunt's place:** There's probably a relative or friend of a friend willing to let you sleep at their place for a night or two.

THINGS TO DO IN BERLIN

- **Be spied on:** Not only are the Western intelligence services incredibly active in Berlin, there's also the East German Ministry for State Security (Staatssicherheitsdienst, SSD – more commonly known as Stasi), spying on its own population. So if you are from East Berlin, you're most definitely spied on.
- **Clubbing:** You are not supposed to be adolescent and bored in Berlin, as the divided city is the showcase of both systems. There are many night clubs aimed at youth, and there is also a vibrant music scene in Berlin. The East Berlin authorities consider the Western pop culture to be decadent and fascist, but that doesn't stop East Berlin youth from tuning in to Radio Luxembourg or the radio stations from West Berlin.
- **Culture:** Berlin is somewhat of a cultural capital in Europe, with twelve symphony orchestras, and a celebrated opera and theatre culture. There's also a vibrant cinema industry on both sides of the Wall. Of course, movies from the western side are considered ideologically unhealthy in the east, and are rarely shown there.
- **Protest:** There are regular protests in West Berlin, against the Soviets, the police, the West, the government, nuclear weapons, Stasi, the Wall, and just about everything you can imagine. In East Berlin, not so much.
- **Shopping:** For an East German, West Berlin is a wonder of Western consumer goods, electronics, fashion and food. For someone from Western Europe, consumer goods and electronics are generally more expensive than in the rest of Europe. High fashion, however, is still attractive.

WHY BERLIN IS IN YOUR ADVENTURE

- **Big badaboom:** The Octopus has a secret plan to provoke an armed conflict between East and West by detonating a stolen American atomic bomb in East Berlin. Only the characters can stop this heinous plan, as East German authorities would only consider a formal warning to be part of a capitalist destabilisation ruse.
- **Escape from Berlin:** Hedwig Braun is a friend of the characters. She has a niece who is stuck in East Berlin, and the characters have to help her across the border to West Berlin. But the niece is actually not Beate, but an imposter and spy from the Soviet Union who is using Hedwig's concern to infiltrate the West.
- **The Joy of Chemistry:** Professor Florian Hoffman, an East German professor of chemistry, has invented zero-calorie chocolate. Get your hands on the formula! But it's not that easy – agents from Swiss and Belgian chocolate manufacturers want it destroyed, while the CIA, acting on behalf of a number of American companies, is after it.

BUENOS AIRES

> **Buenos Aires in a nutshell**
> **Foundation:** 1536 CE
> **Population:** 7,549,000
> **Area:** 203 km²
> **Elevation:** 27 m
> **Climate:** Subtropical
> **Notable landmarks:** National Museum of Fine Arts, River Plate soccer stadium, Calle Florida, Palermo Park

Fair winds were important to seafarers in the colonial age. When the new colony at the mouth of Rio de la Plata was founded by sailors having crossed the Atlantic and the equator, it was named "Real de Nuestra Señora Santa María del Buen Ayre" – "Our Lady Holy Mary of the Fair Winds". Eventually it was shortened to the more manageable Buenos Aires.

The city has a humid subtropical climate, reaching 43 °C in January – Buenos Aires is in the southern hemisphere, with summer in January – and an average mean temperature of about 18 °C ± 5. It rains a lot in the summer, which can sometimes lead to floods.

Buenos Aires is a bustling city. 7.55 million people live in the Greater Buenos Aires area. They often identify as *porteños*, people who live in a port city. The port is indeed one of the busiest in South America. The architecture is a broad mix of styles from Art Noveau and Art Déco to Neo-Gothic and French Bourbon styles. It would remind you of Madrid or Paris, if it wasn't for the grid layout typical of cities in the New World.

Historically, Buenos Aires has been Argentina's venue for liberal, free-thinking and foreign ideas. The schism between *porteños* and Argentinians in general is wider than just ideology: the urban identity mixed with mainly European, but also Chinese and Japanese origin, clashes with the rural colonial origin of the rest of Argentina. This schism often leads to open hostilities between the government and the citizens, even resulting in war and revolutions.

Languages in Buenos Aires
Although Argentina does not have an official language, Spanish is the de facto common language of the country

and of Buenos Aires. Being a hot spot for immigration, Buenos Aires is very diverse. However, it is part of the Hispanophone world, meaning that it may be tricky to get by using French or English only.

Languages in Buenos Aires	Chance (%)
Spanish (Rioplatense dialect)	95%
English	45%
French	25%
Mandarin	15%
Cocoliche Italian (pidgin)	10%
Galician	10%
Yiddish	5%
Belgranodeutsch (pidgin)	5%

Money in Buenos Aires

The official currencies of Argentina are the peso moneda nacional ("m$n", paper bills) and the peso oro sellado (coins). They are not equivalent, since the peso oro sellado is worth its weight in gold or silver, and the peso moneda nacional is fluid.

HOW TO GET TO BUENOS AIRES

If you go to Buenos Aires by air, you will most likely land at *Ministro Pistarini International Airport* (IATA code "EZE"), often called Ezeiza Airport after the suburb in which it lies. BOAC has a weekly Concorde service, and daily flights using Boeing 707s and Vickers VC10s for economy flights. Air France also offers daily Boeing 707 flights. Air Majestique has a weekly Concorde service from Paris.

You may also land at *Aeroparque Jorge Newery* (IATA code "AEP"), but that is primarily used for domestic flights and regional flights to neighbouring South American countries.

Ferry services connect Buenos Aires to cities in Uruguay and Montevideo, and more than a million people use the ferry service every year. Several shipping companies run transatlantic ocean liners to Buenos Aires, but the age of ocean liners is in decline.

A permit is needed for bringing typewriters, portable radios and cameras into the country. Be sure to declare them in customs. Speaking of cameras, there are very few photo shops that can develop colour film, and film may be hard to get outside Buenos Aires – especially colour film.

WHERE TO STAY

- **The Plaza (Retiro district):** The Plaza, a modern and beautiful hotel and the finest in South America, is popular among American tourists. It is expensive, and tipping is customary.
- **Alvear Palace (Recoleta district):** Although less expensive than The Plaza, Alvear Palace is a place with a good reputation. Guests typically include artists and actors.

THINGS TO DO IN BUENOS AIRES

- **Horse racing:** Horse racing is particularly popular in Argentina, and the race track in Palermo, Buenos Aires, holds 30,000 visitors. Horse betting is one form of gambling which is not restricted, and is very popular.
- **Opera:** The Teatro Colón is said to be the largest opera house in the world, and the pride of Argentina. The theatre has a National Symphony Orchestra with 100 pieces, and its own opera and ballet company. Fancy attire is a must on gala nights.
- **Shopping:** Alligator leather articles are much cheaper in Buenos Aires than in Europe or America, as are furs and ponchos.

WHY BUENOS AIRES IS IN YOUR ADVENTURE

- Smugglers steal the pet bird of an acquaintance in Buenos Aires, and she asks the characters to track down the smugglers and retrieve the animal.
- The Octopus has a camp in a monastery on the Pampas, where they train agents in sign language, explosive bolas and riding. They also develop weird drugs from the local flora.
- A plane has crashed in the Andes, and the characters are recruited to find it and find the cause of the crash.

CAIRO

Oh, Cairo! The city of a thousand minarets, but also the double crown of Egypt, straddling the Nile in both the land of the living and the land of the dead. With almost 5 million inhabitants, Cairo is one of the largest cities in Africa and more populous than any in the nearby Middle East.

Egypt is a young nation. The country declared itself independent in 1922, but remained a British protectorate until the revolution in 1952. Because of that, Egypt is trying to find its identity. The country is caught in a constant tug-of-war between militarism, Islam, Westernisation, and the heritage of its ancient past.

The city of Cairo is similarly influenced, with the Citadel being the headquarters of the powerful Egyptian army, an old town with a multitude of mosques, a rapidly expanding modern economy, and the Giza plateau with its Great Sphinx and the pyramids of Khufu, Khafre and Menkaure right next door.

Located at the upper end of the Nile delta, Cairo is a city with a history that stretches into the ancient past. Nearby Memphis was the capital of the old Egyptian kingdom, so the area has long been a focal point for trade and politics.

The problems of the day

Islamism is not a big issue for Egypt in 1965. On the contrary, Egypt is moving towards Westernisation. Most of the Islamist leaders are behind bars for plotting an assassination attempt against the president in 1954.

Rather, the animosity between the Arab countries and Israel is the most important issue for Egypt. And since Israel is allied with the United States, Egypt has to ally itself with the Soviet Union, meaning that the armed forces mostly have Soviet equipment.

Languages in Cairo

Being at different times a former Ottoman province and British protectorate, Cairo is remarkably multilingual. Arabic and English are spoken side by side, and a portion of the population learns French. There are also Italian, Armenian and Greek immigrant communities.

Languages in Cairo	Chance (%)
Arabic (Egyptian or Sa'idi)	97%
English	85%
French	15%
Turkish	15%
Italian	5%
Armenian	5%
Greek	5%

Money in Cairo

Egypt has recently left the pound sterling behind, and instead pegs its Egyptian pound to the dollar at a rate of EG£1 to US$2.3. British pounds can be used in some districts, and the souks are always hungry for dollars.

HOW TO GET TO CAIRO

You need a passport and visa to enter Cairo. You may need a smallpox certificate if you come from certain countries, and travellers from Africa must prove that they are vaccinated against cholera and yellow fever.

Cairo International Airport (IATA code "CAI") is in Heliopolis just north of Cairo. Formerly a US Army Air Force base from the Second World War, the civilian authorities have since taken over its operation.

By train, you arrive at Ramses Railway Station. The Egyptian National Railway stretches along the Nile all the way up to Aswan, and along the Mediterranean coast to Sallum near the Libyan border, with an extensive network in the Nile Delta and spurs to oases and the Red Sea coast.

Cairo also has its tram network, and a growing political will to extend the network of roads. As a result, the taxi industry is booming.

WHERE TO STAY

- **Nile Hilton Hotel:** The newly built Nile Hilton Hotel with its more than 400 air-conditioned rooms overlooks the Nile. It has its own nightclub, where belly dancer Soheir Zaki often performs.
- **Shepherds Hotel:** In the European district lies this fine hotel, with freshly installed air conditioning. The service is excellent.

THINGS TO DO IN CAIRO

- **Egyptology:** The natural activity for any inquisitive character in Cairo is of course Egyptology, with the Egyptian Museum in the city and the necropolises in Saqqara, Giza, Darfur and elsewhere right on Cairo's doorstep.
- **Explore the Nile:** The Nile has forever been the lifeblood of Egypt. In ancient times, practically all transportation was accomplished by boat along the Nile. In modern days, one can still sail on a felucca, or on a cruise ship which also functions as a floating hotel.
- **Souqs:** There are numerous souqs, bazaars and flea markets in Cairo. Khan el Khalili, the biggest souq and one of the oldest, is the historical centre of Cairo. Beware, though: the souqs are tourist traps.

WHY CAIRO IS IN YOUR ADVENTURE

- The Octopus has a base in secret chambers under the Sphinx, where they are experimenting with a new mind-control field which could be projected globally using an emitter at the top of the Great Pyramid. Up until now, nobody knew about the hidden chambers, but recently, evidence of their existence emerged in the form of hieroglyphic inscriptions on the tomb walls inside the Great Pyramid.
- Newly uncovered papyrus scrolls hint at the location of a forgotten pyramid in the desert. These scrolls are held in the Cairo museum, where the curator Saib Nafiz is trying to put together an expedition to visit the site. It is ominously referred to as "the Traitors' Pyramid" and it served, if the scrolls are to be believed, as a prison where those who displeased Pharaoh would be made immortal and then entombed alive, keeping them locked away from the land of the gods forever. But this is just a legend, right?

HONG KONG

> ### Hong Kong in a nutshell
> **Foundation:** 1842 CE
> **Population:** 3,015,000
> **Area:** 2,755 km²
> **Elevation:** 0–957 m
> **Climate:** Humid subtropical
> **Notable landmarks:** Kowloon Walled City, Macau, Victoria Harbour, The Peak, The Big Buddha at Lantau Island, Man Mo Temple

Ever since the British East India Company stuck its flag on Hong Kong island, the colony and the surrounding territory and islands have been in turmoil. With all the trouble to have occurred in the area – the Boxer Rebellion, the opium war, the Japanese occupation, protests and riots – few would have believed that such a small colony was destined to become a centre of international trade and commerce.

The British Crown Colony of Hong Kong is at a turning point. With a successful public education and health-care policy, many Hong Kong Chinese side with the British authorities, but there is also a large group of disaffected, partially influenced by Maoists.

The relationship between the British colony and the People's Republic of China is sometimes strained. Hong Kong buys water from China, and sometimes China turns off the water supply in times of conflict.

With three million inhabitants, half of which are under the age of 25, Hong Kong is not only marked by political chaos but also by economic growth. Quite a lot of the economic growth comes from the textile and construction industries, and Hong Kong is growing rapidly with new districts in the New Territories, leased from China.

With the economic expansion came new opportunities, but also a cultural shift. The Chinese family tradition is challenged by long work hours in the many factories, and women have also entered the labour force en masse.

KOWLOON WALLED CITY

Originally a Chinese fortress, the Walled City in Kowloon became occupied by squatters, while its walls were demolished and used to build the Kai Tak airport in Victoria Harbour. Unable to drive out the squatters, British authorities eventually let them be. This lack of action has led to the city being controlled by the triads, which run the numerous opium dens and brothels.

Kowloon Walled City is a hodge-podge of modular pre-fabricated sections piled on top of one another, up to 13 or 14 stories high. There's no particular planning for infrastructure or architecture. Electricity and water mains are mostly just hooked in wherever they are needed or there is space available.

The city is a tightly knit community, where everyone helps everyone else. Since there's so little light in the often covered alleys, rooftops and the centre square (yamen) have become important focal points for the community.

Languages in Hong Kong

Most people in Hong Kong speak Cantonese, but as Hong Kong is a British Crown Colony, many people also speak English or only English. There is a significant Mandarin-speaking immigrant minority from the mainland, and also small minorities from Singapore and Macau.

Languages in Hong Kong	Chance (%)
Cantonese	95%
English	75%
Mandarin	25%
Portuguese	5%
Malay	5%

Money in Hong Kong

Being a crown colony, the Hong Kong dollar is tied to the pound sterling at a rate of 1 shilling 3 pence to the dollar. US dollars and British pounds are also commonly accepted, at least in the tourist and shopping districts.

HOW TO GET TO HONG KONG

The fastest way of getting to Hong Kong is by air. Most major airlines fly to Hong Kong, including Air France, Air Majestique, BOAC, Pan Am, Qantas and Swissair.

Kai Tak International Airport (IATA code "HKG") in Kowloon is often regarded as "the most extreme airport in the world". Not only is it one of the busiest, with passenger planes and transport planes sharing one runway only; it is also infamous for the "Checkerboard" approach. It is the air approach from the west to runway 13, and includes a sharp right turn to narrowly miss Beacon Hill, followed by a steep descent between skyscrapers to land on the single runway on a narrow strip of land in Victoria harbour. It is not an approach for the faint-hearted, especially in crosswinds.

The most comfortable way of getting to Hong Kong is by boat, especially by cruise liner. It takes a lot longer – from London by way of the Mediterranean and the Suez canal takes just over two weeks, and from San Francisco, it takes about 21 days.

The land route to Hong Kong goes through China, and although it is a lot easier for Westerners than for mainland Chinese (who are generally not allowed to go abroad, but do so anyway as refugees), it is still not particularly easy to navigate the Chinese bureaucracy or roads.

A passport and visa are required for Hong Kong entry, as well as proof of smallpox vaccination and cholera inoculation if arriving from certain countries.

WHERE TO STAY

- **The Peninsula:** This colonial-style luxury hotel in Kowloon was opened in 1928 by the Kadoorie family, and is known as the finest hotel east of Suez. It has a fashion arcade which not only houses international brands, but also Hong Kong brands such as Betty Charnuis Clemos.
- **Miramar:** The Miramar, a tall, glass-covered skyscraper, is Hong Kong's first post-war hotel, built in Tsim Sha Tsui in Hong Kong in 1957.
- **Repulse Bay:** Situated on the beach of the same name in the southern district on Hong Kong Island, Repulse Bay hotel is a building in British style with first class service.

THINGS TO DO IN HONG KONG

- **Movies:** Hong Kong has the third largest movie industry after Indian cinema and Hollywood, with themes ranging from Cantonese opera to low budget martial arts films. There is a sharp rivalry between production companies over whether they should make movies in Cantonese or Mandarin. Since there is a law mandating movies to be subtitled in English, and the producers often add subtitles in other languages while they're at it, this rivalry is somewhat moot.
- **Trade and investments:** The Hong Kong stock exchange and commodities market is one of the biggest in the world, and the Hong Kong dollar is a powerhouse on the international currency market. Because of the peculiarities of Cantonese culture, it is very hard to make deals by mail or telephone. Deals in Hong Kong are best made face-to-face.
- **Fashion:** The fashion scene in Hong Kong is vibrant, partially due to the blending of Eastern and Western culture, but also because of the textile industry in Hong Kong. Here you can get a traditional well-made suit or gown, traditional Chinese fashion, or any kind of fusion of the two, ranging in quality from ultra-cheap copies and affordable but high quality hand-sewn clothes, to expensive haute couture.
- **Food:** Don't forget to try the true Cantonese kitchen! It's the real deal, nothing like the faux Chinese restaurants that are opening across Europe and America.
- **Martial arts:** As religion is strongly discouraged in mainland China, and many martial schools are connected to temples, some of them have sought refuge in Hong Kong. Some of the students have become little more than thugs for the triads, while others have become movie stars.
- **Chinese New Year:** The Chinese New Year is celebrated between January 15 and February 15. It is a colourful event with dragon dances and fireworks.

WHY HONG KONG IS IN YOUR ADVENTURE

- The triads are smuggling drugs from the Golden Triangle, hidden in hollowed-out, ancient Chinese jade statuettes. One of those, including a package of opium, ends up at the wrong address – the characters'.
- Industrial espionage is fun! The characters are unknowingly used as couriers by spies on a visit to Hong Kong, and are caught by the British authorities who "recruit" them to expose the contact and unravel the spy ring.
- Rumour has it that Chinese sorcery is used to control the minds of kung fu students, making them into slave fighters or workers for the triads. And it seems to actually work, as the characters find out when they are subjected to this ancient sorcery.
- Niu Tou is a respected businessman in Hong Kong, with links to the Triads. He is rarely seen in public, but when he appears, he never touches anyone. This has led to a rumour that he is actually an ancient god whose body is trapped in the underworld, capable only of projecting his spirit into this world. It is prophesied that he must marry a girl with characteristics that could match one of the characters, or one of their friends, in order to finally free himself from imprisonment.

ICE STATION X-14

Deep in the Antarctic in the shadow of Mount Kirkpatrick at about 82°20' S, Ice Station X-14 sits on the glacier, slowly drifting with it.

Ice Station X-14 consists of a central corridor made of prefabricated half-cylindrical sections, with science and habitation wings jutting off at right angles from the central corridor. Two larger sections stick out at the end, one being the garage for snowmobiles, tracked snow vehicles and snow homes; the other being a hangar for the ice station's two helicopters – one Chinook 234LR and one Bell 204, both modified for arctic conditions. There is also a fuel dump nearby, which provides fuel for the vehicles, helicopters and power generator.

The habitation wing has social areas with pinball games, a ping-pong table, a small library with predominantly scientific literature and lewd magazines, and a very small gym.

There's not much privacy at the station, because it is very expensive to get the prefabricated sections there. Station Chief Robert Emerich has a room big enough to have not only a desk and a proper bunk bed, but also two couches and a small coffee table. Stationed personnel get very small cubicles combining a desk and a bunk with a locker, while guests have to make due with triple-bunk beds in a small room.

Showers, washrooms and a laundry room are also available to the staff. Laundry duty rotates among the personnel. The sick bay is compact but well equipped, and there is even an isolation lab with four beds, just in case something contagious breaks out. Luckily, so far it has never been used.

The kitchen is compact but well-stocked, if by "well-stocked" you limit yourself to anything that is frozen, canned, dry, freeze-dried, powdered or otherwise can be stored for at least 12 months. Fresh produce is a rare luxury, limited to the Antarctic summer and the supply flights.

The science wings contain drilled-out ice cores, the equipment to study them, a biology lab (mostly dedicated to microbiology and lichen), a medical lab, a high energy lab used to study cosmic rays, and an astronomical observatory. There is a closed-off lab for the US Air Force which nobody can enter except Chief Emerich, Doctor Staedler and the occasional visitor with proper authorisation.

Languages at Ice Station X-14

Being an international research station, everyone uses English as the standard language, but various personnel also speak German, French, Soviet, Norwegian, and sometimes other languages depending on who is visiting at the time.

Languages at Ice Station X-14	Chance (%)
English	100%
Norwegian	25%
French	15%
German	15%
Russian	15%
Any other language	5%

Money at Ice Station X-14

There's really nothing to buy at Ice Station X-14, so this is one of the few places in the world where money has little value. US dimes are in some demand for the pinball machines, but the key to the coin slot doors is in the lock. There's a local custom to leave some of your country's currency pinned to the wall in the social area.

HOW TO GET TO ICE STATION X-14

Ice Station X-14 is as remote as remote can be. There are two ways of getting there: by air from McMurdo station on the Antarctic coast, or by trekking across the vast glaciers by ski, dogsled, or snow vehicle.

There is one supply flight utilizing a C-130 Hercules, modified with ski gear, from the US Air Force at McMurdo Station every two weeks in the summer months (November to February) if weather permits. It's not easy to get on that flight unless you are attending to legitimate business. It's probably easier to charter or rent a plane on your own than to cut through the red tape to get on the Air Force's C-130.

Challenge: Get on the supply flight

Contacts, to know who can get you a seat.
Red Tape, to get through the bureaucracy.
Science, to have legitimate business.
Status, to be important enough to be flown there.

Modifications

Having a really good reason: +2 pips to all task checks.

Not having a reason, or not wanting to state the reason: –2 pips

Outcome

Great outcome: You get a seat on the next supply flight.

Good outcome: Your application takes **1d6** days to process,

Limited outcome: Your application takes **2d6** days to process, after which you get a seat on a flight in **1d6** days. If the Antarctic winter hits in February, the slot rolls over to next summer in November.

Bad outcome: Your application is denied.

Abysmal outcome: Your application is accepted after **1d6** days, but the flight is cancelled at the last moment due to engine problems and you find yourself stuck at McMurdo Station instead.

Challenge: Charter or rent a plane

Contacts, to know someone who knows someone who owns planes adapted to Antarctic conditions.
Credit, because renting a plane is expensive.
Red Tape, to get the flight permits in order.

Modifications

+2 pips on **Credit**, but **–2 pips** on **Red Tape** if a character can fly the plane and you don't have to pay the pilot.

Outcome

Great outcome: Travel permit and visa application accepted after **1d6** days.

Good outcome: You get a plane from New Zealand with a stopover at the New Zealand Scott Base or the US McMurdo Station. The entire trip, including arrangements, takes **2d6** days in the Antarctic summer.

Limited outcome: You get a plane from Argentina with a stopover at Belgrano station, but you have to bribe some officials to make it happen. The entire trip takes **3d6** days in the Antarctic summer, and you get a **–2 pips** modification on the next **Credit task check**.

Bad outcome: There's no plane or pilot available.

Abysmal outcome: You get a plane, but there's a mechanical failure forcing the plane to land, and you are now stranded on the ice shelf. Hopefully someone will come to the rescue.

Trekking across the ice will take a month, so you better start in December at the latest if you plan to return. It is also extremely demanding, and requires meticulous preparation and anyone making the attempt to be in peak physical condition.

Challenge: Trekking across the ice

Alertness, to spot dangerous terrain or shifting weather in time.
Credit, to afford the equipment.
Endurance, for the exhausting journey.
Red Tape, to get through the bureaucracy to have your expedition cleared.
Survival, to prepare for the journey and survive on the ice.

Modifications
–5 pips on all task checks if the characters make the journey between March and October.

Outcome
Great outcome: The trip takes **2d6** fewer days than planned.
Good outcome: After about a month, you arrive at Ice Station X-14.
Limited outcome: You are caught in a blizzard and forced to bivouac for **2d6** days, **1d6** random characters get snow blindness and are **Blinded** for two days when you arrive, or you are all **Exhausted** when you arrive. Choose one.
Bad outcome: You are forced to give up and return to base.
Abysmal outcome: A catastrophic mishap happens, and you are stranded on the ice.

WHERE TO STAY

There's not much choice on where to stay: you get a bunk in the barracks, or you can sleep on the floor or on the couch in the communal area. You can also risk sleeping outside in a tent or one of the snow vehicles or mobile snow homes, but it is strongly discouraged unless you have to.

THINGS TO DO AT ICE STATION X-14

There isn't all that much to do at Ice Station X-14 beyond whatever brought you there in the first place. It's a science station, not a tourist resort, and basically everything is a luxury.

- **Science!** Ice Station X-14 is focused on meteorology, climatology, biology and astronomy. Equipment is limited to what you can fit into an airplane, but for some fields of science, the location is second to none!
- **Explore the glacier:** Borrow or hijack a snowmobile to make a trek on the glacier. But beware, weather is a killer. Often it is impossible to even exit the barracks for weeks at a time. All you can do is wait out the storm.
- **Pinball:** On the last Saturday of every month, there's a pinball tournament among the station's personnel. After pinball, sleeping is the favourite activity when off-duty. Living so close together makes being alone very valuable, and you're usually exhausted from working very long hours anyway.
- **Repair things:** The extreme climate tests the infrastructure of the ice station, and things must always be repaired, from snowmobiles to the barracks themselves. For any expedition on the glacier, you are dependent on your equipment. If it fails, you die.

WHY ICE STATION X-14 IS IN YOUR ADVENTURE

- Ice Station X-14 is actually a secret biolab, and a virus is spreading. The characters have to contain it. The effect of the virus may be strange but harmless (turning the infected green), or potentially deadly.
- There are rumours of an abandoned secret Nazi base nearby, possibly connected to Project Haunebu and Nazi UFOs. Usually people just laugh at the rumours, but people have found a huge and concentrated magnetic anomaly under the ice not far away from the ice station. The anomaly is circular in shape and the magnetic field is pulsing around the edge. Could there be some truth to the rumours, or even a UFO from another planet buried in the ice?
- There are strange ruins in the nearby mountains that appear to be vastly older than humans. They have a weird angular architecture with inscriptions that seems to look like both Sumerian/Babylonian cuneiform and the Minoan language Linear A. An expedition of archaeologists under the leadership of Howard Lecamp and supported by the characters is sent using Ice Station X-14 as a base camp to explore the ruins and their hidden secrets.
- A passenger plane with the son of the President has crashed on the Antarctic ice, and Ice Station X-14 is the closest location that can serve as a base camp for the rescue expedition. Being known for surviving the most adverse conditions, the characters' expertise is needed. But it's not that simple – the expedition also includes several people who would like to hurt France: the very same people who sabotaged the crashed plane.

KYŌTO

The old imperial capital of Japan was generally spared from Allied bombing in the Second World War. Suffering only a few small air raids, many of the old pre-war buildings and temples avoided destruction.

Kyōto sits in the Yamashiro basin in the eastern part of the Tamba highlands. Because of that, Kyōto has hot humid summers and cold winters with occasional snow. Like the rest of eastern Japan, Kyōto is prone to typhoons from September to October.

Kyōto is the capital of the Kyōto prefecture and the fifth largest city in Japan. Originally, the city was arranged in accordance with Chinese feng shui, with the Imperial Palace facing south. The city, with its strange mix of the modern tech industry and traditional crafts, is renowned for its kimono weavers and sake brewers, which sit side by side with new tech companies springing up in the post-war economic miracle.

There are ten wards in Kyōto, with Nakagyō-ku being the administrative centre of the city. Together with Kamigyō-ku and Shimogyō-ku, these three wards form the city centre. The three northern wards, Kita-ku, Sakyō-ku and Ukyō-ku are mostly forested and the least densely inhabited.

Kyōto's six *hanamachi* ("flower town") districts date back to the 17th century and the early Tokugawa era when the geisha institution was introduced to Japan. There are tea houses where guests can be entertained by *geiko* (as *geisha* are called in Kyōto) or *maiko* (apprentice *geisha*), women trained in the ancient traditions of art, dance, song and conversation. There are also dance halls for traditional dances, kabuki theatres and puppet theatres, restaurants, bars, pachinko halls and much more in the hanamachi districts. These districts still have 16th century buildings with narrow cobbled streets.

Languages in Kyōto

Naturally, Japanese is the dominant language in Kyōto. English is taught in schools, and many younger people speak English, although often with a heavy accent and limited vocabulary. Some of the exchange students and foreign students in the university struggle with the Japanese language and its writing system. Official road signs are bilingual, but beyond that, a foreign visitor must often get help with translation.

Languages in Kyōto	Chance (%)
Japanese	100%
English	35%

Money in Kyōto

The Japanese yen is the only legal tender in Japan. However, it is easy to exchange currencies, as money exchange offices and banks are able to help almost everywhere. The yen is tied to the US dollar at an exchange rate of ¥360 per US$1. Some stores in towns near US military bases often accept dollars too.

HOW TO GET TO KYŌTO

To enter Japan, you need a passport. A visa is not necessary for short visits (less than 72 hours) but is required for longer stays.

Kyōto does not have an airport of its own, but nearby Ōsaka International Airport (IATA code "ITM") – commonly known as Itami Airport – is easily accessible by train.

The star of travel to Kyōto is the Tōkaidō Shinkansen, the main trunk line between Ōsaka and Tōkyō. The Bullet Train takes half an hour to reach Ōsaka (there's also a stop at the airport), and two hours forty minutes to reach Tōkyō. The magnificent conveyance is a marvel of speed and comfort. Many other railways converge on Kyōto Station as well, connecting most of the west coast of Japan.

In ancient days, Kyōto was also accessible from the sea by rivers, lakes and canals, but these days, the canals are only used for sightseeing and occasionally private boating.

Within Kyōto, there is an extensive bus, tram and trolleybus network that reaches all over the city. Kyōto is also very bike-friendly, with plenty of bike rental stations to be found.

WHERE TO STAY

- **Miyako Hotel Hachijō:** This hotel is one of the most luxurious in Japan, with a grand view over Kyōto.
- **Kyōto Station Hotel:** Kyōto Station is one of several Western-style hotels, mainly with services aimed at attracting tourists who aren't as familiar with Japanese accommodations.
- **Tawaraya:** A traditional Japanese inn or "ryokan", which may be the finest in Japan. Conveniently located in downtown Kyōto, but Westerners may not be used to the etiquette.

THINGS TO DO IN KYŌTO

- **Cultural sites:** Since Kyōto was relatively untouched by Allied bombing campaigns during the war, a lot of cultural sites survived intact, including Buddhist temples, Shinto shrines, gardens, castles and other places of great natural beauty. There are about 1,600 Buddhist temples and 400 Shinto shrines in the area. Don't forget the Imperial Palace, which is open to the public.
- **Sports:** Japan is really into baseball, and has been since before the war. Kinugasa Stadium has been the home of local Central League teams for a long time. Football is also popular, and the Kyōto Nishikyogoku Athletic Stadium hosted football matches in the 1964 summer Olympic games.

- **Study:** Kyōto is a centre for academics in Japan, with many institutions and universities. Kyōto University is ranked as the second university after Tōkyō U, with many opportunities even for foreign students.
- **Drink tea with a *geisha*:** There are many tea houses in the hanamachi districts, where you can enjoy a tea ceremony with a *geisha*.

WHY KYŌTO IS IN YOUR ADVENTURE

- Doctor Senku Ishigami (who has *ten billion percent* in the **Science** Skill) has created a giant robot – because why not? – and he needs some brave person to be its test pilot. However, the huge robot has also attracted the attention of less savoury types who want to use it as a weapon against their enemies.
- A giant sea monster attacks ships in the Sea of Japan, but an analysis of the wreck of one ship, Kobayashi Maru, reveals a particular kind of clay that only exists in the Kyōto area. The monster is actually a submarine, built by the Octopus in order to hurt the Japanese economy.
- The Octopus is searching for Izumi, a young girl with amazing combat prowess on the run in Kyōto. She was kidnapped and brainwashed into becoming a super-soldier before she escaped. The Octopus wants that technology for their own minions. She is hiding somewhere in the industrial district of Kyōto.

Illegal samurai swords

Japan has strict weapon laws, particularly regarding swords. Any blade longer than 15 cm is considered illegal, unless properly registered at the Prefectural Education Board, or if it is a training sword that can't be sharpened. Only traditionally-made nihontō can be licensed. This means that the sword has to be either antique or made by a contemporary licensed smith. Foreign swords and mass produced swords from the Second World War are not eligible.

Note that it is the sword that is licensed, not the owner. The license must stay with the sword at all times, usually attached to the scabbard or the storage bag.

Some swords can be designated cultural property or national treasures. Such swords may not leave Japan, and if sold, the government reserves the right to buy the sword for a fair market price.

Feel free to ignore these laws in your game for drama purposes. Do not ignore them in real life.

LENINGRAD

Leningrad in a nutshell
Foundation: 1703 CE
Population: 3,677,000
Area: 1,439 km²
Elevation: 13 m
Climate: Humid continental
Notable landmarks: Senate Square, Winter Palace, Peter and Paul Fortress, The Hermitage

Languages in Leningrad	Chance (%)
Russian	100%
German	35%
Polish	23%
English	15%

Russia's big problem has always been its lack of access to the sea. Arkhangelsk on the White Sea is closed in winter, and Crimea was controlled by the Turks. Tsar Peter the Great's solution was to build a new city in the west at the estuary of the Neva river at the eastern end of the Gulf of Finland. He had to expel the Swedish Nyenskan first, of course, but that was not a problem since Sweden and Russia were at war.

The new city was named Saint Petersburg, and with its Italian-inspired baroque design and many canals criss-crossing the islands of the estuary, it was often called the "Venice of the North". For a short time after the outbreak of the Great War, the city was called Petrograd, but on January 26, 1924, five days after the death of Lenin, the city was renamed Leningrad in his honour.

Summers in Leningrad are short, warm and humid, about 23 °C at the warmest, while winters are long, wet and moderately cold at about –8 °C. The Neva river usually freezes up between November and April.

Leningrad is the second largest city in the Soviet Union after Moscow, with a population of 3.8 million. Most people are ethnic Russians, but many other ethnicities from around the Soviet Union live there.

Saint Petersburg was intended to be Russia's gateway to the west, and under the new name of Leningrad, the city remains a gateway, even if it is behind the Iron Curtain.

Languages in Leningrad

You're lucky if you find anyone speaking English in Leningrad as the Russian language dominates the Soviet Union and its satellite states. You may find someone who knows Polish or German due to the proximity to Poland or the German Democratic Republic.

It is easy to find translation services for tourists, though: just contact the nearest tourist centre and they will gladly help you. If you travel as a tourist, it is likely that you will get a guide for your group who speaks perfect English or French, has a friendly smile, and who spies for the KGB.

Money in Leningrad

The Soviet Union has recently had a monetary reform, and the Sixth Soviet Ruble is what you pay with now. However, there are specific tourist shops and hotels where you only can pay with Western currencies.

There are also black market exchanges which can offer better conversion rates for any Western currency than you might get through official sources, but there is always a certain risk associated with it. Western currencies are also highly attractive to anyone, since they enable ordinary Soviet citizens to buy stuff in the shops aimed at Western tourists. Blue jeans are particularly desirable.

HOW TO GET TO LENINGRAD

You need a visa and passport to enter the Soviet Union.

Up until recently, you could not go by air from the West directly to Leningrad but had to make the final leg by train from Finland or by Aeroflot domestic flights from for instance Moscow. However, Shosseynaya Airport has just opened for international flights, and Aeroflot, SAS, Air France and BOAC have opened services to Saint Petersburg (Pan Am and other American airlines have not).

Going by train is a lot easier. There are five railway stations, including Finlyandsky Station which has train services to the north and to Vyborg and Helsinki, Finland, and Moskovsky Station from which the Moscow-Leningrad rail service operates. Suburban rail ends in Baltiysky station.

Within Leningrad there are tram lines, buses, trolleybuses and the Leningrad Metro, serving millions of people daily. Taxi boats operate along the canals and the Neva river when it is not frozen, and hydrofoils serve the Neva river and the coastal communities around St Petersburg.

The Leningrad tram network is the largest in the world, and the Leningrad Metro is one of the deepest metro services in the world due to the geology of the Leningrad area. Admiralteyskaya is 86 meters below ground. The metro stations are among the world's most beautiful, elaborately decorated with marble and bronze.

To get to Leningrad or anywhere in the Soviet Union from the West is tricky but not impossible. You have to apply for a visa at a Soviet embassy or consulate and get it approved, which usually requires navigating the Soviet bureaucracy. It is not quite as tricky for a Soviet citizen to get to Leningrad, but you still have to apply for a travel permit.

Challenge: Getting to Leningrad

The challenge should be used when it is appropriate. If the characters are really bad at the Skills below, or if you want to be sure that the characters can enter Leningrad, either don't use this challenge, or modify the **Bad** and **Abysmal outcomes** so that the characters are allowed entry but there are consequences for the characters while in Leningrad.

Credit, to afford the trip
Red Tape, to navigate the bureaucracy
Status, because life's not fair
Contacts, because it is a lot easier if you know the right person

Modifiers
Soviet citizen: +2 pips on all checks
Western citizen: –2 pips on **Contacts**

Outcome
Great outcome: Travel permit and visa application accepted after **1d6** days.
Good outcome: Travel permit and visa application accepted after **3d6** days.
Limited outcome: Your visa is accepted after **3d6** days. Choose one of the following: going through customs takes **2d6** hours and they will confiscate one gear kit of the Director's choice; you are now on the watchlist of the KGB; or you have to wait **1d6**+1 months for your visa application to be accepted instead of **3d6** days.
Bad outcome: Visa denied.
Abysmal outcome: Visa denied, and you are now on the watchlist of the KGB.

WHERE TO STAY

All hotels are run by Intourist, the official state travel agency in the Soviet Union. The agency has offices all over the world and arranges trips to the Soviet Union.

- **Hotel Astoria (St Isaac's square)**: Astoria was built as a luxury hotel for the 300 year jubilee of Romanov rule, but has survived into the Soviet era. It is said that Rasputin met his lovers here.
- **Hotel Leningradskaya (St Isaac's square)**: Originally called Hotel Angleterre, then Hotel International and now Hotel Leningradskaya, the building sits side by side with the more luxurious Astoria. The upper guest room floors are interconnected.
- **Oktyabrskaya Hotel (Vosstania square)**: Oktyabrskaya is within sight of the Hermitage and the Museum of History of Religion and Atheism (formerly the Kazan Cathedral). Each room at the hotel is unique and differs from every other room.
- **Hotel Evropeiskaya (Nevsky prospekt)**: One of the great 19th century hotels, Evropeiskaya has an interior of marble and gold, sweeping staircases and elegant furniture.

THINGS TO DO IN LENINGRAD

- **Be spied on**: As a foreigner, you are always a suspect. In fact, everyone is a suspect, but foreigners much more so. The KGB will always keep a watchful eye, especially if you are someone who is someone.
- **Culture**: Leningrad has a rich culture, not only for being associated with Peter the Great and Catherine the Great, but also for the momentous events that happened here recently, including the Russian revolution and the siege of Leningrad – of which the tour guides are very happy to tell you about. The Hermitage Museum is the second largest art museum in the world.
- **Ballet**: The Vaganova Academy of Russian Ballet has produced some of the best dancers Russian ballet has ever had, from the strictly classical tradition of Russian ballet to more avant-garde dancers. Of all the culture in Leningrad, ballet is still the dominant and best regarded form.
- **Get educated**: The Leningrad State University is one of the best universities in the USSR, and is to some extent open to foreigners. Leningrad Polytechnic Institute is regarded as one of the finest universities in the world and a world-leader in hydro-aerodynamics, but attendance is generally limited to Soviet citizens.

WHY LENINGRAD IS IN YOUR ADVENTURE

- Kirill Tostobrov, a defector friend of the characters, still has family in Leningrad, and has asked the characters to help them over the border to Finland. This of course will be tricky, as the KGB border guards regularly check any train that crosses, and there are road checkpoints at the border as well.

- Not only are the Leningrad metro stations some of the deepest in the world, they also hold a secret: an Octopus base, probably built with the tacit support of someone inside the Soviet system. And because of that, the investigators in Leningrad Oblast cannot directly take care of the issue themselves. Instead, they ask some international experts who have a history

of dealing with the Octopus to help them. It is good to have someone else to blame in the Soviet Union.

- Two new Fabergé eggs have been found, from 1904 and 1905. Officially, Fabergé did not create any eggs in those years. Now everyone wants them: the Communist party wants them because they are Soviet property. The KGB wants them in order to destroy them because they contradict history. The Fabergé family in exile in Switzerland wants them, because they made them 60 years ago. An old lady, Anna Romain, claims to be a surviving Romanov princess, and wants the eggs to prove her identity. And they just happened to fall from the luggage shelf into the lap of one of the characters.

WEIRD LOCATIONS AROUND THE WORLD

Roll a **d%**, or pick an interesting location for an adventure.

d%	Where?	What?
1–3	41.73° N, 49.94° W	The wreck of RMS Titanic, with its secret cargo of byzanium.
4–6	Achenberg, Austria	A sealed-off tunnel with a lost Nazi train carrying several billion pounds in fake 5 pound bank notes.
7–9	Akira, Katsutori	The location for the first operating fusion reactor in the world, and the target of industrial spies.
10–12	Al Bichou, Al Ansur	An oasis used for millennia by desert caravans, known for its caves haunted by a lost Roman legion.
13–15	Artemovsk, USSR	An archeological excavation of possibly a Neanderthal city from 20,000 BCE.
16–18	Bergen, Norway	A circle of stones high up in the mountains, with a magic runestone said to open a gateway to the realm of the trolls.
19–21	Breuil-Cervinia, Italy	A secret Octopus base under Matterhorn, not far from the ski resort.
22–24	Bumbugur, Mongolia	Reputed to be the location of the grave of the Great Khan.
25–27	Falcon, Alabama	A sleepy American small town with a top secret high energy laboratory.
28–30	Fujiyoshida, Japan	A small town near mount Fuji, best known for its hot spring bath and old ghost stories, and also the location of UFO sightings.
31–33	Grand Central Station, New York, USA	A hidden Octopus base with secret elevators for entire trains.
34–36	Groom Dry Lake, Nevada, USA	A secret air force base where the CIA and the US air force develop airplanes and test captured Soviet airplanes. No UFOs, promise!
37–39	Guiana Space Centre, French Guiana	The space centre and launch site for future French space missions, including Kaguyahime-class atomic rockets.
40–42	Ilonga, Democratic Republic of Congo	Last known location of the de Huiis expedition of 1955. Its last radio message mentioned "flying lizards".
43–45	Kanoskaye, USSR	The sad ruins of the Czar's boarding school for the children of powerful nobles, where the children were kept as hostages to keep the nobles in line.
46–48	Kirkenes, Norway	A hidden genetic lab in a warehouse in the harbour.
49–51	Kiruna, Sweden	Under the guise of a civilian rocket launch facility, the Swedish army hides evidence of a crashed UFO.

d%	Where?	What?
52–54	Pfalzdamm, East Germany	A secret KGB training facility where Soviet and East German agents are trained to infiltrate the west.
55–57	Point Nemo, Pacific Ocean	The "pole of inaccessibility", the most distant point from any land, and also a satellite graveyard since many spent satellites are aimed at this point when they are deorbited.
58–60	Naganohara, Japan	The construction site of a huge black tower, so far several hundred meters high.
61–63	Nevada desert, USA	The ruins of a ghost town constructed as part of nuclear tests a decade ago.
64–66	Piuramarca, Peru	Said to be a gateway to a lost Inca realm.
67–69	Queen Maud Land, Antarctica	A Nazi u-boat base, inhabited by Ahnenerbe personnel who managed to escape Nazi Germany's defeat.
70–72	Ramstein, West Germany	A KGB safe house, staffed by Herr and Frau Schmitt, a sweet old couple and KGB assassins.
73–75	Sheik Wahai, Jordan	A resort for the ultra-rich on the coast of the Red Sea.
76–78	Skull Island, Bermuda	An island hidden in the mist, where an abandoned British destroyer from the Second World War is anchored in the lagoon.
79–81	Tanegashima Island, Japan	Centre for the Japanese space exploration agency, and the launch site for the Kaguyahime Moon rocket.
82–84	Tsingy de Bemaraha, Madagascar	Not only a strict nature reserve, but the razor-sharp rocks also hide an Octopus base.
85–87	Venice, Italy	Hidden in the catacombs under the town is an Octopus science base, working mainly on mind control drugs.
88–90	Victoria Harbour, Hong Kong	A secret MI6 base is constructed inside the wreck of the Cunard liner RMS Queen Elizabeth.
91–93	Waldenhaus, East Berlin	An abandoned grand mansion, under which a hidden bunker reveals a secret listening station.
94–96	Woolabalou, Australia	An illegal opal mine on sacred Aboriginal ground.
97–99	Zimmerthal, Switzerland	A chocolate factory producing the only zero-calorie chocolate in the world, a secret that people would kill for.
00	Tycho Crater, Moon	Rumoured to be the location of US Moon base, Alpha. The rumour is obviously false, since the 1964 Kaguyahime expedition is the only manned spaceship that has reached the Moon.

FRANCE

Since the end of the War, there has been an economic boom in France like nothing before. It has fully recovered from the War, and is steadily rising on the international arena. The French standard of living is now one of the highest in the world, and there is no sign of an end to the boom.

France is the fourth nuclear power, after the United States, the Soviet Union and the United Kingdom, but before the People's Republic of China. France is also a leading nation in nuclear power production, and is rapidly expanding its capacity.

Together with the UK, France has built the first supersonic passenger plane. France has just launched its first supersonic service from Orly, Paris to John F Kennedy International Airport, New York using the new Concorde.

The country's crowning achievement is the joint French-Japanese mission to the Moon in 1964. France and Japan are now deliberating on how to continue their presence in space. One option includes continuing to operate together, but from a French site in addition to the Japanese site at Tanegashima Island from which the 1964 Moon mission was launched. Another option is that they operate independently, but build the rockets jointly. A third option is that France and Japan go separate ways. The current president favours the joint operation option, but the opposition prefers some degree of divorce. In either case, France is constructing their own space centre in Kourou in French Guiana.

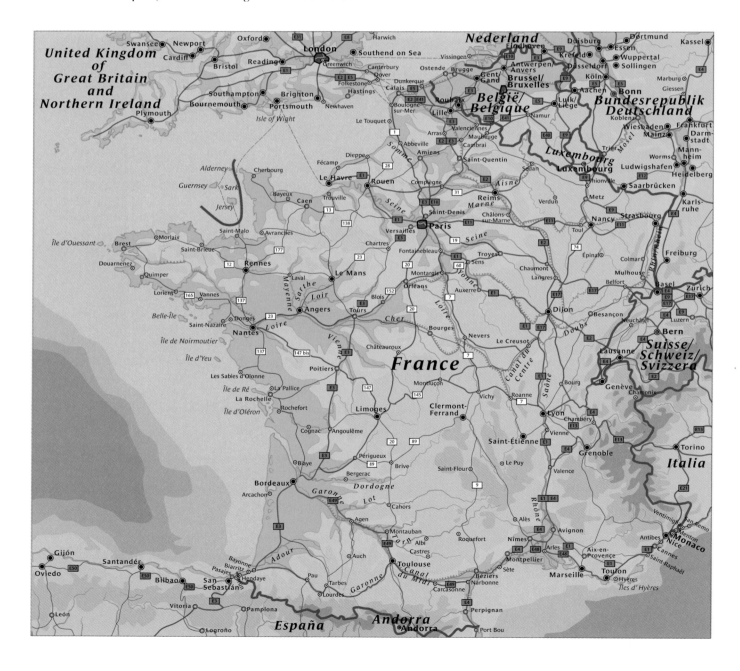

WEIRD LOCATIONS IN FRANCE

Roll a **d%**, or pick an interesting location for an adventure.

d%	Where?	What?
1–4	Amboise	In the gardens of Château d'Amboise, you can find the chapel of Saint-Hubert, the final resting place of Leonardo da Vinci.
5–8	Amiens	In Amiens cathedral, there is a relic said to be the head of John the Baptist, resting on a silver plate.
9–12	Aubeterre-sur-Dronne	With almost 20 metres to the ceiling, a winding staircase hewn out of the rock, and many passageways including a necropolis with over 80 sarcophagi, the church of Saint-Jean is the largest underground church in Europe.
12–16	Auvergne	The Jonas cave system is completely man-made, cut from the limestone rock. The excavation began in pre-history, with the site being converted into a monastery that housed up to 600 people during the middle ages.
17–20	Bugarach	Pic de Bugarach has an interesting geology: its top layer is an overthrust that is older than its bottom layer. It is said to be the place most visited by UFOs in Europe.
21–24	Chartres	The labyrinth at Chartres cathedral is surrounded by myth and legend, and is said to be the tomb of the structure's unknown builders. Underneath, there's an ancient crypt that, according to legend, dates back to a holy site from the age of the druids.
25–28	Dinan	The only walled city in France, and it still has its medieval buildings intact.
29–32	Landrethun-le-Nord	Hidden underground in this hamlet lies the bunker intended for housing the "London Gun", also known as Vengeance weapon 3 ("V3") or *Hochdruckpumpe* ("High pressure pump"), a cannon intended to shell London.
33–36	Lille	Bibliophiles in France flock to La Vieille Bourse, the old stock exchange which is now a vibrant second-hand book market. You can even find Franco-Belgian comic books here.
37–40	Maincy	When the Château de Vaux-le-Vicomte was opened with a lavish banquet intended to impress king Louis XIV, it ended with its owner, finance minister Nicolas Fouquet, being sent to prison for the rest of his life.
41–44	Marseille	Château d'If was used as a prison, and gained notoriety after Alexandre Dumas used it as the jail for Edmond Dantés in the book *The Count of Monte Cristo*. One of the cells has been designated as his, despite the Count never existing.

d%	Where?	What?
45–48	Montségur	Formerly a Cathar stronghold, it is said that their treasure was kept here but moved by four Cathar knights before the castle fell – some say that the Holy Grail was among their collection.
49–52	Paris	The house of the renowned alchemist Nicolas Flamel, supposedly the discoverer of the Philosopher's stone, and the oldest stone building in Paris, now an atmospheric restaurant.
53–56	Porquerolles	A sparsely populated island next to the Côte d'Azur. The explorer François Fournier bought the entire island as a wedding present for his wife.
57–60	Puy de Dôme	A huge lava dome from a young but dormant volcano. There has been a lot of construction activity in the region lately.
61–64	Rennes-le-Château	The castle used to belong to the Blanchefort family, formerly grand masters of the Knights Templars.
65–68	Rouen	The author Gustave Flaubert left a strange collection of medical relics from the 18th and 19th century, now on display in a museum in his home.
69–72	Saint-Cloud	In the basement of the international Bureau of Weights and Measures sits the kilogram prototype, a platinum alloy cylinder that by definition weighs one kilogram, and to which all other kilogram prototypes are compared.
73–76	Saint-Georges-d'Oleron	Off the coast between Île-d'aIx and Île d'Oléron sits Fort Boyard, still protecting the strait against an English invasion fleet that never came.
77–80	Saint-Guilhem-le-Désert	An isolated village in the Occitanie region that hasn't changed since the middle ages, and the location of a Benedictine abbey.
81–84	Sers	The mapping of the Moon in preparation for the Kaguyahime Moon landing was done from the observatory at the Pic du Midi observatory, high in the Pyrénées.
85–88	Sète	A small port town in Languedoc, famous for its canals and an annual jousting tournament on the Grand Canal.
89–92	St. Nazaire	The preserved Kriegsmarine u-boat pens from the Second World War
93–96	Tonnerre	Fosse Dionne is a natural wellspring in a sinkhole, surrounded by an amphitheatre built by the Romans. People have died in the sinkhole, diving for treasure and artifacts.
97–00	Villefranche-sur-mer	La Rue Obscure is a hidden street under the picturesque village, which has gradually been built-over by the village, and is now mostly subterranean.

PARIS

Paris, the city of light, dreams and romance! It is also the capital of France, the hub of French transportation and bureaucracy, and one of the major centres of finance, diplomacy, fashion, science and arts of Europe since at least the 17th century. One in five French live in the greater Paris region. In France, all roads lead to Paris, not Rome.

Paris hugs an arc of the river Seine with the two islands Île Saint-Louis and Île de la Cité, the oldest part of the city. Although mostly a flat city, there are some prominent hills rising almost 100 metres over the lowest point.

Why Paris?

When we started writing *The Troubleshooters*, we considered many "default starting locations", including Brussels, Strasbourg and Amsterdam. We finally settled on Paris because everyone has an image of Paris, no matter where in the world you live. Even if you have never been to Paris, you still know about it. As long as you can imagine yourself walking on the boulevards and bridges in Paris, you will do fine even if that image is factually wrong!

The city of Paris is divided into twenty administrative districts, *arrondissements municipaux* or simply *arrondissements*. They should not be confused with the sub-divisions of departments in government bureaucracy, which are also called arrondissements. But fear not: if anyone says arrondissement, they almost always refer to one of the districts of Paris.

Modern Paris owes much of its city plan to Napoleon III and his prefect, baron Georges-Eugène Haussmann, who had the city centre rebuilt with wide boulevards, squares and parks. Buildings in the city centre are required by law to not exceed 37 metres, forcing the city to expand outwards rather than upwards. More than half of the buildings are from before the War.

The suburbs are somewhat disconnected from the city centre. All suburbs are administratively handled as one region, but because it is so large and spread out, it is an administrative nightmare. New cities (villes nouvelles) are being built to offer low-cost housing for the rapidly growing population.

The old social stratification from the 19th century is still part of Paris: the affluent and upper classes live in the west and southwest or in some areas of historical importance, while the lower middle class and working class live in the north and east. The middle class live everywhere else.

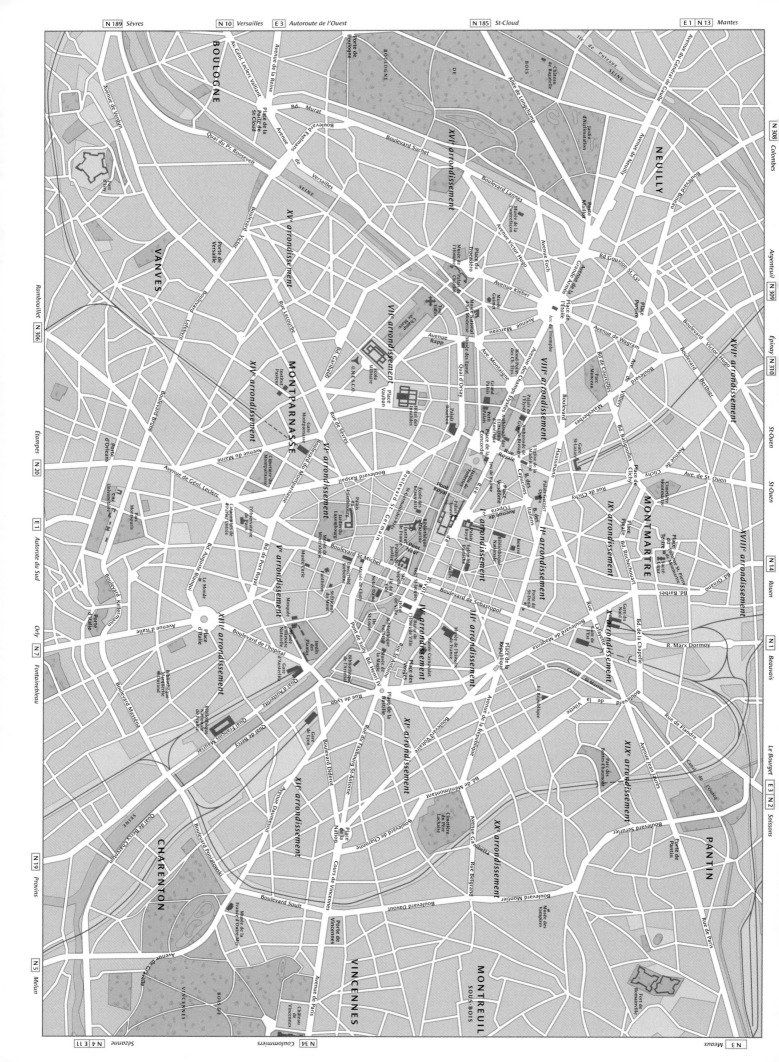

PUBLIC TRANSPORT IN PARIS

Paris has a very good public transport service. It mostly escaped wholesale destruction during the Second World War, and has been expanded since because of the economic boom.

Fare on public transport is 40 centimes.

Métro: With 14 lines, the Paris Métro is the second busiest underground service in Europe, only surpassed by the Moscow metro. The first métro lines opened in 1900 in conjunction with the World's fair.

Transilien: The commuter train network serving the greater Paris region, Île-de-France, brings thousands of workers in and out of Paris itself. The upgrade from steam to electrification, and the proliferation of automobile congestion, has led to an upswing of passengers after the War.

Buses: There are over 50 bus lines in the Paris area criss-crossing the city.

Railway stations

The railway stations not only serve long distance trains, but also the Transilien regional trains. Some of the major train stations in Paris are:

Gare d'Austerlitz: Trains to central France, Toulouse and the Pyrenees

Gare de l'Est: The oldest station in Paris. Serves trains travelling to eastern France, Germany and Switzerland.

Gare de Lyon: Trains to southeastern France and Languedoc-Roussillon.

Gare Montparnasse: Trains to western and south-western France.

Gare du Nord: Trains to northern France, Belgium, the Netherlands and Germany, and the Golden Arrow to Calais and London via ferry to Dover.

Gare Saint-Lazare: Trains to Normandy.

Airports in Paris

The two airports in Paris serve domestic and international flights, and most international airlines have services to one or the other of the airports.

Le Bourget: The original airport of Paris, before Orly became the main airport after the War. Charles Lindbergh landed here after his historic transatlantic flight in 1927, and in 1961, the Soviet ballet dancer Rudolf Nureyev defected here. You can take the Transilien, regular bus or airport coach to and from Le Bourget.

Orly: Originally, Orly was a secondary airport to Le Bourget. After the liberation of Paris, the United States used the airport as an Army Air Force base, until it was returned to the French government in 1947. Now it is the main airport of Paris. Airport coaches will bring you from Orly to Gare de Lyon.

Public transport in your adventures

Most of the time, public transport is just a means of moving across Paris. But sometimes, it is more than that.

Traffic jams: The traffic in Paris is unforgiving, and traffic jams are frequent obstacles on the streets of Paris. These could be a reason for one of the task checks in a chase Challenge.

Underground fights: The subways and trains could be an interesting setting for a fight with some horrible monster from beyond the stars, a rogue Octopus sentinel, or pale-faced vampires hiding in the catacombs.

The oldest of games: Stalking someone on the métro, or being stalked, is a classic way to spend your time there. The strange flickering lights, the claustrophobic atmosphere and the limited ways out could make for a really scary situation.

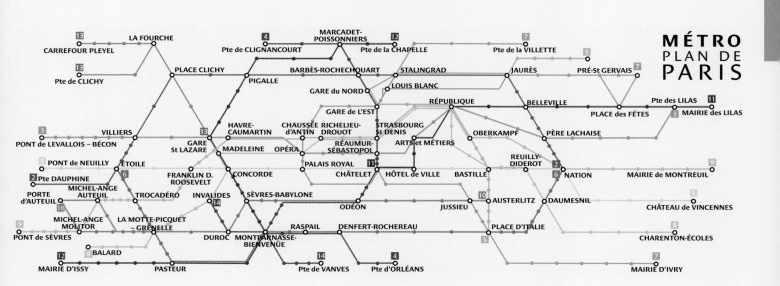

INVESTIGATIONS

There are wild ideas of installing a telephone terminal hooked up to all kinds of services, from library searches to table and ticket bookings, but truth be told, even if it would be technically possible, it is not feasible for decades to come. In this pre-internet age, information is not available by electronic means. You have to look in archives and libraries, and ask experts at museums and universities, for the information that typical troubleshooters would need for their investigations.

Much of the information is in the artefacts themselves or printed in books, but sometimes it may have been photographed and stored on microfilm.

Investigations in your adventures

There are many ways you can use museums, archives and libraries in your adventures.

Expert help: Have an expert at one of the locations help the characters find a piece of critical information, maybe even a photocopy of whatever they are looking for.

Help in a challenge: If you use a challenge to reveal clues, give the characters a +2 or **+5 pips modifier** if the characters think of using a proper resource, such as an archive or library. The investigation takes a little longer (estimate at least half a day per task check), but it may be worth it.

Break-in: There may be valuables in a museum, or a particular artefact that the characters need and can't get by legal means. Optionally, someone else is out for those valuables or that resource.

Table: List of some libraries in Paris

Library	Location	Subject	Skill
Bibliothèque Forney	Rue du Figuier, IVᵉ Arrondissement	Decorative arts	**Entertainment, Humanities**
Bibliothèque de l'Arsenal	Rue de Sully, IVᵉ Arrondissement	French literature, medieval manuscripts, charts and plans	**Humanities, Languages**
Bibliothèque Mazarine	Quai de Conti, VIᵉ Arrondissement	Oldest library in France, originally cardinal Mazarin's private library	**Humanities, Languages**
Bibliothèque Marguerite Durand	Rue Nationale, XIVᵉ Arrondissement	Feminism, suffragettes; letters, biographies, photographs, letters and more	**Humanities**
Petite Bibliothèque Ronde	Rue de Bretagne, Clamart	Newly opened children's library	**Humanities, Charm**
Bibliothèque de la Sorbonne	Rue de la sorbonne, Vᵉ Arrondissement	University library	**Engineering, Humanities, Languages, Medicine, Science**
Bibliothèque nationale de France	Quai François Mauriac, IXᵉ Arrondissement	Medieval and modern manuscripts, ancient history, scientific history, genealogies, Masonic collections etc. Copies of every book published in France must by law be deposited here.	**Humanities, Languages**

Table: List of some museums in Paris

Museum	Location	Subject	Skill
Bibliothèque-Musée de l'Opéra National de Paris	Rue Scribe, IXᵉ Arrondissement	Library and museum about the Paris Opera	**Entertainment, Humanities**
Catacombes de Paris	Avenue du Colonel Henri Rol-Tanguy, XIVᵉ Arrondissement	Underground ossuary with the remains of over six million people	**Humanities, Science**
Musée de la Contrefaçon	Rue de la Faisanderie, XVIᵉ Arrondissement	History of counterfeits	**Subterfuge**
Musée Curie	Rue Pierre et Marie Curie, Vᵉ Arrondissement	History of radiology research and the work of Pierre and Marie Curie	**Science**
Musée de l'Homme	Place du Trocadéro, XVIᵉ Arrondissement	Anthropology, human evolution and the history of human sciences	**Humanities, Medicine, Science**
Musée de l'histoire de France	Rue de Francs Bourgeois, IIIᵉ Arrondissement	History, documents from the Archives Nationales	**Humanities, Languages**
Musée de Minéralogie	Boulevard Saint-Michel, VIᵉ Arrondissement	Geology, minerals, rocks, ores, gems, artificial minerals	**Science**
Musée des Égouts de Paris	Quai d'Orsay, VIIᵉ Arrondissement	History of the Paris sewer system, sewer workers, water treatment and tours of the sewer system	**Humanities, Subterfuge**
Musée du Louvre	Rue de Rivoli, Iᵉ Arrondissement	Art and art history from all over the world, including the Classical world and the Near East.	**Humanities, Languages**
Musée National d'Art Moderne	Place Georges-Pompidou, Iᵉ Arrondissement	Modern and contemporary art	**Humanities**
Musée des Vampires et des Monstres de l'Imaginaire	Rue Jules David, Les Lilas	Vampirism, demonology, occidental folklore and tales of the macabre	**Humanities**

FOOD AND DINING

There is a revolution happening in French cuisine, possibly as an effect of the War and possibly due to immigration. Nouvelle cuisine is moving towards shorter menus, lighter sauces, and a celebration of produce and vegetables. At the same time there is an influx of Vietnamese, Chinese, African and Italian cuisine.

Cuisine classique: For much of the century, the classical French high-culture kitchen has been practiced in grand restaurants and hotels in Europe. Complex dishes and formalised presentations of dishes, served one course after another ("service à la russe"), marks cuisine classique.

Nouvelle cuisine: "The new kitchen" is in a sense a rebellion against the extravagant classic cooking. It puts emphasis on natural flavours, simple preparation, lighter sauces, shorter menus, and shorter cooking times.

Bistro: In the many small bistros in Paris, you can get a simple meal for a modest price. The food is often regional and slow-cooked, like a rich casserole with beans.

Brasserie: A wider array of choices than the bistro and more professional service can be found at any brasserie. A meal typically has a single dish, unlike the classical or new kitchen. Steak frites – fries and steak – is a typical dish.

Guide Michelin

Guide Michelin was created by the tire manufacturer to encourage people to drive more, so that they would need to buy tires more often. The famous grading system works like this: a restaurant with a single star is worth stopping by if you are going that way. Two stars means that the restaurant is worth a detour, and three stars means that it is worth planning an entire trip just to go there.

Parisian café: A Parisian café is not just a place to get coffee, they offer a complete kitchen with a restaurant menu, often a bar and even a wine selection. They are the hub of social life, where you can sit for hours and watch life pass by.

Nine delicious places to get a bite

Restaurant	Location	Menu
Bouillon Camille Chartier	Rue Racine	Traditional Parisian food
La Petite Simone	Rue Caumartin	Nouvelle cuisine
Le Train Bleu	Gare de Lyon	Cuisine classique
Restaurant Italien	Rue de Ponthieu	Italian from the Po valley
Le Grand Véfour	Palais-Royal	Traditional French cuisine
Dingo Bar	Rue Delambre	American food and alcohol.
Ma Bourgogne	Place de Vosges	Bistro, Burgundian cuisine
Pondichéry	Passage Brady	Indian food
Yeng et Chen	Rue Bargue	Frenchified Cantonese

DINING IN YOUR ADVENTURES

Most of the time, dining is just a filler (pun intended) or statement of style. But sometimes, it can be more than that.

Start an adventure: It is a rather common ploy to start an adventure with the words "you are at a tavern", and you can often use this ploy in *The Troubleshooters* too – we have found that it is often a good way to get the characters together after the **Plot Hook** handouts are given to the players. This usually happens spontaneously, so just let it play out.

Meet a contact: Shady contacts generally want to meet in shady bars or sleazy diners, where they can slide an envelope full of information to the characters without any prying eyes taking notice.

LA RÉPUBLIQUE

La République is an independent newspaper based in Paris. Although it sells moderately well with about 200,000 copies daily, it does not count as a newspaper of record like *Le Monde* or *Le Figaro*.

Politically, *La République* is somewhere between its main rivals, the centre-left *Le Monde* and the left-wing *L'Humanité*. No matter which party is in power in France, *La République* is critical of the government. Of course, they're more critical if the government is right-wing.

Robert Legros is the current editor in chief.

Reception: Reception is always manned during office hours. They can help visitors with most issues, or call someone that can help them.

Switchboard: Like reception, the switchboard is also manned during office hours. The all-female staff answer incoming calls and connect them to the correct person, and make calls over the PA if they do not answer.

Mail room: The mail room is mostly busy in the morning, where bags with incoming mail are sorted and then delivered to the recipients in the building. Most mail is actually not for the newsroom or editor, but for the sales department – especially ads for print or complaints about subscriptions.

Teleprinter room: The teleprinter room is the second noisiest place at *La République*, but not by much. Rows of teleprinters print out news from agencies all around the world on long rolls of paper.

Newsroom: In the newsroom, teleprinter news, telephone interviews and hand-written notes are converted into news stories that can be set and printed.

Setting room: You can't just take a typed story and put it in a printer. It has to be set, and that happens in the setting room. *La République* has brand new electronic phototypesetting machines which can set an amazing 600 characters per minute.

Sales department: The sales department sells three things: private subscriptions, retail subscriptions, and advertisements, both personal and commercial. Salespeople are ready to receive your call to place an ad or start a subscription during office hours.

Editor's office: Robert Legros, the editor in chief, is the one ultimately responsible for the content of the newspaper. Most of the time, he delegates to his editors to decide what stories to run. If there is a big scoop, the editors and journalists come to monsieur Legros to inform him and get his approval on the story. It doesn't happen that often, but sometimes he orders the printing presses to stop, while a last minute breaking story is inserted.

La République
1. Reception
2. Switchboard
3. Mail room
4. Lunch room
5. Storage
6. Printing press room
7. Loading dock
8. Archive
9. Sales room
10. Conference room
11. Teleprinter room
12. Setting room
13. Newsroom
14. Editor's office

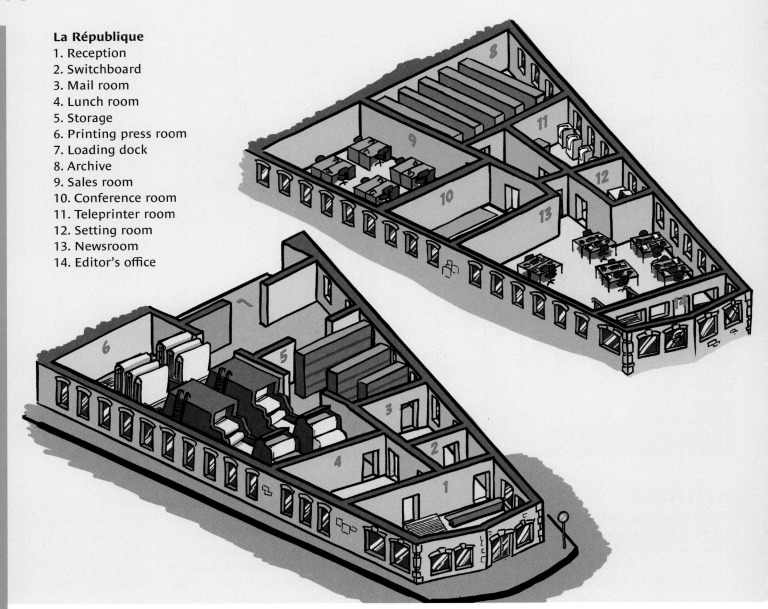

Archive: In contrast to the hubbub around the print shop and the news room, the archive is the most silent place at *La République*. Here, hard-bound compilations of every issue are kept, and articles and news stories are also indexed, transferred to microfilm and stored.

Printing presses: The print shop is the noisiest place at the newspaper by far. The huge presses prints thousands of copies every hour for distribution around the world.

Loading dock: From the loading dock, bundles and pallets of freshly-printed newspapers are sent out all over Paris and France. Loading the trucks starts very early in the morning.

Distribution trucks: *La République* still uses their old Renault trucks for distribution within Paris.

La République in your adventures
La République can help the characters, but the relation is often business-minded: the paper expects something in return, even if it is an "I owe you".

Patron: *La République* may sponsor the characters' adventures in return for the rights to the story.

Archives: The archives contain every printed issue, either bound or on microfilm, since the start of the paper in 1857 except for 1940–1945 due to the Nazi occupation. If the characters dig in the archives, make an **Investigation task check** or a challenge for **Investigation**, **Red Tape** and **Search**.

Contacts: *La République* has foreign correspondents all over the world. Either they meet the characters when they arrive, or they can easily be found with a **Contacts task check**.

POLICE

How good the French police are depends on which police force you are talking about. The Sûreté and the Gendarmerie are generally seen as competent police forces, while the municipal police are the target of some ridicule for having sleepy police officers in sleepy French towns.

The different police forces generally cooperate well due to clearly defined jurisdictions, but there can be clashes at times.

Sûreté nationale: The civilian police force was a pioneer in policing when it was formed in the 19th century, and was the model for Scotland Yard and the FBI. It is responsible for most of the larger urban areas, for instance Paris. A reform of the Sûreté is being considered, and may happen as early as 1966.

Gendarmerie nationale: The Gendarmerie is a military police force which is responsible for policing most of the countryside and small towns, as well as protecting military installations.

Police municipale: The municipal police are responsible for some 3,500 towns all around France, larger than those that the Gendarmerie are responsible for, but not the urban centres.

Death is only the beginning

Worth mentioning is the *Institut Médico-Légal* at Quai de la Rapée, the Paris morgue and forensic medical institute. If you meet a violent end in Paris, or happen to be famous, this is your penultimate destination before the grave.

The police in your adventures

Most of the time you *don't* want the police in your adventure. If the villains are arrested, then the characters will have nothing to do, and if the characters are arrested, then there won't be an adventure and the villains will probably win.

The police therefore work best if you keep them as a pacing mechanism, to stop the characters temporarily if they steam on too fast, or as a device for generating humour.

When you want to slow down the tempo, the police can bring the characters to the station for questioning. Then have the players squirm a little as you ask uncomfortable questions.

If the characters are arrested for doing something incredibly stupid (like murder, theft, abuse, break and entry etc), use the following guidelines:

Fines/warning: If it is a minor transgression, like a fist-fight, speeding, trespassing and so on, let them go with a warning or with a ticket **–2 pips** on the next **Credit task check**). You can also order them to turn up at a magistrate's court to have the book thrown at them, but until then they're free to go.

When they show up in court, make it a challenge for **Contacts**, **Investigation**, **Red Tape** and **Subterfuge**. Depending on the outcome, the characters may be fined (**–2 pips** or more on the next **Credit task check**), have to pay damages (**–2 pips** on one more **Credit task check**), or even jailed for a short time.

Don't leave town: If the police can't pin the characters to a crime, but they are among the main suspects, they may be forced to hand over their passports and ordered to remain available.

Out of the game: If it is a major transgression or if the characters are obviously dangerous (for instance they openly used firearms), they are locked up. Effectively, they are out of the game. If it is a serious crime like murder or abuse, the character is out of the game for the foreseeable future, and the player should make a new character. If it is a less serious crime, they may be out of the game for this adventure. Have the player play a temporary character, perhaps by taking over a Director character, for the rest of the adventure.

Sometimes, you *do* want the police in the adventure. When the characters have figured out everything, but are not proficient enough in combat to take care of things by themselves, it is a good time to send in the police. Then the problem is just persuading the police to do it. It may require that the characters present evidence, successfully argue for intervention (you can use a challenge for it), and bring in a prosecutor to handle the police and the bureaucracy of the judiciary.

EYES ONLY

The following material is PROTECTED
under article 413-9 of the Penal Code.
For the Director of Operations' eyes only.

THE DIRECTOR

Do you want to dominate the world? Good luck! I won't let you do that, because that is reserved for me! But I will allow you to control your game as the Director of the local Octopus operation.

In fact, I encourage you to do just that! It is good fun, and in this chapter I will teach you all about it.

If you are a player, you should stop reading now. This section of the book is for the Director of Operations' eyes only. If you are the Director of Operations, please continue.

THE DIRECTOR OF OPERATIONS' JOB

The Director of Operations is the person in charge of the game. Your job is to drive the story and entertain the players. This can be condensed into seven primary tasks:

- Hosting the game
- Moderating the table
- Presenting the setting
- Challenging the players
- Interpreting the rules
- Acting
- Having fun

HOSTING THE GAME

Very often, the Director is also the host of the evening. It doesn't have to be the Director, but it usually works out that way.

- Make sure that basic amenities are available. Expect toilet breaks.
- Offer coffee, tea or something to drink, and maybe some snacks. It's quite common for players to be expected to bring their own drinks and snacks.
- Prepare a place to play. A kitchen table works perfectly fine: just make sure that players have space for their stuff and somewhere to sit somewhat comfortably, and that you can play without too much interruption.
- Have some accessories available, like tokens, cards, pen, paper, erasers etc.

MODERATING THE TABLE

One of the most important tasks is moderating the table. You want everyone to be satisfied with the time they get in the limelight, and you want the session to be played in an orderly fashion.

Sometimes, you have to stop one player to give another player time to have their say or act out the actions of their character. Sometimes it may be tricky to notice when to do this, especially if a player is a bit shy, introverted or socially uncomfortable.

One way of giving the quiet players an opportunity to express themselves is to have the active player's actions result in things that directly affect a quiet player's character, forcing them to tidy up the mess.

However, it is a tricky balance. Sometimes, giving too much attention to a player makes them uncomfortable. Don't force players to take the limelight if they don't want to, and don't punish them for not wanting to be the focus of the session.

PRESENTING THE SETTING

You have to present the setting for the players. There are many tricks you can use, but the main tool is the characters' senses. Describe what they see, hear, smell and feel.

Use pictures if you can. Maps are good too, but give the players a helicopter view of the place. Pictures are generally from a more down-to-earth perspective. Steal them from the internet – and of course, they don't have to be from the actual place. If the picture fits the general atmosphere of the adventure, use it, even if the place it shows is from somewhere else.

Remember that you are the players' eyes. By describing the setting, you create a window into the world of the Troubleshooters. The wider you can open this window, the better they can imagine the world and live it.

CHALLENGING THE PLAYERS

At its core, any game is about choices. Should you do this or do that? What are the consequences of each decision? Roleplaying games work just the same, except that you make those choices as your character and some choices are adjudicated by the Director rather than the game's rules. But it is still about making choices.

Something to keep in mind is that problems are most fun to solve when there are multiple solutions, each with a distinct outcome. Roleplaying games are uniquely suited to this end as they are not limited to a board and the rules. What's more, the randomness of the dice adds a level of uncertainty to every situation.

Most of all, though, it's the intellectual challenge that makes roleplaying fun. It's not just about creating a story together, but encouraging both the players and their characters to constantly come up with and act out new ideas that propel the story forward.

So throw challenges at the players.

- Give them tricky puzzles to figure out.
- Let them try to discover the weaknesses of their enemies.
- Have them face tricky moral choices.
- Let them create a plan for reaching their goals.

Part of challenging the players is also challenging their characters, by pushing them to the limit. Let them shine with their Abilities and high Skills by putting obstacles in their path and forcing them to overcome them. Never let their victories be too easy.

There are plenty of obstacles you can use to increase the difficulty and drama of a scene.

- Be more liberal with hard modifiers as characters get skilled and players get cocky.
- Note the Complications of the characters, and give the players an excuse to activate them (they probably want the **Story Points** anyway).
- Ask for task checks and Skill challenges involving Skills with lower Skill values.

A big part of ensuring the players are properly challenged happens when you prepare their adventures. This can't be overstated. It is such an important aspect of the game that we have given it a rather large section of its own.

INTERPRETING THE RULES

Roleplaying games have rules for the simple reason that it feels more fair that way. It's easier for players to accept an outcome if it was the dice – not the Director – that decided their fate.

The rules of the game are generic enough for most situations, but that also means that you need to interpret

the rules to figure out how you should apply them in any given situation.

In most circumstances, you can apply the standard rule: declare an action, decide which Skill applies, and make a task check for it. Then again, you might instead decide to make a Skill challenge (keep a Skill list handy). In some special situations, you use the fight rules, or the rules for Abilities and Complications. Knowing what rule to use is half your job as Director. You can even make rules up on the spot, usually based on task checks or Skill challenges.

One important thing to remember is that you should never make a rule with an outcome you don't want. Don't make a rule for not being crushed by a collapsing tunnel unless the outcome of characters being crushed is within the realm of desirable outcomes. If the narrative calls for a collapsing tunnel but you are not prepared to let the characters end up flattened under tonnes of rock and rubble, make the rule about something else, like avoiding having their equipment crushed, getting separated or even becoming trapped underground.

ACTING

The final job of the Director is to give a voice to all the people in the game world not controlled by the players. You decide how they act, what they say, and in the case of more important characters, instill them with memorable personalities.

Most of the people in the game world are minor characters that you don't have to spend much energy on. They're templates and stereotypes, and you can treat them that way.

Unlike the cast characters, your Director characters get very little stage time. For them to have any discernible personality at all, you need to exaggerate certain features or traits to make them stand out.

Here are some examples of how you can express your characters.

- Stand up when acting as Graf von Zadrith, or whoever your main villain is. Or hunch forward like a vulture when acting as Doctor Cutter or any mad scientist.
- Vary your voice. Use pitch, intonation, loudness, vocabulary – anything you can think of – to express the character.
- Give them a few trademark phrases, from Graf von Zadrith's "A-haha-haha" to Harry's aunt's "Pish-tosh!"

Villains and the Art of Camp

Speaking of acting, the best villains are often portrayed as camp. They are ostentatious, exaggerated and theatrical. That includes Graf von Zadrith himself, with his stylised purple dress suit and monocle, outlandish laughter and speeches, and ridiculous plans for world control.

The best way to portray villain is to make them camp. The essence of camp is the love of the unnatural, the artifice and exaggeration. Make your villains larger than life, go over the top, *but do it utterly serious*. Try to not make it as a joke, but embrace their nature of camp.

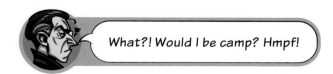

What?! Would I be camp? Hmpf!

CREATING ADVENTURES

An adventure is a self-contained story framework that you and the players flesh out by playing in one or more sessions. One of your main jobs as Director of Operations is to create the adventures for your players.

A QUICK RECIPE FOR ADVENTURES

The quick way to get an adventure is simply this: *steal!* If you're short of ideas, and only have a few hours prep time, you can use this recipe for making an adventure:

1   **Pick up any comic book from the genre:** or watch an episode of *Lupin III* or *The Saint*.

2   **Steal the story:** Where does the story take place? What happens? What has to be done? Who besides the main characters are in the story? What's the twist? How is it resolved? What's the climax?

3   **Define the opposition:** Use recurring Director characters for the main antagonists if you can. Use generic characters for the rest. Write up stats for the more interesting new characters.

4   **Replace the main character with the cast characters:** Use a patron and/or two matching **Plot Hooks** to get the characters involved. Create **Plot Hook** handouts.

5   **Plan for what happens if the characters are captured:** Identify when the characters are most likely to get captured and plan for it.

6   **Make or steal the necessary maps:** Also, create clues if you need them and have the time.

This should quickly give you at least an outline of a playable adventure. Since you're not creating a computer game, an outline of a playable adventure is all that you need for running it.

Example: *In the* Blake & Mortimer *two-volume adventure* "The Mystery of the Great Pyramid", *the deciphering of a newly discovered papyrus scroll points to a secret chamber in the Great Pyramid where the mummy of Akhenaten and his treasure lies buried. A recurring villain has a mole in the Cairo museum and learns the secret too. Posing as a famous Egyptologist, the villain gets away and finds the passage to the secret chamber. Stopping the villain is straightforward in the beginning: just get to the secret chamber first.*

In the story, there's the curator of the museum, his assistant (the mole), the head of Cairo police, an antique dealer, a famous Egyptologist, his assistant (a henchman to the villain), and a mysterious old man in the desert, plus supporting villains, police officers and other cast.

There are several twists: the villain posing as the famous Egyptologist, the assistant being the henchmen of the villain,

and of course the old man in the desert. In the album, the story is resolved with a little bit of deus ex machina, which the Director can keep as a reserve outcome if things go poorly.

The locations are the Cairo museum, the antique dealer's shop, the Egyptologist's home, the dig at the Giza plateau, the tunnels beneath the pyramid, and the chamber itself. The Chamber of Horus is the location of the climax of the story.

The Director doesn't have to change much: the story is set in the 1950s, so it just needs to have slightly more modern technology. She decides to use Baroness Zonda as the villain, searching for the treasure at the behest of the Octopus. Otherwise, she keeps the rest as is, and uses the stats for generic Director characters.

The Director toys with the idea of moving the story to England and having it be about the standard of the IX Legion hidden at Stonehenge, but eventually decides to keep it in Egypt.

*The Director then goes on to map the tunnels under the Great Pyramid, and of course the Chamber of Horus. She invents a few nasty traps and hidden passages, and creates the necessary challenges. She also decides to use the **Looking for the Past** and **Friends in High Places Plot Hooks** to get Paul Marchand and Frida Bäckström on the case.*

There are a few situations where the characters can get caught: at the antique dealer's, at the Egyptologist's home, and of course in the Chamber of Horus. In the first case, the characters will just be tied up and kept in the basement with a lot of antiques. In the second case, the police will storm in if things take a turn for the worse and it all hits the fan. In the third case, the strange old man will reveal himself to be the head priest of Aten, the protector of Akhenaten's treasure, and will appear to save the day with the power of the sun god Aten (or hypnotism, sleeping gas or whatever).

The last thing to do is to google for maps of Cairo in the 1960s, and then the Director is set for an exciting adventure.

If more time was available, she could make clues from hieroglyphs for the players to crack, handouts of secret doors to open, more backstory on the cult of Aten and the history of Akhenaten, and so on. But right now, the players are arriving.

STORY

The core of any adventure is that somebody (the antagonist) wants to do something, and someone else (the protagonist – the characters in this case) need to do something about it. You can often find ideas in your campaign notes.

● **What happens?** If you don't have any other ideas, the antagonist can always be the Octopus. So what do they want to do? They may be looking for a strange mineral called ruritanium, kidnapping an influential countess to prevent a top meeting, setting up a mind control device to control the French government, or attempting to murder a defector.

- **What has to be done about it?** Well, that's the characters' job. It could be that the characters steal the ruritanium mineral first, find and destroy the mind control device, free the kidnapped countess and smuggle her across the border, or figure out who the murderer is.
- **How do the characters get involved?** When you know what happens and what has to be done, you look at the characters' **Plot Hooks** or patron and figure out how to get the characters involved. Write the startup handouts that you need.
- **Where will the characters have to go?** Exotic locations are more fun than mundane ones. Why go to a generic big city when you can go to Hong Kong? Once you have an idea of the location, find a few interesting landmarks and get inspired. Prepare a few scenes – a meeting with a contact, a clue, an ambush – just to frame the location and get the action going.
- **What should they do when they get there?** That's the final thing: how do you finish the story once the players get to the right location? Be sure that whatever happens makes for a satisfying conclusion.

When you have the core of a story, you can expand upon it with red herrings, alternative solutions, additional locations, and so on.

PLOT HOOKS

To start the adventure, you can use **Plot Hook** handouts. If you are running a published adventure, there are about 4–6 prepared **Plot Hook** handouts in the adventure book. Pick two of them, and make sure that they apply to two different characters, and use them to kick off the adventure.

If you're creating an adventure for yourself, you just pick two characters, choose one **Plot Hook** for each, and create a **Plot Hook** handout for those characters.

A **Plot Hook** handout should do the following:

- Set up a problem.
- Offer a lead-in to the adventure.
- Motivate the character to solve the problem.
- Set the tone of the adventure.

Make sure that your **Plot Hook** handouts fulfil these requirements.

The characters who receive the **Plot Hook** handouts are the **Plot Hook** characters for that adventure. They are expected to drag the other characters into the adventure – they get free improvement ticks if they do. They are also the "main characters" of the adventure,

and the other players are motivated to make them feel like main characters – those players get free improvement ticks if they help the **Plot Hook** characters stand out and seem special.

Some **Plot Hooks**, like **Arch-Enemy: The Octopus** or **Secret Service**, can easily dominate a campaign. Avoid using the same **Plot Hooks** every time.

It is important to rotate the role of Plot Hook characters, so that no player feels as if they are being left out or treated unfairly.

ACTS

A good way to set up your adventures is to plan it in acts. The three-act model has an Introduction, a Development, and a Climax. The five-act model has an Introduction, a Development, a Twist, a New Development, and a Climax.

These are not the only models, and they are also linear, but they have the advantage of being simple and understandable, while still providing a template for a story that a less experienced Director can use to make adventures.

Introduction: In the introduction, the problem is presented to the characters, the characters find motivation to go on an adventure, and the story starts up.

The typical introduction starts with **Plot Hook** handouts, or a patron asking the characters to complete some task or another. You can have an action scene or two and leave a few clues to further motivate the characters to have an adventure. There can even be travel scenes and socialising scenes as the characters go to the location of the adventure.

Development: The development act is for elaborating on the story. This is where the characters investigate the problem, or the problem comes to the characters (or both). The development act often forms the bulk of mystery adventures. The goal is to reveal some kind of truth that can lead to a climax.

Twist and New Development (Optional): In a five-act adventure, you often have a twist and a new development. The twist means that something happens that turns the characters' theories on their heads, or messes with their plans so that they have to start over. There can be a new travel scene as the twist takes them to a new location.

After that a new development act happens revealing the actual truth, which leads to the climax.

Climax: The final act is the climax. It can be a big fight, or a big reveal, or a big chase scene, but whatever it is, the story is concluded. Not all loose ends have to be tied up (you will need a new adventure in the future anyway), but the core of the story should have a natural ending.

SCENES

Most scenes are created and framed on the spot, as they are needed. Some key scenes may be planned in advance, for instance the big villain shootout, the key interrogation scene etc. It is common to have at least one scene that defines the act of your story:

- **Introduction:** You need one scene per startup handout, plus a scene where everyone gets together and comes up with a plan. You can add an action scene for getting the plot going.
- **Development:** This is the part where the characters find clues. Some of the clues may need social scenes, others may require that the characters engage in semi-legal or illegal activities (breaking and entering), and some may be research scenes. Use the Clue sheet (see below) as a checklist to figure out what clues you need and how to distribute them.
  - For **social scenes**, define who knows what: decide which Director character has the information the characters are looking for. There may be some sort of quid pro quo involved.
  - For **research scenes**, define what the characters can learn at a location. The characters can get some clues automatically by looking in the right place. Use task checks for additional clues on top of the automatic clues. You can also use challenges for the same effect.
  - For **breaking-and-entering scenes**, you can steal or quickly make a map. Add some challenges, like alarm systems, locks, guards etc. Plan for the eventuality that the characters are captured.
  - You can add an **action scene** involving villains trying to stop the characters' investigation, either by trying to kidnap them, steal their clues, silence them or attack them.
  - **Travel scenes** need to establish a change of location. Such scenes could consist of planning for the journey, maybe some task checks or a challenge, followed by a bit of description of the new location. The introduction of a contact at the airport or train station and checking into a hotel is usually a good way of establishing the new location, and gives the characters a base of operations.
- **Twist and new development:** If you have a twist planned, you need to plan the scene where the twist is revealed. Handle the new development just like the first one.
- **Climax:** You need to plan for a climax scene, preferably before it is about to happen. Non-planned climax scenes often fall a bit flat. You don't have to plan the climax scene before starting the adventure, but it is often useful to have it planned in advance since you then know where to lead your players.

MAPS

There are two kinds of maps: setting maps and location maps.

Setting maps exist to give the players a sense of their characters' world. One advantage of the setting of Earth in the 1960s is that it is easy to find setting maps. The disadvantage is that there are no fictional countries or locations on those maps – there are no countries like Sitomeyang, Arenwald or Sylveria. You have to insert those on your own.

One solution is to use real maps for an overview, and then add in your own countries wherever you want them.

Location maps are for places that the characters visit: villages, towns, castles, apartments, Octopus bunkers and so on. Sometimes you can borrow these from other sources, and sometimes you have to draw them on your own.

If you suspect that a fight will happen at a location, or plan for it, remember to divide the available space into zones (see *Zones* on page 89) and make sure the terrain will help make the fight more interesting.

CLUES

A mystery adventure is an adventure built on clues. If you use the act model, finding and interpreting the clues mostly happens in the Development act. A way to plan clues is to list the characters' Skills, and then invent at least one clue for each Skill at 45+, and at least two clues for Skills at 65+. Focus on social and **Investigation** Skills. Background, action and Combat Skills are not that important. You probably need one set of clues for each development act. Also, you need to create clues for Abilities and Complications, and even **Plot Hooks**.

You can do this using a clue sheet. A clue sheet is just a table of characters as columns, and Skills, Abilities, **Plot Hooks** and Complications as rows.

Clues consists of one small fact, like "footprints in the snow", "a handgun in the closet", "the maid lacks an alibi" and so on. They can be elaborated upon with a little story or even a handout, but at its core, it's just a small fact.

You can never have enough clues! If your adventure is a mystery in which your players need to figure out something to get to the next location, double down on the amount of clues that would get them there.

Be generous with clues. Hand out a clue if someone is at the right place and has the right Skill, or if they ask for it. Elaborate on the clue (i.e. give them another clue) if the players use their Skills to investigate further.

Never interpret the clues! That's a job for the players. If they don't get it, give them another clue instead of telling them what a previous clue means.

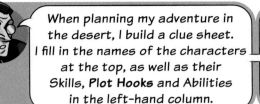

When planning my adventure in the desert, I build a clue sheet. I fill in the names of the characters at the top, as well as their Skills, **Plot Hooks** and Abilities in the left-hand column.

And then I go nuts, inventing clues for as many rows as I can! I note that none of the attending characters have **Humanities**, which means that they probably won't understand much of the Egyptology. Too bad.

This is what the clue sheet looks like when I'm about halfway through.

Character:	FRIDA	PAUL	ELEKTRA	ÉLOÏSE	
Agility		Traps (too late)			
Alertness	Antique dealer, hidden door Cairo Museum, stalked		Antique dealer, hidden door Cairo Museum, stalked		
Contacts		Captain Mubarrak, Cairo Police			
Electronics				Cairo Museum, alarm system sabotaged	
Engineering				Invoice listing machine components for high-powered drill	
Investigation				Cairo museum, CCTV feed connected to transmitter Antique dealer, fake authenticity certificates	
Prestidigitation		Antique dealer, stealing letters			
Ranged Combat	Stalker has a gun in shoulder holster				
Science				Cairo museum, C14 dating of artifacts older than the pyramid	
Search		Antique dealer, hidden door		Antique dealer, hidden door	
Security		Cairo museum, alarm Antique dealer, alarm			
Subterfuge	Egyptologist's false beard				
Vehicles	Recurring tyre tracks		Recurring tyre tracks		
Born Behind the Wheel			BMW brand		
Been Everywhere			Aziz, truck driver, driving supplies to dig		
Media Darling			Journalist hints of unlicensed dig		
Military Rank	Persuade Cairo police				
Secret Service	Baroness Zonda				
Lock-Picker		Antique dealer, locked safe			

ENEMIES

You need a supporting cast for your adventure. Some of them will be enemies trying to stop or capture the characters (maybe even kill them, but that's not really true to the genre).

Balancing enemies can be tricky. Encounters can often be made too easy or too hard. Here are some guidelines that may help:

- **One boss:** One Boss may be enough if it can counter-attack, or has multiple attacks, area attacks or similar ways to damage several characters in the same turn. One Boss can also be enough if it can delay characters, for instance by being terrifying or huge. Make sure the Boss has enough **Vitality**.
- **A boss or lieutenant with underlings/mooks:** With Underlings and Mooks, a Boss may be less dangerous – maybe even a Lieutenant. Area attacks and multiple attacks are not that important with Underlings and Mooks. A reasonably even fight is one Boss or Lieutenant, plus one *Underling* per character or two Mooks per characters.
- **A bunch of underlings:** You can have a fight with just Underlings. One Underling per character, plus an additional Underling per fighting character (any Combat Skill at 65% or more) is usually a good mix.
- **Cannon fodder:** Cannon fodder is for making the players feel awesome and competent. About twice as many Mooks as characters is usually a cool fight. Two fighting characters against ten Mooks is challenging, and one fighting character against ten Mooks is stressful and borderline impossible (and sometimes hysterically funny)!

Sometimes you don't want a fair fight. Maybe you want to discourage the characters from fighting at all, or you want them to be captured. Then you need some time for the enemies to deal enough damage to the characters. Here are some things you can do to make fights more challenging:

- **More opponents:** Every extra opponent buys more time for the Bosses and Lieutenants. They also offer the characters more chances for that sense of accomplishment that comes from taking out an opponent.
- **More Vitality:** More **Vitality** buys your Director characters more time to be dangerous, but also has the disadvantage of making the fight into a slow and tedious grind.
- **More protection:** Heavy protection has the same effect as **Vitality**, only less reliable.
- **More damage:** If enemies inflict more damage, it will be easier to knock out characters.
- **More attacks:** More attacks shorten the duration of a fight, measured in turns. Counter-attacks are a

nasty surprise to characters, and will force them to think about how to take on a Boss.

- **Area effects:** Area effects are dangerous as you can knock out several characters in one single attack. Player characters are not invulnerable.
- **Neutralising attacks:** When player characters become stuck, separated, scared, paralysed etc., the group's overall damage per turn goes down, allowing you more time for the bad guys to do their thing.
- **Stopping attacks:** If the opponent is huge or immaterial, the characters can't attack it right away. They need to find a way around the tag that prohibits them from causing it harm.
- **Tactics:** A simple and dangerous trick is to have the enemies think tactically, using the terrain to their advantage, cooperating to take down one character at a time (especially fighting characters), etc.

OTHER PEOPLE

You need other people in your adventures as well: contacts, people with clues, ordinary people to flesh out the world. Often, you just need a name, a role, an associated clue, and nothing else.

If you need rules for them, you only have to set the **Vitality** score (usually 4), the **Basic** Skill value (usually 35%) and the **Specialist** Skill value (usually 65%). Sometimes you can add an Initiative score and some Attacks (somewhere between **Basic** and **Specialist** Skill values). Optionally, you can also add a Defence score (usually slightly higher than the **Basic** Skill value) and some Skills for colour. You can find more advice and examples on creating Director characters in chapter 17, *The Threat Files* on page 204.

One thing that is handy to have is a list of names. Whenever the characters meet a random Director person, pick a name from the name list instead of trying to improvise it. It improves the flow of the game a lot. Don't forget to note the random person and the name for future use.

ENDINGS

Usually, adventures end. Mostly, an adventure is about villains trying to do something and the characters trying to foil those plans. If the characters succeed, all is well in the world. The characters may also get stuff as a result: artifacts and treasure from lost civilisations, tools of destruction, secrets not meant for the public etc. Consider what you want to happen to them.

It should always be a possibility that the characters fail. In this situation, it's the plot of the villain that advances. Decide what will happen if the villain wins, and how that will affect future adventures. It may even open up new adventures!

- If the Octopus gets hold of secret Nazi accounts in a Swiss bank, they can finance another goal, maybe an expedition to the Antarctic where there was a lost Nazi base with flying saucers.
- The Octopus has been chasing the characters and their Tibetan mushroom across the world and finally gets hold of it. Maybe they didn't need it to make a new drug, but for the more mystical purpose of opening a sacred vault in the catacombs beneath Venice.

There is an exception: in campaign play, adventures may overlap so that it is hard to tell where one adventure ends and another begins. Still, it's a good idea to plan milestones that resemble the end of an adventure.

TRAVEL

For the ordinary person, intercontinental travel is an adventure in and of itself. Few can afford it, and even then, only once or twice in a lifetime. The characters, however, are meant to go on adventures and are not limited to Europe. So travel should not be a showstopper. There are several ways of solving the problem:

- At least one character has a high **Credit** Skill value.
- At least one character has the Old Money or Nouveau Riche Abilities.
- Introduce a patron that can finance the characters' travels around the world.
- Allow for two modes of travel, a cheap way (third class, steerage, the long way around) and an expensive way if they make a **Credit task check** (fast, direct, comfortable).
- Don't worry about it – the characters can travel wherever they want to if it's in line with the adventure.
- Make the travel into a challenge, involving for instance **Vehicles** (if they go by car), **Survival** (if they trek by foot or ride animals) or **Credit** (if they go by any other means), **Endurance**, **Languages**, **Red Tape** and **Search**. This spreads out the risk while still allowing for the unexpected to happen. On a **Good outcome**, the journey goes as planned.

WHEN CAPTURED!

Thanks to the **Out Cold** Condition and the **Story Point** mechanic, it is likely that player characters will be captured during a mission, often in adventure acts that involve:

- Breaking into the villain's lair
- Illegally searching for clues
- Attracting too much attention

When you plan your adventure, expect that the characters will be captured at least once.

- Create a place where the characters will be locked up. Will they be tied up? Create a Challenge to escape from that location, and be ready to improvise.
- Their possessions will be taken from them. Where will they be stored? Can the characters possibly take something else (and do they have to use **Story Points** to get it?)
- Someone may interrogate the characters. What will they brag about during the interrogation sequence? What will they reveal? Do the players have to use **Story Points** for the villain to reveal something?

You may need more than one plan, depending on your adventure and the number of possible outcomes. For instance, you may need a plan for if the characters are captured when they sneak into Castle Sagvár in Sylveria (they may be captured by Sylverian security forces), another if they are captured smuggling the artifact across the border to Arenwald (they may be arrested by an Arenwaldish border patrol), and yet another if the car chase in the Austrian alps ends badly (they may be arrested by Austrian police or kidnapped by Sylverian agents).

Keep in mind, getting captured is not necessarily a bad thing, as it is one of the few occasions when the player characters have an opportunity to interact with the villain. That's why getting captured is rewarded with **9 Story Points**.

However, getting captured by the police is a special case. It usually happens if the characters are involved in something suspected to be illegal or dangerous. But unless the characters blatantly broke the law, such as by trying to kill someone, or there is a serious risk that they will flee the country, they are likely to be released as soon as it no longer serves the investigation to keep them locked up. Bail bonds are not common in Europe. Rather, the detained may get certain restrictions, such as being ordered to turn over their passport, stay in the country, always be available for questioning, etc. Eventually, the characters may be summoned to court, either as the accused or as a witness.

> Sometimes, being captured by the police is not a special case, and you will just treat it as being captured by anyone else.

> The characters are locked up, their possessions are taken from them, and they have to escape from prison somehow. This is more common in a heist campaign, where prison break episodes could even be their own adventures. I have been in a few, and it is usually pretty fun!

Nine things which fit well in a Troubleshooters game

- **A country you never heard of before:** As said earlier, *The Troubleshooters* is about fantasy tourism. So pick a place that the players have never heard of before, or make one up. Don't be so picky about reality: it is malleable.
- **Hilarious plots for world domination:** If it involves a rubber band, a particle accelerator, octo-rays and a super-bouncy coating made from moon dust, that's completely plausible. Have mind control projectors installed on the Eiffel tower. Invent a secret language in counter-culture books that sends people into a shared hallucination. Make Octopop snacks that contain a drug which will make consumers pliable and open to suggestions from anyone dressed in purple. The more ridiculous, the better!
- **Clumsy or incompetent police officers:** It's not fun if the police solve the characters' problems for them. So of course they can't: they are not interested, the characters are a nuisance, the police draw the wrong conclusion, they think too slowly, they stumble over their shoelaces, or something similar. Only when the adventure is effectively over and the characters have presented the evidence to the police can they arrest the villains.
- **Moustache-twirling villains:** Ah-haha-haha! Of course there must be moustache-twirling villains, even when the moustache-twirling is only figurative.
- **Exotic locations:** Underground bases. Ancient temples. Old castles. Tropical beaches. Cozy cafés. Luxury ocean liners. Picturesque country towns. Glittering casinos. If you consider somewhere to be familiar, it is not a good place to have an adventure.

- **Weird science:** Science really doesn't work like here and now. There are strange particles and even stranger rays, mysterious diseases and creatures that time forgot. Robots are almost practical with a positronic brain rather than a computer, you can build a flying saucer, and you can distill a superb fuel from purple mushrooms. These things are not common for ordinary people, though: you need a mad scientist to perform mad science, and you can't mass-produce mad scientists. But it is quite likely that your characters will encounter their creations, and the mad scientist who came up with them.
- **Travels across the world:** Not only should you go everywhere, you should go there in style. Preferably, a highly varied style too: one journey could be on a luxury ocean liner or supersonic jet, the next in a smoking Toyota Landcruiser, by camel, or in a surplus Russian propeller transport biplane.
- **Everyday problems:** Make everyday problems part of the adventure. The characters' luggage is displaced. There's an exam tomorrow. There's a red light in the middle of a car chase. The characters forget their car keys. There's no food in the fridge. It's even better if you can tie these everyday problems to the characters' Complications – then they never feel out of place and add colour to your adventures.

OTHER GENRES

Bande dessinée are broad and span over several genres and styles, from fantasy to history to present day to science fiction, from drama and romance to action and adventure, and yes, erotic stories too.

We have focused on international mysteries and adventures in the modern era, but there is nothing stopping you from experimenting with other genres and eras.

COMEDY

The Troubleshooters is a light-hearted game. It's supposed to be fun and generate laughs, and comedy is a big part of it.

Comedy is often a balance act. It is about violating the audience's sense of how things ought to be, but in a benign and non-threatening way where the audience can see both sides of the contradiction. The reason that comedy sometimes fail is often that the audience feels that they are directly or indirectly the target of the joke (i.e. the joke feels threatening or non-benign), or that the audience is incapable of seeing both sides (the joke flies over their heads).

You know your players better than we can ever do, so we can't say what works for you. However, here are some simple tricks that you can use:

- **Failing is fun:** Allow for some slapstick when people fail. On a failed **Sneak** roll, don't just have the person make a noise. It could be that someone makes a noise which at first is not noticed, but it kicks off a small argument which ends up in someone yelling in anger. When your players knock out villains, describe a fun way of how the villains are **Out Cold**. Describe them flip backwards, knock them out of their boots, or fall out of the building.

- **Build up to the joke:** A joke is not just the fun punchline. The best jokes are those that you build up to and has a story. This allows you to build up to challenging how things ought to be. Integrate the story of the joke into the story of the adventure
- **Kick upwards:** To make the joke non-threatening, make sure that you never joke about minorities. Rather, kick upwards: aim your joke upwards at the elite or at institutions.
- **Timing:** A lot of the effectiveness of comedy is timing, to make the right joke at the right time. Don't forget that often, the right time is when it is completely unexpected.

PLAYERS CAN DO GAGS TOO!

Allow and encourage players to describe their gags, especially if they fail. Encourage players to make their own running gags. This is basically what the "entertain the table" option is about – you want to reward players for making good comedy.

Don't be afraid of modifying or houseruling Abilities or situation to player gags. This is how the option to throw out a Mook from the scene using the Judo Blackbelt Ability came to be.

- **Make running gags:** Find something that you can make fun of, and do it again. Variation makes repetition better: don't do exactly the same gag every time, just have the same theme. Have the same police inspector turn up every time, and invent a new way of him always drawing the wrong conclusion. Make a Director character mispronounce a character's name all the time, but in different ways (and prepare a list of things to call the character every time).

CREATING A CAMPAIGN

Campaigns are long-running games that are not finished in a few nights. While a single adventure is self-contained, a campaign can often meander as the players branch off, exploring any number of detours in the story. Campaigns can have a common thread linking individual adventures together, consist of several unrelated adventures with no connection to one another, or be one really huge adventure. The one thing campaigns have in common is that they span multiple, even dozens, of sessions.

CAMPAIGN OUTLINE

The campaign outline is what you present to the players at Session Zero to give them a rough idea of the campaign and setting, so that the players can create suitable characters or adjust their character ideas to fit the concept.

You can make the outline as ambitious as you like. It may consist of just a few sentences, a so called "elevator pitch" to sell the idea to the players, or you might go so far as to make a comic book cover mock-up: a front cover page illustration with the title and a rear cover page with text. If you can, draw the cover illustration;

if not, use whatever fitting illustration you can find. If you print the cover on large and sturdy A3 paper, it can also be used as a folder for the handouts that you give to the players and a place to collect their passports.

CAMPAIGN PLAN

The campaign plan is a living document describing the plot of your campaign in broad strokes. It helps you plan your adventures, but it isn't necessary, especially if your campaign just consists of several unrelated adventures.

If you have an overarching story for the campaign, you can organise the campaign plan as a list of episodes, each with a short synopsis, leading up to the final adventure in the story.

This is a living document which is supposed to help you plan future episodes and give your campaign direction. You can change the document as much as you like. Update it regularly, and feel free to insert more episodes as the campaign unfolds.

An easy way to make a campaign plan is to imagine that you're making a television series.

- Write up about ten names for episodes that outline the story arc of your campaign. Then make a brief synopsis, "elevator pitch", for each episode.
- Elaborate on the first episode and make it into an adventure, so that you have something to use for the first session.
- After Session Zero, the players have made their characters. With the knowledge of the cast characters, adapt the elevator pitch to fit the characters and their **Plot Hooks**. Spread episodes evenly among the characters.
- You can write extra episodes (name and elevator pitch) which focus on the characters. 1–3 episodes per character is a good amount. At least one character episode per character should be early in the campaign plan. You should now have about 15–20 episodes in your campaign plan.
- Update the campaign plan after each adventure. Adjust episode order and elevator pitches as necessary.

Do not write more than the elevator pitch until you are prepping that particular adventure. Chances are that events in your adventures will make the campaign plan and any extra prepping that you have done outdated.

EPISODE	NAME	ELEVATOR PITCH/SYNOPSIS
1	The Smile of a Twin	The characters stumble upon a Mona Lisa portrait, which is authenticated to be real by art experts. So what actually hangs in the Louvre?
2	The Ghastly Secret of Château de Skeuvre	In a cozy country château, a fungus experiment goes horribly wrong.
3	Last Train to Istanbul	The Orient Express is suddenly the target of a train heist as it crosses the Alps.
4...		

THE "WHAT'S REALLY HAPPENING" DOCUMENT

It is a good idea to have a "what's really happening" document, even if all you plan to run is stand-alone adventures. This document is about the different factions in the game, what they want to accomplish, how they want to do it and with what resources.

Exactly how you organise the "what's really happening" document depends on the purpose. A mindmap is good for mapping the relations between your different factions and gives you a great overview of possible conflicts that you can make adventures from. A hierarchical word document is easier to organise and search in. Of course, you can have both.

You can use the "what's really happening" document to plot out adventures, even if you're planning for all of them to be independent of one another. Just find one faction opposed to the players, or better yet, two

factions opposed to both the players and one another, take the role of the faction leader, and create a heinous plan that will affect the players.

The "what's really happening" document, or documents, should be updated continuously, just like the campaign plan. After the campaign, you can show it to the players and brag about the villains and their evil plans that have been developing from the very first session.

BACKGROUND FOR PLAYERS

You may need one last document to cover background information that will be known to the player characters when the campaign is starting up.

The background document is not updated as much as the campaign plan or the "what's really happening" document. It may be amended, for instance when the characters get a patron or settle in a new location. Other than that, the background is handled by the players as they get clues and handouts, and keep track of what happens on their own.

SESSION ZERO

"Session Zero" is the session before play actually starts, where the players create their characters and set up the group, and where you as a group define the outline of the campaign.

- As the Director, you should come to Session Zero with a campaign outline, which covers the central concept of the campaign. It's a good idea to have a prepared adventure as well, to use after Session Zero, since it rarely takes that much time to create the group.
- The players should come to Session Zero with an open mind and a willingness to adapt to the campaign idea, but it helps if they have some understanding of the kinds of characters they want to play and what they want to accomplish.

Session Zero usually follows this pattern:

Present the outline: The Director presents his campaign outline, telling the players the central idea about the campaign, and what kind of characters he imagines will work in the campaign and what kind of characters won't fit.

- As a Director, you want to communicate your idea for the campaign, and make any needed adjustments based on feedback from the players.
- As a player, you want to understand the concept of the campaign and think of a way to fit your character idea into it.

Brainstorm: The players discuss ideas about the team, characters, and their overall expectations. The Director participates in the brainstorm, moderating the discussion, and keeping the ideas somewhat in line with the campaign outline. The Director probably has ideas about the theme of the campaign, but the player can of course provide input.

The meat of the brainstorm phase is the players' character ideas. You can use the Templates as a starting point for the discussion, so have the core book at hand and open to the *Templates* chapter.

The goal is for the players to have ideas that inspire them to create their characters, while the Director should understand the players' expectations and wishes – what kind of characters they want to play, what the characters' goals are, and what kind of stories the players want to participate in.

Do not make any characters yet! Wait until you reach a consensus about the characters: not only should each player be happy with their character concept, but all other players as well as the Director should agree that the concept is appropriate for the campaign. It is more common for the Director to think a particular idea doesn't fit the campaign outline than for the players to take issue with each other's concepts.

- As a Director, you want to end this step with a general understanding of the characters, their goals and expectations, and the stories the players would want to take part in.
- As a player, you want to end this step with an idea about your character, and a general understanding of the other characters.

Create characters: Next, get the passports and make characters. This usually doesn't take much time, though having only one core book at the table will naturally slow things down a bit, as players often have to wait while someone else is looking through it. The second most common reason for this step to drag on is if a

player is being indecisive. Other participants can minimise the waiting time this creates by helping the player and making suggestions.

There are some things that have to be done collectively (**Plot Hooks** and how you met), but it is always a good idea to treat the entire character creation process as a group activity. You can ask for advice and give feedback, as well as adjust your own choices to fit the group.

- As a Director, you want to end this step with players with finished characters, and you want to know their **Plot Hooks**, Abilities, Complications and some important Skills.
- As a player, you want to end this step with a complete character and your Passport filled out.

Complete the team: When the players have finished putting the details of their characters down on paper, take some time to present them to one another. The best time to do this is when you decide how the characters met.

- As a Director, you want to end this step with all the characters feeling like a functional team.
- As a player, you want to end this step with an idea of who the other characters are and how you work as a group, and what role your character plays within that group.

Start playing: Session Zero usually takes about an hour tops, so there may be time left to start playing. That's why it's a good idea to have a scenario prepared.

THE FIRST ADVENTURE

The very first adventure takes over after Session Zero. The biggest challenge for you as the Director is that the first adventure needs to do a few things, but that you have to prep it without knowing who the characters are.

Don't do everything: Take it slow. You don't have to introduce the big plot. Instead, start small with just an isolated adventure. It can tie in to the big plot later on or in retrospect, but for the moment, you just want to get the group going.

Introduce the setting: For the first adventure, you should be vivid in your descriptions. Include all the senses. Describe little details, like the baker who greets a character in the morning, the florist flirting with someone, the landlord's grumpy demeanour, the flaking wall plaster on an old buildings, wet cobblestones, landmarks they see in the background – just pepper your descriptions with such details. It sets the tone and helps the players imagine the setting by painting a picture of it in their heads.

Meet the characters: It is a good idea to take the time to learn about the characters. You automatically get the chance to introduce the **Plot Hook** characters, but also make sure to highlight their strengths and weaknesses as you give them their startup handouts.

Then do the same for the non-**Plot Hook** characters. Give each character a scene to show how great they can be.

As it is likely that you will play the first adventure at the end of Session Zero, you may not know what characters you have to work with. The trick is to look at your prepped adventure, and then divide its scenes among the characters according to what they are good at, so that each character gets the necessary introduction.

Learn the rules: If it is your first time playing *The Troubleshooters*, it's a good idea to learn the rules of the game. For that, you need a few scenes:

● One scene just doing things and making task checks.
● One scene with opposed task checks
● One scene with a Challenge.
● One fight scene.

Identify fitting scenes in the adventure, and use them to try the rules. While you're at it, use these scenes to introduce the characters (see Meet the characters above). For instance, a Fight scene is perfect to introduce a Muscle character, while Challenge scenes are good for Investigators, Fixers and Specialists.

Allow for mistakes: After the first adventure, allow the players to adjust their characters according to *Step 8: Customise your character* on page 34, before you make improvement checks and Learning checks.

Have fun: This is the most important part!

My First Adventure usually has a very simple plot: something happens that involves two of five **Plot Hooks**. Then something else happens that has the players try out a task check.

This leads to a third thing which involves some sort of investigative challenge. The investigation leads to a break and entry challenge. The break and entry ends with a fight. After the fight, there's another challenge to find the lair, and a puzzle to sneak in. Once inside, there's a boss fight, or a big reveal scene, or both.

After the players make their characters and I know what to expect from them, I adjust the scenes to fit them better.

Maybe they don't have an investigator in the team, but more of a femme fatale: then the investigative challenge is replaced by a social challenge, perhaps a seduction. Maybe they don't have a proper muscle type character: then the first fight only has Mooks, and there won't be an end fight with a Boss, but instead a big reveal scene.

It usually doesn't take much time making these adjustments. Often I can do them at the table as the players finish their characters.

PATRON

A patron is someone that is willing to support, protect and provide for the characters. The relationship is much less formal than that of an employer. There's not necessarily a contract, but more of a mutual understanding.

A patron is also very useful for starting adventures, offering up assignments rather than having a problem that the characters need to solve.

Here are a few ideas:

A newspaper: As soon as the players get a case, the newspaper can fund their journey across the globe (within reason), provided that they get an exclusive and exciting story out of it. They also have contacts and local correspondents that can help.

An eccentric scientist: An eccentric scientist may always have an idea that has to be tested or something that must be collected, often far away in a distant land. Such a scientist may have crazy ideas, but also a lot of contacts among colleagues across the globe.

A wealthy businessman: The big advantage of wealthy people is that they are not bound by any particular rules. If the adventure sounds exciting or profitable to them, they may happily sponsor it. The drawback is that you have to persuade the patron to provide the funds.

A university: The downside of having a university as a sponsor is that they are accountable, either towards the foundation that funds them or to the taxpayers. So there's a bureaucracy to navigate before going on an adventure. Of course, you might be able to handle that by having someone else do the work. The funds are often limited, but on the other hand, they have access to all the knowledge in the world and contacts in other universities. There's also the "Old Boys network" to rely on.

A law enforcement or intelligence agency: For a regular police or spy action, have the patron be a law enforcement or intelligence agency.

Within reason and based on the interests of the patron, a patron can help the characters with the following:

- **Kick off an adventure:** The patron asks the characters for their help, or offers an assignment to them.
- **Fund travel and boarding:** Realistically, travel and boarding would probably be reasonable but not fancy, but that's not as fun as excessively luxurious or dirt cheap. So don't be afraid to send your characters to a luxury hotel using a Concorde or private jet, or to have them hop on old World War 2 biplanes and stay in a cockroach-infested hostel with one common toilet and no shower in the middle of nowhere.
- **Provide equipment:** The patron can provide the equipment for the assignment. Keep the equipment basic and don't provide everything that the players ask for – it will be a boring game if the equipment solves all the characters' problems for them.
- **Provide help:** The patron may have contacts in the area who can help the characters. You can use the patron to fill gaps in the characters' fields of knowledge, for instance a pilot for a helicopter, a translator for the local languages, a guide who knows the area, and so on. You can also use contacts to give the characters clues if necessary. But remember, like equipment, it's not fun if the contacts solve the characters' problems.

IN MEDIAS RES

You don't have to use **Plot Hooks** to start an adventure. Patrons are another common way of kicking things off, where the patron asks or employs the characters to undertake an adventure. Another way is to have adventures happen when the player characters are doing something else, like having a vacation.

One good way of starting adventures is *in medias res*, "in the middle of the action". In this way, you start in the middle of the adventure with some kind of action or fight scene. Then the characters are already invested in the story.

You can go back and tell how they got to that point, but it isn't entirely necessary to play that part out in detail. A short retelling is often enough, and sometimes not even that.

> So you are on the good ship MS Nords... Nordstjernen... did I pronounce it right? Anyway, it's a Norwegian ship on the Hurtigruten route from Bergen to Kirkenes.

> Uhm, why are we here?

> It had something to do with Éloïse's mother's former boyfriend, but anyway:

> ... as you are having breakfast in the ship's restaurant, there's suddenly a loud bang outside. When you look outside the window, you can see a submarine with an Octopus logo painted on the fin docked next to MS Nordstjernen, and soldiers in purple uniforms are climbing up rope ladders to board the ship! You have only a few seconds before they storm the ship. What do you do?

> Which is better, **Plot Hooks**, patrons or in medias res?

> Well, the good thing is that you don't have to choose. Each has its uses, and they can all be used in the same campaign and even the same adventure. For instance, we will often use the newspaper *La République* as a kind of "semi-patron" in our adventures, on top of kicking off the adventure with **Plot Hooks**.

> When you design your adventures, you can often use your patron to kick off an adventure. Your players already know and trust the patron, so it's almost a given that they will accept a mission from them. Since the patron is often your and your players' creation, it's tricky for us to write adventures that will use your patron. We can hint at ways to use a patron to start the adventure, but it may not suit your patron at all, and we can't go into details since every group's patron will be unique.

> In our adventures, we will often use the **Plot Hooks** mechanism, and in medias res less often. It is very easy to design adventures around **Plot Hooks**, even without knowing the characters. Doing so also has the advantage of making **Plot Hook** characters the main focus of the evening. In medias res is also very easy to design adventures around, but sometimes it feels cheap, especially if written for somebody else's characters.

> **Plot Hooks**, in medias res and patrons require that the players accept the concept. If they don't, and instead respond "why do we care?" there won't be an adventure.

HANDLING THE SESSION

There are some practical things to consider as the Director of the session. Here is a short list of things you have to do.

PREP

For the Director, the game begins before the session even begins.

- **Prep an adventure:** Either you write an adventure of your own, or you buy a published adventure. Either way, it's good to be prepared. Make sure there are startup handouts available. If you have a published adventure, never assume it is written for you. It isn't: it's written for everyone. Read through the adventure at least twice, make notes, and change whatever you must to fit the characters.
- **Have a place to play:** Either you are the host (see *Hosting the game* on page 180), or someone else is. Make sure that everyone knows where and when.

STARTUP

The start of a session is important. It gets everyone into the mood, kicks things off, and takes care of a few loose ends.

- **Handle leftover experience:** Some players may have been absent last time, or had to rush before they could make improvement and Learning checks. Do that now if you have to.
- **Handle leftover downtime:** As you start the new adventure, you may have given the players too few downtime periods last time, meaning that they should have a few more downtime periods to use. Also, players who were absent last time or players who had to leave early also have to handle downtime.
- **Set up Story Points:** A player always starts with at least **4 Story Points**. They can get more **Story Points** because of downtime.
- **Recap the last session:** Remind players of what happened last time, so that they are up to speed on the story. This is especially important if the session is the continuation of a previous adventure.
- **Declare Plot Hook characters:** If you start a new adventure, it is time to declare which characters are **Plot Hook** characters this time. Then pass out the startup handouts to those players.
- **Start playing!**

PLAYING

The startup is done. Now you just play and do awesome stuff.

- **Food:** It is good to consider what everyone wants to eat, even if you just tell the players to show up fed. You can take a dedicated food break, eat together before the session, bring food or have food delivered and eat it at the table, eat after the session, or not eat at all. Just make sure that you all know and agree on the final decision.
- **The show must go on:** One of your tasks will be to keep the story going. If the players seem stuck, there are three rather reliable methods to get things moving again: give the players another clue, have the characters be captured, or ninjas attack! It doesn't have to be ninjas, of course. The important thing is that the action doesn't stall. Be sure to drop a few clues at the end, to help the players out.
- **Describe a lot:** The players rely on you to inform them of what their characters are experiencing in the game world, so describe what they are seeing, hearing, feeling and smelling all the time.

THE PLAYERS TELL YOU WHAT THEY WANT

Players are expecting a particular story about their characters. If they don't tell you this directly – and you should learn about the character's expectations during Session Zero – they will tell you indirectly, through the background story of their characters, their choice of Template, Abilities, Complications and Skills, and especially through their activities in downtime.

Be open to adding elements of the players' creations to your campaign. It will make your job easier and satisfy the players.

- If a player describes a nemesis in her background story, she doesn't want to just defeat that nemesis. That would be unsatisfactory. She wants it to be a struggle! In that case, you should consider swapping out a Lieutenant, or even the main villain, for that nemesis.
- If a character is from another country, you want to do more than just mention that country now and then. You will often find that the player has a fascination with that country and culture, so consider placing an entire adventure there.
- A player who puts a high Skill value in **Melee**, picks the Swordsman Ability and chooses a Samurai Sword gear kit wants to show off with his Skill. You can handle that by adding a similar swordfighter to the opposition who would like to pit herself against the character, or by modifying a Director character to that effect.

This is not limited to just swordfighting skills, but any specialist area, no matter if it is a classical violin player, a horse-riding Cossack, or a skilled cat burglar. In some cases, it's easier to make stories and challenges that fit the character, but it's trickier with artistic characters. Add particular clues that are only open through artistic expression: you can only meet the mysterious corporation leader if you're a skilled violinist, or the only way to get to the secret bunker without the KGB stopping you is to get the help of the local Cossacks. Or make an adventure about a Stradivarius violin.

WHO TELLS THE STORY?

One of the more important aspects of the Director's job is to keep the narrative going. But you don't have to tell the story all by yourself. Players often yearn to tell the story too. Let them!

Here are some ideas:

- Let the players describe how their action succeeded, given the outcome of their rolls and any damage inflicted.
- Inventors will create weird stuff. Give the player time to describe it.
- Ask another player to describe a failed action, preferably taking the fail-forward principle into account.
- Have players whose characters are not present in the scene take temporary control of non-player characters, even villains.

"YES, BUT" – THE FAIL-FORWARD PRINCIPLE

Straight up failing a task check is boring. Not only does it stop the narrative dead in its track, it also incites the other players to attempt the same task. For starters, don't allow other players to attempt that task: the failure counts for the whole group.

One way of avoiding a second attempt by another player, and also keeping the narrative going, is to handle it like the chase of the secret agent on page 85: the task is technically a success, but then something else happens. Instead of not catching up with the agent at the Austrian border, they caught up with the secret agent, who then took Éloïse as a hostage and drove off.

This technique is called "yes, but…", or fail-forward. Instead of stopping the narrative because of a failed task check, the action succeeds but the outcome is something other than what the characters wanted.

The technique requires that you improvise, which isn't as difficult as you might think and gets easier with practice. One way to start training is to have a Faustian approach, and imagine that you're the devil dealing with the players and their souls.

- If the characters do what they intend to, is there any way that you can twist it for the worse?
- If it is an opposed check, how can the opponent snatch victory from the jaws of defeat in the last moment?

Sometimes you can't fail-forward. In that case, you have to accept that the players just failed, and try to get the narrative going anyway. Don't let any other player make another attempt, though.

There is a difference between fail-forward and **Bad Karma**, maybe best expressed as "no, and" rather than "yes, but" – "no, it definitely didn't work, *and* something else happened." The important thing here is the "something else happened" part – something happens, and thus the narrative moves forward.

"Yes, but…" the bédé way

What happens if a famous rally princess held for questioning by the police wants to use her beauty and fame to get away? You could say no, which is boring. You could use a task check for **Charm** to determine the result, which is almost as boring. Or you could say yes, but… the rumour of the famous rally driver in this little French village suddenly spreads like wildfire, and before you know it the whole village has lined up for autographs on anything from car parts to their plaster cast, and with triple cheek kisses to everyone!

"Yes, but…" is a well-known technique in roleplaying games: don't just succeed, but let something unexpected happen, and see what the players do to deal with the result. And since this is a bédé roleplaying game, let the unexpected thing spin out of control in a ridiculous but humorous way.

Karma (good or bad) can also result in similarly ridiculous but humorous events.

IN CASE OF DEATH

Even if it is hard to die in *The Troubleshooters*, characters still die at times. As it is mostly through player choice, it is only fitting to give the character a proper send-off.

- First, allow for a few last words in the scene where the character died, maybe handing over the final vital clue or something like that.
- Remind the players that there will be a funeral scene in downtime, and that they should think of One Nice Thing to say.
- At any time after the death of the character, the player should create a new character. One or more existing character knows the new character: roll on the *Meet-up Location table* (page 37) to see where they met, and spin a tale about what happened.
- In downtime, add a funeral scene. The funeral does not count as a downtime period, but it happens during downtime. At the funeral, each other participant, including the Director, should say One Nice Thing about the character. Remind the players at the death scene to figure out what they want to say at the funeral, so that they have time to come up with One Nice Thing.

Death is not the only reason to create a new character. It is more common that players retire their characters or that a new player joins the group after some time. In any of these cases, the player has to create a new character.

As a guideline, allow the player two "death dice" per session played in your campaign.

Death dice can be used in three ways:

- **Get ticks towards a language:** Pay one death die to get one tick in a language. You can pay the entire cost now if you want.
- **Get ticks towards an Ability:** Pay one death die to get one tick in an Ability. You can pay the entire cost now if you want.
- **Improve Skills:** Allocate any number of death dice to your Skills. When all death dice are allocated, roll

1d6 for each death die on a Skill and add the outcome to the Skill. However, no Skill can be raised higher than 85% in this way.

Death dice are allocated after you have decided how you met (*Step 10*, page 36).

DEBRIEFING

After the session, it's the post-session phase. Make sure to have ample time for it – about 20 minutes is usually enough. The post-session phase looks like this:

- **Use experience ticks:** The players use the experience ticks next to their Skills to improve Skills, learn languages and learn Abilities.
- **Hand out free improvement ticks:** Give the players free improvement ticks according to the list of criteria on page 127.
- **Use improvement ticks:** The players then use their free improvement ticks as they like to improve Skills, learn languages and learn Abilities.
- **Recalculate Vitality (if necessary):** Check if **Vitality** has changed, according to the rules on page 129.
- **Determine downtime:** If you know how long time it will be (in game) until the next adventure starts, tell them how many downtime periods they will get. If you don't know, the players get one downtime period now, and possibly extra downtime periods at the start of the next session. The players then use their downtime periods according to the options on page 129.
- **Ask for feedback and suggestions:** Allow the players to give feedback on the session – what you did well and what you did less well – and listen to it. Also, ask for suggestions for future sessions.
- **Set the date and time for next session:** The players bring out their calendars, and together you agree on the date for the next session. If you have a regular time, like every other Thursday, check that everyone is still available.

Some final tips

It's okay to make mistakes. Nobody is perfect. You will make mistakes. The best way to handle them is to just move on. *"Sorry, I forgot that rule, but done is done, let's just try to remember that one in the future, okay?"*

Be prepared. You don't have to know the rules by heart, but you need to know where to find stuff in your adventure and the rule book.

Expect the unexpected. Your players will do things you didn't anticipate. That's okay, it's part of the fun of being the Director of Operations. The trick is to roll with the punches, adapt and improvise.

Let everyone participate. If you have silent players, involve them by having them notice cool things. If you have players that take too much of the attention, direct the action to other players.

Take notes. You won't remember everything the players do.

Make lists of names. We have provided some lists in the appendices, but feel free to expand on them. When there is an encounter with NPCs, players will invariably ask for their names. Instead of going "uhmmmm, his name is Bob", take a name from the list. (And note who it is.)

Say "yes", or roll the dice. "Can I ride the elephant?" "No" is a boring answer. Instead say, *"Make an **Agility task check** but at **−2 pips** since you've never seen an elephant before"*. Or you can say "yes" and go with it.

Make a new rule to handle situations. Don't say "the ice is too thin for you to crawl out on". Rather say *"make an **Agility task check** at **−2 pips** to crawl out on the ice. If you fail, the ice breaks and you fall in."* Be prepared for smart solutions: *"But I have this plank, I use that to spread my weight." – "Oh. Okay. Make the check without modifiers then, but with the same possible outcomes."*

Give the players a choice. Just look at the situation with the ice above as an example. And you can do it in other situations as well: *"The bridge breaks, and you fall through the hole. Make an **Alertness task check** to react fast enough." – "*✦☼✦*! Failed." – "Okay, you have a choice. Either you're **Out Cold** and **Wounded** and separated from the others, or you lose everything you're holding in your hands, including the rifle and flashlight."*

Don't forget to hand out Story Points for entertaining the table. **Story Points** are fun little awards that give the players a modicum of control, and the players like them. By handing out **Story Points** often, you encourage players to use them.

Start familiar, and tour the world. As we said in the chapter The World of the Troubleshooters, this game is partially about "fantasy tourism". But to be a tourist, you need a home as well. Start in a setting that everyone has some knowledge about, that they can call familiar. Don't bother about being right or wrong: the important thing is that the players can imagine themselves there. For that reason, Paris is an excellent starting choice. Then have the adventures send the players all over the world and explore it instead of having the players read about it.

Communicate. Tell your players what you expect of them during an adventure. Let them tell you what they expect from you. Give feedback. Take feedback.

Be a fan! Be the greatest fan of your players' characters. Imagine them being characters in your favourite television show, and make adventures as if you were writing fan fiction about those characters. Encourage your players to write backgrounds for their characters, learn them, and use them in your campaign. Not immediately, but as the game and setting expands and you find what it's about.

That doesn't mean that they should succeed with everything. It just means that the *cast characters* are the main characters, not Graf von Zadrith. All the nasty stuff you throw at them – including von Zadrith – is supposed to make them look and feel awesome!

Are there other ways of organising campaigns and adventures? Of course there are, but there are books published on the topic and this chapter is big enough as it is. The aim here is to provide simple tools and instructions to create adventures and campaigns that suit the genre, and help new Directors of Operations to run a Troubleshooters game, not to cover every possible way of running the campaign.

This chapter should get you going. Good luck.

THE OCTOPUS

Welcome to the Octopus. No, it is not an abbreviation. What do you take us for, movie villains? "The Octopus" is simply the name of this organisation.

Like our namesake, we are masters of disguise, intelligent and cunning, deadly and stealthy, and have tentacles everywhere. You are one of those tentacles – or rather, you will be, once you have been properly indoctr... introduced.

You will make mistakes, and I encourage you to learn from them. People in the Octopus who do not learn from their mistakes tend to live very short lives. Do you understand?

Good. Please note the trapdoor, controlled by this very button, that you are standing on. The next time you report to me, you will stand on exactly that spot.

Dismissed!

THE ORIGIN OF THE OCTOPUS

The Octopus has a very long history, and like many things in the modern world, it started with the Peace of Westphalia.

The Peace of Westphalia ended the Thirty Years' War. It also reduced the influence of the Vatican and was the beginning of the end of the feudal order. This left the world with a dangerous power vacuum.

As the idea of nation-states started to gain a grip on Europe, a new power emerged to keep the fragmented world together. It didn't have a name at first, but consisted of an uneasy alliance of merchant families and companies from both the Protestant and Catholic side of the war. Inspired by the Capuchin friar Pére Joseph – the original *éminence grise* – the French Delacroix family had a major role in the formation of the alliance. They helped their mentor Pére Joseph and his master Cardinal Richelieu support the Protestant Swedish forces, and had contacts all over Europe on both sides of the divide. Other influential members were the Genovese

Sanpietri, the Hungarian Szentgyörgy, and the North German Kirchner merchant families.

The trade alliance existed behind the scenes as an "invisible hand" guiding the market, as Adam Smith put it. It soon grew to something greater: a network of policy makers that worked in secret to glue the continent back together after being shattered by the Thirty Years' War. It was at this time that the Octopus got its name from the reach of its tentacles. Their greatest triumph was the Concert of Europe, the uneasy balance of power in Europe after the Napoleonic wars.

HIDING IN THE SHADOWS

That changed at the end of the Great War. The Octopus had *influence* over the world, but not *control*. They could not stop the Great War from happening, and it unmade so much of the Octopus' work. In the aftermath of the Great War, fascism and radical nationalism emerged despite the Octopus' influence, and because of the Great Depression, fascism and nationalism gained power and led the world to war. At the end of the Second World War, a new world order emerged with two superpowers dominating the globe, the United States of America and the Soviet Union. Whatever influence the Octopus had before the wars had vanished.

As a result, the Octopus morphed into something new. The Octopus realised it would not achieve its goals by influencing the world from the shadows. Instead, it had to take control directly. It stopped being a network of policy makers, and shifted into a world-wide conspiracy aimed at a purification and rebirth of the world under their banner.

Although powerful, the Octopus is still in the build-up phase and very paranoid about infiltration – especially from the Bolsheviks (by which they mean any state east of the Iron Curtain) and the Liberals (any state west of the Iron Curtain).

So Octopus members stay hidden in underground bases, mention one another only by number, not by name, and slowly infiltrate every nation on Earth, waiting until they are finally ready to take over and unite the world.

At least, that's one story. Others say that they are seekers of knowledge, intending to enlighten mankind, that they are tired of the disharmony of the ordinary world and want to live in an ordered parallel world instead, or that they are simply agents of chaos seeking to profit from destruction. Both sides of the Iron Curtain accuse the other side of being behind the Octopus, both sides are manipulated by the Octopus, and both sides sometimes employ the Octopus' services.

THE OCTOPUS AND THE WORLD

The average Joe has never heard of the Octopus. Most that have think it is a mafia organisation of some kind, and often mix it up with the Italian Cosa Nostra or another mob syndicate.

Those that have heard of the Octopus and know what it is about are often dismissed as conspiracy theorists. They do publish their own magazines and sometimes run conventions to discuss and share clues. These communities are often flat-out wrong about the Octopus, and many of them are infiltrated by Octopus agents that use them to spread disinformation – and also recruit future members.

The intelligence agencies are aware of the existence of the Octopus, but the picture they have of the Octopus is far from clear. Some dismiss the Octopus as a terror group sponsored by their opponents, or as a crypto-fascist cult. Some are actually aware of the identities of ranking members of the group. Almost all of them underestimate the Octopus.

But the Octopus is finally getting ready.

THE STRUCTURE OF THE OCTOPUS

To protect itself, the Octopus is cell-based and hierarchical. Each cell operates independently. They control a number of sub-cells, and report upwards to a master cell. A number of master cells are in turn controlled by a tentacle, a regional (often underground) command base that controls the master cells in its geographical area. Many cells are sleeper cells. They are not active, but can be activated at any time if their master cell so demands.

This way, if discovered, the Octopus can take considerable damage, even losing an entire tentacle base, without being utterly destroyed.

To further protect itself, members of the Octopus never refer to one another by name, only by number.

The higher the number, the lower they are in the hierarchy. #3579 and #86841 are mere henchmen in the Octopus organisation, #812 is their section commander, #47 is their base commander, and #2-#9 are the Octopus Council, with #2 as their leader.

Very few Octopus members are known by name – in essence, council members like Graf von Zadrith (#2), Baroness Zonda (#6) and Comrade Zhyudov (#9) are the only people who most members know by name. Also, most cells and even sections within a particular tentacle command base are kept isolated from one another, making it almost impossible for members to identify anyone beyond those they deal with directly.

TYPICAL OCTOPUS CELL

The typical Octopus cell is little more than an apartment or cellar, enough to house the cell leader and a few members. It always has several escape routes, and well-prepared defences for buying time to destroy evidence and escape. There are weapon caches hidden, both for missions and for defence. It is rather common for a cell's hideout to be rigged with explosives to destroy it if stormed by the police.

TYPICAL OCTOPUS TENTACLE COMMAND BASE

The typical Octopus tentacle command base is an underground facility, well-camouflaged and hidden. You could reach it from hidden doors in basements and metro stations, hidden trap door elevators in alleys and underground parking lots, or unknown side spurs of metro lines. It could be hidden under a mansion outside town and reached from a secret elevator behind a grandfather clock. If it is big, it has several entrances so as not to attract attention from all the people coming and going to weird places.

A common layout is that of an operations station at the centre of a huge domed cylinder, with eight or ten tunnels branching outward, all connecting to barracks, weapon stashes, laboratories, factories, power generation and other things needed to support the nefarious plans of the organisation.

MEMBERS OF THE OCTOPUS

Unless Octopus members are in a tentacle command base, they are rarely uniformed. Instead, they try to look as inconspicuous as possible. You wouldn't know that they were part of an organisation vying for world domination. Even in an Octopus cell, they would look like ordinary people. After all, they are infiltrating the world's government.

In a tentacle command base, things are different. Everyone is uniformed, identical to their role in the Octopus, and refers to one another only by number or rank.

- Single digit numbers are for the Octopus Council. There are eight of them, numbered 2 (Graf von Zadrith) to 9 (Comrade Zhyudov).
- Double-digit numbers are for regional commands. These are the members responsible for a tentacle command base.
- Triple-digit numbers are for section and group commanders. These command a section of a tentacle, or a single cell.
- Four or five digit numbers are for henchmen. These work in a tentacle base or in a cell.

Except for the Council, each number is assigned randomly by a computer. As members advance in the Octopus, they get lower and lower numbers depending on their responsibility, often by just dropping a digit to fit a free

Octopus cell
1. Bedroom
2. Living room
3. Kitchen
4. Hallway
5. Escape ladder
6. Weapon cache
7. Secret exit
8. Hidden door to secret exit

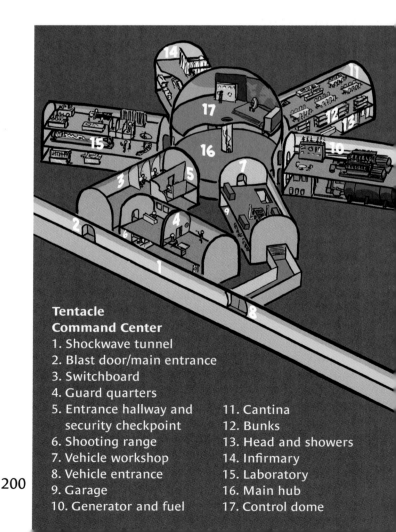

Tentacle Command Center
1. Shockwave tunnel
2. Blast door/main entrance
3. Switchboard
4. Guard quarters
5. Entrance hallway and security checkpoint
6. Shooting range
7. Vehicle workshop
8. Vehicle entrance
9. Garage
10. Generator and fuel
11. Cantina
12. Bunks
13. Head and showers
14. Infirmary
15. Laboratory
16. Main hub
17. Control dome

slot. When #3579 is promoted to section commander, the computer could drop a digit making her #359 instead. If necessary, either one or more digits are changed or two digits swapped, depending on the computer algorithm. If 357, 359, 379 or 579 are all taken, #3579 could perhaps become #367 (changing the 5 to a 6) or maybe #375 (swapping the 5 and 7). It is automatically handled by the computer, which also prints out a new number tag for the member.

The eight Council members are numbered according to rank within the council. The current leader, Graf von Zadrith, holds the #2 position.

Who is #1? That would be telling.

WHEN THE OCTOPUS GETS DEADLY

Assassins and hitmen are often recruited from mafia and terror groups. They are always considered expendable, and are never told more than they need to know: a target, a location, a time-frame, and where to collect the reward.

Sometimes, the Octopus employs some really weird characters with strange outfits and specialties as hitmen and assassins, like Alice, Jack or Santos. Of course, their names are code names. Here are some assassins known to be working for the Octopus:

Alice: An assassin with two custom-made long-barrelled revolvers made in the style of flintlock weapons, dressed in 18th century garb with cape, tricorn hat and a smiling porcelain carnival mask. She prefers to chase her targets into dark alleys before making the kill, and always leaves a red rose on her victims.

Jack: Dressed as a gentleman from Victorian England, this killer prefers knife-work over guns. He keeps his long and very sharp knife hidden in his cane.

Santos: Santos is an example of the less theatrical Octopus assassins. He's an ordinary guy of rather nondescript Southern European appearance. He is an excellent sniper and kills with a precision rifle at very long distances.

External resources are always referred to by code names, not by number and never by their real name.

Only when the Octopus gets desperate do they use their own members as assassins, killers or hit squads. They don't want to get blood on their own hands – not because they are good guys, but because murder attracts attention, and it is always better if nobody pays attention to the Octopus. That's also the reason the Octopus sometimes employs such theatrical killers: that way everyone pays attention to the killer, and not the hand leading them.

TECHNOLOGY OF THE OCTOPUS

Despite its size, the Octopus is still limited in numbers compared to the armed forces of the world (in particular the super-powers). To compensate, the Octopus relies on very advanced technology.

Octobots: To increase the number of the Octopus' disposable soldiers and handle menial and/or dangerous tasks, the Octopus manufactures robots. There are three main types:

- **Service drones:** single-wheeled robots with two arms that are used as assistants and servants. They are equipped with an artificial voice generator and a positronic brain. They are the smartest of the octobots, with some intelligence to obey commands and a very basic capacity for taking the initiative in order to ensure the safety of their owners.
- **Sentry drones:** bipedal robots with two arms and a disneuro ray in the right arm. They are used as sentries and guards inside tentacle command bases. They can be mass-produced and equipped with normal assault rifles to act as soldiers when the revolution comes. Their intelligence is tactical but limited.
- **Sentinels:** dome-shaped robots with eight tentacles folded underneath them and two eyes constantly scanning around them. They are slow and heavy but armoured, and are equipped with powerful lasers and disneuro rays in their eyes. They are used as point defence and surveillance for remote tentacle bases. The intelligence of sentinels is severely limited, set to either defend an area or to search and destroy intruders.

Reverse encephalography projectors: A sinister method of the Octopus is "reverse encephalography", which uses the same technology as a normal encephalogram, the monitoring of brain activity, but runs backwards to imprint brainwaves into the subject. It is used in two forms:

- REP fields are often used in a tentacle command base to project a field which makes unprotected subjects generally more susceptible to commands and more

loyal. The technique cannot be used to imprint specific or detailed behaviour, but it can be used to reinforce broad behaviour patterns and can cover a wide area.
- REP imprints are used in training programs for Octopus members and to program sleeper agents. REP imprints are more detailed than REP fields, but can only affect one subject per machine at a time. It can be combined with hypnotic suggestion. The combination is very powerful and can be used to modify behaviour, insert or remove memories and programmed behaviour, and teach skills. An Octopus member will have had at least one REP imprint in her life.

Disneuro rays: The disneuro ray is a non-lethal weapon that projects a short-range ion field which temporarily locks up the somatic and sensory nervous system in the subject by overcharging the neural pathways. The result is that the subject is **Paralysed** for a few hours. The paralysis can be counteracted by grounding the subject and sending an electric shock from the head to the groin – basically, from the brain to the end of the spinal cord. The projector looks like a small flashlight connected to a big battery pack, usually attached to the belt by means of a clip. It is often used by guards in tentacle bases to capture trespassers for interrogation. The trespassers are then dumped some distance away using an octopod, after having their memories of the experience removed.

Octopods: The octopod is a personal flying transport, with an spherical cockpit and a round ring around it. The ring contains a magnetic drive and a huge fan, which allows the octopod to hover and fly with a swooshing sound. It is highly manoeuvrable and the shape is almost invisible to radar, but it is subsonic and can't fly faster than about 900 km/h. The octopod has two seats and a luggage area that can carry two more passengers if comfort is not a problem (for instance, after being zapped by disneuro rays). Octopods can be armed with lasers and missiles.

THE OCTOPUS AND YOU

The beauty of the cell structure of the Octopus is that even if a regional tentacle tries a plot to take over the world and fails, the damage can be compartmentalised. It also means that if you make an adventure where you portray the Octopus in one way, and there is an official adventure that contradicts it, there's not really a problem: different tentacles run things differently.

You have to decide what you want your Octopus tentacles to be like. Here are some examples:

- **The mad scientist:** Perhaps your Octopus tentacle has a cunning machine that uses Reverse Encelography Projectors to brainwash people into loyal minions, or has an army of robots standing by. All that is needed is to insert some plucky heroes that can foil their plan.
- **The coming invasion:** Your Octopus tentacle may be planning for an upcoming invasion. Before you know it, vital targets will be hit, and when the country is paralysed, the invasion force will storm the beaches.
- **The mad dictator:** Perhaps this particular tentacle of the Octopus operates more out in the open than others: they have taken over a country somewhere, and their current glorious leader is actually an Octopus agent. Using that country as their base, the Octopus will destabilise the region and invade their neighbours.
- **The secret conspiracy:** Maybe the Octopus is hidden deep within the world's governments, in conspiracy cells using secret organisations to promote their goal of world domination.
- **The terror network:** Your Octopus tentacle could consist mostly of hidden cells of terrorists, assassins, hit squads, and even thieves and robbers. They have agents deep within the government, and they are just waiting for the right time to strike – not to take over the country, but to crack it.
- **The mafia organisation:** Your Octopus tentacle could also be just another organised crime syndicate, running extortion rings, drug distribution and other things that mafia syndicates do.
- **All of the above:** Feel free to combine them if you have to, or invent other natures for the Octopus. Also feel free to change your stance between adventures.

IN YOUR ADVENTURES

When you plan your adventures with the Octopus, never give the players more than one piece of your grand plan (if you even have one for them). The Octopus works a lot better if they don't hatch a new plot for world domination every week, but instead play a long game over your entire campaign.

By having a "chess move per session" rather than a "chess game per session" mentality, the characters get to foil one step in the Octopus' grand plan, without unravelling the whole thing. Then the Octopus will have to regroup and rethink their strategy.

This gives you a follow-up adventure almost for free, while the Octopus feels more threatening and has more longevity.

Most of the time, the Octopus is the adversary. They may not be a clear adversary, instead remaining hidden under layers of deception and false leads.

Sometimes, they may be temporary allies. This could happen if a tentacle goes rogue, or if there is a common enemy. This puts the characters between a rock and a hard place: don't help the Octopus and thereby ensure the world's destruction, or help the Octopus and have them get closer to their goal of world domination.

STARTING AN OCTOPUS ADVENTURE

The obvious way to start an adventure with the Octopus is to use the **Arch-Enemy: The Octopus**, **Secret Service** or **Looking for a Case Plot Hooks**.

Looking for a Case: This **Plot Hook** assumes that the player will go for a case if it looks interesting. If you use this **Plot Hook**, all you have to do is create an interesting case. You don't have to mention the Octopus at the outset, but you need to make the case interesting and a part of the Octopus' plans. You can reveal the nature of the enemy later.

Arch-Enemy: The Octopus: This **Plot Hook** may open like the **Looking for a Case** option. The difference is that it has to mention the Octopus, because that is their raison d'être.

Secret Service: The **Secret Service Plot Hook** is an excellent way to start an Octopus adventure. You can do it in a straight-forward way, by sending the character on an assignment. You can be open about the Octopus from the start, or keep its involvement hidden until later. You can also be devious, and have an Octopus infiltrator in the character's organisation.

The not so obvious way is to start an adventure as something else – a spy ring plot, an expedition to Antarctica or Tibet, helping a scientist friend with an experiment – and then reveal that the Octopus is behind it all or are racing you towards the same goal. You build those adventures like you would any adventure, but you add the Octopus as a twist.

This method has the advantage of involving the Octopus, but without any Octopus-focused characters stealing the show. It also allows you to add nuance to the Octopus, and even have them as unlikely allies from time to time.

THE THREAT FILES

What the ☠️💫🌀 were you thinking?

It's not my fault!

Not your fault? We're on a mysterious island that time forgot, and the first thing you think of when you see a giant egg is quiche lorraine?

We haven't eaten in three days, okay?

We haven't been eaten in three days either! And I want to remain not eaten!

HOW TO USE DIRECTOR CHARACTERS

There are many dangers in the world, but that's a good thing. If there weren't, most adventures would end up pretty boring. Director characters are one of those dangers, and they serve several purposes in the game:

Interaction: The obvious use of Director characters is to give the players someone other than themselves to interact with.

Pacing: Using Director characters, you can slow down or speed up the game. Use them as opposition to slow down the game, and to hand out clues and provide aid if you want to speed things up.

Introduce uncertainty: As soon as the players oppose a living breathing opponent, you cannot be completely certain of the outcome.

Create puzzles: Players will often want to bypass enemies. This creates puzzles very naturally. Use Director characters to let the players figure out how to get past them.

Atmosphere: Your Director characters are a part of the world and breathe life into it.

SKILLS OF DIRECTOR CHARACTERS

Director characters do not necessarily have the same Skills as player characters. Often, they are completely different. It is also not always a full set of Skills, but only some attacks, maybe defence and some Skills to add a bit of unique flavour. The one Skill all director characters have is the **Basic** Skill.

THE BASIC SKILL

The **Basic** Skill is a Skill that only Director characters have. It is used as a fallback for every task check that there isn't a Skill for. The **Basic** Skill usually has a Skill value between 25% and 45%.

THE SPECIALIST SKILL

The **Specialist** Skill represents any topic, subject or Skill that the Director character is supposed to be proficient at. If there isn't a specific Skill that fits the situation, and it falls within the character's area of expertise, use the **Specialist** Skill. In a few cases, such as wildly improvised characters, the **Specialist** Skill can be used for attacks. The **Specialist** Skill usually has a Skill value between 55% and 75%.

IMPORTANT SKILLS

Director characters may have any number of Skills, but they're not bound to the same Skill list as the characters. Some Skills only cover a very narrow concept. "Seduction" may be one such Skill. Important Skills usually have about the same Skill value as the **Specialist** Skill, within ±10%. Important Skills may be listed even if they have the same value as the **Specialist** Skill to indicate that they specifically have that Skill.

FLAVOUR SKILLS

Some of them may be Flavour Skills, like "Bark Orders 75%" or "Bravely Run Away 55%" – these are intentionally a bit silly and intended to illustrate certain aspects of the character's behaviour. Usually, Flavour Skills have quite high Skill values – above 50% – but some may be lower than the **Basic** Skill to accentuate that the Director character is really bad at it. One example may be "Humour 15%" to indicate that the character has no sense of humour.

ATTACKS

Attacks are listed separately. Many Director characters have at least one attack, and some have more than one which gives the Director an interesting choice and also becomes a nasty surprise for the cast characters. Attacks also have a Damage value and may also have one or more tags.

Attacks usually have a Skill value in the same range as the **Specialist** Skill.

DEFENCE

Some Director characters have a Defence value. It's used for Defence task checks. Most Unimportant characters and all Mooks lack a Defence value. If there is a Defence value, it is usually a little bit higher than the **Basic** Skill, by maybe 10% or 20%. A high Defence value will always make fights a lot longer, so Defence should rarely be over 50% except for the most powerful Bosses.

TAGS FOR ADVERSARIES

Amphibious: The creature can move unhindered in water and on land, but still has to breathe air.

Aquatic: The creature can move unhindered in water.

Beast: The creature is an animal. It will not fight to the death unless it has to (for instance because it is protecting territory or cubs, it cannot run away, is desperate due to hunger or because it is trained to), but will try to escape if it loses **Vitality**. If **Vitality** runs out, it is either **Out Cold** or it runs away.

Boss: The character can take the **Wounded** Condition once instead of **Vitality** loss. The character may also take the **Mortal Peril** Condition once instead of **Vitality** loss. The character is dead if **Vitality** runs out and they have the **Mortal Peril** Condition; otherwise they're just **Out Cold**.

Counter-attack: Immediately after being attacked, the character makes one counter-attack against the person that attacked them, if that person is within range.

Flips (X): The adversary can flip X task checks in a fight scene.

Flying (X): The creature flies and must either move X zones every round as its Move action, or take a **–2 pip modifier** on its attacks until it takes a Move action.

Frightening: If the characters face an adversary with this tag, they get the **Frightened** Condition.

Guard Beast: Although the creature is a Beast, it's flight instinct is overridden if its handler or trainer is present.

Huge (X): The creature is so huge that it cannot be attacked until immobilised, or with specialised or heavy weaponry. Immobilising the creature is a Skill challenge of five (5) non-Combat Skills of the character's choice that can be reasonably justified to confuse the creature, tie it down, lure it into a narrow space, trap it under debris etc. Each Skill use is a main action, and X is the modifier of all task checks in the challenge. Challenging (0) is for beasts the size of a rhino, great white shark, or grizzly bear; Difficult (–2) for beasts the size of an elephant or allosaurus; and Very difficult (–5) for beasts the size of a diplodocus. The outcome of the Skill challenge determines how long it is immobilised.

- **Great outcome:** The creature is **Restrained** and can be attacked for **1d6+2** rounds, after which it is free at the start of its turn. It cannot break free until then.
- **Good outcome:** The creature is **Restrained** and can be attacked for **1d6** rounds, after which it is free at the start of its turn. It cannot break free until then.
- **Limited outcome:** The creature is **Restrained** and can be attacked for **1d6** rounds, after which it is free at the start of its turn. The creature can try to break free on its turn as a main action.
- **Bad outcome:** The creature is **Restrained** and can be attacked for 1 round, after which it breaks free again at the start of its turn.
- **Abysmal outcome:** The creature is not **Restrained** at all, but royally pissed! All future attempts to immobilise the creature are at **–2 pips**, which stacks.

Leader (X): The character can instead of taking any main actions of their own order X allied Mooks to make one main action at the Leader's initiative, in addition to any action they would take on their own initiative. Other allies can also be ordered, as long as they are lower than the Leader. Underlings count as two Mooks, and Lieutenants count as four Mooks.

Lieutenant: The character can take the **Wounded** Condition once instead of **Vitality** loss.

Mook: If an attack against a Director character with the *Mook* tag has **Good Karma**, the Mook is **Out Cold**.

Multiple Attacks (X): The character may perform X attacks as their main action. Unless an attack has the Multiple Strike tag, each attack can be used once. The number of times each attack can be used during a turn is in parentheses after the name.

Pack Hunter: The creature has **+2 pips** on its attacks per extra pack member attacking the same target.

Slow: The creature has no Move action, but can move as their Main action.

Terrifying: If the characters face an adversary with this tag, they get the **Terrified** Condition.

Trained Beast: Although the creature is a Beast, it's flight instinct is overridden if its handler or trainer is present.

Underling: If an attack against a Director character with the *Underling* tag has **Good Karma**, the Underling is immediately **Out Cold**.

TAGS FOR ADVERSARIES' ATTACKS

Concealable: See *Equipment*, page 115
Counter: Use this attack for counter-attacks.
Dangerous: See *Equipment*, page 116
Long reach: See *Equipment*, page 115
Loud: See *Equipment*, page 115
Noisy: See *Equipment*, page 116
Non-lethal: See *Equipment*, page 115
Paralytic: See *Equipment*, page 115
Precise: See *Equipment*, page 115
Pushing: On a successful attack, push the target into a zone
Really Dangerous: See *Equipment*, page 116
Recharge (X): The attack can only be used once. At the end of its turn, the attack can be recharged with a roll of X on **1d6**.
Reload (X): See *Equipment*, page 115
Restraining: The target makes a **Strength task check** against the Attack check in addition to any Defence check. If the Attack check beat the task check, the target is **Restrained**, regardless of whether or not the Defence check beat the Attack check.
Short Range: See *Equipment*, page 115

Single Shot: See *Equipment*, page 115
Silent: See *Equipment*, page 115
Smoky: See *Equipment*, page 116
Snaring: See *Equipment*, page 115
Suffocating: The attack also counts as if the target is Drowning.
Swift Reload: See *Equipment*, page 115
Unreliable: See *Equipment*, page 116
Terror: If the target's **Vitality** runs out, the target can't take the **Wounded** Condition. Instead, the target can take the **Frightened** Condition and **Vitality** is restored to max. If the target already has the **Frightened** Condition, the target can either upgrade **Frightened** to **Terrified** instead, or be **Out Cold**. If the target is already **Terrified** when **Vitality** runs out, the target is **Out Cold** instead. **Frightened** and **Terrified** cannot be stacked.
Thrown: See *Equipment*, page 115
Tiring: See *Equipment*, page 116
Tripping: See *Equipment*, page 115
Unwieldy: See *Equipment*, page 115
Worn: See *Equipment*, page 115

GENERIC CHARACTERS

Generic Director characters should be considered templates and examples of Director characters. You can use them as is when you have to improvise a Director character on the spot, or flesh out and customise them for your adventure. We also use them as the basis for our threat files.

SUPER-GENERIC SPECIALIST

Every Director may find themselves in a situation where they need stats for a character that they have improvised on the spot. The characters may haggle with a random salesperson that you invented, or there may be a bar brawl with some drunken sailors because of **Bad Karma** on an **Endurance task check**.

Here's a rule of thumb for any such situation:

- **Basic:** 35%
- **Specialist** Skill: 65%
- **Vitality 4**
- **Initiative 5**
- Generic attack **4dX** (use **Specialist** or **Basic** Skill for Attack checks)

Use the super-generic specialist as a baseline for other characters, increasing or decreasing any given stat, or adding stats as needed.

BOSS CHARACTERS

Boss characters are the big bad villains of *The Troubleshooters*. Boss characters usually have more than one attack and a Defence value. Their **Vitality** is often rather high, at 7 or even higher, and they can take the **Wounded** Condition.

Boss characters may also take the **Mortal Peril** Condition. Use that sparingly – only for the end fight of the campaign. This means that Boss characters that can take the **Mortal Peril** Condition are subject to the same "no character death" rule as the cast characters.

Boss characters are always named.

Boss characters are used for three purposes:

Drive the story: Most of the time, the Boss acts behind the scenes to drive the story. They are the reason that the story is actually happening.

End fight: At the end of the adventure, you may need an end fight to reach a satisfying climax. That is the most likely time for your characters to meet a Boss. As the players often prepare carefully for this fight, pad it with at least a Lieutenant and a number of Underlings. If you want the end fight to be epic, throw in a ninja horde of Mooks too.

Exposition: If the characters are captured, the Boss may use the opportunity to brag about their plan. This is a great exposition moment, when the characters may find out what the Boss was actually planning.

- The **Basic** Skill
- About half a dozen important Skills
- A few Flavour Skills
- More than one attack
- Defence value
- High **Vitality** (often 7+)
- May take the **Wounded** Condition
- May take the **Mortal Peril** Condition
- May flip task checks

> ### Generic Boss
> **Tags:** Boss, Flips (4), Counter-attack, Multiple Attacks (3)
> **Initiative:** task check   **Vitality:** 8
> **Attacks:**
> - Katana (2): 75%, 5dX
> - Desert Eagle .357 Magnum (1): 75%, 6dX, Loud, Short Range (3), Reload (8–0), or
> - Uzi 9 mm submachine gun (1): 65%, 5dX, Loud, Reload (9–0)
>
> **Defence:** 45%
> **Skills:** Basic 45%, Specialist 75%, Alertness 65%, Strength 65%, Endurance 65%, Vehicles 75%, Barking Orders 85%, Intimidate 65%, Brag About World Domination 85%

LIEUTENANT CHARACTERS

Lieutenant characters are the Boss character's minions, and are similar to Boss characters. Lieutenant characters usually have more than one attack and a Defence value. Their **Vitality** score is often 6 or higher, and they can take the **Wounded** Condition instead of **Vitality** loss.

The difference to Boss characters is that Lieutenants can't take the **Mortal Peril** Condition. When **Vitality** reaches zero, they're **Out Cold** and may or may not be out of the game.

Lieutenant characters should be named.

There are four main uses for a Lieutenant:

Major opposition: If you need a mini-boss that is not the actual Boss, but will still provide noteworthy resistance for the characters, use a Lieutenant. Pad with Underlings if necessary.

Exposition: Lieutenants know more than Underlings and can provide some background for the plot, either by bragging, being captured and interrogated, or playing both sides against each other (who said that Lieutenants are always loyal?).

Interaction: Lieutenants are named and may have priorities of their own. They can be used for exposition, but also to create rivalries or inspire romantic flings.

Save the boss: In the final fight, you can use Lieutenant characters to take the bullet instead of the Boss, thus prolonging the fight or giving the Boss a chance to escape and return in the next adventure.

- Name
- The **Basic** Skill
- About half a dozen important Skills
- A few Flavour Skills
- More than one attack
- Defence value
- High **Vitality** (often 6+)
- May take the **Wounded** Condition
- May flip task checks

> ### Generic Lieutenant
> **Tags:** Lieutenant, Flips (2), Multiple Attacks (2)
> **Initiative:** 7   **Vitality:** 5
> **Attacks:**
> - Nasty dagger (1): 65%, 4dX, Precise
> - Desert Eagle .357 Magnum (1): 65%, 6dX, Loud, Short Range (3), Reload (8–0), or
> - FA-MAS (1): 55%, 6dX, Loud, Reload (9–0)
>
> **Defence:** 35%
> **Skills:** Basic 45%, Specialist 65%, Alertness 65%, Agility 65%, Vehicles 65%, Sneak 65%, Take a Bullet for the Boss 55%, Steal the Hero's Heart 55%

UNDERLING CHARACTERS

Underling characters are the staple Director characters.

Underlings don't have a Defence value. They have a **Vitality** score, usually around 5, but it may be higher. They can't take the **Wounded** Condition, and when their **Vitality** reaches zero, they're effectively out of the game. They also often have a fixed Initiative score, around 7. Underlings are also out of the game if they are hit with **Good Karma**.

There are two general uses for Underlings:

Padding: You have a Lieutenant or Boss, but you need to keep characters occupied. Use Underlings as padding during a fight scene to match the characters' numbers.

Random roadblock: If you need stats on a random Director character that will force the characters to look at another solution before they start a fight, use an *Underling*.

- The **Basic** Skill
- A few important Skills
- Optional: A few Flavour Skills
- One or more attacks
- Moderate **Vitality** (5)
- Fixed Initiative (≈7)

Generic Underling

Tags: Underling
Initiative: 7   **Vitality:** 5
Attacks:
- A fistful of hurt: 55%, 2dX
- 9 mm Beretta: 55%, 5dX, Loud, Short Range (3), Reload (9–0), or
- 9 mm H&K MP5: 45%, 5dX, Loud, Reload (9–0)

Skills: Basic 35%, Specialist 55%, Agility 45%, Strength 55%, Obey Orders 55%

MOOKS

Mooks are a special kind of Unimportant characters. They have the **Basic** Skill, possibly a few Flavour Skills, one or more attacks, no Defence value, a fixed Initiative score of about 5, and low **Vitality**. Mooks are also out of the game if they are hit with **Good Karma**.

There are two obvious situations for using Mooks:

The ninja horde: if you want a fight scene where the characters can shine and the players get to feel competent and powerful, use Mooks.

Random minor roadblock: If you need stats for a random Director character that is not a complete roadblock if a fight breaks out but still requires some effort to get past, use Mooks.

- The **Basic** Skill
- Optional: A few Flavour Skills
- One or more attacks
- Low **Vitality** (2)
- Fixed Initiative (≈5)

Generic Mook

Tags: Mook
Initiative: 5   **Vitality:** 2
Attacks:
- Generic fist: 45%, 2dX
- Generic gun: 45%, 4dX, Loud, Short Range (2), Reload (9–0)

Skills: Basic 35%, Specialist 45%, Dogpile 55%, Just One Purpose (that is not combat) 65%

LAW AND ORDER

Going on adventures is dangerous business, and the characters may end up on the wrong side of the law.

INVESTIGATOR

If a crime is committed, it is the investigator's job to look into the crime, using basic methods like knocking on doors and taking notes, as well as complex forensic tools such as blood tests, fingerprints, fibre analysis and even computer databases, in order to produce a case for a prosecutor to bring to the court.

Forensic Investigator
Tags: Lieutenant, Flips (2), Multiple Attacks (2)
Initiative: 7 **Vitality:** 5
Attacks:
- 9 mm Beretta (1): 65%, 5dX, Loud, Short Range (3), Reload (8–0)
Defence: 35%
Skills:
Basic 45%, Specialist 65%, Investigation 65%, Forensics 75%, Law 75%, Build a Case 65%, Intimidation 65%, Interrogation 75%

STREET COP

The ordinary patrol officer is often the first on site if something happens. His job is to maintain law and order, secure a crime scene so that it is not contaminated, and sometimes chase down and arrest the crook.

Street cop
Tags: Underling
Initiative: 4 **Vitality:** 3
Attacks:
- Truncheon: 55%, 3dX
- 9 mm Beretta: 55%, 5dX, Loud, Short Range (3), Reload (9–0)
Skills: Basic 35%, Specialist 55%, Agility 45%, Strength 65%, Secure the Scene 65%, Catch the Perp 55%

BORDER GUARD

Depending on the organisation, the border guard may be part of the police force, part of the armed forces, or a separate force altogether. The individual border guard is usually bored out of his skull, as the job typically consists of opening the border, closing the border, and checking papers, passports, vehicles and luggage of those crossing over.

Border Guard
Tags: Underling
Initiative: 4 **Vitality:** 3
Attacks:
- Truncheon: 55%, 3dX
- 9 mm Beretta: 55%, 5dX, Loud, Short Range (3), Reload (9–0)
- 9 mm H&K MP5: 45%, 5dX, Loud, Reload (9–0)
Skills: Basic 35%, Specialist 55%, Agility 45%, Strength 65%, Search for Contraband 55%

PRIVATE EYE

The private eye is not part of a law enforcement agency, but operates independently and investigates stuff on his own – performing background checks on presumptive employees, runaway kids and infidel husbands and wives. In Europe, their mandate is heavily restricted, so they are usually not as exciting as the pulp novels would indicate.

Private Investigator
Tags: Lieutenant, Flips (2), Multiple Attacks (2)
Initiative: 7 **Vitality:** 5
Attacks:
- Fists of steel (2): 65%, 4dX, Precise
- Smith&Wesson revolver (1): 65%, 5dX, Loud, Short Range (3), Reload (8–0)
Defence: 35%
Skills: Basic 45%, Specialist 65%, Alertness 65%, Agility 65%, Illegal Entry 65%, Vehicles 65%, Sneak 65%, Find Clues 75%

SECURITY GUARD

Security guards are not law enforcement per se: they just guard a location. They may be employed by a security firm or the owner of the location.

> ### Security Guard
> **Tags:** Underling
> **Initiative:** 4   **Vitality:** 3
> **Attacks:**
> - Truncheon: 55%, 3dX
>
> **Skills:** Basic 35%, Specialist 55%, Agility 45%, Strength 65%, Guard the Perimeter 55%

> ### Guard Dog
> **Tags:** Trained Beast, Guard Beast, Frightening
> **Initiative:** 5   **Vitality:** 5
> **Attacks:**
> - Vicious bite: 65%, 3dX, Restraining
>
> **Defence:** 35%
> **Skills:** Basic 45%, Specialist 65%, Run 75%, Jump 75%, Bark 65%, Not be Fooled by Yummy Steaks 55%

THE MOB

La Cosa Nostra, Yakuza, the triads – there are many forms of criminal organisations with less ambitious aspirations than the Octopus. Surprisingly often, troubleshooters end up opposing them.

CAPO

At the top of a mafia organisation, hidden in the shadows, always untouchable, is the capo, the head. He is the boss and the mastermind behind the mob's operations. Often, it just takes a whisper or a suggestion, and someone's life is ruined.

> ### Generic Mob Boss
> **Tags:** Boss, Leader (4), Flips (4), Counter-attack, Multiple Attacks (3)
> **Initiative:** task check   **Vitality:** 8
> **Attacks:**
> - Baseball bat (2): 75%, 4dX
> - Smith&Wesson .357 Magnum (1): 75%, 6dX, Loud, Short Range (3), Reload (8–0)
>
> **Defence:** 45%
> **Skills:** Basic 45%, Specialist 75%, Alertness 65%, Fashion 55%, Intimidate 85%, Hosting Spectacular Parties 85%, Let Someone Else Take Care of It 85%

CONSIGLIERE

A consigliere advises the capo, and takes care of delicate problems for him so that the capo's hands don't get dirty.

> ### Generic Lieutenant
> **Tags:** Lieutenant, Flips (2), Multiple Attacks (2)
> **Initiative:** 7   **Vitality:** 5
> **Attacks:**
> - Colt M1911 .45 pistol (2): 65%, 6dX, Loud, Short Range (3), Reload (8–0), or
> - .45 Thompson submachine gun in violin case (2): 45%, 6dX, Loud, Reload (9–0)
>
> **Defence:** 35%
> **Skills:** Basic 45%, Specialist 65%, Intimidate 75%, Take a Bullet for the Boss 55%, Destroy Evidence 75%

FOOT SOLDIER

Even the mob has its brutes, the generic enforcer whose main talent is loyalty and muscles.

> ### Mob Foot Soldier
> **Tags:** Underling
> **Initiative:** 7   **Vitality:** 5
> **Attacks:**
> - Knuckle dusters: 55%, 3dX
> - Smith&Wesson revolver: 55%, 5dX, Loud, Short range (3), Reload (9–0)
>
> **Skills:** Basic 35%, Specialist 55%, Rough 'Em Up, 55%, Obey Orders 55%

THE ARMY

Although the world is undergoing an economic boom, there's the ever-present threat of the next world war. In bases throughout Europe and all over the world, army personnel are waiting for the order to roll out.

ARMY GRUNT

The regular army grunt is actually a simple person: give him a rifle and point him towards the enemy, and he knows exactly what to do.

> **Army Grunt**
> **Tags:** Underling
> **Initiative:** 4   **Vitality:** 3
> **Attacks:**
> - 7.62mm H&K G3 assault rifle: 55%, 7dX, Loud, Reload (8–0)
> - Hand grenade: 55%, 6dX (3dX in adjacent zones), Thrown
> **Skills:** Basic 35%, Specialist 55%, Endurance 45%, Strength 65%, Obey Orders 55%

SPECIAL FORCES

There are many kinds of special forces. Some specialise in parachuting behind enemy lines. Some infiltrate by boat or by car to take out strategic targets. Some dive into enemy harbours. Some specialise in counter-terrorism and hostage-rescue. All receive way better training and equipment than the regular army grunt.

> **Special Forces Soldier**
> **Tags:** Lieutenant, Flips (2), Multiple Attacks (2)
> **Initiative:** 7   **Vitality:** 5
> **Attacks:**
> - Dagger (2): 65%, 4dX, Precise
> - FAMAS (2): 75%, 6dX, Loud, Reload (9–0)
> - Hand grenade (1): 65%, 6dX (3dX in adjacent zones), Thrown
> **Defence:** 45%
> **Skills:** Basic 45%, Specialist 65%, Alertness 65%, Agility 65%, Vehicles 65%, Sneak 65%, Parachuting 75%, Scuba Diving 75, Blow Things Up 85%

ARMY OFFICER

Soldiers need leaders, and armies need hierarchies. That's where officers come in: they're meant to have an overview of the situation and lead the men to victory.

Meant to – some officers are just there for the bling, some like the authority of rank, and some, supposedly, are good officers.

> **Army officer**
> **Tags:** Boss, Flips (2), Leader (4)
> **Initiative:** 7 **Vitality:** 5
> **Attacks:**
> - Officer's baton (2): 65%, 3dX, Non-lethal
> - MAC 50 9 mm pistol (2): 75%, 6dX, Loud, Short Range (3), Reload (8-0)
> **Defence:** 55%
> **Skills:** Basic 45%, Strategy 65%, Instill Patriotism 75%, Yelling Orders 85%, Impressive Hat 105%

SECRET AGENTS

The many secret services in the world are not too fond of troubleshooters. Troubleshooters often ruin their long-standing operations and stir things up unnecessarily. It is entirely likely that the characters will find themselves face to face with secret agents.

HANDLER

The Handler is generally a bureaucrat, sitting in the embassy handling a number of spies recruited from the enemy. The handler meets them, handles deliveries through dead-drops, and passes on the gathered intelligence to an analyst. Sometimes it's up to the handler to do something for the spies when they are in trouble, like smuggling them and their family out of the country. That can be dangerous business, so handlers are often former agents.

Handler
Tags: Boss, Flips (4), Counter-attack, Multiple Attacks (3)
Initiative: task check   **Vitality:** 8
Attacks:
- Close quarters fighting: 75%, 3dX
- Silenced 9 mm Beretta: 75%, 5dX, Short Range (3), Reload (8–0), or
- H&K 9 mm submachine gun: 65%, 5dX, Loud, Reload (9–0)
Defence: 45%
Skills: Basic 45%, Specialist 75%, Alertness 65%, Strength 65%, Endurance 65%, Vehicles 75%, Intimidate 65%, Security Access 85%

BRUTE

Brutes are just muscle, and not much brains. It's an old tradition.

Brute
Tags: Underling
Initiative: 4   **Vitality:** 3
Attacks:
- A fistful of hurt: 55%, 2dX
- 9 mm Beretta: 55%, 5dX, Loud, Short Range (3), Reload (9–0), or
- 9 mm H&K MP5: 45%, 5dX, Loud, Reload (9–0)
Skills: Basic 35%, Specialist 55%, Agility 45%, Strength 65%, Obey Orders 55%

AGENT

An agent is a special operative who does the dirty work for an intelligence agency. They're well-trained in many different fields and very competent. Agents often make first contact with spies and get them to begin a job, and then hand them over to a handler.

Agent
Tags: Lieutenant, Flips (2), Multiple Attacks (2)
Initiative: task check   **Vitality:** 7
Attacks:
- Nasty dagger: 65%, 4dX, Precise
- Walther PPK: 75%, 4dX, Loud, Short Range (2), Reload (9–0)
Defence: 35%
Skills: Basic 45%, Specialist 65%, Alertness 65%, Agility 65%, Vehicles 65%, Sneak 65%, Tail Someone 55%, Seduce 55%

RAVEN/SWALLOW

A special kind of agent is the "raven" (male) or "swallow" (female), the KGB term for an agent seducing their target and blackmailing them by having the affair taped, thus turning them into an unwilling asset. Despite the Soviet origin of the term, virtually every intelligence agency uses it.

Raven or Swallow
Tags: Lieutenant, Flips (2), Multiple Attacks (2)
Initiative: 9   **Vitality:** 5
Attacks:
- Surprise kung fu: 75%, 3dX
- Hidden switchblade: 65%, 4dX, Precise
- Makarov Pistol 9 mm: 65%, 5dX, Loud, Short Range (3), Reload (8–0)
Defence: 35%
Skills: Basic 45%, Specialist 65%, Alertness 65%, Agility 75%, Sneak 65%, Find a Way Out 75%, Steal the Hero's Heart 55%

THE OCTOPUS

The Octopus is a secret organisation striving for world control.

The Octopus is a secret organisation striving for world control. Their tentacles are everywhere: in corporations, among world leaders, in organised crime.

GRAF VON ZADRITH, #2

The current leader of the Octopus is graf Albrecht Vogelin Erwin von Zadrith. He is almost mythical in the Octopus. Few in the Order have ever met him. Still, he is one of the few in the Octopus who is actually known by name and not by number.

Outside the Octopus and in business clothes, he is not a remarkable man. He would just look like a thin, well-dressed, middle-aged gentleman with a receding hairline. You wouldn't look twice at him if you met him at the airport.

Chances are that you actually have.

Graf Albrecht Vogelin Erwin von Zadrith

Tags: Boss, Flips (4), Leader (8), Counter-attack, Multiple Attacks (3), Frightening

Initiative: task check   **Vitality:** 8

Attacks:
- Disneuro ray (1): 75%, 4dX, Paralytic, Reload (0)
- Cane sword (2): 65%, 5dx, Counter

Defence: 45%

Skills: Basic 45%, Specialist 75%, Alertness 65%, Strength 65%, Endurance 65%, World Domination 75%, Barking Orders 85%, Intimidate 65%, Ominous Pipe Organ 105%

BARONESS ZONDA, #6

If there is anyone that could compete with von Zadrith, it is Baroness Zonda. Perhaps that is the reason she is "merely" #6 in the Octopus. Rumour has it that she is actually a "product" from a Soviet program to create a super-human, but was instead recruited by the Octopus.

Baroness Katerina Zhurova Zonda

Tags: Boss, Leader (4), Flips (3), Multiple Attacks (3), Counter-attack

Initiative: task check   **Vitality:** 8

Attacks:
- Rapier (2): 75% 5dX, Counter
- Martial arts (1): 65% 3dX, Counter
- Poison stiletto heel needle (1): 55% 4dX, Single-use, Worn, Paralysing Poison 75%, Deadly Poison 65%
- Two Desert Eagle .357 Magnum (2): 65%, 6dX, Loud, Short Range (3), Reload (8–0), Counter

Defence: 55%

Protection: 1dP Kevlar combat catsuit

Skills: Basic 35%, Specialist 65%, Alertness 75%, Nine Lives 75%, Sadistic Interrogations 75%, Seductive Interrogations 85%, Strength 85%, Endurance 75%, Over-complicated Planning 75%

DOCTOR CUTTER

The stuttering doctor Cutter is a genius in high-power physics, robotics and the emerging field of genetics. He is highly driven and ambitious, although fiercely loyal to the Octopus. He sees the Octopus as a tool enabling him to make the Superman possible.

Doctor Cutter
Tags: Lieutenant, Frightening, Flips (2)
Initiative: 5   **Vitality:** 4
Attacks:
- Experimental death ray: 55%, 7dX, Short Range (2), Reload (8–0)
- Reprogramming disneuro ray: 55% 5dX, Single Shot, Non-lethal, Special: target's brain is reprogrammed to include brain patterns of a random animal until it can be reset by a good night's sleep (the target takes on some behavioural traits of an animal); if the target is Out Cold, the random animal brain pattern overwrites the target's brain completely for 24 hours.
- Exoskeleton metallic fists: 55% 5dX
… any other weird experiment you can think of.
Skills: Basic 35%, Specialist 65%, Science 95%, Obscure Knowledge, Muahahahaha! 75%, Focus on Experiment 55%

OCTOPUS SCIENTIST

Octopus scientists work in many fields, from rocketry and atomics, to biology and virology. Don't expect them to fight for the Octopus, unless they have invented a giant robot with themselves at the helm. They may still have delusions of grandeur, though.

Generic Octopus Scientist
Tags: Underling
Initiative: 2   **Vitality:** 2
Attacks:
- Lab equipment: 45%, 3dX, Brittle
Skills: Basic 35%, Specialist 65%, Science 95%, Obscure Knowledge 75%,

OCTOPUS BRUTE

The generic Octopus brute is hired for loyalty and strength, not intelligence. Don't expect any conversation deeper than "resistance is futile", "silence!" or "keep moving!"

Octopus Brute
Tags: Underling, Pack Hunter
Initiative: 4   **Vitality:** 3
Attacks:
- A fistful of hurt: 55%, 2dX
- Disneuro projector: 55%, 4dX, Short Range (2), Reload (9–0), Paralytic
Skills: Basic 35%, Specialist 55%, Agility 45%, Strength 65%, Obey Orders 55%

OCTOBOT SERVICE DRONE

The Service drone is a single-wheeled robot, keeping its balance with an advanced, miniature gyro in its body. It has two arms with six degrees of freedom, and a head with sensors, artificial voice generator and a positronic brain. They are the smartest of the octobots, with some limited intelligence, the ability to obey verbal commands (to the letter) and a very basic and enervating habit of acting to ensure the safety of their owners.

Service Drone
Tags: Mook
Initiative: 2   **Vitality:** 2
Attacks:
- Grapple: 45%, Non-lethal, Restraining
Defence: 35%
Skills: Basic 45%, Serve Tea, Beverages and Food 65%, Utter Useless Warnings 55%, Restrain Violent Humans 55%, Literal Interpretation of Commands 85%

OCTOBOT SENTRY DRONE

The Sentry drone is a skinny bipedal robot with a disneuro ray in the right arm. Sentry drones are used as sentries and guards inside important Octopus command bases. They can be mass-produced and equipped with regular firearms to act as soldiers when the revolution comes.

Their intelligence is tactical but limited. Their positronic brain only recognises commands from Octopus personnel with the right security level, but they obey them to the letter. They have an artificial voice generator, but it is severely limited.

Sentry Drone
Tags: Mook, Pack Hunter
Initiative: 3 **Vitality:** 2
Attacks:
- Disneuro ray: 45%, 4dX, Paralytic, Reload (0) or
- CAM 7.62mm assault rifle: 45%, 6dX, Load, Reload (8–0)
Skills: Basic 35%, Scan for Targets 65%

OCTOBOT SENTINEL

The dome-shaped, four metre Sentinels are used for point defence around Octopus bases. The top of the dome rotates around, their eyes constantly scanning their surroundings.

Sentinels are slow and heavy, but armoured. They use tentacles for locomotion as well as for attacks. They can ensnare a victim or electrocute them. The eyes have laser rays as well as disneuro rays for attack.

Their positronic brains are limited, set to either defend an area or search out and destroy non-authorised personnel. They don't talk, but they coordinate by radio.

Sentinel
Tags: Underling, Frightening, Multiple Attacks (3), Slow, Pack "Animal"
Initiative: 2 **Vitality:** 12
Attacks:
- Disneuro ray (1): 55%, 4dX, Paralytic
- Laser ray (1): 65%, 5dX, Short Range (2), Counter
- Tentacles (2): 65%, 8dX, Long Reach, Restraining
Protection: 3dP Armour
Skills: Basic 35%, Scan for Targets 65%

JACK

Jack is one of the Octopus' go-to guys when they want to get rid of people. He's discreet when doing his work, preferring blades to guns. He keeps his long and very sharp knife hidden in his cane.

He's not as discreet when walking around – he's dressed as a gentleman from Victorian England, but with a mask when he does his job. It may work to his advantage, though: people always remember the top hat, the dress and the cane, but not the face. It is doubtful that he would be recognised after just a quick change of clothes.

Jack
Tags: Boss, Frightening, Multiple Attacks (3)
Initiative: task check **Vitality:** 8
Attacks:
- Sharp dagger (2): 75%, 4dX, Precise
- Cane (2): 85%, 3dX, Non-lethal
Defence: 55%
Skills: Basic 45%, Alertness 65%, Disappear in Shadows 75%, Sneak 65%, Medicine 95%, Specialist 75%

ALICE

More flamboyant is Alice, an assassin with two custom-made, long-barrelled revolvers made to look like converted flintlock guns with intricate etchings and inlays. She is dressed in 18th century style with cape, tricorn hat and a smiling, porcelain carnival mask. Highly acrobatic and capable of running across the rooftops, she prefers to chase her targets into dark alleys before making the kill, and always leaves a red rose on her victims.

Alice takes most of her contracts in Italy, but has been seen all over the world.

Alice
Tags: Boss, Frightening, Multiple Attacks (2), Counter-attack
Initiative: task check **Vitality:** 8
Attacks:
- Revolver (2): 65%, 5dX, Loud, Reload (9–0), Counter
- Karate kicks (2): 75%, 3dX, Counter
Defence: 55%
Skills: Basic 45%, Alertness 65%, Agility 75%, Rooftop Acrobatics 75%, Sneak 65%, Find the Target 75%, Specialist 65%

SANTOS

Santos is an example of the less theatrical Octopus assassins. He's an ordinary guy with a nondescript, Southern European appearance. He is an excellent sniper and kills with a precision rifle at very long distances.

Rumour has it that Santos was a veteran for the communists in the Spanish civil war, then escaped and was trained as a terrorist in Cuba. He occasionally takes on jobs for other organisations besides the Octopus.

Santos
Tags: Boss, Counter-attack
Initiative: task check   **Vitality:** 8
Attacks:
- Sniper rifle: 95%, 7dX, Loud, Single Shot
- 9 mm Beretta: 65%, 5dX, Short Range (3), Reload (9–0), Counter
- Sambo (Soviet martial art): 55%, 3dX, Counter
Defence: 55%
Skills: Basic 45%, Alertness 75%, Disguise 75%, Smuggling 75%, Specialist 65%

ANIMALS AND BEASTS

Not only are there dangerous humans to contend with, but the world is full of deadly animals too. Here are some examples.

Tiger
Tags: Beast, Flips (2), Multiple Attacks (3)
Initiative: 8   **Vitality:** 8
Attacks:
- Tiger bite (1): 65%, 6dX, Restraining
- Tiger claws (2): 55%, 5dX
Defence: 35%
Skills: Basic 45%, Specialist 65%, Sneak and Ambush 75%, Track by Smell 85%, Swim 55%

Lion
Tags: Beast, Flips (2), Multiple Attacks (3), Pack Hunter
Initiative: 7   **Vitality:** 8
Attacks:
- Lion bite (1): 65%, 6dX, Restraining
- Lion claws (2): 55%, 5dX
Defence: 35%
Skills: Basic 45%, Specialist 65%, Run 75%, Jump 75%

Elephant
Tags: Beast, Huge (–2), Flips (2), Counter-attack
Initiative: 5   **Vitality:** 16
Attacks:
- Stomp: 65%, 6dX
- Tusk: 55%, 5dX, Throwing
- Trunk thump: 55%, 4dX, Counter
Defence: 35%
Protection: 1dP Elephant hide
Skills: Basic 45%, Specialist 65%, Trumpet 65%, Strength 75%

Crocodile
Tags: Beast, Amphibious, Ambushing, Flips (2)
Initiative: 7   **Vitality:** 10
Attacks:
- Snap: 65%, 6dX, Restraining
- Death roll (Restrained targets only, in water only): 55%, 8dX
Defence: 35%
Skills: Basic 45%, Specialist 65%, Hide in Water 75%, Swim 75%

Constrictor

Tags: Beast, Amphibious, Ambushing, Flips (2)
Initiative: 2   **Vitality:** 5
Attacks:
- Catch: 65%, 3dX, Restraining
- Constrict (Restrained targets only): 65%, 6dX, Suffocating

Defence: 35%
Skills: Basic 45%, Specialist 65%, Hide 65%, Swim 65%, Hold 75%

Hippo

Tags: Beast, Amphibious, Huge (–2), Flips (2)
Initiative: 5   **Vitality:** 12
Attacks:
- Stomp: 65%, 6dX
- Tusks: 55%, 5dX, Throwing

Defence: 35%
Protection: 2dP Hippo hide
Skills: Basic 45%, Specialist 55%, Swim 55%

Wolf

Tags: Beast, Flips (2), Multiple Attacks (3), Pack Hunter
Initiative: 8   **Vitality:** 6
Attacks:
- Fangs of the wolf (1): 65%, 5dX, Restraining
- Claws of the wolf (2): 55%, 4dX

Defence: 35%
Skills: Basic 45%, Specialist 65%, Run 75%, Jump 75%, Coordinated Attacks 65%, Howl 85%

Grizzly Bear

Tags: Beast, Flips (2), Multiple Attacks (3), Huge (0)
Initiative: 8   **Vitality:** 12
Attacks:
- Bear bite (1): 65%, 6dX, Restraining
- Bear claws (2): 55%, 5dX

Defence: 35%
Protection: 1dP Bear hide
Skills: Basic 45%, Specialist 65%, Climb 75%, Track by Smell 85%, Swim 55%

Polar Bear

Tags: Beast, Flips (2), Multiple Attacks (3), Huge (0)
Initiative: 8   **Vitality:** 14
Attacks:
- Bear bite (1): 65%, 6dX, Restraining
- Bear claws (2): 55%, 5dX

Defence: 35%
Protection: 1dP Bear hide
Skills: Basic 45%, Specialist 65%, Track by Smell 95%, Swim 65%, Survive the Arctic 75%

Coyote

Tags: Beast, Multiple Attacks (2), Pack Hunter
Initiative: 5   **Vitality:** 4
Attacks:
- Fangs of the coyote (1): 65%, 3dX, Restraining
- Claws of the coyote (2): 55%, 4dX

Defence: 35%
Skills: Basic 45%, Specialist 65%, Run 75%, Jump 75%, Coordinated Attacks 65%

Cougar

Tags: Beast, Flips (2), Multiple Attacks (3)
Initiative: 10   **Vitality:** 4
Attacks:
- Cougar fangs (1): 65%, 3dX
- Cougar claws (2): 55%, 3dX

Defence: 35%
Skills: Basic 45%, Specialist 65%, Run 75%, Jump 75%, Ambush 65%

Horse

Tags: Beast, Huge (–0), Counter-attack
Initiative: 5   **Vitality:** 12
Attacks:
- Front kick: 65%, 4dX
- Rear kick: 55%, 5dX, Throwing

Defence: 35%
Skills: Basic 45%, Specialist 65%, Gallop 65%

Moose

Tags: Beast, Huge (–0), Counter-attack
Initiative: 5   **Vitality:** 14
Attacks:

- Vicious antlers: 55%, 5dX, Restraining (bulls only)
- Antler charge: 55%, 7dX, Pushing, Recharge (5–6)

Front kick: 65%, 4dX
Rear kick: 55%, 5dX, Throwing
Defence: 35%
Skills: Basic 45%, Specialist 65%, Gallop 65%

Tyrannosaurus Rex

Tags: Beast, Huge (–5), Flips (2)
Initiative: 5   **Vitality:** 20
Attacks:

- Bite: 65%, 6dX
- Stomp: 55%, 5dX, Throwing
- Tail thump: 55%, 4dX, Counter

Defence: 35%
Protection: 1dP Dinosaur hide
Skills: Basic 45%, Specialist 65%, Roar 65%, Very Short Arms 75%

Triceratops

Tags: Beast, Huge (–5), Flips (2), Counter-attack
Initiative: 5   **Vitality:** 16
Attacks:

- Horns: 65%, 6dX
- Ramming: 55%, 8dX, Throwing, Recharge (5–6)
- Tail swipe: 55%, 4dX, Counter

Defence: 45%
Protection: 2dP Head shield
Skills: Basic 45%, Specialist 65%, Veggiesaurus 85%, Strength 75%

Allosaurus

Tags: Beast, Huge (–5), Flips (2)
Initiative: 5   **Vitality:** 16
Attacks:

- Bite: 65%, 6dX
- Stomp: 55%, 5dX, Throwing
- Tail thump: 55%, 4dX, Counter

Defence: 35%
Protection: 1dP Dinosaur hide
Skills: Basic 45%, Specialist 65%, Roar 65%

Utahraptor

Tags: Beast, Flips (2), Multiple Attacks (3), Pack Hunter
Initiative: 8   **Vitality:** 8
Attacks:

- Sharp teeth (1): 65%, 5dX, Restraining
- Searing sickle claw (2): 55%, 7dX

Defence: 35%
Skills: Basic 45%, Specialist 65%, Run 75%, Jump 75%, Coordinated Attacks 65%, Clever Girl 75%

Velociraptor

Tags: Beast, Pack Hunter
Initiative: 5   **Vitality:** 5
Attacks:

- Tiny sharp teeth (1): 65%, 3dX
- Small sickle claw (2): 55%, 4dX

Defence: 35%
Skills: Basic 45%, Specialist 65%, Run 75%, Jump 65%, Coordinated Attacks 75%

Pterosaur

Tags: Beast, Flying (2)
Initiative: 5   **Vitality:** 5
Attacks:

- Claws: 55%, 4dX
- Strike from above: 65%, 6dX, Recharge (5–6)

Defence: 35%
Skills: Basic 45%, Specialist 65%, Walk 25%, Fly 75%, Spot Prey 75%

Plesiosaur

Tags: Beast, Amphibious, Ambushing
Initiative: 8 (in the water), 4 (on land)   **Vitality:** 8
Attacks:

- Bite: 65%, 4dX, Restraining
- Drag Down (Restrained targets only, in water only): 55%, 8dX, Suffocating

Defence: 35%
Protection: 1dP Slippery hide
Skills: Basic 45%, Specialist 65%, Swim 85%, Ambush Hunter 75%, Moving on Land 15%

APPENDICES

CALENDAR 1965

	January			February			March	
1	Friday	New Year's Day	1 ●	Monday		1	Monday	
2 ●	Saturday		2	Tuesday		2	Tuesday	
3	Sunday		3	Wednesday		3 ●	Wednesday	
4	Monday		4	Thursday		4	Thursday	
5	Tuesday		5	Friday		5	Friday	
6	Wednesday		6	Saturday		6	Saturday	
7	Thursday		7	Sunday		7	Sunday	
8	Friday		8	Monday		8	Monday	
9	Saturday		9 ◑	Tuesday		9 ◑	Tuesday	
10 ◑	Sunday		10	Wednesday		10	Wednesday	
11	Monday		11	Thursday		11	Thursday	
12	Tuesday		12	Friday		12	Friday	
13	Wednesday		13	Saturday		13	Saturday	
14	Thursday		14	Sunday		14	Sunday	
15	Friday		15	Monday		15	Monday	
16	Saturday		16 ○	Tuesday		16	Tuesday	
17 ○	Sunday		17	Wednesday		17 ○	Wednesday	
18	Monday		18	Thursday		18	Thursday	
19	Tuesday		19	Friday		19	Friday	
20	Wednesday		20	Saturday		20	Saturday	March equinox
21	Thursday		21	Sunday		21	Sunday	
22	Friday		22	Monday		22	Monday	
23	Saturday		23 ◐	Tuesday		23	Tuesday	
24 ◐	Sunday		24	Wednesday		24	Wednesday	
25	Monday		25	Thursday		25 ◐	Thursday	
26	Tuesday		26	Friday		26	Friday	
27	Wednesday		27	Saturday		27	Saturday	
28	Thursday		28	Sunday		28	Sunday	
29	Friday					29	Monday	
30	Saturday					30	Tuesday	
31	Sunday					31	Wednesday	

April		May		June	
1	Thursday	1 ● Saturday *Labour Day/May Day*		1	Tuesday
2 ●	Friday	2 Sunday		2	Wednesday
3	Saturday	3 Monday		3	Thursday
4	Sunday	4 Tuesday		4	Friday
5	Monday	5 Wednesday		5	Saturday
6	Tuesday	6 Thursday		6 ◑ Sunday *Whit Sunday*	
7	Wednesday	7 Friday		7 Monday *Whit Monday*	
8	Thursday	8 ◑ Saturday *WW2 Victory Day*		8	Tuesday
9 ◑	Friday	9 Sunday		9	Wednesday
10	Saturday	10 Monday		10	Thursday
11	Sunday	11 Tuesday		11	Friday
12	Monday	12 Wednesday		12	Saturday
13	Tuesday	13 Thursday		13	Sunday
14	Wednesday	14 Friday		14 ○	Monday
15	Thursday	15 ○ Saturday		15	Tuesday
16 ○	Friday *Good Friday*	16 Sunday		16	Wednesday
17	Saturday	17 Monday		17	Thursday
18	Sunday *Easter Sunday*	18 Tuesday		18	Friday
19	Monday *Easter Monday*	19 Wednesday		19	Saturday
20	Tuesday	20 Thursday		20 Sunday *Father's Day*	
21	Wednesday	21 Friday		21 Monday *June Solstice*	
22	Thursday	22 Saturday		22 ◑	Tuesday
23 ◑	Friday	23 ◑ Sunday		23	Wednesday
24	Saturday	24 Monday		24	Thursday
25	Sunday	25 Tuesday		25	Friday
26	Monday	26 Wednesday		26	Saturday
27	Tuesday	27 Thursday *Ascension Day*		27	Sunday
28	Wednesday	28 Friday		28	Monday
29	Thursday	29 Saturday		29 ●	Tuesday
30	Friday	30 ● Sunday *Mother's Day*		30	Wednesday
		31 Monday			

July		August		September	
1	Thursday	1	Sunday	1	Wednesday
2	Friday	2	Monday	2 ◑	Thursday
3	Saturday	3	Tuesday	3	Friday
4	Sunday	4 ◐	Wednesday	4	Saturday
5 ◐	Monday	5	Thursday	5	Sunday
6	Tuesday	6	Friday	6	Monday
7	Wednesday	7	Saturday	7	Tuesday
8	Thursday	8	Sunday	8	Wednesday
9	Friday	9	Monday	9	Thursday
10	Saturday	10	Tuesday	10	Friday
11	Sunday	11	Wednesday	11 ○	Saturday
12	Monday	12 ○	Thursday	12	Sunday
13 ○	Tuesday	13	Friday	13	Monday
14	Wednesday *Bastille Day*	14	Saturday	14	Tuesday
15	Thursday	15	Sunday *Assumption of Mary*	15	Wednesday
16	Friday	16	Monday	16	Thursday
17	Saturday	17	Tuesday	17	Friday
18	Sunday	18	Wednesday	18 ◑	Saturday
19	Monday	19	Thursday	19	Sunday
20	Tuesday	20 ◑	Friday	20	Monday
21 ◑	Wednesday	21	Saturday	21	Tuesday
22	Thursday	22	Sunday	22	Wednesday
23	Friday	23	Monday	23	Thursday *September Equinox*
24	Saturday	24	Tuesday	24	Friday
25	Sunday	25	Wednesday	25 ●	Saturday
26	Monday	26 ●	Thursday	26	Sunday
27	Tuesday	27	Friday	27	Monday
28 ●	Wednesday	28	Saturday	28	Tuesday
29	Thursday	29	Sunday	29	Wednesday
30	Friday	30	Monday	30	Thursday
31	Saturday	31	Tuesday		

October		November		December	
1	Friday	1 ◑	Monday All Saints' Day	1	Wednesday
2	Saturday	2	Tuesday	2	Thursday
3	Sunday	3	Wednesday	3	Friday
4	Monday	4	Thursday	4	Saturday
5	Tuesday	5	Friday	5	Sunday
6	Wednesday	6	Saturday	6	Monday
7	Thursday	7	Sunday	7	Tuesday
8	Friday	8	Monday	8 ○	Wednesday
9	Saturday	9 ○	Tuesday	9	Thursday
10	Sunday	10	Wednesday	10	Friday
11	Monday	11	Thursday Armistice Day	11	Saturday
12	Tuesday	12	Friday	12	Sunday
13	Wednesday	13	Saturday	13	Monday
14	Thursday	14	Sunday	14	Tuesday
15	Friday	15	Monday	15 ◑	Wednesday
16	Saturday	16 ◑	Tuesday	16	Thursday
17	Sunday	17	Wednesday	17	Friday
18	Monday	18	Thursday	18	Saturday
19	Tuesday	19	Friday	19	Sunday
20	Wednesday	20	Saturday	20	Monday
21	Thursday	21	Sunday	21	Tuesday
22	Friday	22	Monday	22 ●	Wednesday December Solstice
23	Saturday	23 ●	Tuesday	23	Thursday
24	Sunday	24	Wednesday	24	Friday Christmas Eve
25	Monday	25	Thursday	25	Saturday Christmas Day
26	Tuesday	26	Friday	26	Sunday St Stephen's Day
27	Wednesday	27	Saturday	27	Monday
28	Thursday	28	Sunday	28	Tuesday
29	Friday	29	Monday	29	Wednesday
30	Saturday	30	Tuesday	30	Thursday
31	Sunday			31 ◑	Friday New Year's Eve

NAME LISTS

FRENCH NAMES

Male names	Female names	Surnames
Adam	Adrienne	Albert
Adrien	Aimée	André
André	Alice	Barre
Baptise	Arianne	Beaufort
Bernard	Avril	Bellerose
Cédric	Blanche	Bonnaire
Christian	Brigitte	Caron
Cyprien	Caroline	Clément
Daniel	Cécilia	Colbert
David	Christiane	Comtois
Dorian	Colette	Delacroix
Émile	Délia	Denis
Eugène	Dominique	Dufour
Félix	Élodie	Fabien
François	Emma	Favre
Gaspard	Fabienne	Garçon
Guy	Félicie	Gauthier
Henri	Francine	Giroux
Hugo	Gisèle	Herbert
Jacques	Hannah	Janvier
Jean	Jacqueline	Jordan
Jean-Luc	Jessica	Lamar
Jules	Julie	Lambert
Laurent	Léa	Leclerc
Léon	Lisette	Lucas
Lionel	Louise	Lyon
Lucien	Madeline	Maçon
Marceau	Marie	Michaud
Mathis	Mireille	Moreau
Nathanaël	Nina	Olivier
Olivier	Odette	Perrin
Oscar	Orianne	Petit
Pascal	Pascale	Poirier
Pièrre	Pauline	Romilly
Quentin	Rachel	Roussel
Raoul	Rébecca	Roy
Raymond	Roxane	Salmon
Remy	Sabine	Sault
Robert	Séraphine	Sauvage
Sébastien	Simone	Séverin
Simon	Sophie	St Martin
Stéphane	Sybille	Tailler
Théo	Sylvie	Thomas
Thibault	Valérie	Travert
Thierry	Véronique	Victor
Victor	Virginie	Villeneuve
Vincent	Yvette	Vincent
Xavier	Zoé	Voclain

GERMAN NAMES

Male names	Female names	Surnames
Adolf	Adelheid	Bauer
Albrecht	Agata	Berlitz
Aldo	Amalia	Braun
Benedikt	Angelika	Eisenhauer
Berndt	Anneke	Färber
Berthram	Beate	Fischer
Bruno	Belinda	Fleischer
Diedrich	Bertha	Fuchs
Dieter	Brigitte	Grün
Eberhart	Cäcilie	Hahn
Eckhardt	Eleonore	Hammerstein
Emil	Elfi	Herrmann
Ernst	Elfriede	Hitzig
Eugen	Elisa	Hofmann
Florian	Elli	Huber
Franz	Elsa	Kantor
Friedrich	Emelie	Kappel
Gottlieb	Felicie	Kaufmann
Heinrich	Frauke	Klein
Heinz	Frieda	Koch
Hermann	Friederike	Köhler
Johann	Gabriele	Kohn
Jürgen	Gertrude	König
Karl	Grete	Krause
Klaus	Hanne	Krüger
Kolman	Hedwig	Kuper
Konrad	Ilsa	Lehmann
Lewenhart	Jannike	Meier
Lothar	Juliane	Mencken
Manfried	Karoline	Metzger
Max	Käte	Müller
Moritz	Kirsa	Raabe
Odo	Lise	Rosenthal
Reinhardt	Magda	Schäfer
Rickert	Maria	Schlesinger
Rolf	Mina	Schmidt
Siegmund	Mitzi	Schneider
Stephan	Renate	Schröder
Theodor	Rosa	Schuhmacher
Udo	Sara	Schultz
Uwe	Selma	Schwarz
Valentin	Sofia	Spreckels
Waldemar	Theresia	Walter
Waldo	Ulrike	Weber
Walther	Viktoria	Weiss
Wilhelm	Walburga	Werner
Willi	Wibeke	Wolf
Wolfgang	Wilhelmina	Zimmermann

RUSSIAN NAMES

Male names	Female names	Surnames
Abram	Alexandra	Ananyev
Alexander	Anna	Anosov
Alexey	Anzhelika	Azarov
Anatoli	Darja	Bazhanov
Andrei	Ekaterina	Berezin
Anton	Elena	Bukov
Arkady	Elizaveta	Desjatkov
Arseny	Elvira	Djatlov
Boris	Emilia	Dryagin
David	Emma	Golovchenkov
Dmitry	Eva	Goryunov
Eduard	Fedosiya	Gryaznov
Evgeny	Galena	Ilyukhin
Gavril	Inessa	Ipachev
Gennady	Inna	Ivashin
Georgy	Irina	Kasatij
Gerasim	Iskra	Kolobkov
Grigory	Jana	Koryavin
Ignaty	Jaroslava	Krutin
Igor	Klara	Kutikov
Ilia	Klavdiya	Lebedev
Ivan	Kseniya	Ljagushkin
Jakov	Larisa	Lubashev
Jegor	Lidija	Matveyev
Josif	Ludmila	Mishutin
Juri	Marija	Nedelyayev
Kirill	Marina	Nikulin
Konstantin	Nadezhda	Osokin
Leonid	Natalja	Revyakin
Maxim	Nika	Rusakov
Mikhail	Nina	Savasin
Nikita	Oksana	Smolyanov
Nikolai	Olesja	Solodskik
Oleg	Olga	Telitsyn
Pavel	Polina	Tolstobrov
Pjotr/Peter	Rada	Ulyanin
Ruslan	Raisa	Vazov
Sergej	Sofiya	Vershinin
Stanislav	Svetlana	Vikashev
Stepan	Taisiya	Yelagin
Vadim	Tatyana	Yenin
Valentin	Uljana	Yermushin
Valery	Valeria	Yolkov
Viktor	Vera	Vochakov
Vyacheslav	Veronika	Zadoroshniy
Vladimir	Viktoriya	Zharkov
Vladislav	Zhanna	Zhilov
Zakhar	Zinaida	Zvyagin

DUTCH NAMES

Male names	Female names	Surnames
Aalt	Aleid	Aalves
Boudewijn	Angelien	Bonnekers
Cees	Carolien	Brus
Cornelis	Christiane	Cloeck
Diederik	Doortje	Drijhuis
Erasmus	Eva	Effsinck
Frans	Femke	Frieselder
Geert	Gerdi	Giersiepen
Gustaaf	Grietje	Hekkelman
Hannes	Hadwych	Horn
Huibert	Hendrika	Jager
Jakob	Johanna	Kappers
Joop	Katelijn	Limbeck
Klaas	Liesje	Meeuisse
Lieven	Maaike	Nijenhuis
Mozes	Mieke	Ostendorp
Rutger	Paulien	Pietersen
Sebastiaan	Renate	Reesinck
Svart	Saskia	Stemerdinck
Theunis	Sofie	Thushuisen
Urian	Truus	Uwland
Willem	Viona	Villekes

POLISH NAMES

Male names	Female names	Surnames
Andrzej	Anilea	Adamski
Aron	Beatrycze	Chmielewski
Bartosz	Czeslawa	Czarnecki
Czeslaw	Dita	Czerwinski
Dominik	Elzbieta	Gorski
Eliasz	Fryderyka	Jasinski
Felicjan	Grazyna	Jaworski
Gerwazy	Irena	Kalinowski
Grzegorz	Iwona	Kucharski
Iwan	Jadzia	Maciejewski
Jacek	Lechoslawa	Olszewski
Jerzy	Miroslawa	Ostrowski
Karol	Natasza	Pawlak
Leszek	Radomila	Sawicki
Mieczyslaw	Roksana	Sobczak
Przemko	Seweryna	Sokolowski
Radoslaw	Sylwia	Szczepanski
Sebestyjan	Tekla	Tomaszewski
Swietomierz	Wera	Walczak
Wislaw	Wiga	Wieczorek
Wojciech	Zofia	Wysocki
Zbigniew	Zuzanna	Zawadski

APPENDICES

CZECHOSLOVAKIAN NAMES

Male names	Female names	Surnames
Anton	Ana	Cizeek
Bohdan	Anezka	Fiser
Cenek	Barbora	Havel
Dobromil	Dusanka	Hruska
Dusan	Eliska	Janecek
Evzen	Frantiska	Klima
Georg	Hedvika	Kovar
Holic	Irena	Martinek
Ivan	Jaromila	Musil
Jaromir	Julia	Nemec
Karel	Kamila	Neuman
Ludvik	Katica	Riha
Marek	Lenka	Skala
Pavel	Milena	Slavik
Radoslav	Nada	Soukup
Simon	Pavla	Strnad
Stepan	Ruzena	Sykora
Tibor	Sobeska	Tichy
Vasil	Svetla	Urban
Vladimir	Tereza	Vacek
Yanko	Vera	Valenta
Zdenek	Zdenka	Zelenka

ITALIAN NAMES

Male names	Female names	Surnames
Adolfo	Aria	Agnelli
Antonio	Bernadetta	Bello
Beppe	Carla	Buffone
Bruno	Chiara	Costanzo
Cesare	Cristina	Drago
Dino	Delia	Falco
Ennio	Domenica	Franzese
Federico	Elettra	Gimondi
Giuseppe	Eva	Guerra
Gustavo	Fabia	Locatelli
Leandro	Fiorenza	Lupo
Luca	Isidora	Marchetti
Maria	Laura	Morello
Nicolò	Lilia	Nicolosi
Orsino	Lucia	Orsini
Peppe	Maria	Pedrotti
Renato	Mirabella	Ricchetti
Santino	Nadia	Russo
Stefano	Nicoletta	Selvaggio
Tino	Paolina	Toloni
Uberto	Sabina	Uberto
Vittore	Valentina	Valerio

SPANISH NAMES

Male names	Female names	Surnames
Adolfo	Anabel	Aguado
Albert	Andrea	Belmonte
Bernado	Blanca	Campana
Carlos	Carmela	Cruz
Claudio	Consuela	Domínguez
Edmundo	Daniela	Esparxa
Emilio	Emilia	Félix
Felipe	Fabiola	Giménez
Geraldo	Francisca	Hernández
Hernando	Graciana	Herrero
Jacinto	Inés	Maradona
Jorge	Joana	Moralez
Luis	Julia	Núñez
Marco	Leandra	Olmos
Miguel	Lola	Pérez
Pablo	Mónica	Quintana
Roberto	Noela	Ramírez
Sebastián	Oriana	Sánchez
Sergio	Paloma	Tomáz
Toni	Roberta	Ureña
Vito	Rosarita	Vargas
Xavier	Sabina	Vásquez

GREEK NAMES

Male names	Female names	Surnames
Aris	Aleka	Andreas
Christos	Artemis	Antonis
Dimitris	Dimitra	Botsaris
Emilios	Ekaterini	Christakis
Filippos	Evangelia	Demetriou
Georgios	Filippa	Floros
Iakovos	Iliana	Giannis
Kostas	Iris	Giannopoulos
Marios	Katina	Ioannidis
Michalis	Konstantina	Karavitis
Panagiotis	Kyveli	Konstantinidis
Periklis	Marika	Kyriakous
Silas	Melina	Lambrakis
Spiro	Nikoletta	Leandros
Stavros	Olympia	Liourdis
Stephanos	Persefoni	Marinos
Stylianos	Sibylla	Megalos
Takis	Sofia	Michelakos
Themistoklis	Stella	Papadopoulos
Vasileios	Valentina	Stavros
Vlassis	Xenia	Stefanidis
Yiannis	Zenovia	Xanthopoulos

CHARACTER TRAITS

INDIAN NAMES

Male names	Female names	Surnames
Ajeet	Aishwarya	Abbasi
Chiranjivi	Anjali	Anand
Dhananjay	Bhavana	Bachchan
Dinesh	Devika	Banerjee
Ghulam	Divya	Chaudhari
Girish	Esha	Das
Gobinda	Gayathri	Gadhavi
Harendra	Harshada	Gupta
Indra	Hema	Jain
Jagadish	Ila	Kaur
Jasvinder	Indira	Kumar
Kunal	Jaya	Misra
Mahendra	Kamala	Nagarkar
Mayur	Kishori	Narang
Nagendra	Lilavati	Patil
Neelam	Meena	Rao
Nirmal	Nirmala	Singh
Prabhakar	Priyanka	Sultana
Ramesh	Rupa	Tamboli
Shankar	Sarita	Udayar
Vikram	Sima	Vemulakondo
Vijay	Vasanti	Vishwakarma

JAPANESE NAMES

Male names	Female names	Surnames
Akio	Airi	Ando
Ayumu	Ami	Hara
Daichi	Asami	Imai
Eiji	Ayaka	Jouda
Fumio	Eri	Kawano
Goro	Haruka	Kojima
Hachiro	Hitomi	Kouda
Hajime	Kaede	Kouki
Hisao	Kimi	Kouno
Isamu	Kotone	Makida
Jiro	Miyu	Maruyama
Kaito	Nanami	Miyazaki
Michi	Noa	Morita
Noburo	Rei	Nakayama
Ryo	Rio	Ojima
Sadao	Saki	Sakai
Seiji	Sayuri	Shibata
Shigeru	Shika	Takaki
Tetsuya	Shun	Takeda
Toshio	Suzume	Taniguchi
Yori	Umeko	Ueda
Yuuto	Yuka	Yokoyama

d%	Trait	d%	Trait
1	Accommodating	51	Intimidating
2	Alert	52	Inventive
3	Ambitious	53	Lazy
4	Amiable	54	Loud
5	Angry	55	Lustful
6	Authoritative	56	Meek
7	Awkward	57	Menacing
8	Bland	58	Miserly
9	Blunt	59	Mournful
10	Calm	60	Observant
11	Cautious	61	Open
12	Charming	62	Overbearing
13	Cold	63	Perky
14	Conceited	64	Pious
15	Confident	65	Plain-spoken
16	Controlling	66	Principled
17	Corrupt	67	Punctual
18	Courageous	68	Puritan
19	Deceitful	69	Rational
20	Defiant	70	Rebellious
21	Dignified	71	Reckless
22	Diplomatic	72	Resourceful
23	Distrustful	73	Respectable
24	Dithering	74	Rugged
25	Dull	75	Rustic
26	Eager	76	Sarcastic
27	Eloquent	77	Seductive
28	Emotional	78	Selfish
29	Energetic	79	Self-righteous
30	Fearful	80	Sleepy
31	Flamboyant	81	Slick
32	Focused	82	Smug
33	Foolish	83	Soft-spoken
34	Forgiving	84	Stammering
35	Friendly	85	Stoic
36	Generous	86	Stubborn
37	Gossipy	87	Submissive
38	Graceful	88	Superstitious
39	Greedy	89	Thorough
40	Gruff	90	Tidy
41	Gullible	91	Understanding
42	Hard-working	92	Unkempt
43	Helpful	93	Unpredictable
44	Honest	94	Violent
45	Honorable	95	Voracious
46	Humble	96	Whiny
47	Icy	97	Wily
48	Idealistic	98	Wise
49	Incorruptible	99	Witty
50	Ignorant	100	Youthful

PROFANITIES

The problem with profanities is that they are rude, so you can't use them. Before the 1990s, actual profanities were almost non-existent in bédé, and they were rare even after that. Instead, profanities were cleaned up for the young reader. It was never "proper" censorship, but rather a matter of culture, good behaviour and not making a scandal.

If you had to depict a swearing character, it was much more common to draw a series of colourful pictograms, or misspell profanities and treat them like onomatopoeia – monsieur Prunelle's "*Rogntudjû!*" is a classic example, a garbled "*Nom de Dieu*" meaning "in the name of God". This practice is actually very old – King John of England's favourite curse was "*gadzooth*", a corruption of "God's teeth". Using God's proper name as an expletive was sensitive stuff – "thou shalt not take the name of the Lord thy God in vain", you know.

Another way to get around the limitations of good behaviour was to not use profanities, but express words as if they were. Yell "*sabre de bois!*" angrily enough and people will back off, even though it just means "wooden sword" (Captain Haddock is the undisputed master of this technique).

You can also swear in another language, especially if you use non-profanities. Examples include "*donnerwetter!*" which is German for "thunderstorm"; "*santa vaca!*" is Spanish for "holy cow"; or "*baka*", Japanese for "idiot".

You could get away with one real profanity per album, reserved for extreme situations and very angry characters, but you would have to write it as the first character followed by ellipsis. You never wrote "*Merde!*", but "M…!"

Remember that profanities are not for everyone. It is a class issue. Heroes swear rarely if ever. Neither do gentlemanly villains. Ladies never ever swear. Curses are used by lower class characters, uneducated or proletarian characters, and even they stay within the rules above.

Rude, but not actual swear words	
Emplâtre	Dummy. Unisex.
Triple buse	Fool. Unisex.
Imbécile	Imbecile. Unisex.
Idiot	Idiot. Female is "Idiote".
Cornichon	Litterally a pickle. Male.
Mufle	Rough type, crude, ungentlemanly person (usually from a lady). Exclusively male.
Brute, brute épaisse	Brute, thick brute. Unisex.
Blanc-bec	Someone who is naive, young, inexperienced (male).
Butor	Someone who is the opposite of a gentleman, a brute, and stupid at that. (male). Originally the name of a swamp bird.
Forban	Pirate, bandit, brigand (male).
Foutriquet	Young and lazy man/boy.
Godiche	A silly or naive woman.
Gourgandine	A cheap seductress, a tart.
Cuistre	An ignorant man.

Rude, but not actual swear words	
Ganache, Vieille ganache	An old and rambling person. Litterally means "old horse jaw".
Malappris	Stupid, ignorant, litterally "who received a bad education". The feminine form is "malapprise", but almost never used.
Malotru	Rude person.
Maraud	Litterally "pillager". Used by people of superior status to qualify evildoers.
Maroufle	Rude character.
Olibrius	A man who has an extravagant and outlandish behavior.
Ostrogoth	A rude or violent man.
Paltoquet	Used by nobles to qualify people who have "peasant manners".
Pourceau	"Pig". Self explanatory…
Ribaud	"Ribald".
Sagouin	Small south american monkey. Feminine is "sagouine", but never used because it sounds like it implies homosexuality.

Curses from the 60's through 80's

Sapristi!	Anything from "FUCK!" to "Oopsie-daisies".	Expresses surprise and astonishment.
Fichtre! Bigre!	"I am stumped!"	Expresses astonishment in the face of a difficulty or an obstacle, not necessarily a danger... translated as "damn, this puzzle is tough!" or "damn, that opponent is huge!"
Mazette!	Oh my!	Expression of admiration and felicitation.
Saperlipopette! Saperlotte!	Anything from "FUCK!" to "Oopsie-daisies".	Surprise, for the older people or old-fashioned.
Enfer! Damnation! (or even better: Enfer et damnation!)	"Hell!" "Damnation!"	Used mainly when your plans have been foiled.
Sabre de bois!	"Wooden sword!"	Favorite expletive of Comte de Champignac.
Peste!	"Ah, pox!"	Mainly used by the rich.
Zut! Flute!	"Damn!", "Dang!", "Gosh!"	
Non!	"No!"	Simple, but effective.
Par tous les saints! Bonté divine!	"By the saints!" "Goodness gracious!"	It's quite rare to see anyone refer to religion explicitely, but when they do, this is more interesting than "by god" or "holy virgin".
Scrogneugneu!	"Blast!"... When you want to say something rude or blasphemous, you eat your words and say "scrogneugneu" instead.	Expresses anger, surprise, and so on, generally in quiet circumstances (i.e. not when one is in danger, as opposed to "sapristi").
Ça alors! Ça par exemple!	Oh my! (meaning Wow! Holy shit!)	Surprise, astonishment.
Par (insert name of a non-christian god or gods, such as Jupiter, Allah, Vishnu, Odin, Le Vent du Sud...)	"By (...)!"	Calling to a pagan god, for foreigners, cultists and people from the past, was sadly perfectly acceptable in the eighties, as opposed to mentioning the Christian god).
Oh la la!	"Oh dear!"	A bit mild, even in the sixties, but still in use by prude characters.
Bon sang! Bon sang de bonsoir! Bon sang de bois!	"Good grief !", "By golly!", "For God's sake!"	Expression of shock and surprise in the face of adversity.

Continued on next page

Continued from previous page

Curses from the 60's through 80's		
Par ma barbe !	"By my beard!"	Only used by older, bearded characters.
Nom d'une pipe ! Nom d'un chien ! Sacré nom d'une pipe ! Nom d'un petit bonhomme ! Nom de nom ! Crénom de nom !	"Blast!"	Surprise and anger. Perfectly acceptable replacement for nowadays "putain" and "merde". This is once again "in the name of…" where "god" has been bowdlerized.
Cornegidouille !		Comical expletive for surprise. Literary. Invented by Alfred Jarry for his plays.
Nom de (…)	"Holy (…)!"	Insert a noun appropriate for each situation, just like Robin in the 1966 Batman series.
La barbe !	"You are boring me", "I am fed up with this"	

d%	Ways of saying *"by God"* without using *God*		d%	Ways of saying *"by God"* without using *God*
01–05	Palsambleu !		51–55	Sacredieu !
06–10	Ventredieu !		55–60	Cadédis !
11–15	Mordieu !		61–65	Jarnibleu !
16–20	Morbleu !		66–70	Maugrebleu !
21–25	Mordious !		71–75	Corbleu !
26–30	Sacrebleu !		76–80	Crébleu !
31–35	Vertudieu !		81–85	Crévindiou !
36–40	Vertuchou !		86–90	Crévindjeu !
41–45	Diantre !		91–95	Vindiou !
46–50	Crénom !		96–100	Roll twice and use both.

CLUE SHEET

Character:

CLUE SHEET

INDEX

1   2   3

SKILLS COMPÉTENCES KOMPETENZEN

Agility Agilité/Beweglichkeit	☐	**Melee** Corps-à-corps/Nahkampf	☐
Alertness Vigilance/Wachsamkeit	☐	**Prestidigitation** Passe-passe/Taschenspielerei	☐
Charm Charme/Charme	☐	**Ranged combat** Tir/Fernkampf	☐
Contacts Contacts/Kontakte	☐	**Red tape** Bureaucratie/Bürokratie	☐
Credit Ressources/Kreditwürdigkeit	☐	**Science** Science/Naturwissenschaften	☐
Electronics Électronique/Elektronik	☐	**Search** Fouille/Suchen	☐
Endurance Endurance/Ausdauer	☐	**Security** Sécurité/Sicherheit	☐
Engineering Ingénierie/Ingenieurwesen	☐	**Sneak** Furtivité/Schleichen	☐
Entertainment Spectacle/Unterhaltung	☐	**Status** Statut/Status	☐
Humanities Sciences Humaines/ Geisteswissenschaften	☐	**Strength** Force/Stärke	☐
Investigation Enquête/Nachforschungen	☐	**Subterfuge** Tromperie/Täuschung	☐
Languages Langues/Sprachen	☐	**Survival** Survie/Überleben	☐
Machinery Mécanique/Maschinerie	☐	**Vehicles** Pilotage/Fahrzeuge	☐
Medicine Médecine/Medizin	☐	**Willpower** Volonté/Willenskraft	☐

Vitality/Vitalité/Vitalität

Story points/Points de récit/ Handlungspunkte

ABILITIES CAPACITÉS FÄHIGKEITEN

....

....

....

....

....

....

....

....

COMPLICATIONS DÉSAVANTAGES KOMPLIKATIONEN

....

....

DESCRIPTION DESCRIPTION BESCHREIBUNG

....
Profession/Profession/Beruf

....
Name/Nom/Name

....
Given name/Prénom/Vornamen

....
Residence/Domicile/Wohnort

....
Height/Taille/Größe

....
Colour of eyes/Couleur des yeux/Augenfarbe

....
Colour of hair/Couleur des cheveux/Haarfarbe

....
Special peculiarities/Signes particuliers/Unveränderliche Kennzeichen

....
Date of birth/Date de naissance/Geburtsdatum

....
Place of birth/Lieu de naissance/Geburtsort

....
Holder's signature/Signature du titulaire/Unterschrift des Passinhabers

VISA STAMPS VISAS VISASTEMPEL

LICENCES FOR DANGEROUS ITEMS
PERMIS POUR OBJETS RÉGLEMENTÉS
LIZENZEN FÜR VERBOTENE GEGENSTÄNDE

Item/Objet/Gegenstand   Tag/Étiquette/Etikett

.... ☐
.... ☐
.... ☐
.... ☐
.... ☐
.... ☐
.... ☐
.... ☐
.... ☐
.... ☐
.... ☐
.... ☐
.... ☐
.... ☐
.... ☐

Native language/Langue maternelle/
Muttersprache

....

....

Fluent languages/Langues parlées/
Sprachkenntnisse

....

....

....

CONTACTS   CONTACTS   KONTAKTE

....

....

....

Plot hooks/Accroches scénaristiques/Handlungsstränge

VISA STAMPS   VISAS   VISASTEMPEL

QUAE GRAVIS LUDOS

EMERGENCY PASSPORT
PASSEPORT TEMPORAIRE
PASSERSATZ

....

No of Passport/No du Passeport/Nummer des Reisepasses

....

Name of bearer/Nom du titulaire/Name des Passinhabers

NATIONAL STATUS   NATIONALITÉ   STAATSANGEHÖRIGKEIT